The Restless Art

By the same author:

IMAGES OF AMERICAN LIVING:
Four Centuries of Architecture and Furniture
as Cultural Expression

Alan Gowans

THE RESTLESS ART

A History of Painters and Painting

1760—1960

J. B. LIPPINCOTT COMPANY

PHILADELPHIA AND NEW YORK

A
JULIO ACUÑA

Pintor de asuntos profundos y excelente dibujante,
Compañero de trabajo e íntimo amigo mio durante muchos años,
Quien, por abstracta que sea su obra, nunca se olvida de que
La meta propia del artista es la Belleza.

Preface

THE GENESIS of this book was in the 1953 University of Michigan summer session program, which had for its theme The Popular Arts, and in which I gave a course on the arts of caricature, illustration, cartooning, advertising, motion pictures, and comics, as cultural expression, and first had to consider seriously how these arts differ from the "fine art" of painting in means, ends, and social function. When, in the summer of 1956, I returned to Ann Arbor to repeat the Popular Arts course and had paired with it a course on Modern Painting, I began to see how the two were so tightly interrelated that the history of painting proper is not fully intelligible without taking the development of the popular arts into account. Since coming to Delaware in the fall of 1956, I have been able to work out this interrelationship, using as a vehicle the concepts of Beauty and Reality, by offering both courses on a regular basis; this present work is the result. Writing it has been decidedly a spare-time project, so that it is my wife and family who have in effect made the most practical contribution to it. I am grateful also to Dr. John Dawson, Director of the University of Delaware Libraries, for providing me with a study in which the final writing was done, and to my Dean, G. Bruce Dearing [now President, Harpur College], for thoughtfully overlooking how often I have been in that office instead of in my own.

A. G.

Newark, Delaware
June 28, 1964

Contents

CONTENTS

CONTENTS

Illustrations

ILLUSTRATIONS

ILLUSTRATIONS

Overheard at the Washington Square Outdoor Art
Exhibit, sneakered man to sneakered girl, "Sure I like
beauty, but I have no use for art."
—*The New Yorker,* Talk of the Town, Sept. 24, 1960

M ost of what is called "painting" today does not
look like what was called "painting" two hundred or even one hundred
years ago. That is, to say the least, obvious. Not so obvious, perhaps,
is the fact that it actually *is* different. Yet that is the case. "Painting" as
generally known and practiced in the mid-20th-century represents a different kind of activity in ends, means, and social function from what it
was then.

In 1750, it was taken for granted that the ultimate object of painting
was to embody, and a painter's proper business was to discern and
perpetuate, something called Beauty. In 1950, the ultimate object and
concern of painting and painters was something quite different from
Beauty, and equally difficult to define, called Reality. The change is
more than a matter of aesthetics. It is both a result and a cause of a
fundamental alteration in the concept of what painters are and what
painting does in society. And this altered concept in turn is the product
and expression of those deep shifts in social structure, in economics, in
religious belief, that have created the modern world. That is the basic
concern of this book.

THE TRADITIONAL THEORY
OF BEAUTY

1750-1840

We BEGIN this history with Sir Joshua Reynolds, not because he was anything like the greatest of painters, but because he was a culminatingly representative figure of that concept of what painting is and what painters do in society which the 18th century had inherited from centuries and millennia past and which we can call most simply the traditional theory of Beauty.

There is little need to describe in detail what the theory of Beauty involves. Even after two hundred years of steady and often violent attacks on it, most people today not only take it for granted, but criticize all painting in its terms, without being aware of holding any theories about art at all. They assume first that the object of painting (when not obviously communication, as in advertising) is to provide substitute images of "beautiful objects" in Nature. The businessman whose hobby is duck-shooting expects painters to provide his den with "beautiful" pictures of ducks rising into the sunset sky, to solace him during the fifty weeks of the year when the real thing is unavailable. His wife, who enjoys flowers but finds the real ones always either budding or wilting, captures forever the instant of perfect bloom, the ideal arrangement, with pictures on her living-room walls. The soldier in barracks carries in his wallet photographic substitute images of his family, puts pin-up substitutes above his cot, and so on. And all these people assume, secondly, that there is a self-evident way not only to determine which objects in Nature are beautiful and which are not, but also to make value distinctions among the beautiful objects themselves. It all depends on the power of objects to generate "beautiful feelings" in those who look at them. Those which do not generate such feelings—garbage pails, dead snakes, telephone poles, for instance—are by that token ugly, unworthy of any painter's attentions. Those which do—the human figure, flowers, flights of ducks, mountains, sailboats—are beautiful, and the painter's proper subjects. Quite as clearly, different objects generate different kinds of beautiful feelings, some more beautiful than others. The feelings aroused by human figures are in general more "beautiful" than those aroused by flowers or ducks; but among human figures again, it is

3

obvious that a noble pioneer in front of his cabin or a great statesman rising to address his people in a moment of crisis are more "beautiful" objects than a small boy playing with his dog or Maud Muller raking the meadow sweet with hay, and that a finely proportioned youthful physique pleases the aesthetic sense better than one fat and fifty.

Finally, there is also in the popular mind no question as to what the painter is supposed to do with these beautiful objects. He is expected to heighten their beauty by a process of abstraction and selection. In painting a human figure, he is expected to omit all nonessential blemishes and imperfections; a cowboy may be dirty, but not pimply. In a landscape, he is expected to eliminate the billboards and telephone poles; in a flower painting, any "unsuitable" background; in a seascape, litter on the beach. He is expected, in a word, to improve on Nature.

This concept of what painting is and what painters do was held almost universally at the beginning of the 19th century. Though painters like Reynolds and Delacroix, Blake and Ingres and Constable might put primary emphasis on very different aspects of it, all agreed on the essential core. All took for granted that a painter's job was to choose objects beautiful in form, and capable of generating beautiful feelings, and to make both forms and feelings more beautiful by judicious selection and abstraction from Nature. And all were therefore bound by certain limitations on their activity which to mid-20th-century painters seem at best galling, at worst stultifying. But with these limitations came enormous advantages. The most obvious were that painting then had self-evident standards by which it could be judged and that painters then had a self-evidently valuable and useful place in society.

Ideas about what constituted beautiful forms and feelings might vary widely from epoch to epoch—the Middle Ages, for example, thought more of spiritual and theological Beauty than of the physical Beauty sought after in classical Antiquity and the Renaissance—and there was never entire agreement as to precisely what degree of selection and abstraction from Nature was best. But essentially, a fairly valid system of categorization obtained in classical and Western civilization, to all intents and purposes, from the beginning of the classical Greek era down to the middle of the 19th century. Whether embodied in a temple metope or a cathedral tympanum, the floor of a Roman villa or the wall of a Byzantine church or a Renaissance easel painting, "the noble human form in noble action" was accepted as the most beautiful of objects, and within that category, the noblest feelings were those evoked by acts of religious connotation, the next noblest by heroic acts in history, the least noble by genre scenes from everyday life. The lowest category of beautiful forms was accepted as still life and landscape. Thus when you called Praxiteles's *Cnidian Aphrodite,* or the *Beau Dieu* at Amiens, or Leonardo's *Last Supper* "great" works of art, you were not merely saying you happened to like them, you were making an objective estimate from fixed premises. And when you said that so-and-so was a great painter, you were not merely saying that his "style" (or his manners, or his wife, or whatever) happened to appeal to you, you were objectively judging how well he had succeeded in doing a job whose demands were reasonably self-evident.

It had taken many centuries and generations to reach the point where the artist's job was fully respected and rewarded. But by the middle of the 18th century, it was so even in England. Solely by skill in his art, an unknown of middling family like Joshua Reynolds could achieve a respected and secure place high in society, capped with a knighthood. Centuries of struggle to emancipate artists from the ranks of artisans-craftsmen and establish them as the professional equals of poets and scholars had finally been consummated. The President of the Royal Academy of England could stand on state occasions next to the Archbishop of the established Church and alongside peers of the realm, secure in the knowledge that his place, won by rigorous apprenticeship and long years of study in an intellectual discipline, was as firmly fixed and essential as theirs. Painting was recognized as an activity based, like science and theology and law, on the great principle on which Western civilization had been built: there is an Order behind the ephemera of appearances which it is the duty and glory of thinking men to discover and reveal and employ. Beauty was the painter's way of expressing that Order, and society was prepared to honor him accordingly.

Yet in two centuries more, all this had gone. The traditional theory of Beauty, on which the painter's place in society depended, had disintegrated and collapsed. From being a discipline as steady and rigorous as medicine is now, painting had become, in the estimation of as keen an observer as George Orwell, "the only profession that can be practised without either talent or hard work." * How this came about, how and why the traditional theory of Beauty disintegrated and collapsed, is the theme of the first section of this book.

* *Burmese Days,* (New York, Popular Library Edition, 1934), p. 80. Notice he says "can be," not "is"; but two hundred years ago the very idea was unthinkable.

I

Beauty Is No Object:
Dissolution of the Traditional Theory of
"Beautiful Form"

ACCORDING TO THE TRADITIONAL THEORY STILL DOMI-
nating Europe in the 1750s, Beauty in painting was attainable in two
ways: as Form (which included both the subject matter and its mode of
composition, selection, and arrangement) and as Feeling (i.e., a
heightened awareness of the divine, noble, sublime, or pleasurable
produced by given classes of objects and situations). Between these two
kinds of Beauty no really rigid demarcation was either possible or
desirable in practice, of course; for—like body and spirit, order and
variety, reason and imagination, education and intuition, logic and
romance—both are part of the permanent makeup of every human
creature, and a painting embodying beautiful forms must in the nature of
things produce beautiful feelings in the spectator as well. Nevertheless,
just as reason may tend to rule imagination in some cases, or intuition
overcome logic in others, so some painters showed a predominant interest
in Form, others in Feeling.

In the first half of the 19th century, it was common to make a
distinction between "classicists" and "romantics," which more or less
corresponded to these two points of view. We no longer think of it quite
this way. In retrospect it seems that practically all painters from the
1780s into the 1840s shared a common romantic attitude. If we group
together Reynolds, David, Ingres, Constable, and Corot as representatives of "the classical tradition of form," and Delacroix, Blake,
Goya, and Turner as representatives of "romantic expression," it is less
to imply any ultimate distinction of means and ends than simply for
clarity of organization. In the work of the first group, we can most
conveniently trace progressive stages in the dissolution of the traditional

6

theory that beautiful forms are a painter's business; in the second, a parallel dissolution of the traditional concept of beautiful feelings. The story begins with Reynolds.

1

Beauty by Common Consent:

Sir Joshua Reynolds (1723–1792)

Joshua Reynolds always had a strong interest in the theoretical side of his profession. Even before he became Sir Joshua and as founding President of George III's Royal Academy of Painting had to deliver annual lectures (or "discourses," as he preferred to call them) on the subject, he associated by choice with men of letters, most notably those in Dr. Johnson's circle, with whom he could talk not merely about the technical problems of concern to painters, but of painting in its widest perspective, of the whole range of relationships between art, life, and society.

Like most men whose lives spanned the 18th century, Reynolds inherited, and held throughout his life, the traditional concept of the painter as being primarily concerned with Beauty; with beautiful objects in general, that is to say, arranged, selected, and abstracted in a beautiful manner; and with the human form in particular, which of all possible objects had the most potential for Beauty. That might have been discouraging, perhaps, for someone who, like Reynolds, had to make his living depicting the prosaic sort of aging human forms that could most often afford to make their way to a portrait painter's studio. Fortunately, however, Reynolds had also inherited a conviction that the ultimate purpose of all art is to make men better, nobler, and wiser. This in practice meant that the portrait painter not only could but should depart from raw nature as it sat before him, should make it conform, insofar as he could without violating common sense, to an ideal standard of Beauty. And that standard, too, Reynolds had inherited from the past. It was classical art, as represented by the great works of Greek, Roman, and Renaissance artists, that ultimately and always determined for him what Beauty was; if, as he said in the *Third Discourse,* "the wish of the genuine painter . . . is to improve mankind by the grandeur of his ideas," then to make portraits more closely approximate classical Beauty by judicious generalization and modification was not only permissible, it was what artists ought always to do.

Needless to say, a portrait painter with principles like these was bound to be popular. If it flattered Reynolds to think that he was being true to the highest mission of art when he based portraits on Michelangelo's majestic forms, or the *Apollo Belvedere,* or the *Mona Lisa,* the resemblance flattered his sitters even more, of course. Never before, indeed, had an English artist commanded such high renown, esteem, and (not so incidentally) fees. But for all the success his principles brought him, Reynolds never took them for granted. He was forever exploring the theory of Beauty he had inherited from the past, trying to establish its rationale; and in the *Discourses* that he had to deliver to the Royal Academy students he had a great opportunity to put his thoughts in order. In that series of addresses he kept coming back again and again to the same central problems: What ultimately determines standards of Beauty in art? On what rational grounds (for this was, after all, the Age of Reason) can we decide what is beautiful and what is not? And if his answers have not entirely stood the test of time, it was hardly for lack of force or logic, but because essentially they address the kind of problems the human mind has never been fitted to answer with finality. Certainly the questions are still open today.

Why do we like the lines of one chair, say, better than of another very similar? Or the design in one drapery fabric more than another? Or prefer the columns of the Parthenon to squat inverted posts? Because in the one case there is a balance, harmony, unity, or good proportion that is lacking in the other? But that only moves the problem one step back; why should we prefer balance to imbalance, harmony to discord, unity to confusion? On what grounds can we consider some ratios of load to support, or height to width, as being "better proportion" than others? On what, in short, do our judgments—any judgments—of what constitutes Beauty ultimately depend?

Now on this question there are two possible lines of thought. The one usually followed in the earlier 18th century was an inheritance from the theoreticians of the Renaissance, who in turn found their authority in classical Greece. It held that the idea of Beauty is innate. A faculty for recognizing and responding to beautiful forms is born into us, as much an inherent part of our mental furniture as the faculty of reason or of speech. It was one of those faculties, indeed, wherewith God endowed man to differentiate him from animals. It was, therefore, absolute—not a human creation for man to mold or modify, but a divine revelation for him to accept and perpetuate. The classic exposition of this theory is by Plato, who attributes its origin to Socrates's controversy with certain Sophists claiming to be able to "teach" Virtue (i.e., Beauty; in Greek thought both were essentially the same). This claim, according to Socrates, was nonsense; the thing could not be done. Virtue and Beauty were not skills to be acquired or information to be gathered—like carpentry, say, or economic statistics; they were innate ideas and, as such, unteachable. We can never be taught them, because we knew all there was to know from the moment we were born. The most education can do is "remind" us of our knowledge, help bring us to full awareness of it. Like a sculptor who chips away superfluous stone until the idea in his mind when first he faced the block stands clear to the world, the wise educator works only to clear away whatever accumulation of trivia and misinformation may cloud our understanding and prevent our realizing the truths we inherently know; Socrates demonstrated the point by proving how, through skillful questioning, even the most illiterate slave boy could be made to realize abstruse geometrical propositions.

If Beauty cannot be learned by teaching, then, it follows that artists cannot be made by teaching, either. The great painter must be born with a superior faculty for recognizing Beauty, just as the great orator or writer must be born with a "gift for language," the athlete with muscular coordination, the musician with an "ear." Certainly this gift or faculty may be developed; but if it is not there in the first place, no amount of education can create it. The only really appropriate training for painters is, therefore, apprenticeship. Through apprenticeship to an older master, the gifted youth may learn the practical problems and technical media of his profession: how to mix paints or cut stone, how to draw a blueprint or calculate stresses so as best to express and transmit that awareness of Beauty which he already possesses; but he cannot "learn" Beauty itself. True artists, in short, are always born, never made.

But the spirit of his age in general and his country in particular, his own temperament, and his professional aspiration all combined to make this line of thought difficult if not impossible for Reynolds to accept. Advanced 18th-century thought was everywhere challenging the principle of hereditary excellence—the idea of one class having innate talents for government or war which another could not possess. And just as the theory of kingship by divine right was being rejected by contemporary

9

political thinkers, so Reynolds was predisposed against any assumption that one painter could have some innate superiority of talent or perception over another. Living in the country that above all others exalted Reason and Natural Law, that had defied autocratic rule wherever it appeared, that had destroyed James II's absolute government at home and Louis XIV's absolute powers abroad, it was hardly to be expected that Reynolds would be happy with any theory that made Beauty absolute, arbitrarily imposed by fiat from above, incumbent on all men everywhere. As a theoretician, he was furthermore by nature suspicious of anything so vague and spontaneous as to be unteachable. But most of all, perhaps, as President of the Royal Academy he felt that the classical theory, if true, doomed all his hopes of seeing a great school of painting develop in England. And training first-rank painters was imperative, he was convinced, if England were properly to play the great-power role 18th-century history seemed to have destined for her. In literature, England had Shakespeare, Milton, and now Johnson—world figures, all of them. In music there was Purcell, and now Handel; in architecture, Jones, Wren, Gibbs. But in painting, Reynolds could almost have said to

1. *Sir Joshua Reynolds:* Sarah Siddons as the Tragic Muse. *San Marino, California, Henry E. Huntington Art Gallery.*

Painted in 1784, this portrait of actress Sarah Siddons is, in basic composition, pose and setting, a free and obvious composite of two of Michelangelo's Sistine Ceiling figures (the prophet Isaiah and the Delphic Sibyl). A summation of that Grand Style which Reynolds practiced throughout his life and preached to two generations of students at the Royal Academy, it illustrates Reynolds's conviction that a painter's ultimate object must always be to "improve mankind" by leaving the world fuller of "great and ideal beauty" than he had found it. When he proclaimed that the standard for this ideal Beauty was not to be sought in the realm of absolute and innate ideas, but based on a reasoned agreement of the "generality of mankind" as to what was greatest and best in earlier art, Reynolds unwittingly helped begin that breakdown of the traditional theory of Beauty as the painter's proper concern which opened the way for a new concept of painting to develop in succeeding generations.

Gainsborough, "There have only been two significant English painters—
you and me," and added, like the fisherman of folk wit, "I'm not so sure
about you." (Gainsborough, in Reynolds's opinion, painted in the old-
fashioned frivolous Rococo manner and relied far too much on spontaneous "genius" instead of disciplined study.) To admit that painters could
not be "made" would mean that all institutions which professed to
produce them, like the Royal Academy, were fundamentally futile.
Reynolds would not admit it. He would challenge the classic theory,
analyze it, find flaws in it, and produce another more in accordance with
what his times, tastes, and hopes demanded.

If, as the traditional theory held, the idea of Beauty was innate, part of
the inherent mental furniture of the human race, then it must be
universal, the same for all men everywhere. Show that it was not
universal, and you would prove it was not absolute. Show that it was not
absolute, and you would prove it must be relative—an idea, that is,
varying according to different men's experiences and backgrounds, no
more than a man-made standard. Show that it was man-made, and you
would prove what Sir Joshua so earnestly wished to believe—that Beauty
could be taught, that artists could in fact be made. All of which, given
18th-century enlightenment, Sir Joshua felt was not difficult at all.

For England in Reynolds's time was in the process of reaping a rich
harvest from her two preceding centuries of exploration, conquest, and
discovery. Not only monetary wealth was accumulating; ideas and
information of all kinds, too, flowed into England from all over the
world. And they seemed to justify a re-evaluation of all those older ideas
that 18th-century Englishmen had inherited from earlier times and more
provincial places, when perspectives were so much narrower and points
of view so limited. The Greek world of the 5th century, for instance.
Had Socrates known of all the strange lands and new places Reynolds's
countrymen had discovered, would he have so confidently assumed that
people everywhere instinctively recognized the same ideal of Beauty?
Certainly not; for from what travelers reported, it was clear their ideals
differed. And as early as 1759, in a treatise on Beauty published in *The
Idler,* Reynolds was making good use of the fact:

> I suppose nobody will doubt, if an Ethiopian were to paint the God-
> dess of Beauty, but that he would represent her black, with thick lips,
> flat nose, and woolly hair. . . . By what criterion will anyone dispute
> the propriety of his idea? We indeed say that the form and color of the
> European is preferable to that of the Ethiopian: but I know of no other

reason we have for it but that we are more accustomed to it. It is absurd to say that beauty is possessed of attractive powers which irresistibly seize the corresponding mind with love and admiration, since that argument is equally conclusive in favour of the white and the black philosophers.

Today, we might not find this argument so convincing. It seems as if Reynolds is confusing the question of universal response to beautiful forms with sexual attraction, which are two quite different things; and closer acquaintance with savages has shown them so far from the innocent and noble creatures 18th-century philosophers supposed that all an argument from Hottentot sensitivities might prove, if it proves anything, is that the more savage men are, the more deeply buried in superstition and error will be any primordial ideas of Truth or Beauty in their minds, and consequently the harder to detect. But that would be beside the point. The point is that for Reynolds the argument was conclusive. One exception to the rule was enough; he needed no more witnesses to establish that the idea of Beauty was not absolute but relative. On this foundation he could go on confidently to build not only his own body of painting but, what is infinitely more important, a fundamentally new aesthetic theory.

If our ideas of Beauty are not innate, they must be formed by environment. We take our standards, that is to say, from the world about us, from the kind of art we have known as children. But as children we are surrounded by all sorts of art—good, bad, indifferent; how shall we know which is which? This is the task of the older generation; it is not only possible for them, but their duty, to instruct the young which models to admire and emulate, and which to shun. And how shall the older generation know? They will know because they have reached the age of reason, and Reason (here speaks the 18th century) tells us that the only true Beauty is that which stands the test of time. There are some kinds of art on whose beauty the wisest men of every rational age have always agreed; such, pre-eminently, is the classical art of Greece and Rome, and of the Italian Renaissance. This classical art, then, provides our standard of Beauty, not because classical art represents some absolute which we are bound to admire because of the structure of our minds, but because its beauty has been validated by the reasoned agreement of the "generality of mankind."

Now at first sight this seemed no more than an academic and idle change in theory, of no practical significance. The fact that he now

13

considered classical standards to be matters of reasoned agreement
instead of absolute canons did not in the least affect the appearance of
Reynolds's pictures. They remained based on classical models, just as
art in the Renaissance tradition had always been. Nor did classical art
become any less binding a standard. Reynolds was fond of telling how,
as a young man making his required Grand Tour of Italy, he had not at
first appreciated the works of Raphael, couldn't, in fact, see anything in
them at all. But being aware that the "generality of mankind" had always
held Raphael to be the Prince of Painters, Reynolds had concluded that
any fault must be in himself, not Raphael. He had set to work
assiduously studying the Master's style day after day, until he could
truthfully say he understood it, that his ideas of Beauty had been raised to
Raphael's standard. And as he had taught himself, he proposed to teach
others. "You must have no dependence on your own Genius . . ."
he told his students in the *Second Discourse.* "With respect to the
pictures you are to choose for your models, I could wish that you would
take the world's opinion rather than your own." Choose classical
models, then, and study them incessantly; that, and that alone, is the sure
way to become a great painter: "Nothing is denied to well-directed
labour, nothing is to be obtained without it."

But however small were the effects of Reynolds's revision of classical
theory in immediate practice, its implications for the future were enormous, ranging far in two quite opposite directions. If, on the one hand, it
were true that great art demanded nothing more than hard work and
study, then any drudge with time and energy enough could claim to be a
great painter. In that direction lay the "academic art" of the 19th
century—vast "machines" of industriously assembled ideas and forms
picked piecemeal from approved models: studied, erudite, pretentious,
dead. Reynolds, of course, was English enough to imagine that such a
catastrophe (which he was quite perceptive enough to consider) would
be forestalled by common sense; how could he have foreseen the coming
social and economic convulsions that would so sadly upset his reasoned
and orderly 18th-century world? But he might, perhaps, have foreseen
more easily the other, opposite, development of his ideas, for it was
inherent in the theory itself. If Beauty is not absolute, but represents
only the agreement of the "generality of mankind," then surely more than
one standard is possible. Could we not extend the basis of agreement
from "the generality of mankind" to "most people"? And thence to "what
some people agree on" and to "what a few perceptive people recognize"?

And finally to "Beauty is what I say it is"? Once at that point, we are talking more philosophy than aesthetics, more about subjective "Reality" than objective "Beauty." And at the end of that road, what Reynolds called painting will be transformed into quite a different kind of activity.

We may be very sure that Sir Joshua had not the least intention of undertaking such a journey, but because of the change in basic theory he (and others in his generation) promulgated, others could start upon it.

One first step in that direction Reynolds did take, but only tentatively. He was quite acute enough to see one inevitable corollary that his shift in the theoretical basis of Beauty involved: if it is true that what we call beautiful is only what everyone is agreed to call beautiful, and if there is some kind of art that everyone is agreed on as the most beautiful art of all, then what reason can there be for not copying that model as closely as possible? Specifically, why bother with Renaissance variants of classical art when the real classical art of Antiquity is available to imitate? If you want to create works of beauty, clearly the way to do it is to copy classical art as closely as possible. And in the 1760s we find Reynolds consciously beginning to follow the leading of his own logic, and in works like *Lady Sarah Bunbury Sacrificing to the Graces* (page 101) deliberately imitating not only general classical principles but the specific forms of Graeco-Roman art. This could have led to a school of neoclassical painting in England comparable to the one appearing in France twenty years later led by Jacques Louis David, and the beginnings of one are apparent in the work of painters like Reynolds's follower Benjamin West in the 1770s. But then the course of English painting turned away from it; and in the van of that reaction was Reynolds himself. By the 1780s he was back to the general position he had held in the 1750s, as *Sarah Siddons* (page 11) shows—basing his art on broad classical principles common to all the Great Masters, handling them with more and more freedom as time goes on (e.g., *Georgiana, Duchess of Devonshire,* 1786).

What happened? First, probably, the workings of English common sense, refusing to carry any theory to extremes when it is obviously leading to absurdity, and assisted by the emerging popular arts, whose leading practitioners, as we shall see (*cf. Ill. 13B.*) (page 103), were quick to puncture the inflated pretensions of neoclassicism. But even more decisive was the influence of Samuel Johnson, Reynolds's great and close friend. Johnson's exact relationship to Reynolds's art is often debated; though few people think nowadays that Johnson wrote much if anything of the *Discourses,* certainly his ideas influenced Reynolds deeply. And Johnson was above all the man of balanced classical Reason, a man whose whole philosophy of life was set against broad theoretical schemes for improving humanity or art or anything else, who insisted on concrete logic over abstract theorizing. Johnson's ideas on classical balance between extremes clearly color the five major portraits of him Reynolds painted. If ever there were a case when Reynolds might have invoked his own idealizing precept—"historians tell us Alexander the Great was mean and low in appearance; the painter ought not so to represent him"—it was in painting Johnson. After his death precisely that precept *was* followed in Bacon's pretentious neoclassical statue of Johnson in St. Paul's, complete with classical toga, bare head, and robust serenity of countenance. But that is not how Reynolds showed him in the definitive portrait of 1778 in the Tate, London. Just as Johnson had condemned the overliteral truth of the 1774–75 portrait of himself squinting at a book—"He may paint himself as deaf as he chuses, but I will not be *blinking Sam"*—so he had condemned the overidealized 1769 Knole portrait of himself as a classical philosopher, had insisted on a compromise which showed him dignified but not pompously pedantic, severely plain but not ugly or deformed, classical in character but English in detail, like Johnson's own conversation.

Common sense saved England from anything worse than a mild bath of neoclassicism. But it was one of the last times for two centuries that common sense played much of a role in shaping the course of theory. For now the center shifted to Revolutionary France; there abstract theory was king, Pure Reason was elevated above common matters to become a goddess, and art, as exemplified in the painting of Jacques Louis David, followed them.

NOTES

There has been no attempt in text or Notes to list all the works of a given painter. The principle has been to include key pictures and especially pictures which may be seen in American museums and galleries.

Where the location of a painting is indicated simply by the name of a city, reference is to the major gallery or museum there (e.g., "London" indicates National Gallery; "Boston" indicates Museum of Fine Arts).

In bibliographical citations in the Notes, the place of publication is New York unless otherwise indicated.

Reynolds came very naturally by his scholarly and theoretical bent; his father, the Reverend Samuel Reynolds, was a fellow of Balliol and headmaster of the grammar school at Plympton, Devon (where Joshua was born in 1723), while clergymen, scholars, and teachers had been numerous in his family for three generations. And although apprenticed for some three years (1740–43) to the fashionable London portraitist Thomas Hudson, in his professional training Reynolds essentially lived up to his own maxim: "Few have been taught to any purpose who have not been their own teachers" (*Second Discourse*). He formed his own mind in art, first by study of Jonathan Richardson's *Essay on the Theory of Painting,* then of the local Exeter painter William Gandy, most of all by a three-year stay in Italy (1749–52). By 1753 he had reached full artistic maturity, settled in London, and almost immediately established that position as unchallenged leader of English painting which he maintained until his death in 1792. When the Royal Academy was founded in 1768, Reynolds was the inevitable choice for first president; he was knighted in 1769 and, despite a stroke in 1782, continued to paint with steady success until partial blindness ended his career in 1789.

Reynolds's reputation in London was first firmly established by the full-length portrait of his early patron *Augustus* (later *Viscount*) *Keppel,* painted in 1753 (Greenwich, National Maritime Museum), in which he first demonstrated how to "improve on nature" by modeling his subject on a classical work of art—in this case, the heroic *Apollo Belvedere.* Similar derivations from Greek, Roman, and Renaissance prototypes can be cited for portraits all through Reynolds's career; a particularly well-known example is *Nelly O'Brien* (1760–62, London, Wallace Collection), based on Leonardo's *Mona Lisa.*

To the period 1768–81, when he apparently felt obliged to demonstrate the principles he was inculcating in the Royal Academy, belong most of his pompous and pedantically classical works, like *Lady Sarah Bunbury Sacrificing to the Graces* (1765), *Anne Hussey Delaval* (1765, Baltimore Museum), and *The Graces Adorning a Term of Hymen* (1774, London).

In 1781 he made a trip to Flanders and Holland; his observations there (reinforcing his own increasing common-sense awareness of the dangers of overworking dogmatic theories, perhaps) resulted in a new directness in most work (with the exception of subjects, like *Sarah Siddons as the Tragic Muse,* which obviously demanded a "grand" setting): e.g., *Colonel George Coussmaker* (1782, New York, Metropolitan); *Georgiana, Duchess of Devonshire* (1786, London); *Lord Heathfield* (1788, London); *The Age of Innocence* (1788, London).

17

Among the more useful books are J. Steegman, *Sir Joshua Reynolds* (London, 1933); E. K. Waterhouse, *Reynolds* (London, 1941); E. K. Waterhouse, *Painting in Britain 1530–1790* (Baltimore, 1953); Derek Hudson, *Sir Joshua Reynolds* (London. 1958).

2

The "Beautiful Society":
Jacques Louis David (1748–1825)

"Classical" is a very complicated and ambiguous word. Essentially, to call a painting "classical" means that it has some relationship to the art of Greece or Rome; the word came into general use at the time of the Renaissance (or rebirth) of Greek and Roman art forms in the 15th century to imply that these were to be considered "classic" or "standard," in contrast to Gothic—i.e., "barbarian"—medieval forms. But that relationship may vary widely. It may involve the direct reproduction of Greek or Roman objects such as vase-paintings, statues, or (in architecture) entire buildings. It may mean borrowing only details or ideas, and using them in original combinations. It may mean simply applying what were considered to be the principles or "spirit" of Greek and Roman art (until quite recent times the two were considered practically identical): balanced composition, clarity of outline, and the like. Or it may mean any combination of these things.

All this adds up to considerable confusion. It may perhaps be helpful to remember that, though "classical" and "classic" are often used indiscriminately in reference to the same thing, a "classic" may be anything that is the "best of its kind," whether a comic strip, a wine, or a novel, but "classical" in the strict sense specifically implies some Graeco-Roman origin or inspiration. And it may help, too, to remember that there are four generally recognized historical phases of classical art. These are:

(1) Graeco-Roman Antiquity, from (roughly) the 6th century B.C. to (with many deviations and permutations) about the 4th century A.D.

(2) The Renaissance of the 15th and 16th centuries, originating in Italy as a "rebirth" of (1) and gradually spreading thence to other countries.

18

(3) 18th-century classicism, which begins about 1720 (particularly in England and France) as a return to the principles of (2) after they had been "corrupted" during the Mannerist and Baroque periods (say 1550–1700). Reynolds is a typical representative of this third phase.

(4) Neoclassicism, a deliberate and studious attempt to revive not merely the principles of (1) but its specific forms as well. As we have seen in the case of Reynolds, this phase begins tentatively as early as the 1750s and -60s; and it is still viable as late as the 1840s. But it was in the years 1780–1820, and in the person of Jacques Louis David, that neoclassicism pre-eminently flourished.

To most people nowadays, neoclassical painting seems so unbelievably stilted, pretentious, melodramatic in the worst sense, that when we read how the exhibition in 1785 of David's *Oath of the Horatii* (page 21)— which effectively introduced the new movement to France—created a commotion and sensation comparable to that of later "modern" exhibitions, we are at a loss to understand why. Yet for its time and place this painting was just as revolutionary as anything by Courbet or Monet, Cézanne or Picasso. Indeed, a direct line runs from it to them; this was, in fact, the first appearance of "modern art."

David was working on the *Oath* at the same time that Reynolds was painting *Sarah Siddons,* and essentially both pictures depended on the new theories of Beauty developing in the 18th century. But David had practised what Reynolds only preached. Where Reynolds's art exemplified the proverbial English genius for pragmatic compromise between theory and practice, David's was characteristic of the equally proverbial French penchant for rushing to logical extremes, pushing every idea to an ultimate conclusion. Englishmen might be content to work towards new ideals, whether in painting or government, by gradual, almost imperceptible degrees; not David. He had the single-mindedness, the impatience, of a born revolutionary. Once accept the principle of "Beauty by common consent," and he must put it into practice immediately. Once define Beauty as determined by the agreement of "the generality of mankind," and once admit that the generality of mankind agrees on the classical art of Antiquity as best representing Beauty, and you have no alternative. There can be only one way to paint beautiful pictures: copy Greek and Roman paintings as exactly as you can. Let no such practical difficulties as our ignorance of what Greek and Roman paintings actually looked like stand in our way. So the only actual remains of Greek painting are a few square inches of ruined wall? So even the Roman copies of Greek paintings that we know now were mostly all unknown to David? No matter; we will use what we have. We will use large clear blocks of primary colors, as ancient authors tell us was the practice of Polygnotus. We will adopt the sharp linear contours that we find on Greek vases. We will copy our figures from statues; and we will arrange them all on a line in the foreground plane, as we see them on vases and in pedimental sculpture. And the result, even if inferior to what might be done could we have had the greatest works of Graeco-Roman painting to copy, will still be immensely more beautiful than the soft pastel shades, the fragile blurred forms floating through intricately composed spatial planes characteristic of earlier 18th-century French painting.

Such a dramatic break with the forms of the preceding Rococo tradition, still the official court style of France, was revolutionary enough. But its forms were the least revolutionary thing about the *Oath*. Far more momentous was its revolutionary content; for in that was implied a revolution in the basic concept of what painting itself is and does, and what kind of people painters are.

The *Oath* was in fact not a painting in the old sense of a "thing of beauty and a joy forever" at all. It was primarily a statement of political belief. Its theme was the superiority of republican over monarchical forms of government. It was in fact what Johnson in England would have called Whiggish prating; and it is no accident that the best parallel to

2. *Jacques Louis David:* Oath of the Horatii. *The Toledo (Ohio) Museum of Art, Gift of Edward Drummond Libbey.*

Small version, painted 1786, of the large picture exhibited in 1785. Neoclassicists, modifying the traditional theory of Beauty, held that of all possible subjects the ideal human form in noble action was the most beautiful, of all forms Graeco-Roman classical the most ideal, of all actions Graeco-Roman history and mythology the most noble. In his large painting of the three sons of Horatius swearing to return victorious or not at all from their forthcoming combat with three Alban warriors (one of whom, for added drama and "beautiful feelings," is betrothed to their sister), David fulfilled this prescription to the letter—and by so reducing it to absurdity, unintentionally helped destroy it.

20

it in literature (though written later, and about a different episode) is in the 1842 *Lays of Ancient Rome* by that greatest of Whigs, Lord Macaulay:

> Then out spoke brave Horatius,
>   The Captain of the Gate:
> "To every man upon this earth
>   Death cometh soon or late.
> And how can man die better
>   Than facing fearful odds,
> For the ashes of his fathers,
>   And the temples of his Gods,
> And for the tender mother,
>   Who dandled him to rest,
> And for the wife who nurses
>   His baby at her breast . . . ?"
>
> "Horatius," quoth the Consul,
>   "As thou sayest, so let it be."
> And straight against that great array
>   Forth went the dauntless Three.
> For Romans in Rome's quarrel
>   Spared neither land nor gold,
> Nor son nor wife, nor limb nor life,
>   In the brave days of old.
>
> Then none was for a party;
>   Then all were for the State;
> Then the great man helped the poor,
>   And the poor man loved the great:
> Then lands were fairly portioned;
>   Then spoils were fairly sold:
> The Romans were like brothers
>   In the brave days of old.

Here are the typical contrived rhythms of neoclassicism (figures composed in three triangles against three arches; methodically uniform lighting so that all elements in the picture get equal emphasis); its self-conscious archaism and uncritical idealization of the virtues of Republican Rome; above all, its concept of "total classicism." Macaulay, writing at the end of the neoclassical era, hardly intended his subtitle—"a lay made about the year of the city CCCLX"—to be taken seriously; but David was in deadly earnest. He intended his painting to be understood as not merely based on Graeco-Roman precedent, but insofar as possible, to *be* a Graeco-Roman painting. It was "totally" classical, revolutionary in the most literal sense. And this was something very new.

When Reynolds had defined the artist's goal as "to improve mankind by the grandeur of his ideas," he meant no more than an obligation to show men the highest kind of Beauty he knew. David, however, understood that goal as a commission to make painting a positive instrument of moral reform. In the *Oath* and a series of pictures following it in quick succession over the next few years, he pointed out the virtues of republican self-government and the vices of absolute monarchy with an uncompromising clarity matching their uncompromisingly classical forms. How, under the heredity rule of degenerate kings and venal noblemen, you could never hope to find citizens with the simple patriotism Horatius's sons learned in their republican home. How only in a republican state could there be a scene like *The Lictors Bringing Back to Brutus the Bodies of His Sons,* because only republican government bred officials honest enough to condemn their own sons' crimes. How free men must always stand guard against that despotism which always lurks ready to pervert their institutions and, as *The Death of Socrates* warns, persecute dissent and destroy the greatest and wisest spirits. David's painting was, in short, frankly didactic, all but overtly preaching and teaching the cause of political Revolution. And that implied an entirely different way of conceiving the nature and function of painting, and of the relationship between artists and society.

We happen to know that David did not personally care much for pure classical forms as such; his taste ran to the Rococo forms in which he had been trained and in which his first works were executed. Only ten years before the *Oath,* when he was leaving to study in Italy after having won the French Academy's *Prix de Rome,* he had declared that "the Antique will not seduce me—it lacks spirit and does not move one." In this he resembles his almost exact contemporary Thomas Jefferson, the great protagonist of neoclassical architecture in the United States, who likewise retained all his life a personal preference for Adamesque-Federal forms. Thinking simply in terms of what appealed to their aesthetic sense, both found pure Graeco-Roman forms frigid and dull. But thinking in terms of these forms as symbols—pictographs, if you like, which could be used to demonstrate and proclaim truths which to them seemed self-evident— classical art appeared in a new light. In other words, they came to value the forms of classical art not for what they were, but for what they could say, as a kind of language. In this was implied a new concept of art altogether, characteristic of the coming Victorian age. Its workings were most obvious in architecture, where very soon one past style after another would be revived for various symbolic purposes: Gothic for Christian virtue, Egyptian for intimations of eternity, and so on. But the idea that a picture could and should "say" something in a literary or didactic sense had an equally important influence on the evolution of painting in the first half of the 19th century—what we can roughly call the Early Victorian age; most of the major disputes in painting throughout that era revolved around it in one way or another.

Even more than it revolutionized the concept of what painting is, David's *Oath* introduced a new relationship between painters and the society they live in. For to begin with it was not a commissioned work. No client or patron ordered it, or supplied ideas for it; David painted it entirely on his own initiative, in Rome, almost in secret. He painted what he wanted to, as he liked, then exhibited it in a salon for the inspection of connoisseurs, critics, and potential buyers. This practice, of course, is so normal for painters today that we find it hard to realize how rare it was before David's time. With certain conspicuous exceptions (the late Rembrandt is one, for instance), painters before 1750 were no more generally expected to invent their own subject matter or work on their own than a modern architect is expected to put up a variety of buildings and hope someone will happen along to buy one. As an architect today still generally begins his career in an established office, then sets up in business for himself when he feels he has become sufficiently known to attract clients, so painters traditionally began as apprentices and only in time set up their own studios and took orders for painting. It was not for them to invent subjects; whether Madonnas or family portraits, frescoes on a Sistine Ceiling or panels in a Barberini Palace, what painters did was determined by whoever commissioned the work. Their concern was merely how best to render their given subjects —how to realize the greatest beauty (spiritual, visual, or whatever), through that sensitivity to line, form, color, and composition which was accepted as their special talent. Literary, verbal ideas they left for those whose special gift was words and abstract concepts—poets, theologians, scholars, genealogists, or whoever. Not David. In the spirit of the coming Revolution, he demanded for painters liberty, equality, and fraternity with other "intellectuals." He demanded for painters the right to determine not only how they should paint, but what. And, defying all official canons, working on his own despite all disappointments, finally seeing his standards triumphant, his academic superiors all abashed, and himself dictator of painting in France, he set a potent example. If today painters can take it for granted that they are entirely free agents to invent whatever subject matter they choose (or ignore it altogether), to scorn any hint of compromise with public taste as an intolerable infringement of their natural rights, they owe much of that freedom to the revolution begun by Jacques Louis David. But they owe his revolution much more than that.

For he actually demanded more than equality for the artist, more than simply freedom not to follow the ideas of patrons and clients; he proclaimed that the artist ought to form and lead them. Painters ought to be, in a word, something like seers or prophets. Earlier artists, concerned with Beauty, had been generally content to leave philosophy to sages (Reynolds, for instance, would confine his speculations largely to aesthetics, let Johnson talk about life); David was not, and the new role he proposed for painters was attractive indeed. "As in Greece," wrote François Benoit,* "where they were the 'key and body of legislation,' the arts must become among the moderns 'a vital institution, a mute and ever eloquent legislation,' which elevates the mind and purifies the heart. What more sublime usage for the arts than this kind of priesthood?" What indeed? And what more flattering pose for the painter? Human nature being what it is, we should hardly be surprised to find that another result of David's revolution was that, as the 19th century wore on, painters began to consider themselves more and more inspired purveyors of Truth (or as they would call it, Reality), less and less humble seekers after Beauty.

For as David conceived his new "total classicism," it went far beyond the older conception of concern for a beautiful subject, beautifully painted. We have it on the best—for David, the unquestionable—authority, that Beauty and Goodness are inseparable. If the Greeks had but one word for both, how then could we presume to make a distinction between art and life? If we agree that nothing less than re-creation of Greek and Roman standards of Beauty in art should satisfy us, then we should likewise never rest until Greek and Roman standards of Virtue have been restored in society. And the painter least of all men should stand aloof from the task. So it is that we find David's total classicism involving him at one and the same time in a revolution in painting and the great Revolution in politics, making him at once the dictator of post-Revolutionary taste in art and a deputy to the National Convention, associate of the Directoire, and fervent supporter of Napoleonic "re-

* *L'art français sous la Révolution et l'Empire* (Paris, 1897).

form." So it is that we find him proclaiming artists to have no higher duty than "to produce work of 'usable application' "; art to have a deliberately "utilitarian aim; not the particular utility of a privileged caste, but the general utility of the nation, of the masses . . ." So it is that we find him proclaiming in theory, and demonstrating in practice, that there is and can be no difference between art and life. And this perhaps implied the most profound revolution of all.

Traditionally, art and life had been considered separate entities. Art reflected life, imitated it closely or at a distance as the case might be, but was essentially independent of it. Even though in David's *Oath* every detail was taken with minute accuracy from the Greek and Roman world (furniture, costumes, sandals, architecture), in this early painting he had still maintained the distinction; what he depicted there—the old Roman and his sons, their wives, the home they were swearing to defend— obviously had an existence independent of the picture; the one is a copy of the other. But by the 1790s, with the Revolution accomplished and David's classicism established both as the rule of art and the guide of life, the distinction blurs. Does David's painting (facing page) "imitate" Madame Hamelin, for instance, or did she "imitate" it? Are the painter's standards drawn from life, or did life take its standards from his painting?

3. *Jacques Louis David:* Madame Hamelin. *Washington, National Gallery, Chester Dale Collection.*

Essentially a new kind of painter, David conceived it his duty to set standards of public taste; the kind of Beauty validated by appeal to the "generality of mankind"—meaning the art of Graeco-Roman Antiquity— ought to be imposed on everyone, a process he felt justified by the Revolutionary doctrine of government by the "will of the people"—i.e., conformity of minority to majority opinion. This portrait of c. 1800 represents a full-scale application of his principles. It is not simply a painting in imitation of classical models; in a real sense, the sitter imitates painting. This Creole born in Santo Domingo, though a leader in Directoire *society, has been made to live in the world of the* Horatii. *The painter's forms and standards have not been determined by the world; it is he, the painter, who determines what forms and standards shall be, and the world takes them from him.*

26

So effectively and thoroughly had David made his art an instrument of moral reform, so successfully had Graeco-Roman standards been imposed on every phase of the intellectual and social life of France in the 1790s, that it would actually be difficult to say. David's goal of total classicism was now completely realized; not only was Beauty entirely identified with the particular forms of classical art, but he had succeeded in thoroughly fusing—or confusing, if you prefer—art and life.

The most immediate result of this, of course, was to establish David as dictator of French art, with powers unheard of before. Just as the political Revolution, by destroying the old distinction between "people" and "State," had made patriotism synonymous with obedience, justified mass military conscription, and given Napoleon "total" powers the French kings could never command, so David's revolutionary obliteration of all distinction between art and life made patriotism synonymous with classical taste, and enabled him to impose total conformity on French art as the old Academicians never dreamed or dared. This phase of David's career was a perfect illustration of the principle expounded in Bertrand de Jouvenel's *On Power,* that the net result of revolutions has always been to increase the powers of the State concerned, so that it pursues historic objectives more effectively than before. Thus, just as Napoleon more efficiently pursued Louis XIV's policies of enforcing conformity at home and French hegemony abroad, so David's official aesthetic position simply restated in a different context the principle of national unity on which Louis XIV's ministers had justified persecuting Huguenots. Once Truth and Beauty are officially proclaimed, other views on the matter are more than error or even mere heresy, they are subversion which cannot be tolerated.

And the end of David's career was an equally cogent commentary on the truism that revolutions destroy those who make them. It was not only that with Napoleon's defeat, the external authority of neoclassical art necessarily collapsed and David himself was exiled to Brussels. The rationale of neoclassicism itself collapsed, because by identifying it so totally with a particular political system, David had to distort it out of all recognition. That process began as early as 1799, when for the last of his series of episodes from republican Roman history David chose one, *The Rape of the Sabine Women,* which illustrated not republican virtue, nor yet (I think) a plea for unity among quarreling Revolutionary factions, but the principle that a noble end justifies ignoble means, thereby providing a useful precedent from Antiquity for Napoleon's aggressive plans to subjugate Europe in the name of liberty, equality, and fraternity. But it reached its absurd climax in David's great panoramas of the Empire, like the *Coronation of Josephine* and the *Distribution of the Eagles*. How could David's original definition of classical art, demanding subject matter and form both drawn from Graeco-Roman art down to the smallest detail, be reconciled with the literal, almost photographic counterfeiting of nature done by David in acquiescence to the Emperor's arbitrary taste? True, David did have an explanation for it. It was not only, he argued, that Napoleon and his circle were "inherently" classical (the Emperor resembled Augustus, his sister Pauline was another Venus, and so on) but that classical art had so far succeeded in determining life that France under Napoleon was a re-incarnation of the Graeco-Roman world, and Napoleon *was* a Roman emperor, hence to paint him as he was, to paint the world as he had made it, was to be classical. But all this was extraordinarily unconvincing. Only a fanatic could fail to see that "classical art is what I believe it to be" is pure solipsism; or, observing how deviously David made classical art conform to the Napoleonic "party line," retain any real respect for it. For most people, "classicism" lost all objective validity; the end result of David's revolution was to destroy the classical tradition of form altogether. A revolution that had begun by proclaiming classical art an absolute canon for painting ended by making it entirely relative to specific times and places. A crusade to integrate painters in society, to abolish all distinction between art and life, ended by vastly deepening the gulf between painter and public, encouraging painters to be independent of the demands of society or patrons, individualistic seers, isolated prophets, living in personal worlds of their own creation. Of course, all these implications were only worked out by slow degrees; that process was begun by Ingres.

NOTES

Appropriately enough, in view of David's contention that art and life are inseparable, the four rather well-marked phases of his life determine the four main phases of his painting. Born in Paris in 1748, David began in the Louis XV manner of his teacher, J. M. Vien, in which he painted *Mars Vanquished by Minerva* (1771, Louvre) and *Antiochus and Stratonice* (1774, Paris, Ecole des Beaux-Arts); in portraiture he retained the essence of it almost to the end of the century—e.g., *Pierre Desmaisons* (1782, Buffalo); *Lavoisier* [the chemist] *and His Wife* (1788, New York, Rockefeller Medical Institute); *La*

Marquise d'Orvilliers (1790, Louvre; replica in New York, Metropolitan). Exhibition of the *Oath of the Horatii* in 1785 began the next phase of his career as influential seer, moral and political reformer, and arbiter of social Reality; characteristic are *The Death of Socrates* (1787, New York, Metropolitan), *The Lictors Bringing Back to Brutus the Bodies of His Sons* (1789, Louvre; replica in Hartford, Wadsworth Atheneum), and the portraits of *Madame Récamier* (1800, Louvre) and *Madame Hamelin*. Intimations of the third phase, in which Napoleonic actuality and classical ideals are commingled, began early in the Revolutionary period, with *The Oath of the Tennis Court* (1791, Louvre; study in Cambridge, Fogg) and *The Death of Marat* (1793, Brussels); the *View in the Luxembourg Gardens* painted while David was incarcerated in the course of upheavals (1794, Louvre) and often cited as a premonition of Impressionist fragmentization of experience and spontaneous composition, also belongs here. But the full Napoleonic phase sets in only c. 1800 and lasts until Waterloo in 1815. To it belong *Napoleon Crossing the Alps* (1800, Versailles); *Le Sacré: Napoleon Crowning Josephine* (1805–7, Louvre) whose sheer 500-square-foot expanse, into which one can walk, breaks down the distinction between art and life as its forms recognize none between the classical and modern worlds; *Distribution of the Eagles* (1810, Versailles); and portraits like *Pius VII* (1805, Louvre) and *Antoine Mongez and His Wife* (1812, Louvre). *Leonidas at Thermopylae* (1814, Louvre), with unmistakable overtones of Napoleon after Leipzig, marks the beginning of David's last phase, in which he returns to neoclassical allusions; it continues during his nine years of exile in Brussels from Napoleon's downfall to his death in 1825 (e.g., *Mars Disarmed by Venus,* 1824, Brussels). And in the portraiture of his last phase he likewise returns to something of his pre-Napoleonic manner; *Emmanuel Joseph Sieyès* (1817, Cambridge, Fogg) is an example.

A useful catalogue of David's works, now somewhat outdated, is Richard Cantinelli, *David* (Paris, 1930). Also dealing with David in English are W. Valentiner, *Jacques Louis David and the French Revolution* (1929); M. W. Brown, *The Painting of the French Revolution* (1938); H. Rosenau, *The Painter: Jacques Louis David* (London, 1948); D. L. Dowd, *Pageant-Master of the Republic* (Lincoln, Nebr., 1948).

3

The Problem of Formal Beauty:

Jean Auguste Dominique Ingres (1780–1867)

Ingres was born at just the wrong moment in history. A "born painter" if there ever was one, he had the kind of precocious and innate gifts characteristic of Great Masters in the old tradition—an exquisite sense for perfectly balanced composition, for perfectly placed line, for precise harmony of color; in a word, for pure form. And he began his career in the traditional manner, going to Italy on a *Prix de Rome* in 1806, devoting himself to a study of Renaissance forms and principles (Raphael's in particular) quite in the spirit of Reynolds's 18th-century classicism, as if determined to ignore everything that was happening to the theory and practice of painting in his time. But of course it could not be done.

Fifty years earlier even, certainly two or three hundred years earlier, he could have devoted himself to this bent for pure form without distraction, while others provided him with subject matter, as they had Michelangelo and Raphael, Rubens and Fragonard, the sculptors of medieval cathedrals and the great temples of Greece. Fifty years later, he could have ignored subject matter and worked out problems of pure form in arrangements of bottles and guitars, or abstract compositions. But Ingres began his career in the early years of the 19th century when David's neoclassical dictatorship was at its height, when a whole generation was being taught that artists must be leaders of society, that form was less an end in itself than a means of saying something of moral or intellectual consequence which it was the painter's duty to invent.

Consequently, though to the end of his life Ingres considered himself, and was considered by others, the great champion of "pure classicism" as opposed to the "Romantic school" led by Delacroix, in fact the celebrated "battle" between them was (as Daumier in his famous satirical cartoons delighted in pointing out) no more than Tweedledum versus Tweedledee. There was no more fundamental difference between "classicists" and "romantics" in painting than between classical and Gothic Revivalists in architecture, because all the leading figures in this early Victorian generation shared the same characteristic assumption about the nature and function of art: though they might reject *what* David had said, they all took for granted his premise that the artist ought to say *something* of moral or philosophical consequence. Though differing on specific choices of forms, all put forms together in the same spirit, and so all belonged to the same ultimately romantic tradition. And this was the root cause not only of Ingres's personal difficulties and frustrations, but of the collapse of that tradition of classical form which he had set himself to represent and defend.

Human beings by nature have different ways of expressing themselves. People with a gift for words, who enjoy working with abstract ideas, seldom like working with their hands, and vice versa. Rare indeed is the person equally talented in both directions. But in the past, generally speaking, nobody had to be, because then most works of art normally involved collaboration between men of ideas, who furnished subject matter, and men of art, who gave it tangible form. Now painters were expected to provide both ideas and forms; they were required to be not only skilled manipulators of paint but also accomplished philosophers and keen commentators on life. And Ingres is a spectacular example of the difficulties involved. The excellence of his pictures varies almost inversely with the degree to which they dealt with a "story." Thus he was always at his best painting portraits or nudes, because in them he had his subjects given him, like the Old Masters, and, having no "story" to bother about, was free to concentrate his whole energies on formal problems.

So it is that his portraits are always objects of beauty, but rarely if ever penetrating psychological studies. The same thing is evident when he paints the nude. In a picture of a single nude seated on a couch doing nothing, like the *Bather of Valpinçon,* where no need for an "action" or a "story" disturbs his concentration on line and form, all the attractive power of the classical tradition of form comes across to us undiminished. When he complicates the issue, as in *La Source,* even to the slight extent of a clumsy classical allusion and pun on "goddess of the spring" and "source of life," our experience of classical form is weakened. And when he incorporates the form of the Valpinçon bather in a larger, complex "scene" of a *Turkish Bath,* it takes a coolly trained sensitivity to separate aesthetic from erotic sensations, and both from ludicrous mental associations with some country-fair peepshow. A comparison of Ingres's unfinished *Odalisque en grisaille* (page 35) in the Metropolitan Museum with others of this genre (for example, the *Odalisque with a*

Slave in the Walters in Baltimore, or the *Grande Odalisque* in the Louvre) illustrates particularly well how Ingres's subject matter clashes with his forms. In all cases Ingres's command of classical form is superb; but we can fully appreciate it only in the *grisaille,* where it has not been buried beneath heaps of Early Victorian romantic story-telling paraphernalia—fans and Oriental rugs and comic-opera stage properties. Yet only by accident was the *grisaille* left in its unfinished state. In Ingres's normal course of procedure, this underpainting, the formal framework of the picture, would have been overlaid with the same sort of details, because Ingres never questioned the assumption that pure form was not enough to make a picture. Yet in retrospect it seems clear that everything added later would have been superfluous, not only in our eyes but, what is more significant, in Ingres's. Although perhaps he never admitted it even to himself, subjects did not really interest him. He was interested in form—classical form, the balanced play of three-dimensional shapes against each other, the interacting pattern of lines, the organization of a comprehensive, organic whole out of independently defined parts. And in this he had no rival; it is his mastery of this, classical form in its purest sense, that makes all his pictures, even those with the most wretchedly mawkish subjects, worth our study today. This was the heart of his painting. Local colorations, the detail, the story, all were subsidiary and superfluous to this painterly core.

All of which became painfully evident when Ingres undertook to fulfill what he conceived to be his obligation to invent subject matter for pictures drawn from history, mythology, religion, or literature. True, he did somewhat better with classical themes than with others; his "classical" pictures rarely descended to the banal, pedestrian or bathetic levels of his Gothic Revival themes, like the successive essays on *Paolo and Francesca,* each worse than the last, or the Baroque Revival *Vow of Louis XIII.* But they were bad enough. Not all his mastery of composition, not all his literal dependence on the revered Iliad could make Ingres's *Jupiter and Thetis* more than ludicrous, or raise the drama of *Stratonice* above the level of waxworks in a museum period room. *Ut pictura poesis,* the classical ideal, was wrecked on this combination of great painting and wretched poetry. In the *Apotheosis of Homer,* superb details and compositional coordination were expended to create an assemblage of corpses. To appreciate the *Apotheosis of Napoleon,* you must turn away from the flatulent painting to the subtle and sensitive preparatory drawings.

33

To following generations in the advance guard, the significance of Ingres's example seemed all too obvious. Painters being the kind of people they are, the more they were made responsible for inventing their own subject matter, the less important subject matter became in painting, so that throughout the 19th century it increasingly came to be considered an obstruction to a painter rather than his inspiration, a barrier to be surmounted rather than a framework on which to build. Increasingly also, therefore, the standards by which painters judged painting and the standards by which the public judged it tended to diverge, the public valuing recognizable ideas, the painter pictorial qualities. Yet in retrospect it is questionable whether Ingres's career demonstrated the obsolescence of subject matter per se, so much as simply Ingres's particular concept of what subject matter ought to be.

Ingres was dedicated to perpetuating the traditional dogma that "the noble human form in noble action" in general, and classical forms in

4. *Jean Auguste Dominique Ingres:* Odalisque en grisaille. *New York, The Metropolitan Museum of Art, Wolfe Fund.*

A "natural painter" who in an earlier era would have happily concentrated on giving exquisite form to subjects set him by patrons, Ingres finds that as a result of the precedent set by David's generation, painters are expected to invent their own subject matter in a sense and to a degree unknown before. Talented in visible and tangible design, not in symbolic or literary abstractions, Ingres manifests what will become the increasing tendency of artists forced to invent their own subjects throughout the century—to treat content as perfunctorily as they can, and concentrate their attention on formal problems of picture-making which temperament and training suit them to understand. A typical example is this painting of c. 1813, which Ingres kept until his death, and which was listed among his effects as ébauche (preparatory). In the artist's eyes it was probably—and in ours it is certainly—a more satisfying work of art than his several finished versions of the same theme, in which superimposition of embarrassingly naïve anecdotal detail from imagined life in an Eastern harem only obscures that stern attention to formal balance, linear composition, controlled organization of light and dark, in which is their great merit.

classical action specifically, still represented a painter's proper subject matter. Yet, at the moment when he lived, classical themes were not only obsolete, they were rapidly ceasing to be viable at all. In part this was a by-product of the triumph of the bourgeois "economic man" in the aftermath of the Revolution. Under the aristocratic and monarchical social structure which had been the mold of Western civilization for so long, grand and noble actions made sense, and even under Napoleon were at least plausible; but once Europe settled into a bourgeois pattern, heroism in art became an anachronism which no longer corresponded to any facts of life. But even more fundamentally, there was an antipathy which Ingres never fully realized between the historic classical tradition and the new romantic approach to art and life characteristic of the rising *bourgeoisie*. In the classical tradition proper, art in general and classical art in particular grew out of and expressed life, were never an escape from it. Once treat classical subject matter in the romantic way, as a means of exciting beautiful feelings through their remoteness in time, in place, from everyday life, and you are no longer working in the classical tradition, no matter what you claim. Not only that, but once accept the premise that art is to be valued more for what it says than for what it is, and you have changed the nature of painting. The "romantic classicists," of whom Ingres was the great representative, thought they were still working in the classical tradition; but actually they had preserved nothing more than the shell of its forms. And how hollow that shell was, how the romantic attitude had emptied classical subject matter of all real significance, was already fully revealed in Ingres's generation by his great contemporaries, Constable and Corot.

NOTES

Ingres was born in 1780. A favorite student of David's (1797–1800), he won the *Prix de Rome* in 1801, but did not use it until 1806. In the interim he painted several works in the official Empire manner, notably *Napoleon as First Consul* (1804, Liège) and *Napoleon in His Coronation Robes* (1806, Paris, Musée de l'Armée), but his *Self-Portrait* of 1804 (Chantilly, Musée Condée) and portraits of the Rivière family (e.g., *Mademoiselle Rivière*, 1805, and *Madame Rivière*, 1806, Louvre) show him departing from it towards the sort of eclectic derivation from Raphael advocated by Reynolds. When he did go to Italy, he stayed 14 years in Rome and 4 in Florence. To this period belong the *Bather of Valpinçon* (1808, Louvre), *Oedipus and the*

Sphinx (1808, Louvre), portrait of *François-Marius Granet* (c. 1810, Aix-en-Provence), *Jupiter and Thetis* (1811, Aix-en-Provence), *Raphael and the Fornarina* (1814, Cambridge, Fogg), the several versions of *Paolo and Francesca* (c. 1814, Chantilly; 1819, Angers, et al.), *Interior of the Sistine Chapel* (1814, Washington), *Roger Rescuing Angelica* (1819, Louvre), and portraits of *Monsieur LeBlanc* and *Madame LeBlanc* (1823, New York, Metropolitan). In 1824, Ingres exhibited *The Vow of Louis XIII* (Montauban, Cathedral) in the Paris Salon with great success and returned to France for ten years, where he was soon made President of the Ecole des Beaux-Arts, painted his most ambitious classical work, *The Apotheosis of Homer* (1827, Louvre) and the very literal *Portrait of Monsieur Bertin* (1832, Louvre). When in 1834 his *Martyrdom of Saint Symphorius* encountered severe criticism, he denounced the "ingratitude" of France and left to direct the French Academy in Rome, not returning until 1841; *Odalisque with a Slave* (1842, Baltimore, Walters) and *Stratonice* (1840, Chantilly) date from this period. His last years, 1841 to his death in 1867, were spent in France as the recognized "last champion of the old classical school"; to them belong *The Golden Age* (commissioned 1839 as a mural in the Château Dampierre, executed 1843–47; a smaller version is in the Fogg, Cambridge), *La Source* (begun 1820, completed 1856, Louvre), portraits of *La Comtesse d'Haussonville* (1845, New York, Frick) and three of *Madame Moitessier* (1851, Washington; 1851, Washington; 1856, London); also *Joan of Arc at the Coronation of Charles VII* (1854, Louvre), and *The Turkish Bath* (c. 1852–63, Louvre).

Of the few monographs on Ingres in English, that in the Phaidon series by Georges Wildenstein (*Ingres,* New York, 1954) is particularly useful.

4

Expanding Concepts of Beauty:
John Constable (1776–1837)

Constable's interest in landscape could only be described as a passion. A born painter like Ingres, Constable was unlike him in that he never even attempted to invent "literary" themes for himself; he was entirely content with the "neutral" subject matter of landscape. For where Ingres had grown up under the shadow of David's demanding theories, Constable had grown up in the rural Stour Valley of East Anglia, and had come to maturity when the English countryside was at its scenic peak

37

(graciously humanized by 18th-century enclosure and landscaped parks, not yet blighted by the railroads and factories of 19th-century industrialism) and when the romantic movement was inculcating a fundamentally new attitude to Nature. He rejected the tenets of 18th-century classicism that "the proper study of mankind is man," that (as Johnson reproved Boswell) "the noblest prospect a Scotsman [or anyone else] ever sees is the highroad to London," where on Fleet Street and the Strand man in all his jostling variety and diverse works may be studied. Constable and people like him felt that man and all his measured little works of reason paled into pettiness beside the spectacle of glancing sun and rippling shadow over open hills, the great gnarled shapes of rugged trees, massy clouds rolling to the horizon, quiet brooks and sparkling waterfalls, reeds and heather. Nature, they felt, provided far fitter objects of awe, wonder, and reverence than any of the puny works or doings of man. Indeed, contemplation of Nature encouraged far deeper and higher religious experience than anything to be found in churches or chapels. As William Cowper put it, in Constable's favorite poem, *The Task,*

> Acquaint thyself with God, if thou wouldst taste
> His works. Admitted once to His embrace,
> Thou shalt perceive that thou wast blind before;
> Thine eye shall be instructed, and thine heart,
> Made pure, shall relish with divine delight,
> Till then unfelt, what hands divine have wrought. . . .
>
> In that blest moment, Nature throwing wide
> Her veil opaque, discloses with a smile
> The Author of her beauties, who, retired
> Behind his own creation, works unseen. . . .
> By the impure, and hears His power denied.

Such a theme, and such a passion, was hardly the highroad to painterly success at the beginning of the 19th century. For one thing, it was flatly opposed to the official position of the Royal Academy, based on the revered theories of Sir Joshua Reynolds. Reynolds had held that standards of Beauty must be taken from the classical world—from the statues and reliefs of the Greeks and Romans, the definitive creations of the Italian Renaissance—in which, he maintained, it was beyond question that man was the measure of perfection. The less directly art dealt with man, therefore, the lower on his scale it came. History, mythology, religion—the highest art must be that which concerns itself with these things. Next on the scale came portraiture, the depicting of man himself

38

idealized and ennobled. Then still life, evidence of man's will to order, even if he himself were not in the picture. Landscape, in which man was reduced to insignificance or eliminated altogether, came lowest of all. The best Royal Academicians could say for landscape was that it might, if "wild" enough (like the works of Mr. Turner, say) inspire noble or sublime feelings; but ordinary landscapes—commonplace rural scenes, the sort of thing Mr. Constable did—could hardly concern a serious painter.

So for Constable recognition came hard; not until he was fifty-three was he elected to full membership in the Royal Academy. And even then, when he paid his new member's courtesy call on Sir Thomas Lawrence, the President, Sir Thomas could not help reminding him how grateful Constable, a landscape painter, should feel to have been elected over the heads of so many "historical" painters. Constable was outraged. It was not so much what he felt as the condescension of a lesser to a greater painter, or even this obtuse doctrinaire insult to his deepest feelings, that angered him; it was that he had been sustained through so many years of difficulty and frustration not simply by some vaguely defined sort of Nature worship, but by a reasoned, logical, and provable conviction that his chosen subject was at least equal, if not superior in Beauty, to the officially approved themes of the Academy—and quite as classical, in every important sense. And it was then, perhaps, that he first determined to set down systematically the principles which he had developed and worked on throughout his life. The result was a series of lectures, given in 1833, entitled "An Outline of the History of Landscape Painting." These lectures represent a milestone in the development of modern art, not so much because they provided a specific apologia for landscape painting, or even because they heightened interest in it (they did not, of course; Constable, like all painters, spoke best through his pictures), but because they demonstrate how surely Reynolds's theory of Beauty contained the seeds of its own destruction.

Reynolds had defined Beauty, not as an absolute idea, but as something determined by reasoned agreement of the "generality of mankind." Very well; this we will accept. But can we, should we take it for granted, as Reynolds had, that the generality of mankind has always been in unanimous agreement on the highest Beauty being "the ideal form in noble action"? By no means. Let us, Constable says, look again and more carefully at Greek and Roman art, in the light of all the latest discoveries: is it indeed exclusively concerned with the human figure?

39

Obviously not. That there were elaborate landscapes on the walls of Pompeii and Herculaneum we know for a fact; that there must have been many other landscapes, now lost, we can certainly infer. Indeed, the whole traditional assumption that Greek and Roman artists preferred human figural subjects may well rest on nothing more substantial than the fact that stone statues survive the ravages of time better than paintings. Even the few paintings we do have prove conclusively that at least some Greek and Roman artists found landscape a worthy subject; probably there were many who did. Or conversely, how about the early Middle Ages? If this were an age of degenerate taste, as all Academicians maintain, then according to their theory it should have been an age of landscape painting; instead, we find it exclusively concerned with figure painting, with (as far as Constable's age could tell) no interest in landscape at all. And as soon as the Renaissance approached, and civilization began to revive, landscape reappeared, in the manuscripts of the late Middle Ages. Then, in the Renaissance itself, was landscape ignored? Certainly not. True, Raphael (for instance) used them only in backgrounds; he never painted landscape alone. But surely that was because he had to paint the subjects his age demanded? Even Reynolds, after all, despite his own theories about the superiority of historical and moral subjects, had to paint mostly portraits in order to make a living. Surely it is obvious that the landscape background of a Madonna by Raphael was put there because the Master felt it was an integral part of the serene, ideal Beauty he wished to convey; surely it is obvious that the historical rarity of pure landscape painting is an accident of circumstances, and no argument at all against its being ranked equally with figure painting? In short, Constable concluded, the fact is that there is no one kind of Beauty you can say "all men are agreed on"; you can say only that Beauty is what "a considerable number of men agree on." Reynolds's standard really justifies several kinds of Beauty. Landscape is one of them.

Furthermore, in composing the great landscapes of his mature period (from about 1811 to 1828), Constable worked in as truly "classical" a manner as even Reynolds might have desired. There was no question of copying direct from nature, any more than Reynolds had exactly transcribed the appearance of a sitter; in both cases, intent and method were the same—idealization, achieved by judicious selection and abstraction from precedents. The difference was that, whereas Reynolds's precedents were from the art of the past, Constable drew on his own. Each of his major landscapes was built up, that is to say, by the most careful process of selection and combination of dozens, perhaps hundreds, of his own sketches. A tall tree here, a low bush there; a bank of cumulus clouds here, the dark shadow of a pond there; here a tiny figure on a bench or a boat, there a grazing cow or a wheeling hawk; all these elements, seen and recorded at many various times and places, are coordinated into one balanced, integrated whole. No detail in *Salisbury Cathedral* (page 43), for instance, "just happens to be there" because it was visible from a given point; everything is disposed and painstakingly arranged. The precise location of the spire, the shape of the trees that frame it, the odd dead branch, the strollers in the close, the glint of water—every detail has its fixed and foreordained place in the grand scheme of the whole, just as in the façade of some classical building each dentil and flute and molding has a calculated relationship to total effect. Even more appositely, perhaps, it reminds us of the construction of a novel by Jane Austen. She, far more than Wordsworth, is the contemporary figure Constable most closely resembles. Not only did she suffer the same criticism and neglect for the "ordinariness" of her themes, but she composed in the same implicitly classical way. Just as in *Pride and Prejudice* or *Sense and Sensibility* no event, no circumstance, no character is casually thrown in because the writer happened to think of it as she went along, just as once we reach the end and see the plot as a whole we realize how each speech, gesture, and development had to come where it did, so nothing in *Salisbury Cathedral,* or the *Hay Wain,* or the *White Horse* is superficial or superfluous. In just as classical a sense as Michelangelo's *Pietà* or Raphael's *Sistine Madonna* or the Olympia pediments, Constable's landscapes are perfectly self-contained; each is a system complete within itself, so that every part takes its meaning and value from the whole. That is especially true of the touches of "realism" that proved such a sensational revelation when French painters first saw Constable's land-scapes at the Paris Salon of 1824. The "true green" of the foliage; the careful, almost meteorological study of clouds; the meticulous accuracy of bark and grass—these, like the deceptively "spontaneous" touches in Jane Austen's dialogue, derive their primary significance not from the actual, visual world outside, but in reference to the internal organization of the picture.

From 1828 on, however, there comes a change. By slow degrees, perhaps perceptible to only the keenest eye, this classical structure begins to dissolve, becomes manifestly less important to the painter. External

41

circumstances undoubtedly had something to do with it; in a very real sense the death of Constable's wife in 1828 must have destroyed that mood of confident serenity which is always essential to the classical world outlook, while his election to the Academy in effect relieved him of any earlier compulsion to "prove" his classicism. But fundamentally the change came from within; it was inherent in the rationale of Constable's art. Once you admit Beauty may have not one standard but several; once admit all men can never agree on it, and define it variously according to different minds and circumstances, sooner or later you must come to the point of realizing that there may be as many standards as there are minds, that Beauty can be a private affair, relative to one individual alone. It must eventually be defined, in short, as what a given painter chooses to think it is. Constable apparently (as far as we can judge from the somewhat fragmentary later lectures of his series) was never willing to go that far in theory. But in his later painting he moved steadily in that direction. Willingly and consciously or not, that dissolution of the classical tradition of form which was inevitably entailed in abandoning a single absolute standard proceeded apace in his last years. He showed less and less interest in "finishing" pictures, in organizing them out of sketched elements in the old painstaking manner. More and

5. *John Constable:* Salisbury Cathedral from the Bishop's Garden. *New York, The Frick Collection. c. 1826.*

Constable justifies a temperamental predilection for landscape by reference to Reynolds's principle that Beauty, instead of being absolute, can be defined as that which a number of people admire. Demonstrating that even the great masters of Renaissance humanism would have painted landscapes if they could, indeed that they inserted landscape background in pictures where their commissions did not require any, he makes landscape a respectable subject for serious painters. At first, he composes his landscapes in the traditional way, selecting, abstracting and collating from nature just as classical painters would treat historical or mythological subjects. In his later paintings and sketches, form as well as subject is increasingly determined by personal likes and inclinations, anticipating in effect the "expressionism" of Van Gogh two generations later.

42

more he began to concentrate his attention on the sketches themselves, on free spontaneous expression of his own moods in the face of nature, made on the spot.

This development was not alone the product of a change in aesthetics, however. For Constable's concept of landscape involved not merely a revolt against the classical theory of Beauty; in a very real sense it involved a revolt against the thinking of most of mankind throughout most of human history. Only very rarely before had anyone tried to maintain its basic premise: that the mind of a great and good God can be seen in the workings of Nature. Indeed, the perfection of each of Nature's creations—the shiny scales of the codfish, the coordination of the leaping rabbit, the majestic oak with its leafy crown—had always seemed to prove exactly the opposite. For consider: if ever in any one year all the offspring of a single pair of cod should survive, every sea would be piled mountain-high with fish; if ever all the offspring of a single pair of rabbits should grow up, no green thing would be left on earth; if ever all the acorns from a single oak tree should grow to maturity, the continents would be one solid mass of tree trunks. It follows that, for every one of Nature's perfect creations that a landscape presents, hundreds of thousands of others, equally perfect, equally admirable in function, have had to be killed. How could the spectacle of such merciless waste, a balance of madly excessive birth and pitilessly constant death, be considered a manifestation of some wise Benevolence, let alone an object of Beauty? Despite Constable's contention in his lectures, the fact is that, whenever landscape had been represented for its own sake in earlier Western art, it was as a foil to enhance by contrast the ordered worlds of human Reason or Divine Providence, much as 18th-century women put beauty patches on their cheeks to show off the whiteness of their complexions. Thus in Renaissance and Baroque painting Nature characteristically appears as evil (as in the background to the *Temptation of St. Anthony* in the Isenheim altarpiece), or mindless (as in Peter Breughel's peasant pictures and *Icarus*), or wild (as in Salvator Rosa), or forbidding (as in Ruysdael's *Jewish Cemetery* in Detroit); self-evidently the work of some evil demon who delights in misery—the Prince of This World. Serene and orderly landscapes (as in the background of Raphael's *Alba Madonna* or Giorgione's *Pastoral Concert*) are highly *un*natural, to be understood as belonging to supernatural or imaginary worlds.

Yet the very fact that men felt Nature to be evil, that they did have the ability to recognize and resent her remorselessness, her cruelty, her chaos, seemed proof enough that human beings were not fully part of this natural world, that they must have been created to live in some other way, by some other Power. To the extent that men share in the mad cycle of illimitable births and the horrors of war, famine, disease and death that are their necessary consequence, they have obviously fallen into the power of the Prince of This World; but there is in them, too, something that encourages them to break out of it. What form this attempt to break out takes is the essence of historic religions, and so in turn determines the character of art in history.

Sometimes the reaction has been ascetic—escape from the world, life in defiance of those urges which Nature implants in you to keep it going. Sometimes the best course has seemed to attempt mystic communion with that Power whose benevolence is evidenced in man's innate awareness of his differences from Nature. But in historic Western civilization, the most characteristic response has been to use that divinely implanted sense for order, man's Reason, to control Nature, so as to create little islands of order in the midst of her chaos and misery. In the Middle Ages this characteristic Western urge for order was manifest in feudal society with its balanced social rights and duties; in systematic theology and philosophy; in the logical structure and controlled ornament of Romanesque and earlier Gothic architecture. In the Renaissance its characteristic forms were clarity of literary expression and that insistence on perspective (i.e., on ordering the world in terms of intelligible human experience) which characterizes painting from the Quattrocento through 17th-century landscapes like Hobbema's *Avenue at Middleharnais* or Vermeer's *View of Delft*. Eighteenth-century classicism was in this same great tradition. Palladian architecture, especially Protestant church architecture, and Reynolds's theory of painting were each in their way expressions of man's defiance and conquest of lawless Nature, and in this sense expressions of the traditional religion of the West.

But in the course of the 18th century a new attitude towards Nature began to develop, which reached maturity in early 19th-century romanticism. The *philosophes* of France, the Deists of England, the protoromantics of Germany, all began to announce that the world was inherently good, that Nature is really orderly. If it seems viciously lawless, they declared, that is only because we do not yet fully understand what its laws are. Ignoring the fact that their new position was only possible because so many generations of slow progress had by the 18th century developed a practical science which was beginning to get Nature under some kind of control, they denounced 18th-century classicism in art, as well as all kinds of systematic theology, as not only cold and lifeless, but in their terms fundamentally irreligious. Religion they defined as something involving emotions, passions, imagination. Such "sensibilities" in themselves became their new religion. After all, if the world of Nature is fundamentally good, what is the point of the old religion with its idea of some divine sacrifice that is to save us from Nature's power? What is the value of a classical tradition which consists in imposing order on something which in fact (could we but recognize it, they say) is divinely ordered already? So by the early 19th century traditional religion and the traditional classical theory of Beauty are put on trial together, and found wanting; and of this attack, Constable's concept of landscape painting is both an expression and a weapon. With it begins a conviction that art can be a religious experience in its own right.

No wonder that Constable's development towards freer, looser, more direct and personal visions was so inevitable, or that critics can see in it premonitions of Van Gogh. Quite as much as Reynolds's, the ultimate significance of Constable's painting was predetermined by the inherent logic of his own theories. True, when he died, Constable was far short of reaching Van Gogh's stage of using landscape as no more than a springboard from which to project his own emotions. But that in Constable's theory lay the ultimate justification of Van Gogh's practise, few can doubt.

NOTES

Constable was born at East Bergholt, Suffolk, in 1776, the son of a miller; his training was haphazard, a combination of informal contacts with connoisseurs like Sir George Beaumont and minor artists like John Thomas ("Antiquity") Smith and Joseph Farrington, and his own study of earlier landscape painting by Claude, Gainsborough, Richard Wilson, and Girtin, among others. In 1799 he was formally entered as a Royal Academy student, but, given the tenor and precepts prevailing there, he had to formulate principles of landscape painting practically independently. His style reached its first maturity c. 1810, as may be seen in *Malvern Hall* (c. 1803, London), *Boatbuilding near Flatford Mill* (1815, London, Victoria & Albert Museum) and *Weymouth Bay* (1816, Hartford, Wadsworth Atheneum); but he remained beset with frustrations and difficulties of all kinds, and without any effective recognition. In 1816, however, his affairs took a marked turn for the better; his long courtship of Maria Bicknell finally ended in a happy marriage, soon after that he received a legacy, and from then until Maria's death in 1828 his painting increased steadily in scope and reputation. To these years belong such works as *Wivenhoe Park* (1817, Washington); *The White Horse* (1819, New York, Frick)—on the success of which he was elected an associate of the Academy; *The Hay Wain* (1821, London; study in the Victoria & Albert Museum, finished work in the National Gallery)—which, when exhibited at the Paris Salon of 1824, caused a great sensation and ultimately affected the whole course of French landscape painting in the 19th century; the great series of cloud studies executed 1820–21 and described in Kurt Badt, *Constable's Clouds* (London, 1950); *View of the Stour near Dedham* (1822, San Marino, Calif., Huntington); *The Leaping Horse* (1825, London, Burlington House); *The Cornfield* (1826, London); *Dedham Mill* (c. 1829, Cincinnati, Taft). The last nine years of Constable's life found him increasingly occupied with landscape as a vehicle of personal expression; more and more of his work is in the spontaneous vehicle of watercolor. Typical are *The Cenotaph* (begun 1832–33, finished 1836, London), *Weymouth Bay* (c. 1830, Philadelphia), *Stoke-by-Nayland* (c. 1836, Chicago), *Arundel Mill and Castle* (1836–37, Toledo, Ohio).

Biographies of Constable include those by C. R. Leslie in 1845 (Jonathan Mayne, ed., 1951), C. J. Holmes in 1902, and R. B. Beckett, *John Constable and the Fishers* (London, 1952). Less ambitious, but useful (particularly for illustrations) are books on Constable by C. G. E. Bunt (Leigh-on-Sea, England, 1948), S. J. Key (London, 1948), J. Mayne (London, 1953), and Lawrence Gowing (1960).

5

The Summing Up:
Jean Baptiste Camille Corot (1796–1875)

Corot was a free man—as painters could never have been before his time, and rarely have been since. He had, in fact, all the important kinds of freedom there are. His living assured by a legacy in force from his twenties on, he was free from want. Unmarried to the end of his life, never (apparently) forming emotional attachments of any kind, he was free from care. And thanks to the revolutionary changes in the status

47

and social function of painting and painters that began at the end of the 18th century, he had a near-complete freedom of thought and action; he could paint what he liked, as he liked, when he liked.

His "easy circumstances" enabled Corot to fly over life in a pressurized cabin, as it were, never quite in touch with the hard ground of fact outside; it is therefore hardly surprising that the saying for which he is best remembered is that (to most people) almost fatuous credo of artistic detachment: "I paint a woman's breast just as I would an ordinary milk can." But this very remoteness from the world of actuality meant that he could afford to bypass conventional taste and pursue painterly experiments at his own contemplative and unsystematic pace. As a result, almost all the important phases in the evolution of the classical tradition of form appeared in his art at one time or another; it was, indeed, a summing up of what that tradition meant both for the past and for the future of painting.

Corot was born in Paris, 1796, of bourgeois parents who for a time put up the usual opposition to his idea of a painting career; but in 1822 his father agreed to it, and settled an allowance on him. Thenceforth Corot's life was an uneventful story of steady fulfillment and success. His earliest works were painted at Rouen, on the Normandy coast, and at his father's house at Ville d'Avray (1822–25); from 1825 to 1828 he was in Rome; thereafter, with the exception of a second short stay in Rome (1834), he lived mainly in and around Paris, at Ville d'Avray, and in the village of Barbizon in the forest (or more exactly, park) of Fontainebleau, whence his association with the so-called "Barbizon School" of landscape painters.

Corot first exhibited at the Salon of 1827 and was represented there every year following, except 1850. His reputation was slow to develop (he sold no pictures until 1838) but once recognized grew rapidly among both painters and the public (for different reasons) until from the late 1850s to his death in 1875 he was one of the most popular painters of the 19th century; his landscapes, especially those in the "fluffy" or "silvery" style he developed c. 1850, remained in such demand that forgeries of them were common down to the time of the Great War.

There was no more rigor in the development of Corot's art than there was in his life. Having no need to fix any particularly salable manner in the eye of public, patrons, or dealers, he could afford to indulge himself in many different directions; at any given period, he might be pursuing several different implications of the classical tradition simultaneously.

But certain more or less easily definable patterns are perceptible.

Possibly because it was in such deep discredit following the Napoleonic collapse, probably because he was always free to indulge the instinctive distaste of born painters for literary inventing—whatever the reason, Corot seems never to have attempted the "total" classical formula of the noble Graeco-Roman theme painted in Graeco-Roman style. Approximations to it are common throughout his work, however. There are, for instance, some examples of classical themes set in a classical landscape, in the manner of the French 17th-century classicist Nicolas Poussin (1594–1665), such as *Homer and the Shepherds* (1845, Saint-Lô). More common are single figures or (occasionally) groups, also set in a landscape, with titles of quasi-classical connotation: *Marietta, the Roman Odalisque* (1843, Paris, Beaux-Arts); *Resting Nymph* (1855–60, Geneva); *Bacchante by the Sea* (1865, New York, Metropolitan). But it is characteristic of these experiments that, while following the letter of the formula, they have little connection with it in spirit. Not only are the background forms freely and loosely painted, but they preserve little or nothing of David's intimations of classical prototypes. Painter, sitter, and spectator are all quite aware that there is no such recreation of the classical world here as in David's work; nor are they even idealized worlds in the Renaissance sense of, say, Giorgione's *Sleeping Venus*. Essentially they are 19th-century people acting picturesque, evocative, nostalgic parts. These pictures have the same relationship to David's classicism that High Victorian buildings, with their miscellaneous piles of elements assembled for eye interest from all over the past, have to the conscientious, methodical symbolism of Classical Revival architecture.

Where Corot comes closest to doctrinaire neoclassicism is in the landscapes done during his first stay in Rome, where he went on the advice of his neoclassical teacher, Jean-Victor Bertin. Typical are the *View at Narni* (1826–27, Ottawa, National Gallery), *Bridge and Castle of St. Angelo with St. Peter's Dome* (1826–27, San Francisco, Palace of the Legion of Honor), *View of the Farnese Gardens* (1826, Washington, Phillips), or *Island of San Bartolomeo* (1826–27, Boston). These are not strictly neoclassical pictures in the original Davidian sense of simulating actual Graeco-Roman art; but to the extent that they are scenes of Rome with actual classical monuments, conceived as solid precise forms composed in broad areas of primary colors, in balanced arrangement and controlled space, they are essentially neoclassical experiments, representing the classical tradition of form both in what is represented and how.

From the 1830s on, the stage of classicism represented by Ingres's portraits and history paintings appears—pictures no longer explicitly classical in content but still "noble" in the traditional sense, and composed with classical formality. Typical of this stage in his earlier work are landscapes like *Jamièges* (1829–30, Northampton, Smith College), *Chartres Cathedral* (1830, Louvre), *Pont-au-Change and the Palais de Justice, Paris* (1830, Philadelphia), and *Florence from the Boboli Gardens* (1835–40, Louvre); in his later work, figure studies like the *Blonde Gascon Girl* (c. 1850, Northampton, Smith College), *Interrupted Reading* (1865–70, Chicago), *Woman with a Pearl* (1868–70, Louvre), and *Young Greek Girl* (Emma Dobigny, 1868–70, New York, Metropolitan), ringing "modern" variants on old classical prototypes like the *Mona Lisa* and Graeco-Roman busts.

At almost the same time he begins experimenting with "ordinary" themes rendered with classical precision, clarity, and balance in the manner of Constable's landscapes of the period 1810–25; representative are *The Quay at Honfleur* (c. 1830, New York, David Rockefeller). *M. Henry's House and Factory* (c. 1830, Philadelphia), and *View near Volterra* (1838, Washington). And the inevitable change follows— once classical form is separated from classical content, it begins to change into a vehicle for personal expression. This is evident as early as the *Quarry at Fontainebleau* (1830–35, Ghent), and proceeds through the

6. *Jean Baptiste Camille Corot:* Young Girls of Sparta. *Brooklyn, N. Y., The Brooklyn Museum, Gift of Mrs. Horace Havemeyer.*

Corot represents the new type of painter made possible by 19th-century capitalism—the man whose private income frees him from social obligations to an unprecedented degree, while at the same time dissolution of the old absolute standards frees him to experiment with pictorial form as he chooses. This picture of c. 1870, with its treatment of a classical theme in terms of contemporary fact, and its impressionistic form, illustrates how in the course of his long life Corot used his freedom to explore a full range of possibilities for classical, romantic, and "realistic" painting.

1840s (*View Near Naples* 1841, Springfield, Mass.). By 1850 only the broadest principles of formal classical organization remain in his studies of *Breton Peasant Women* (e.g., c. 1850, Philadelphia); precise outlines and defined color blocks are all fast dissolving in loose masses of brushwork, and this development proceeds apace in succeeding years. Thenceforth classicism in any essential sense is abandoned, at least in the major pictures Corot exhibited in the Salon. Sometimes their subjects were ostensibly classical, like the *Dance of the Nymphs* (1855, Louvre), or *Souvenir of Mortefontaine* (1864, Louvre); sometimes romantically medieval, as in the *Distant View of Saint-Lô* (1850–55), which makes such a striking contrast with the *Chartres* of twenty years before, *Gallic Horsemen* (c. 1854, Montreal), or *Cathedral of Mantes* (1868–70, Reims); sometimes neither, like the *Return to the Stable* (*Environs de Gruyères,* 1850–65, Philadelphia), *Villa of the Parasol Pine* (c. 1860, Kansas City, Mo.), or *Ophelia* (1871, Boston). But their subjects hardly mattered any longer, for in all alike subject was entirely subordinated to picturesque effect. These were the pictures on which Corot's immense 19th-century popularity was based, and with good reason, for they perfectly suited High Victorian taste. Their eye-appealing picturesqueness, variegated outlines, vague blurry images, and loose silvery-gray overcast created an air of nostalgic "pastness" in general, perfectly paralleling the mood of Tennyson's or Arnold's philosophic poetry. Corot's painting of the 1850s and -60s was an even more striking counterpart to the concept of picturesque eclecticism which dominated architecture in those years, indiscriminately borrowing from all past styles but subsuming all specific styles in one overall picturesque pile.

Thus Corot's life and art provide a résumé of the whole history of art from the Early Victorian through the High Victorian periods, from the precise literary symbolism of neoclassicism and the Gothic Revival to mid-century picturesque eclecticism, from full classical form to no classical form at all. And he went on experimenting to the end. For example, a work like *The Artist's Studio* (1865–70, Baltimore) might well appear to be the end of a long and consistent evolution on the part of a painter who has gradually exhausted and lost all interest in questions of Beauty and now is steadily moving towards Realism in the manner of Courbet. But not so; for in those same years Corot is also painting pictures which sum up the whole theory, evolution, and dissolution of the traditional classical form. Among the most striking is the *Young Girls of Sparta* (page 51), painted 1868–70. The subject is classical—Sparta, that is, is a classical place name; the story of Spartan girls exercising in the fields outside the town was long a favorite inspiration of classical painters; the pose of the main figure is acceptably classical (like the recumbent figures on sarcophagi, and very like Ingres's *Odalisque*); and the three figures in the back are agreeably reminiscent of that classic classical motif, The Three Graces. And in form the picture shows classical principles, too—the main figure in balanced relationship to the frame and the landscape, a respect for solid massing, for formal structure and organization of pictorial elements, the typically classical serene moment of repose. But all of these classical characteristics are subtly vitiated, in one way or another. These are not ancient Spartans, of course, but modern Greek girls; Corot has long accepted the exhaustion of all potentialities of the strictly Graeco-Roman subject. This classicism is residual, nothing more than a stabilizing framework for depicting the world as it is here and now. To this extent, Corot's painting here reflects the potent tide of Realism in the 1860s. And the manner of painting the background, especially, with its forms loosely indicated in trails of paint, suggests something too of the coming era of Impressionism. But essentially these are peripheral intimations; the central mood is romantic —subject and style both are concerned with things and ideas distant in time and place. The brooding air of melancholy, the vague silvery-blue atmosphere, all this takes us out of ourselves, and belongs to something far other than the classical tradition of form. This is the romantic tradition of expression, the other great root of modern painting; to it we now turn.

NOTES

Illustrations of Corot's major works may be found in Germain Bazin, *Corot* (Paris, 1942, 2nd ed. 1951) and Daniel Baud-Bovy, *Corot* (Geneva, 1957); Henri Marceau, *Corot* (exhibition catalogue, Philadelphia Museum of Art, 1946), provides a useful English text. A standard but outdated *catalogue raisonné* is contained in A. Robaut, *L'Oeuvre de Corot* (Paris, 1905). A good selection of Corot's works is illustrated in Robert L. Herbert, *Barbizon Revisited* (Boston, Museum of Fine Arts, 1962).

II

Varieties of Romantic Experience:
from Sensibility to Self-Expression

"ROMANTICISM," AS IT DEVELOPED IN THE EARLY 19TH century, was both a foil and a reaction to 18th-century classicism. Where the instinct of the classical mind is always to delight in imposing precision and disciplined order on the world around, the romantic instinct is to look for things remote from the everyday world, whose very distance lends enchantment. As a result, there can be no consistent pattern for "romantic" painters. Even among painters working well within the traditional theory of Beauty, those whose emphasis is primarily on beautiful feelings rather than beautiful forms differ from each other in almost every conceivable way, as is abundantly demonstrated in the diverse lives and art of Blake and Goya, Delacroix and Turner. But this one characteristic they all have in common—they are impatient with the classical search for Beauty in objects or in formal visual composition; Beauty for them is decidedly more a matter of feelings than calculation. They look on their art, that is, primarily as a medium for expression of what that age called their "sensibility," which in time will come to include their moods, their aspirations, ultimately their inner selves. And in so doing, they complement the dissolution of classical form, complete the ruin of the traditional theory of Beauty, and lead the way towards a new concept of painting altogether.

54

1

The Personal Vision:
William Blake (1757–1827)

Independence of mind is one sure mark of the romantic. This, more than anything else, was what the romantic tradition bequeathed to modern painting. And this above all is what distinguished the life and art of William Blake. It appears all through his work; the page from *Milton* illustrated on page 57 is a typical example.

The subject of Blake's poem, John Milton, was hardly a "romantic" figure in any proper sense of the word, of course. Where the romantic's characteristic concern is with things marvelous and distant, Milton's was with revealed faith, not speculative imagination as such; with spiritual, not exotic, reaches of time and space. And Milton was very far from any intention of providing a self-conscious record of intuitive insights. *Paradise Lost*, the work that most attracted Blake, was written as a dramatic restatement of traditional Christian cosmology; for all its magniloquence and personal interpretations, the framework remains strictly traditional theology. But these facts (or, indeed, facts in general) interested Blake hardly at all; it was precisely and primarily insofar as *Paradise Lost* was a personal revelation that it attracted him. He was deeply, even fanatically interested in theology; but not in theological systems as such, and certainly not in orthodox or traditional ones. He was interested in his own theology. If he felt, as he proclaimed, a spiritual kinship with the poet ("Milton lov'd me in childhood and shew'd me his face"), it was not so much on grounds of common Christian belief as because he recognized (rightly or wrongly is not the point) another soul who had, like himself, personal revelations and intimations of the supernatural world expressible only in terms of revolt against convention. Blake did not read *Paradise Lost* for instruction; its value for him was as a suitable jumping-off point for expressing feelings, emotions, and spiritual experiences of his own. In fact, the purpose of his *Milton* was to "correct" the pernicious errors in *Paradise Lost*: "I saw Milton in Imagination," he told H. Crabb Robinson (who recorded a good deal of Blake's conversation in his *Diary*) in 1825, "and he told me to beware of being misled by his *Paradise Lost. . . .*" According to this revelation, it was because of his personal experiences (making an unhappy marriage for passion) that Milton had tended in the poem to equate Satan with untrammeled imagination and God with disciplined reason. Of course that assumption was quite in keeping with the traditional view of wild Nature as inherently evil; but Blake, in the van of romantic reaction against 18th-century classicism, saw it otherwise. Things were in fact, Blake maintained, quite the reverse; and in his poem he described how Milton in Heaven also realized this error and returned to earth to expiate it by casting off "selfhood" with the help of Blake's and other cosmic spirits.

In his forms Blake was no less insistent on independence than in his subject matter. In our illustration from *Milton,* for example, the muscular nude derives from Michelangelo and the bearded patriarchal figure from his other great source of inspiration, Gothic sculpture. But the picture as a whole is composed neither on Renaissance nor on medieval, nor indeed on any, principles taught in schools; it depends on Blake's own instinctive sense of design alone, and is reproduced by similarly distinctive, personal, eccentrically unorthodox methods. Such a completely personal approach seemed incompetent nonsense to contemporary critics, not only to those of traditional classical persuasion, but even to the newer school of Romantics. Their problem was that almost before Romanticism had become a conscious and accepted movement Blake had both demonstrated its basic premises and anticipated most of its conclusions.

7. *William Blake:* To Annihilate the Selfhood of Deceit and False Forgiveness, *relief-etched, hand-colored plate from* Milton. *Washington, Library of Congress, Lessing J. Rosenwald Collection.*

Most of this poem was composed, and its illustrations conceived, at Felpham in the years 1800–1804; Blake completed and published it in London, 1808. In the new freedom afforded by an emerging democratic society it became possible for artists to defy convention to an unprecedented degree; such an intransigent spirit was William Blake, justifying complete independence from all externally imposed rules on the strength of "inspiration" and "imagination."

56

To Annihilate the Self-hood of Deceit &
False Forgiveness

In the British Museum there is a copy of Reynolds's *Discourses* once owned by William Blake. On its margins Blake jotted down, about 1808, his reactions to the great man's strictures. Better than anyone of his time, Blake understood the full implications of the shift from absolute to relative standards of Beauty that Reynolds preached there; better than anyone, Blake saw how the theory that Beauty is something rationally determined, that artists can be made, must end:

> Reynolds's Opinion was that Genius May be Taught. . . . [but] Knowledge of Ideal Beauty is Not to be Acquired. It is Born with us. Innate ideas are in Every Man, Born with him; they are truly Himself. The Man who says that we have No Innate Ideas must be a Fool & Knave, Having No Con-Science or Innate Science.

> Reynolds Thinks that Man Learns all that he knows. I say on the Contrary that Man Brings All that he has or can have Into the World with him. Man is Born Like a Garden ready Planted & Sown. This World is too poor to produce one Seed.

These were no sudden outbursts of opinion; they represented Blake's mature, developed thought. Ever since he had sat (very briefly) in the Academy Schools, and heard Reynolds deliver his 1778 *Discourse,* Blake had thought him a fool and knave, had been certain that no living art could ever grow on precepts as dead and false as his. Very well; he would discard the Academic rules entirely. But what should he put in their place? For he must put something; that is what human beings are like:

> How comes it that those who have rejected the Stewards immediately set about making new rules of their own, and that these new rules are substantially the same as the old? A man says, "I have finished with rules; henceforth I will do what I want"; But he finds that his deepest want, the only want that is constant through the flux of his appetites and despondencies, his moments of calm and of passion, is to keep the rules." *

Should it be the authority of classical Antiquity, the new rules Jacques Louis David was at that very moment proposing? God forbid: "The Greek & Roman Classics is the Antichrist" were almost the last words he uttered. Should it be the Significant Form to be sought in landscape, the "great spectacle the Deus Pater Omnipotens spreads before our eyes," as Cézanne described it when searching for rules a hundred years later?

* C. S. Lewis, *The Pilgrim's Regress* (London, 1933), p. 127.

(This was the 19th century's perennial problem.) No; that was no more than a shadowy world of "vegetable existence"; "Nature has no Outline." What, then? For Blake it was simple. He was a mystic, considering himself in the great line of Jakob Boehme and Emanuel Swedenborg, the Hebrew cabalists and the Rosicrucians; for him, therefore, there could be only one source for all rules, anywhere, any time: "I know of no other Christianity," he wrote in *Jerusalem,* "and of no other Gospel than the liberty of body and mind to exercise the Divine Arts of Imagination; Imagination, the real and eternal world, of which this Vegetable Universe is but a faint shadow." Or again, in a "prophetic discourse": "Imagination and Vision was . . . , is, and I hope will always Remain my Element, my Eternal Dwelling place." There could be only one kind of Beauty worth striving for in art—transcendental. And there could be only one set of principles worth following—his own, those his visions dictated. As he declared in *Jerusalem,* "I must Create a System, or be enslaved by another Man's." This was the romantic creed, first made feasible by the new emancipated status of painters established in Blake's time; in Blake's work we are introduced to most of the new problems and developments that it involved for the theory of painting.

It involved, to begin with, a complete independence of mind and attitude. Blake would take dictation from nobody, on themes or technique. If, in illustrating Dante's *Divine Comedy* (page 61), or Milton's *Paradise Lost,* or the *Book of Job,* his drawings followed what the text described (as they often did, closely), that was because the older seers' visions happened to agree with his, not because he felt under any compulsion to illustrate what they had written. Wherever they differed, he felt free to use the subject matter as no more than a convenient springboard from which to project his own flights of pictorial imagination. His supernatural visions, his direct personal contacts with the unseen world, superseded all other authority, and justified independence in anything and everything he might choose to do.

His forms were determined with the same independence. To Blake (and in this he anticipated what came to be normal 19th-century practice) the art of the past was a great reservoir of forms, into which anyone ought to be free to lower a pail. That the forms of medieval art might have developed as the specific vehicle for Christian thought, or that Michelangelo's were conditioned by his fusion of Christian belief and classical principles, was of no concern to him; to study the art of the past systematically, to rationalize the use of forms, would kill their vitality, he thought. Academic theoreticians, like Reynolds (let alone modern art historians!) "are at all times Hired by the Satans for the Depression of Art—A Pretence of Art, to destroy Art"—for their attempt to analyze the principles of art rationally can only lead to such preposterous propositions as the idea that a man can learn to become a painter by travel and study. What nonsense! "The man who on Examining his own Mind finds nothing of Inspiration ought not to dare to be an Artist," he wrote next Reynolds's *Third Discourse*. Inspiration is enough for every need. It will provide all the design a painter requires to unify his work; it will supply all the technical skill necessary. With inspiration, an artist has everything; without it, nothing. Nothing, therefore, must be allowed to stand in the way of his realizing Inspiration and Vision to the fullest. Full and total independence in every way is the least a painter should demand and expect.

Now this is an ideal with universal attraction. There is something in every human being that responds to the urge for revolt against convention, for spontaneous expression—just as there is in every human being a faculty that longs for conformity and order. But, just as it is obvious that too much conformity and order may lead to sterility and vain repetition, so there are problems inherent in entirely untrammeled expression, as Blake would demonstrate to the whole 19th century.

The first is the problem of what kind of activity art really is, and what its relation to society ought to be. Blake's reliance on personal vision encouraged him to write poetry in which, like Humpty Dumpty, he made

8. *William Blake:* Dante and Virgil in the Skiff of Phlegyas, Hailed by Argenti. *Cambridge, The Fogg Art Museum, Grenville L. Winthrop Bequest.*

By the 1820s, the romantic spirit was spreading widely enough that Blake's later paintings, like this, were much more appreciatively received than his earlier works had been. That they were actually any better understood is questionable, however; in Blake's mind this was no romantic play on feelings evoked by things far off in space and time, but something Real, in which he believed—its closest parallel, the "high" or "white magic" of Spenser's 16th-century Faerie Queene.

words mean what he chose them to mean, and to base his art on what, despite the claims of modern "Blake circles," amounts to a private set of symbols. It is true that Blake did write (in *A Public Address,* 1810), "Ideas cannot be Given but in their minutely Appropriate Words, nor Can a Design be made without its minutely Appropriate Execution." But the judge of what is the appropriate Word or Execution turns out to be Blake (or any other artist) himself. Blake in fact recognized no outside standards, only his own private vision. This is all very enchanting, to be sure, and such devotion to ideals of Truth in defiance of the unenlightened multitude is indeed commendable; furthermore, Blake's work has the ring of authenticity that keeps art alive. His language and imagery correspond so tellingly with the revelations of earlier great mystics, and with the imaginative faculties of modern generations, that his art is fresh and treasured while most of his contemporaries' has long since been lost and forgotten. But the question is, what influence did his example have on the status of painting in general? That great art resulted from Blake's insistence on complete self-expression may be true; does it necessarily follow that complete self-expression is a good thing for everybody? That is still debatable. If art is a thing so private as to be fully intelligible only to the painter, if his personal satisfaction is the only criterion of its worth, then how does this activity differ in kind from some solitary hobby like stamp-collecting, model-train-building, or bird-watching? The world may well tolerate it, as long as it is socially unobjectionable; but what reason is there to expect anything more? Why, that is, should the world pay any attention to art, if painters pay no attention to the world?

Then again, there is the problem of standards and judgment. Once, during Blake's early and short stay in the Royal Academy school, he had been criticized by Sir Joshua himself, told to work "with less extravagance and more simplicity" and correct his drawing; Blake never forgave it. Always aware that he had some technical deficiencies, Blake excused himself on the grounds that too much attention to formal training, any self-conscious studying of "style," would ruin his or any other painter's spontaneous vision, desiccate his imagination, inhibit all his creative faculties. All of which is undoubtedly true; but how much is "too much"? Works without faith are dead, to be sure; but then, it is equally true that faith without works is blind—and blind men are so easily imposed on. Blake was indignant at the idea of some blockhead presuming, on the strength of technical training alone, to be another

Michelangelo; but why could not any incompetent, on the strength of imagination, presume to be another Blake? Blake talked much about "Mechanical Excellence" as "the Only Vehicle of Genius"; but since he made painters themselves judges of what "mechanical excellence" might be, what was to prevent the appearance of a great horde of charlatans, devoid of either talent or ideas, justifying pretensions to be painters by chanting Blake's own famous litany: "I will not reason and compare: my business is to Create"?

But all these were problems for a more distant future. For his own time, Blake's example raised another and different question. Already the artist and the man of ideas, the intellectual and the craftsman, had begun to dissolve their ancient partnership, which had created so many great works of art in the past; now a further and equally disastrous split began to appear—between Order and Imagination. In the past they, too, had worked together as natural complementaries; in the "high" eras of art (High Gothic, High Renaissance, High Baroque) artists had combined spontaneous direct vision and the discipline of accepted rules to satisfy both mind and eye, appealed at once to love of order and delight in spontaneous expression, and so spoken to the whole man. Even Reynolds would never have denied that some imagination was essential in great art. But now Blake proclaims one element alone sufficient. And perhaps that is why, compared to earlier times, the 19th century seemed to lack giants in painting; why, instead of Titians or Rembrandts or Michelangelos, we see innumerable small groups and single individuals picking independent paths across it—most of them to founder in bogs of emotion or a wilderness of formalism. William Blake largely escaped these dangers, though his mysticism, unsupported by any systematic theology, did undeniably go soggy at times. But those who tried to follow him, with less talent, less vision, or less single-minded conviction, were not always so successful.

NOTES

Blake's life spanned the years from 1757 to 1827, during which English taste passed from the Georgian classicism of the age of Johnson to Early Victorian romanticism, but he himself had little part in influencing the trend. Almost from beginning to end, he remained an isolated and unknown figure

63

—as shadowy to the outside world as the outside world was to him.

Blake's father was a middle-class Dissenter, attracted to the doctrines of Emanuel Swedenborg, and Blake himself formally joined the Swedenborg sect early in life; this religious background undoubtedly stimulated his mystic faculties, but he soon left the orthodox New Church and all other creeds behind to fashion a cosmology of his own. In 1771 he was apprenticed to an engraver, James Basire, and earned most of his later living as an engraver and printseller; throughout his life he maintained that outline was the essential and only proper vehicle for a true artist and deprecated all "painterly" qualities (chiaroscuro, etc.) as materialistic and chaotic—a conviction which, antithetical to the Grand Style as it was, hastened his departure from the Royal Academy school soon after his admission to it, in 1778. Typical of his work at this period is *Glad Day* (1780), explained by the lines "Albion arose from where he labour'd at the Mill with slaves: giving himself for the Nations he danc'd the dance of Eternal Death." In the early part of his life, Blake's creative energies were expended more on poetry than painting, however; he had, as Professor Blunt comments, "little natural facility as a painter"—in this respect curiously anticipating the careers of the great Post-Impressionists Cézanne, Van Gogh, and Gauguin.

Blake married in 1782, and succeeding years were devoted to writing and illustrating poetry—*Songs of Innocence* (1789) being the first major product. In the 1790s Blake, like so many intellectuals of the period, was preoccupied with schemes for social and moral regeneration, inspired both by his own visions and the atmosphere of ideas engendered by the French Revolution; these were expressed in the *Marriage of Heaven and Hell, Visions of the Daughters of Albion, America* (c. 1793), *Songs of Experience, The Book of Urizen, Europe* (c. 1794), *The Four Zoas* (1795–1804). Again like so many contemporaries, he was disenchanted by the obvious perversions of the original goals of the Revolution, and gradually turned away from social concerns to concentrate on the life of the inner man; the change was marked externally by his leaving London to live for three years in the village of Felpham (1800–1804) and in his work by the poems *Milton* and *Jerusalem,* both conceived around this time, and illustrations of Blair's *Grave* (1807) and *Paradise Lost* (begun 1808).

In 1804 Blake returned to London and soon fell into poverty; an exhibition of his paintings (1809) was dismally unsuccessful, and the descriptive catalogue he wrote for it, however interesting a revelation of his mental processes to 20th-century critics, was a disaster in his own time. Calling himself a "mental prince," Blake castigated all Venetian and Flemish painters as "demons," declared with what seemed fantastic arrogance that "till we get rid of Titian and Correggio, Rubens and Rembrandt, we shall never equal

Rafael and Albert Durer, Michelangelo and Julio Romano," and claimed that he

> having been taken in vision into the ancient republics, monarchies, and patriarchates of Asia has seen those wonderful originals . . . the cherubim . . . erected . . . among the Rivers of Paradise, being originals from which the Greeks and Hetrurians copied Hercules Farnese, Venus of Medicis, Apollo Belvidere and all the grand works of ancient art. . . .

A hundred years later, and Blake might well have become a celebrity; but in 1809 such claims served only to establish him, as a review in the *Examiner* put it, as "an unfortunate lunatic, . . . whose personal inoffensiveness secures him from confinement, and consequently, of whom no public notice would have been taken, if he had not forced himself on the notice and animadversion of the *Examiner*. . . ." Blake replied in 1810 with *A Public Address* and notes on his *Vision of the Last Judgement,* but these were not published; henceforth he lived in retirement, kept barely alive by a few engraving commissions and especially by the patronage of John Linnell, a successful painter, who began buying his works in 1818. It was Linnell who commissioned Blake's illustrations of the *Book of Job* (1825) and Dante's *Divine Comedy,* by which he is most widely known today.

Besides his illustrated books, of course, Blake produced throughout his life a great number of prints and drawings on allegorical, visionary, and Biblical themes. Particularly notable are the two large sets of Biblical subjects executed for his early friend and patron Thomas Butts, one in tempera (1799–1800) and the other in watercolor (c. 1800–1805).

Literature on Blake is voluminous and reflects almost every conceivable shade of opinion. The nine books published on Blake by Geoffrey Keynes between 1927 and 1957 are among the best known. The *Life of Blake* was first written by A. Gilchrist in 1863; a new edition was published in London by R. Todd, 1942. The best single shorter account is Anthony Blunt, *The Art of William Blake* (1959), with a critical bibliography. Good introductions to Blake's significance in the history of letters are Bernard Blackstone, *English Blake* (1949), and William Gaunt, *Arrows of Desire* (London, 1956).

2

The Art of Politics:

Francisco José de Goya y Lucientes (1746–1828)

In 1951 a book by Czeslaw Milosz, entitled *The Captive Mind* was published which described how intellectual life in postwar Eastern Europe was being determined, permeated, and guided by a principle Milosz called "Ketman":

> The inhabitants of Western countries little realize that millions of their fellow-men, who seem superficially more or less similar to them, live in a world as fantastic as . . . Mars. They are unaware of the perspectives on human nature that Ketman opens. Life in constant internal tension develops talents which are latent in man. He does not even suspect to what heights of cleverness and psychological perspicacity he can rise when he is cornered and must either be skillful or perish. . . . Just as theologians in periods of strict orthodoxy expressed [heretical] views in the rigorous language of the Church, so the writers of the people's democracies make use of an accepted special style, terminology, and linguistic ritual. What is important is not what someone said but what he wanted to say, disguising his thought by removing a comma, inserting an "and," establishing this rather than another sequence in the problems discussed. . . .

Old Spain was never as thoroughly totalitarian a state as the old Islamic despotisms, let alone the new "people's democracies." But by the time of Goya, centuries of the most autocratic rule in Europe had produced a habit of mind in Spain which, if not precisely the "Ketman" Milosz describes, is certainly something very like it.

There has always been a certain enigmatic quality in Spanish painting, an habitual predilection for symbolic allusion rather than direct statement, for allegory over anecdote, for double meanings and interpretations easily adjustable to circumstances, protecting artist and patron alike. Among "Old Masters," Velasquez is the prime example. When critics of the 1920s and -30s, living in a world made safe for political democracy and objective analysis, wrote encomiums about Velasquez' courageous glorification of the downtrodden Spanish proletariat in *Las*

Hilanderas (*The Weavers*), they overlooked the fact that such obvious and specific social criticism would have been suicidal in Old Spain; and so the later discovery that Velasquez' actual subject was not *genre,* but the classical myth of Arachne challenging Athena to a weaving contest, should not have come as a surprise. But why present a classical myth in so oblique a way, with large figures of peasants at spinning wheels in the foreground and the main subjects—Arachne, Athena, and the competition tapestry—far in the background, out of optical focus, painted so loosely that only the keenest eye can recognize them? It remains a mystery; but then, much about Spanish painting is mysterious. "Why?" is the question we are always asking in Spanish art; and seldom are there any altogether satisfactory answers. That is particularly true of Goya.

The *Marquesa de Santa Cruz* (page 69) is typical. Did Goya choose to abandon the 18th-century academic manner of his earlier portraits and paint her like *Madame Récamier* or *Madame Hamelin* because he had become a great admirer of the neoclassical aesthetic theories and portrait formulas of Jacques Louis David? Or was it because he, or the Marquesa and her circle, wanted to imply their faith in the Revolutionary principles of Liberty, Equality, and Fraternity? Or was it possibly simple expediency to show admiration for French taste in 1804, when Napoleon's star was rising to its zenith and already casting long shadows over Spain? Who knows now? Or who can tell why, compared to the elegant sophistication of *Madame Récamier* or *Madame Hamelin* (page 27), the *Marquesa* seems such a travesty? Surely this creature with her stupid, vacuous face, her bizarre crown of laurel leaves, and her oversize lyre must be meant as some kind of monstrous joke! But a joke on what, or whom? On the classical pretensions of French intellectuals and their art? But pictures like this do them no harm; it is their Spanish imitators that look ridiculous. A jibe at the provinciality of the Spanish intelligentsia? (Perhaps the sitter did in fact look and act the fool.) If so, why was the portrait accepted and kept in the family with (as far as we know) no protest against such an outrageous and merciless exposé? Or perhaps, again, there was a broader implication; perhaps the painter intended to indict the follies of mankind in general, as he did in series of etchings like the *Caprichos* or the *Disparates?* There is no way of telling. It may be that the painter was being deliberately ambiguous. Or it may be that there was a particular significance which was so cleverly disguised and so carefully guarded that the few who knew it took it to their graves with them. Whatever the real explanation, whatever the painter's actual motives, we shall never know for sure. And this mystery is typical of all the most famous of Goya's works.

Goya's official portraits of the royal family of Spain, for instance. Some critics see Goya as the fearless foe of hereditary privilege and divine right who does not hesitate to show his queen an idiot, his king a dotard, the *Family of Charles IV* collectively "a grocer and his family who have just won the Grand Lottery." But can it really be that Goya's royal patrons were so obtuse as not to notice how he has flouted the traditional expectation that painters should beautify and idealize their subjects—"historians tell us Alexander the Great was mean and low in appearance; the painter ought not so to represent him"—or so indulgent as to ignore it? Can we really believe, as others maintain, that Charles IV and Maria Luisa were extraordinarily advance-guard connoisseurs of art for art's sake, spiritual ancestors of the Steins and the Guggenheims, who were prepared to accept anything their court painter gave them on grounds that a genius like Goya must not be inhibited from expressing himself, even to the extent of countenancing deliberate satire on themselves? That seems even more unlikely; but what the full explanation may be, we have no idea.

Neither do we know why Goya painted a pair of *Majas*—one nude, the other clothed. In fact, there is even some controversy over precisely what a *maja* was. We hear that gay blades of the period sometimes had

9. *Francisco Goya:* The Marquesa de Santa Cruz as a Muse. *Los Angeles County Museum of Art, Allan C. Balch Endowment Fund.*

In the decadently authoritarian atmosphere of Spain, Goya for reasons of prudent policy perfected a deliberately allusive and ambiguous presentation of themes, and a loose form appropriate to it. This portrait is typical. In 1804, when it was painted, Napoleon Bonaparte's power was supreme in Europe, and already casting long shadows over Spain; but it would be impossible to say whether Goya here intended a flattering imitation of portraits like Madame Hamelin *or* Madame Récamier *in the reigning neoclassical manner of David, or a patriotically inspired parody of them; all we can say for certain is that its loose painterly handling of the form perfectly complements its ambiguous content.*

double portraits painted of their mistresses, arranging them one above the other so that at the pull of a string the clothed figure would drop out of sight leaving the naked one hanging in its place. Were Goya's two *Majas* no more than a titillating souvenir of his supposed romance with the Duchess of Alba? Or were they intended as something like Titian's *Sacred and Profane Love* which, though literally illustrating a poem by Poliziano, could be interpreted as a commentary on the two natures of Woman, the two faces of love? Is the *Procession of the Flagellants* a mercilessly satirical attack on Spanish superstition, or a moving record of mystic fervor? There is evidence in the picture to support either interpretation. Does *The Bewitched* depict a devout priest resisting a temptation of the Devil, or a renegade fearfully performing some rite of black magic? You could read it either way.

And so it goes; "Life in constant . . . tension" had, as in other times and places, developed "talents which are latent in man" for instinctively veiled meanings and vague allusions. If Goya remains a mystery, it is ultimately because critics raised to take straightforward expression for granted cannot indeed "suspect to what heights of cleverness and perspicacity" an artist "can rise when he is cornered and must either be skillful or perish."

Content inevitably affects form; and so it is not surprising that when Manet and other painters like him later in the 19th century became impatient with photographic precision of form, and began looking for means of getting away from meticulous description to broad impressions of the world, they found their great models in Spain. There, where treatment of subject matter by inference, allusion, and implication had been an enforced habit of mind for generations, painters had long since perfected a correspondingly loose, blurred, painterly technique for embodying it. In a world where no one dared speak directly, where unmistakable meanings were too dangerous to utter, they had cultivated the means of expressing themselves by implication; had made sure that, if cornered, they could at most only be accused of giving this or that "impression"—which they could always claim was misunderstood. Long before it became a self-conscious aesthetic creed, "impressionistic form" had become an habitual and natural technique in Spanish painting.

A typical example of how Spanish painters could use impressionistic form to disguise meaning is provided by Goya's *Disasters of War*. When Goya conceived the series and began to make sketches and first plates, it was not at all sure that France would be defeated, or that Napoleon and his heirs might not rule Europe forever. From inherited generations of experience he knows better than to speak out plainly against the conqueror, as his contemporary Gillray, the political cartoonist, was doing in England. He chooses rather to speak in ambiguous generalities, in unimpeachable platitudes. To say that "war is hell" may involve an implicit condemnation of French aggression in Spain, but it is not explicit; they can hardly guillotine you for pointing out the obvious fact that warfare breaks through the thin humanized crust of civilization to reveal an underlying abyss of barbarism and brutality. And his formal language perfectly complements this kind of content. He develops an etching technique which negates all precision of line, composes in strong separate masses of grays and whites set against varying degrees of darkness—or alternatively, in dark blacks and grays against white; the result is a loose, free effect like the bold brushwork of his oils which later Impressionists admired so much. And with this technique he dissolves all specific content. The soldiers might be any army, so ill-defined are their uniforms; the sufferers might be any war victims, so loosely are they characterized. *Tampoco* (page 73), for instance, presumably is an indictment of French atrocities; but you could never prove it in court. Does the artist mean to say that the French (assuming that it is a French officer, though you can hardly tell from the uniform) have wantonly executed hundreds of harmless peasants, or only two or three guerillas who have committed acts of war against them? Impressionistic technique makes the shadowy line of hanged figures so indistinct, fading off into such immeasurable distance, that it could be argued either way.

That Goya's ambiguity of content and form is quite calculated becomes apparent in 1814, when six years of fighting and French occupation end with Wellington's victory at Vittoria and Joseph Bonaparte's expulsion from Spain, Ferdinand VII returns to the Spanish throne spewing promises of reform, and a new age of free speech seems about to begin. In the brief months of political liberalism which follow, Goya paints two large pictures and makes several prints worked up from sketches for the *Disasters* in a strikingly new manner. In the *Riots of the Puerta del Sol* there is no equivocation; nobody can doubt that Goya sees them as directly caused by French folly in garrisoning Madrid with Moorish auxiliaries. Nobody can doubt whose firing squads are shooting down the pathetic bands of arrested rioters in the subsequent lamplight *Executions of the Third of May*—nor where the painter's sympathies lie,

71

for the composition is dominated by a helpless victim repeating the pose of Christ on the cross. And in these paintings form is likewise used not to obscure but to clarify and dramatize the meaning: bold color exciting noble feelings, a disciplined organization recalling Velasquez' great piece of self-evident history painting, *The Lances*. From this brief period, too, date etchings like *Spanish Superstition* and *The Ruptured Eagle*—no longer blurred allusions, but crisply incised and unmistakable statements of opinion.

But the new era comes to an early end; repression and absolute government set in again, and Goya soon rediscovers, like Winston Smith in George Orwell's 1984, that in a totalitarian state "the only thing you can really call your own is the few square inches inside your own skull." He retires from active life to meditate on the basic nature and problems of power; he expresses his thoughts in necessarily veiled allusion and impressionistic brushwork. A series of paintings of witchcraft on the walls of his country house, the Quinta del Sordo, records how he, like Winston Smith in the Ministry of Truth, came to realize that power is essentially a thing of the mind. On mental delusion the power of witches depends; on mental superiority depends man's power over brute nature, as expressed in Renaissance art by the symbol of man on horseback, and in Goya's by *Judith* in the Quinta del Sordo and the *Tauromaquia* series.

10. *Francisco Goya:* Tampoco ("Nor This"). *No. 36 in the* Disasters of War *series.*

The enigmatic title, completing No. 35, No se puede saber por qué ("Nobody can tell the why of it"), *is characteristic of Goya's four great series of etchings carried out in the last thirty years of his life. Presumably a record of French atrocity and Spanish suffering during the Peninsular War, the* Disasters *are in fact universal. Though sometimes considered an early demonstration of art used as a political weapon, these prints were too limited in circulation, printed too late (between 1811 and 1821, and not published until 1863), and too general in theme to have much specific import. However, their characteristic qualities of generalization, deliberately vague meaning (subjects implied rather than stated), and correspondingly loose technique and broad massings were Goya's heritage to 20th-century painting.*

But increasingly it becomes apparent that the essence of power is control over Reality, the power to define what Reality is and impose it on other men's minds. This brings Goya to explore the idea of insanity, in paintings like *Saturn Devouring His Children,* and the late series of etchings, *Disparates (Proverbs).* Here, veiled under ostensible representations of classical myths, Goya points out that insanity is not merely a matter of failure to perceive physical realities—like some pauper writing a check for a million dollars; in totalitarian societies, it means failure to conform to dictated truth. There, sanity or insanity is determined by collective solipsism; he who says two and two make four is insane in a world where everyone is made to believe that two and two make five. A whole civilization may be insane in terms of another: could we be transported back to the Byzantine Empire in Justinian's time, for instance, we might find that what we consider the curious artistic convention of representing people as automatons with wide staring eyes and puppetlike limbs was intended as actuality, that people whom we might consider raving visionaries were then considered the norm, and people like ourselves insane deviants. Believers in reasoned and objective methodology would find themselves madmen in the Dark Ages when emotion and impulse and superstition ruled men's minds. People in Goya's time who believed that the divine right of kings was part of the order of the universe necessarily considered republican government and religious toleration to be symptoms of insanity.

On these and related matters the aging Goya pondered, and painted increasingly mysterious pictures. Summing them all up, perhaps, was the *City on a Rock* (New York, Metropolitan), enigmatic and ambiguous in subject, loose and painterly in style. Like all Goya's great pictures, it can be read in many ways: as a symbolic vision of future technology, or of the folly of human presumption, depending on whether the flying men are seen as anticipating space fiction or restating the Icarus myth; or as a self-portrait of a deaf man's isolation from the world. My own guess would be that it is an allusive representation of life in a totalitarian world, where men live alone and in fear of each other; where the air is filled with crazy distorted communications; where the ultimate freedom is freedom to be sane, to say that two and two make four. But whatever it is, the picture remains witness to the appearance of a new kind and use of painting— painting whose primary concern is with the inner workings of the painter's own mind, which presents to the spectator only a private world of symbols and imagination.

In Goya's particular situation this kind of painting was entirely justified. Deliberate vagueness and generality, "impressions" rather than definitions, a private imaginative world made more valid than the objective, physical universe—in some political circumstances, these are the only means of genuine expression an artist has, the only way he can keep art alive. But is it appropriate at all times and places? Because Goya was necessarily concerned with "expressing the inexpressible," does it follow that painters any time, anywhere, are justified in following his example and cultivating vagueness for its own sake, considering formlessness somehow meritorious in itself? Goya himself suggested the answer in the clear and unequivocal pictures he produced during the short period of social and political freedom in Spain after 1814. But later generations largely missed that point. "What would be the result," wrote Blamire Young eagerly in the 1920s,

> at the end of 25 years supposing the Education authorities were to hang a carefully reproduced and enlarged copy of the *Colossus* in every schoolroom in the country? . . . One imagines that a nation which kept before the eyes of its children a conception of human life so exalted and so hopeful would reap later on a bountiful harvest of manliness and courage in the lives of the next generation.*

We do not have to speculate; that very experiment was tried, with the same sort of ambiguously generalized painting, by admirers of Mondriaan's abstractions and Kandinsky's nonobjective exercises in spirituality after the Great War, and we know the answer—nothing. Goya could have told them; but each generation has to learn for itself.

NOTES

Born in 1746 into a Spain sinking into political impotence and cultural bankruptcy, Goya began by imitating the grandiose Italian Rococo style practiced by José Luzan, the local master of his birthplace, Saragossa. More direct contact with it came through the visit of Giovanni Battista Tiepolo to Spain (1762–70) and Goya's visit to Italy (1770–71); by 1776, when he was first appointed to make designs (cartoons) for the Royal Tapestry Factory at Santa Barbara, he had mastered it. Typical of his some sixty paintings for tapestries in the next few years are *The Crockery Vendor* (Prado), *Flower Girls* (Prado), and *Gossiping Women* (Hartford, Wadsworth Atheneum). As he began to move in court circles, he gained access to the royal painting

* *The Proverbs of Goya* (Boston, n.d.), p. 155.

collection, discovered the great 17th-century Spanish master Velasquez, and made a series of 18 etchings (begun 1778) after works by him, experimenting in the new medium of aquatint which, by a special process of acid-biting a metal plate, made possible greater gradations of light and shade than in ordinary etching. Study of Velasquez, and also the Venetian masters in the royal collection, increased Goya's painterly breadth and virtuosity, and ensured a steady rise in his reputation; in 1785 he became Assistant Director of Painting at the Academy of San Fernando, in 1786 official painter of the tapestry works, and in 1789 court painter to Charles IV, a position he held until 1802. Characteristic of his official work in those years is the portrait of the *Duke of Osuña* (1785, New York, Frick); of *Don Manuel Osorio de Zuñiga* (c. 1787, New York, Metropolitan); of the *Marquesa de la Solana* (1791–95, Louvre); the frescos for the church of San Antonio de la Florida (1798); and the *Family of Charles IV* (1800, Prado; two studies for it, of *Queen Maria Luisa* and the *Infanta,* are in the Metropolitan, New York).

Paralleling these, however, were works of a new, personal, and eccentric character, apparently occasioned by his severe illness in 1792, which resulted in total deafness; in 1793 he sent eleven paintings of this "new" type to the Academy of San Fernando, with a covering letter explaining that ". . . to occupy an imagination mortified by the contemplation of my sufferings, . . . I fell to painting a set of pictures in which I have succeeded in giving observation a place usually denied it in works made to order, in which little scope is left for fancy and imagination." *The Burial of the Sardine* and *The Procession of the Flagellants on Good Friday* (1793, Madrid, San Fernando) were presumably among these eleven; typical of the new trend also are the "witching" pictures made for the Duke of Osuña (e.g., *The Bewitched,* 1798, London, and *The Lunatic Asylum,* 1800, Madrid, San Fernando), which show a new interest in states of superstition bordering on insanity, but this trend's great monument was the etched series *Los Caprichos* (published 1799, but sale soon stopped).

From 1802 to 1814 Goya retreated increasingly into private life. *Majas on a Balcony* (New York, Metropolitan) and *The Forge* (New York, Frick) probably belong early in this period; the *Maja Nude* and *Maja Clothed* were presumably painted about 1804 for Manuel Godoy, the power behind the throne in Spain and a consistent patron of Goya's. During the political upheavals of these times, which began with Charles IV's enforced abdication in favor of his son, Ferdinand VII, his replacement in turn by Joseph Bonaparte, and final return, Goya continued to paint whatever portraits successive ruling factions in Spain demanded, being court painter under both rival kings, and in 1812 painting the *Duke of Wellington* (London, Wellington Collection). His real interest in these years, however, was the *Disasters of War* series (begun 1810, completed about 1820). In 1814 Goya emerged briefly into active life with his *Riot at the Puerta del Sol* and *Executions of the Third of May* (Prado), patriotic commemorations of the events of 1808 which had sparked a national uprising against the French, but with the return of reactionary policies he fell under political suspicion, was harassed by the Inquisition for having painted the two *Majas,* and finally left Madrid, first for Seville, then to a country home, the Quinta del Sordo (House of the Deaf Man), which he purchased in 1819. Among the famous "black paintings" which decorated it were *Saturn* and *Judith* (Prado); to this period also belong *The City on a Rock* (New York, Metropolitan), *The Pilgrimage of San Isidro* (Prado), and *The Artist with his Physician, Dr. Arrieta* (1820, Minneapolis). In 1820 a revolt momentarily established a liberal government in Spain and Goya once again spoke up unequivocally in its favor, for which temerity he had to pay with exile when Ferdinand VII was restored in 1823; he fled to political asylum in Bordeaux in 1824. There he enlarged the *Tauromachia* (first published 1816) with a set of lithographs (*"The Bulls of Bordeaux,"* 1825), completed the *Disparates,* his last enigmatic commentaries on life and power (1820–24), and died in 1824.

On the portrait of the Marquesa de Santa Cruz, see *Bulletin of the Art Division,* Los Angeles City Museum, X, 1, 1958. Two standard references on Goya are the books by A. Mayer (1923) and F. J. Sanchez Canton, *Vide y Obras de Goya* (Madrid, 1951) on which latter Pierre Gassier, *Goya* (Geneva, 1957) is largely based. For Goya's drawings, see A. Malraux, *Goya's Drawings from the Prado* (London, 1947); for his etchings, E. L. Ferrari, *Complete Etchings of Goya* (1962). Biographical and critical works include books on *Goya* by Charles Poor (1939), R. Moynihan (London, 1951), F. S. Wight (1954), J. Emmons (1955), A. Malraux, *Saturn* (1957), Dino Formaggio (1961).

3

The Early Victorian Romantic:
Eugène Delacroix (1798–1863)

In contrast to Goya and Blake, who overtly or covertly lived at odds with their society, and whose influence was much greater on later generations than on their own, Delacroix and Turner were from youth widely known and accepted leaders of painting in France and in England. Delacroix especially was an entirely typical representative of the prevailing spirit of his age—almost a stock figure of the Romantic Man who became the dominant type of European intellectual from Waterloo nearly to the middle of the 19th century.

Delacroix's kind of romanticism did not initially mean any break with the traditional theory of Beauty inherited from the 18th and earlier centuries. Quite the reverse; to the end of his life Delacroix never varied in his conviction that the proper end and goal of painting was to create Beauty. When he said, "I am a rebel, but not a revolutionary," he meant it; his intention was only to correct within the traditional theory what he felt to be an overemphasis on beautiful form at the expense of beautiful feelings of which he felt David, Ingres, and their followers were guilty. This demanded in the first instance more emphasis on the means of evoking beautiful feelings—on free brush stroke and exciting color—and less on means of defining beautiful form. Where Ingres proclaimed linear composition to be the foundation of art, Delacroix maintained that beautiful painting must begin with a "painterly" style, emotional and spontaneous, suggestive in all senses of the word, creating a world for itself that imagination could feed on. It followed that, where neoclassicists had proclaimed the highest Beauty to be found in Raphael and Phidias, Delacroix took his ideals and inspiration from the great Venetian colorists Titian and Tintoretto, and the Flemish masters of robust pictorial masses and flashing brush stroke, Peter Paul Rubens and Anthony Van Dyck. But while romantics and classicists might differ as to means, they were in basic agreement on the goal towards which a painter's activity should be directed. In this respect the celebrated rivalry of Delacroix and Ingres that "raged" in their lifetimes in France was no more significant than Tweedledum's squabble with Tweedledee; the real gulf is between painters like Delacroix and Ingres, dedicated to Beauty in differing ways, and the "Realists" who appear at mid-century. Delacroix and Ingres together were the last great champions of the traditional theory of painting; after them, the deluge.

Yet there was one respect in which Delacroix, as unwittingly in his way as Reynolds and David in theirs, was a major contributor to the collapse of the traditional theory. This was in the content of his painting. For while he could find evocative techniques in the works of orthodox Old Masters, when it came to subject matter he had to break new ground. Nowhere was he more typically romantic than in his conviction that there was nothing to paint in the world around him which could evoke the kind of beautiful feelings he wanted. Too young to understand properly what horrors were involved in the Revolution, or what monstrous suffering Napoleon had inflicted on France, the generation of intellectuals that came to maturity in France just after Waterloo knew only that those times, with all their glamor and excitement, were gone. All they could see was a Europe made safe forever, apparently, for drab little men of business, content in stodgy bourgeois routines of clock-watching and ledger-keeping. Mediocrity seemed to be glorified; energy, action, and vision useless except for making money. The present had no interest, the future no promise. The only thing to do was escape, to get as far away as possible, into the past, when life had vigorous purpose, or into remote and exotic lands, where it still had color. So it is that the generation after Napoleon is the generation of romanticism in France; and Delacroix was its great perennial advocate and representative. To this extent he is a forerunner of the Bohemian artist, the alienated intellectual; and to this extent he breaks with the traditional concept of what painting is. Content, much more than technique, is what made Delacroix an advance-guard painter and a spiritual ancestor of modern painting; and this is the point of view from which it is most instructive to consider his paintings as evidence for the history of art and European culture.

With few and minor exceptions, all Delacroix's subject matter has one principle in common—he rejects and ignores the 18th-century classical concept of an ordered world under man's reasoned control. In its place he chooses to exhibit the effects and manifestations of super- or non-human powers. Since in fact 19th-century technology, spurred by the social system of the dull and despised *bourgeoisie,* was actually increasing man's powers over Nature at a steadily accelerating pace throughout the Early Victorian period, it follows that in all Delacroix's work (as in all romanticism, especially in the architectural Revival styles then flourishing) there was an obvious element of what could be called at best theatrical make-believe, at worst hypocrisy or phoniness. In some cases, however, this element is conscious and deliberately calculated for effect, whereas in others it is inherent. On this basis Delacroix's works can be divided into two broad categories—those in which romanticism is consciously artificial, deliberately anticlassical; and those in which it is more positive, the artificiality being an unself-conscious part of the total concept of art.

In the first category belong the "romantic classical" pictures that made Delacroix famous in the 1820s—*Dante and Virgil in Hell* (1822, Louvre), *The Massacre on Chios* (1824, Louvre), *Sardanapalus* (1827,

Louvre). They were for Delacroix what the *Oath* had been for David, a vehicle for defining a new romantic concept of and approach to the classical tradition. Where David had emphasized identification of painting with life, and chosen orthodox themes of noble human forms in noble action, Delacroix by contrast chose themes which, despite unmistakable classical allusions, exhibited the effects of human folly and futility—Michelangelesque forms writing in hell, latter-day Greeks overcome by latter-day barbarians, a mighty king of Antiquity perishing in his self-made holocaust. How thoroughly their effect depended on "beautiful feelings" of pity or awe or terror evoked by remoteness from actual life is illustrated by Delacroix's one essay in the old neoclassical tradition—*Liberty Leading the People,* inspired by the revolution of 1830. Though the picture was admired and bought by the new King, Louis Philippe, Delacroix never again painted a current event in France, for even had this revolution not proved a disappointment, he as an orthodox romantic could never have been satisfied with life as it is; like the perennial "seeker" in religion, the last thing Delacroix wanted was to find anything in the here and now.

Consciously anticlassical, too, were Delacroix's paintings of the Arab world. In *The Woman with a Parrot* (1827, Lyons) or *The Woman with White Stockings* (1832, Louvre), he found foils to what he considered the stultifying conventions of classical dogma and bourgeois morality, dramatic contrasts to the formality of Ingres's posed *Odalisques;* in an Arab *Lion Hunt* (1834, 1861, Chicago) or *Turkish Women Bathing* (1854, Hartford, Wadsworth Atheneum), life, raw and remote, excited "beautiful feelings" far better than anything in civilized, classical, bourgeois France. The same spirit informs Delacroix's portraiture. Whereas for Ingres portraits afforded an opportunity of escaping any compulsion to invent literary subject matter and concentrating whole heartedly on problems of form, Delacroix was interested only in portraits which did have a "story," in painting people whose souls were "tortured" by life in the bourgeois world and who in consequence provoked an emotional response in the spectator, people like *George Sand and Frederic Chopin* (1838; originally a single painting, now split, *Sand* in Copenhagen, *Chopin* in the Louvre), the consumptive *Alfred Bruyas,* connoisseur of painting (1853, Montpellier), and, of course, Delacroix himself (e.g., *Self-Portrait,* 1837–38, Louvre).

Finally, it is as an anticlassical expression that we can best understand Delacroix's religious painting. Its background was the romantic "re-

80

vival" of Christianity in reaction against the 18th-century classical view of the world represented by men like Châteaubriand in France and Pugin in England, whose point of departure was not so much the truth of Christianity as its power to evoke beautiful feelings through the associations (especially of its Roman Catholic branch) with vast Antiquity and the colorful Middle Ages. So Delacroix's themes are chosen not for theological significance but to excite the imagination and provoke emotional reactions. His *Resurrection of Lazarus* (1850, Louvre) or *Jacob Wrestling with the Angel* (1853–61, Saint-Sulpice, France) conjure up an unclassical world in which superhuman forces dominate reason. His half-dozen versions of the *Crucifixion* make it a typically romantic spectacle, a moment of dramatic suspense before a triumphant climax, all executed in flaring color, vibrant brushwork, dynamically violent composition. Particularly appealing to Delacroix's romantic temperament was *Christ on the Sea of Galilee,* of which he made at least seven versions (e.g., 1853, New York, Metropolitan; 1854, Baltimore, Walters). Instead of choosing the moment when Christ miraculously stills the waters, Delacroix depicts the preceding moment, when the terrified disciples drift in their open boat on the storm-tossed sea. The romantic reason is obvious—if and when God manifests His powers directly to men, the feelings evoked will hardly be beautiful in a romantic sense; but the power of Nature (which we only pretend to be beyond our control) is.

The "open boat on the storm-tossed sea" introduces us to the second category of Delacroix's subjects—those in which the romanticism is inherent. It is a stock item in the romantic repertoire; *The Shipwreck of Don Juan* (1840, Louvre) or *After the Shipwreck* (1841, Moscow, Pushkin) are typical examples in Delacroix's work, free of artificially anticlassical religious overtones. Here we have a spectacle of the power of wild Nature, which we can contemplate with nostalgic regret and delicious shivers because technology is making our experience of it daily more remote. Irrational animal passions provide subjects of the same sort; now that they no longer represent any real danger, the romantic can delight in contemplating a *Young Tiger Playing with His Mother* (1830, Louvre), *Horse Devoured by Lioness* (1844, Louvre), or *Horses Fighting in a Stable* (1860, Louvre).

Delacroix's kind of history painting is also inherently romantic. Eighteenth-century rational criticism, smashing and revising old institutions, had so effectively freed Europeans from their bondage to the past that now in the 19th century it was possible to look back on history in a different and more pleasing light. Where for Bayle or Johnson, Gibbon or Voltaire, history had been a record of vice and stupidity and suffering to be preserved only as a warning to more enlightened ages, the romantics saw it as a glamorous panorama whose color and violence made an ever more captivating contrast to the stodgy bourgeois world, the farther it receded into time. Delacroix as a history painter was in fact the precise counterpart to the Early Victorian architectural Revivalists. Like those architects who knew iron and glass and concrete but felt that the materials were somehow too dull and uninteresting to use, and so decked out buildings in Gothic pinnacles and Roman columns and Saracenic towers, Delacroix ranged far across the past in order to find those beautiful feelings that everyday routine was incapable of arousing: from *The Assassination of the Bishop of Liège* (1829, Louvre) to *The Entry of the Crusaders into Constantinople* (1840, Louvre), from *The Battle of Taillebourg*'s feudal glories (1837, Versailles) to Near Eastern episodes from the history of the Templars (*Abduction of Rebecca,* 1846, New York, Metropolitan; also 1859, Louvre).

History so conceived became a kind of religion, glorifying the Tragic Hero who in less prosaic times than ours struggled against Fate. Such was Columbus; it is no accident that *The Return of Columbus* (1839, Toledo, Ohio), is modeled directly on Titian's *Presentation of the Virgin.* Such, too, were *Hamlet and Horatio* (1859, Louvre), *Melmoth the Wanderer* (1831, Philadelphia), Goethe's Goetz von Berlichingen (*Capture of Weislingen,* facing page) and *Faust* (c. 1826, Cambridge, Fogg), Ariosto's *Marfisa* (1852, Baltimore, Walters). And it was on this kind of dramatized and sanctified history that the cult of nation worship characteristic of 19th-century Europe was built. Nineteenth-century nationalism and 19th-century romanticism matured together, so

11. *Eugène Delacroix:* The Capture of Weislingen. *Saint Louis, City Art Museum.*

Painted in 1853, this is a typical picture by the archetypal romantic. Like the architecture of the same Early Victorian age, romantic painting characteristically relied heavily on literary sources—in this case, a scene from Goethe's 1773 play Goetz von Berlichingen.

82

that Delacroix's history painting is the perfect counterpart to such romantic monuments to national cultural heroes as the Valhalla at Regensburg, the Pantheon in Paris, the Scott Monument in Edinburgh, the Houses of Parliament in London with their twelve hundred plinths and pillars commemorating the men who built the British Empire, or the Albert Memorial in London with its hundred and sixty-nine images of artists of all ages surrounding the Consort.

To the romantic, of course, the greatest and most tragic of cultural heroes is The Artist himself. Again it is Delacroix who best epitomizes the new spirit, with paintings like *Michelangelo in His Studio* (c. 1850, Montpellier), *Tasso in the Madhouse* (1827, Winterthur) and his own self-portraits. In such works a fundamental change is evident in society's attitude to art and artists. Once upon a time the artist had been honored as someone whose privilege and pleasure it was to give fame, to idealize and immortalize great men and their deeds. Now his highest aspiration is to get fame; to idealize his own deeds and immortalize himself. And at this point Delacroix the orthodox romantic links ideas with isolated seers like Blake and occult prophets like Goya in a chain leading towards a basically new concept of art.

NOTES

The centenary of Delacroix's death in 1863 provoked a spate of books and exhibition catalogues, of which one of the most elaborate was Raymond Escholier, *Eugène Delacroix* (Paris, 1963), based on his 1926 biography. Among the more useful English books were Yvonne Deslandres, *Delacroix, a Pictorial Biography* (London, 1963), and Lee Johnson, *Delacroix* (1963). A translation of *The Journal of Eugène Delacroix* by Walter Pach was published in 1937.

4

High Victorian Romanticism, the Cosmic and the Picturesque:

J. M. W. Turner (1775–1851)

"If I were reduced to rest Turner's immortality upon any single work, I should choose this." So John Ruskin judged *The Slave Ship* (page 87), in the first volume of his *Modern Painters: their superiority in the art of landscape painting to all The Ancient Masters proved by examples . . . of J. M. W. Turner, Esq., R.A.,* published in 1843. Ruskin was young when he wrote *Modern Painters*—so young, in fact, and so unknown in art circles, that he felt obliged to use the pseudonym "A Graduate of Oxford" if what he said were to be fairly heard. His intention was not to "discover" Turner; Joseph Mallord William Turner was a known and respected name in British art before Ruskin was born. Rather, "it was," as his editor put it, ". . . the change in Turner's later manner, and the contemptuous misunderstanding of this change on the part of the critics, that called Ruskin into the fray."

Turner had begun his professional career as a precociously successful and popular painter of precisely the kind of landscape late 18th-century taste liked best—"sublimely" hoary fortresses, moss-grown abbeys, and misty glens in far-off counties; vistas of wild and forbidding Nature which reduced man to a puny antlike creature, overwhelmed into insignificance by great banks of mighty storm clouds, towering peaks, and lashing waters. No wonder that the same critics who thought Constable's tranquil and classically controlled landscapes were minor productions, enthusiastically acclaimed Turner: "The tumult and grandeur of this wonderful picture"—this is a characteristic review, describing his *Fall of the Rhine at Schaffhausen* (Boston) in the *Monthly Magazine* for May 1806—"cannot be described or communicated to those who have not seen it. The whole is singularly awful and eminently impressive." No wonder that, where Constable found the road to recognition so hard and long, Turner was already an Associate of the Academy at the age of twenty-four, and a full member at twenty-seven.

But gradually, as time went on, Turner's art began to change, both in subject and form. In place of exotic scenery, he painted local and contemporary events. Instead of comfortably conjectural terrors, he confronted his viewers with the disconcerting and unpleasant truths of man's precarious state in this world and the next. The decisive turning point was marked by several paintings of *The Burning of the Houses of Parliament,* inspired by a spectacular fire which destroyed the centuries-old Palace of Westminster on October 16, 1834. Here was a demonstration of Nature's destructive powers quite different in implications from open boats on storm-tossed seas or remote waterfalls on the Rhine. It was real; it was immediate, witnessed by thousands of Londoners lining the riverbank; and whatever the feelings evoked by Turner's glaring prophecies of the eventual and inevitable ruin of all human works great or small by the elemental forces of Nature, they were not romantic in the orthodox sense. Neither were the reflections that "Time, like an ever-rolling stream, Bears all her sons away; they fly forgotten as a dream Dies at the opening day" implicit in *The Burial of Sir David Wilkie at Sea.* In the case of this painter, early in the century regarded as a rival of Michelangelo and Rembrandt but already beginning to fall into the near-

12. *J. M. W. Turner:* The Slave Ship (Slavers Throwing Overboard the Dead and Dying—Typhoon Coming On). *Courtesy, Museum of Fine Arts, Boston. 1839–40.*

Like Delacroix's, Turner's romanticism depended heavily on literary sources; here it is a passage from that long-lived favorite The Seasons *by James Thomson (1700–1748), specifically a description in* Summer *of a typhoon. But Turner goes beyond orthodox evocation of "beautiful feelings" through grand spectacles of Nature, passing from the sublime to the terrible, from local to cosmic. And his style changes accordingly —the more inexorably human futility is proclaimed, the more all precision of outline and definition of form dissolves in masses of paint. The result, though superficially presaging Impressionism, is not scientific Reality but rather the climax of the romantic tradition. Like the poets Tennyson and Arnold, Turner, by demolishing the old order, transcending its limitations and undermining its rationale, fallows the ground for a new planting.*

total eclipse which has since engulfed him, the truth was all too immediate and poignant. What was "beautiful" about the feelings inspired by
The Fighting Téméraire tugged to her last berth to be broken up? This
old veteran of the Napoleonic wars moving off into the sunset symbolizes
the end of a familiar era of wind power that had lasted for all previous
recorded history, while the steam tug that moves her off marks the
beginning of a new technology whose consequences no one can contemplate without at least a twinge of foreboding. This theme is elaborated in
Turner's last great picture, *Rain, Steam and Speed: The Great Western
Railway;* out from the fog of the past hurtles modern progress, only to be
swallowed up again in the mists of futurity that lie at the other end of the
brief bridge of life. In such pictures he has not only gone beyond 18th-
century sublimity or early 19th-century romanticism, he has created their
antithesis. Furthermore, to give up the shallow game of play-acting, to
deal in what can best be called the profound cosmic drama of man's true
and actual state in the world, to devote art to Reality, is not only to
abandon the romantic point of view, it means a new artistic orientation
altogether.

A comparable, and in romantic eyes even worse, change had occurred
in Turner's forms. In place of the precise description and meticulous
draftsmanship of his early paintings, he had begun to paint consistently
"up-sun"—i.e., into the light source—so that all his forms were
dissolved into one suggestive hazy blur. His paintings seemed to have
disintegrated into great blobs of yellow, scarlet, orange, and azure, pieced
out with splatters of black. This also was going much too far for
conventional taste: "It is grievous to us," as a critic in the *Athenaeum* put
the reaction in 1838, "to think of talent so mighty and so poetical running
riot into such frenzies; the more grievous, as we fear it is now past
recall." On every side, Turner's admirers had begun to fall away. And
it was at this point that Ruskin stepped in.

That it should have been a young critic who best understood Turner's
later work, was no accident. For Ruskin belonged to a new generation;
his thought and style of writing represents a new, second phase of 19th-
century culture—what we might call the High Victorian, as contrasted to
the Early Victorian mind. And it was to this new generation, to this new
mind, that Turner now spoke. Just as his younger works had perfectly
embodied the romantic ideal of the earlier 19th century, so the painting
of his maturity was the first great expression of what came to characterize
the High Victorian age—the love of "the picturesque."

"Picturesqueness," as High Victorians used the term, is as hard to define as it is easy to recognize in their art. Explicitly, of course, it means "like a picture"; a picturesque painting, or building, or poem, was one that brought to mind a nostalgic image of something past, or lost, or unattainable. But that image was not, as in the romantic art of, say, Delacroix, something that derived from a specific period or episode in history. Rather, the picturesque was conceived as a sort of emanation of "pastness" in general. It was created by so choosing and combining forms drawn from many ages past as to make real something of the mysterious, misty, depths of history; its aim was to set before both mind and eye a tangible expression of the continuity of human culture, past and present. This is what Ruskin meant when he advocated a new architecture that would already look centuries old when the last stone was put in place. This is the effect that High Victorian architects were after when they broke and blurred the precise outlines of their buildings by irregular, complex, visually arresting combinations of shapes, by eye-catching patterns and textural contrasts of wood and brick and tile and colored stone, by those characteristic ironwork "fringes" that run across their rooftops and towers so that they seem to trail off into infinite space, in the same way as their eclectic forms trail back into infinite time. This is the effect High Victorian poets like Tennyson and Arnold sought, when they wove archaic and contemporary language together into one shimmering web of vague verbal imagery. And this, as Ruskin recognized, is the effect Turner sought, and achieved, in his later paintings. In *The Slave Ship* we can see it perfectly.

Compared with *The Slave Ship,* the typical romantic theme of the open boat on the storm-tossed sea seems simple and playful. This is not some particular image that may amuse or entertain, something you can turn away from and forget when your mood changes. This is a cosmic allegory, a composite image of the nature of man in the world drawn from many levels of time and consciousness. Man's wretched wickedness is made immediately manifest in the cruel slave-trade: the full and original title of the work is *Slavers Throwing Overboard the Dead and Dying.* The eternal insecurity of human life, easily ignored amid urban technological comforts, but vividly present to them that go down to sea in old sailing ships. An apocalyptic vision of the final obliteration of all human endeavor in the vast impersonal workings of Nature. A sublime commentary, fusing the past to the present, and the present to the future. This is the counterpart to Tennyson's *In Memoriam:*

89

> The hills are shadows, and they flow
> From form to form, and nothing stands;
> They melt like mist, the solid lands,
> Like clouds they shape themselves and go

and to Arnold's *Dover Beach:*

> . . . for the world which seems
> To lie before us like a land of dreams
> So various, so beautiful, so new
> Hath really neither joy, nor love, nor light
> Nor certitude, nor peace, nor help for pain
> And we are here as on a darkling plain
> Swept with confused alarms of struggle and flight,
> Where ignorant armies clash by night.

This is what "the picturesque" as contrasted with "the romantic" means.

Not all critics were prepared to understand or accept the change. People like Thackeray, for instance, who (as his novels and art criticism both show) was just old enough to retain most of the earlier 19th century's romantic optimism, and a good deal of that insistence on precise expression bequeathed by the 18th, could never fully feel the vague undercurrent of malaise that beset the more thoughtful High Victorians. But John Ruskin could. Ruskin could understand why the vehicle for expressing sublimely picturesque images had to be vague and general, why cosmic visions of the sort Turner created in his later life had to be manifested in what seemed to Thackeray formless blurs of paint; many of his own ideas had to be expressed in writing of the same sort, and were (and are) similarly misunderstood.

There has been, for instance, a fashion for pretending that Ruskin never really understood Turner's later style at all. Critics point accusingly to the fact that some thirty years after *Modern Painters* first appeared it was Ruskin who led the attack on what superficially appears to be the very similar sort of painting by James McNeill Whistler, mocking Whistler's formlessness and ruining his contemporary reputation by calling him a "coxcomb . . . flinging a pot of paint in the public's face." But this is unjust, I think. Ruskin was not being inconsistent. He recognized—as a good many latter-day critics evidently have not—that there is (literally) a world of difference between what Turner was doing in the 1830s and -40s and what Impressionists like Whistler did twenty or thirty years later. The Impressionists were "modern" painters in the 20th-century sense; Turner was not. For them, the mechanics of painting—color and light—were ends in themselves, the subject merely a means of presenting them. But for Turner, that was never true. Turner remained dedicated to "the object"; he painted pictures *of* something, never "just pictures." If he blurred his forms, if what he depicted often seemed to dissolve into shapeless masses of paint, that was because he knew (as did many other painters, Goya, for instance) that precise delineations and particular descriptions were incompatible with the kind of cosmic or universal ideas he wanted to express, not because he was being subjective, or making things appear as he chose to see them. He blurred his forms by naturalistic means, by painting into the light source, so as never to do violence to the object as it existed; he painted objects as they were. To the end, that is to say, he retained that respect for the beautiful object which is the root of the traditional theory of painting. To the end, the goal of his art remained Beauty—of feelings, and of form. True, the revolution that would change all that was already underway when he died, and it may indeed be that the sudden failure of powers remarked on in the last few years of his life (say 1846–51) may have been caused as much by a disconcerting realization that he had come closer to the "search for Reality" of "modern" painting than he wished as by the feebleness of age; but that is only speculation. If, as Ruskin said, *The Slave Ship* is the single work on which Turner's immortality best rests, it is also in a sense one of the last great monuments of traditional Western painting. It marks the limits to which subject matter and form in the traditional sense could be pushed; beyond that, begins the revolution.

NOTES

Turner was born in 1775. While still a student at the Royal Academy (where he was enrolled in 1794) he was traveling about the country making drawings and watercolors for sale to collectors and publishers of engraved views of the divers "sublime" sights—old castles and churches, seascapes, glens and mountains—in England and elsewhere that were suddenly, at the end of the 18th century, beginning to have an enormous appeal for Englishmen. He began, that is to say, as a topographical draftsman, or "landscape illustrator," and his first important paintings, in both watercolor and oil, were essentially simply blown-up versions of these. Characteristic are *Calais Pier* (1803, London); *The Shipwreck* (1805, London, Tate); *Fall of the*

91

Rhine at Schaffhausen (1806, Boston). They met an instant response. By 1799 he was elected an Associate of the Royal Academy; by 1803 a full member; in 1804 he built a gallery for himself and soon began to get rich on sales. In 1806 he was sure enough of his own worth to begin his *Liber Studiorum*, a series of combined etching and mezzotint prints of his work (vaguely based on the example of the 17th-century landscapist Claude Lorraine) "to make his reputation safe for posterity." In 1807 he was appointed Professor of Perspective at the Royal Academy, and in 1808 and 1809 painted, as if to demonstrate that his powers were not limited to landscape, several figure paintings, among them *The Battle of Trafalgar as Seen from the Mizzen Starboard Shrouds of the Victory* (London), and *Adonis Departing for the Chase* (New York, Huntington Hartford). He had now explored practically all the possibilities of conventional romantic landscape, and, to the increasing dismay of his admirers, he began to experiment more and more with light and color. Already by 1810 he was being called the leader of a new and (to the conservatives) disconcerting "White School" of painting; and for the next three decades he continued steadily on this course, followed at an ever-widening remove by critical opinion. Several visits to Italy, the first in 1819 to 1821, served to increase his interest in the dissolution of form by light; by 1836 criticism was loud and constant, the most famous example being the attack on him in *Blackwood's Magazine* by John Eagles which first inspired Ruskin to undertake the case for the defense. Some milestones on this road are: *Dido and Aeneas,* and *Dido Building Carthage* (1814, 1815, London); *Dordrecht* (1818, London); *Ulysses Deriding Polyphemus* (1829, London); *Antwerp: Van Goyen Looking Out for a Subject* (1833, New York, Frick); *The Burning of the Houses of Lords and Commons* (in several versions after 1834; e.g., Philadelphia, Cleveland); *The Parting of Hero and Leander* (1837, London, Tate); *Fishing Boats* (1837, Chicago); and in 1838–39, *The Fighting Téméraire* (London), and *The Burial of Sir David Wilkie at Sea* (1841, London, Tate).

So far a good many perceptive critics could follow him; the *Téméraire* was received with enthusiasm by most. But after 1840 he began to dissolve his forms almost completely. The *Opening of Valhalla* (1842, London, Tate) is a great monument to the transition from Early to High Victorian attitudes; Turner shows the great monument at Regensburg (built 1830–42), quintessence of Early Victorian romantic nationalism with its concept of undying culture-heroes, as already dissolving in time and space. So are *The Slave Ship, Rockets and Blue Lights* (c. 1841, Williamstown, Mass., Clark), *Steamer in a Snowstorm* (1842, London, Tate), *Rain, Steam, and Speed* (1844, London), and *The Whalers* (1845, New York, Metropolitan). Typical of critical reaction is *Punch* for May 31, 1845: "Whether he calls his pictures 'Whalers' or 'Venice' or 'Noon' or 'Night' it is all the same; for it is quite as easy to fancy it one thing as another." As Finberg sums it up, by 1846 "ill health and old age had brought Turner's active career as a painter almost to an end. The attenuation of form and content in his work had nearly reached its end." He died in 1851, bequeathing his unsold pictures, sketchbooks, and other professional effects to the National Gallery in London (founded 1832).

Working almost from beginning to end of his life with single-minded industry, Turner produced an enormous number of paintings and sketches; despite the great concentration in the National Gallery in London, he is extraordinarily well represented elsewhere in England, in the British Empire (many on loan from the Turner bequest), and in the United States.

The definitive biography is A. J. Finberg, *The Life of J. M. W. Turner,* (Oxford, 1939), a consummation of many earlier studies by the author, including *Complete Inventory of the Drawings in the Turner Bequest* (2 vols., London, 1909), and *History of Turner's Liber Studiorum,* with *catalogue raisonné* (London, 1924). Shorter illustrated books on Turner include those by John Rothenstein (London, 1949), C. G. E. Bunt (Leigh-on-Sea, England, 1948), and Luke Herrmann (London, 1963).

THE FIFTY YEARS' REVOLUTION

1840-1890

POLITICAL HISTORIANS know the 1840s as a decade of short and decisive revolutions, which in a brief span of time consolidated and defined the results of fifty-odd years of varied changes and upheavals and determined the pattern of European development for fifty years to come. Art historians could well look on the 1840s in the same way, for they mark the same kind of watershed in painting. Painting before that time, however wracked by inner change and the pressure of new ideas, still preserved at least the outline of what we may call "traditional" values and standards. After 1840, however strong the reminiscences and vestiges of the older order, there can be no doubt that painting is developing along fundamentally different lines—the pattern for the next fifty years is clearly set.

By the 1840s, the traditional concept is clearly derelict. Step by step, the implications of the revolution in theory begun by later 18th-century painters like Reynolds and David have been worked out; one after another, the old stabilizing precepts have been abandoned, bypassed, outflanked. In the work of Ingres, Constable, Corot, we can trace the inexorable collapse of the neat categories of "beautiful objects." In the work of Delacroix, Goya, Turner, we can see how the classical precision of composition and clarity of form is swept away and dissolved. And the careers of all of them, however various and diverse, manifest one thing in common: the change in the painter's social status, from the commissioned workman, with a definite and recognized function to perform, to an independent entrepreneur who must establish his own place in society, and justify his existence and worth not only to his patrons but to himself. This the traditional goal and concern of painting—Beauty—cannot do; it survives only by default. And when, at this critical moment, three violent and drastic changes occur, which vitally affect both the external and internal circumstances of painting, the result is no contest; the old concept of painting as Beauty evaporates, and a new concept—painting as Reality—begins to replace it. The next fifty years will be concerned with defining, refining, and establishing what Reality is to mean.

The first change was a social revolution. The transformation of society that had begun with the Industrial Revolution, about 1750, was now complete; the old type of aristocrat whose powers and influence rested on land was gone, and in his place the artist had to deal with a new kind of patron, the capitalist or bourgeois, whose powers, values, and judgments derived simply from the possession of money. Then there was the upheaval brought about by photography. Once Daguerre's new process was made public, in 1839, there was no longer any need to attend drawing school, to spend years of training, in order to "catch a likeness"; all at once, anyone could do it. What had traditionally been the painter's most obvious function in society, his most reliable source of livelihood—the making of pictorial records of people and events—suddenly became obsolescent. Finally, there was a series of sudden technological changes in picture-making, the most obvious being the invention of "tin" tubes to hold ready-mixed oil paint (in 1841), and the steadily improving methods of reproduction, especially lithography. Both had the effect of giving "serious" professional painters a new and severe kind of competition; in the one case, from amateurs whom the new tubes freed of all need for specialized professional training in the technical processes of painting, in preparing pigments and planning pictures; in the other, from the trend which at once set in towards buying cheap prints of well-known "safe and certified" paintings, instead of originals by young and as yet unrecognized artists.

To such changes every painter had to make some sort of response. That there would be almost as many responses as men was inevitable; the story of painting in these fifty years is largely the account of the immense variety of reactions to this combination of changed circumstances. But one thing all the changes had in common—they all tended to impel painting away from Beauty and towards Reality as a goal, and to make the painter a person who got fame instead of giving it.

I

New Patrons
and Changing Standards

1

"Realism" in the Popular Arts:

James Gillray (1757–1815)
George Cruikshank (1792–1878)
Gustave Doré (1833–1883)

While upper-class ladies and gentlemen with pretensions to taste in England and France were busy discussing the relative merits of Reynolds's "Grand Style" as against David's "total classicism," and filing into salons and academy showrooms to view the innovations of rising young men like Ingres and Turner, artists of a very different class were unobtrusively developing a fundamentally new sort of art, in quite different circumstances and for a very different sort of audience. Had you, in the years around 1800, chanced to pass along St. James Street in London, you might have noticed a noisy knot of people standing in front of an unpretentious little shop with a big bow window, peering in at a multitude of small colored prints on every conceivable subject: hunting scenes, satires political and religious, commentaries on current events of popular interest, patriotic disquisitions. On inquiry you might have learned that this was the shop of one Mrs. Humphrey, a widow; that the prints were made by one James Gillray, a rather eccentric person who boarded with her (and enjoyed more than ordinary boarder's privileges, some malicious mind might have hinted); and that the prints sold for a shilling or so apiece. To whom? You hardly needed to study them long to guess that; obviously, these prints were made to appeal to the

99

characteristic prejudices and the sense of humor of the lower middle-class Englishman. Here was glorified the stolid, unimaginative, "typical Englishman," stuffed with roast beef and unreflective opinions, contentedly deriding all those comical & despicable foreign "types" across the Channel—the jabbering Froggie with his newfangled political ideas and his ridiculous leader, Little Boney; the prancing and mincing Macaroni with his "arty" airs; the thick-headed Dutchmen from those preposterous little German states. And here were jokes on upper-class pretensions to refined taste, habits, and ideas: two clerks out on a holiday who make fools of themselves by aping the ridiculous manners of the hunt; great lords and ladies of the realm, with all their grand airs, being seduced by footmen and chambermaids; the clergy, those hypocritical paragons of morality, gorging themselves at the punchbowl and leering at shapely parishioners. And here too are plenty of digs at highfalutin "modern" paintings and their connoisseurs: *La Belle Assemblée* (page 103), for instance, with four old crones pretending to be Graces, pouring libations on the altar of love, complete with garlands and lyres and lambs and pigeons! That's what they call "classical" painting, that is. That's what milord likes, but he can have it; give me a good sound man who shows us what's there, like this here Gillray, any day . . . This is "popular" art, art by and for "the people."

If you belonged to any class much above that of the small shopkeepers and tradesmen and clerks that the Industrial Revolution had called into being, you would probably not have seen much in Gillray's prints; you would have thought the "serious" ones clumsy and banal, the "humorous" ones uncouth and vulgar. But whether or not you liked such prints you would probably not have taken them seriously as "art," let alone considered them likely to have any great influence on the future. But in this you would have been mistaken. For the people for whom Gillray's art was intended represented the rising class in England; in the coming century, the sons and grandsons of the kind of men who liked this sort of thing would sit in Westminster New Palace, make England's laws,

13A. *Sir Joshua Reynolds:* Lady Sarah Bunbury Sacrificing to the Graces. *Chicago, The Art Institute, W. W. Kimball Collection.* See 13B, Print satirizing this subject by Gillray.

rule England's conquests—and pay England's painters. And it would take a good deal longer than a generation to move them very far from the aesthetic tastes Gillray so abundantly satisfied. Even when they had come to sit in the seats of the mightiest, they would go on liking art that told simple, straightforward, unambiguous stories like this—popular art, that had mass communication as its goal. And they would always feel that art, to be satisfactory, had to have some kind of moral, "it" ought to expose sin or foibles, encourage "straight thinking." And—most significant of all—that it ought to be "realistic." For the whole point of popular art—of its very existence as well as its humor—is that it shows what purports to be a real, as contrasted to an artificial world. An artist like Gillray is not out to show you Beauty; he wants to amuse you or instruct you, or both, by revealing Reality. Reynolds may show you ladies of society, like Sarah Bunbury, as they pretend to be, or would like to be, or as the fashionable and intellectual world agrees to see them; Gillray claims to show them as they really are.

13B. *Print satirizing 13A by James Gillray:* La Belle Assemblée, *published 1787.*

Towards the end of the 18th century a new kind of upper class began rising to power, composed of newly rich men of middle- and lower-middle-class commercial origin. Its ascendancy produced a crisis in painting, because the ideas and standards of painting held by these new patrons were quite different from those of the old hereditary aristocracy. Fundamentally, they derived from the popular arts—i.e., arts of mass circulation—which had developed in response to the increasing literacy, leisure, and purchasing power of that new middle class, created by the Industrial Revolution, from which the new patrons sprang. Typical of those arts are the cartoons of James Gillray at the turn of the century. Working for a middle-class audience, Gillray derides traditional upper-class attitudes and values in art; the object of his activity is not Beauty but Reality—to show the world as it actually is. His means are humor (incongruity between the ideal and the actual), literary description, and anecdotage. And when men from the middle and lower-middle classes who had been Gillray's patrons rose in a generation or two to upper-class status, they took these values and attitudes with them.

Perhaps the first artist in England to make any serious attempt at this sort of thing was William Hogarth (1687–1764). In such series as *The Rake's Progress* and *Marriage à la Mode,* he proposed to show how the aristocrats really lived, how they couldn't make enough from their estates to live in the proper style, and so had to marry their sons and daughters into the families of merchants and businessmen, how foolish and greedy and vicious they were when you looked at them without preconceptions, instead of at the exalted image they held up for you to see. But Hogarth failed, because he came too soon. The audience to whom his exposés should have had most appeal, the lower and middle classes, were not yet large enough, self-confident enough, or wealthy enough, to buy the prints he tried to circulate, much less the original paintings. And he himself was never really sure what he was doing; he kept vacillating between the old ideal of the painter dedicated to Beauty, and this possible new function of the artist as a "popular" commentator showing society the face of Reality, so that in the end he was neither. Thomas Rowlandson (1756–1827) had somewhat the same problem over a generation later. Rowlandson's natural instincts were so much directed towards the popular arts that he deliberately chose to abandon a possible career as a "fine" artist, and turned his very considerable talents, trained in the Royal Academy schools, to boisterous exposés of the foibles of country folk, aristocrats, and intellectuals alike. But instead of addressing himself to the middle-class audience naturally attracted to such works, Rowlandson preferred to work for the old aristocracy, so that he tended to fall into the role of court buffoon rather than social commentator, and so stultified his creativity.

Gillray was the first popular artist whose instincts and audience coincided. By his time the middle class was large enough to support him reasonably well, thanks to industrialization and urbanization; his prices were lower, thanks to improvements in reproductive techniques; and he himself harbored no paralyzing pretensions to great art. But even Gillray came a few years too soon to enjoy full success; he died in 1815, at the moment when society was decisively settling into a bourgeois pattern, when the new age to which his kind of art was so perfectly suited was about to begin. Complete recognition and success was reserved for the generation of popular artists who followed him, for the cartoonists of *Punch* and *Charivari,* and above all for popular illustrators.

Illustration, in the 19th-century sense, was an essentially new kind of art, created by and for the *bourgeoisie* that the Industrial Revolution had brought into being. Until the 1820s, books were still quite scarce, mostly serious in intent, with publication more often than not subsidized by patrons' subscriptions. In them, "illustration" still meant something like the medieval illumination—that is, designed to enrich a text, either by elucidating its contents (as in treatises on architecture or geography) or by "glorifying" it (as we see in Blake). But when the appearance of a large literate middle class made it possible, and eventually usual, for writers who appealed to this audience to make a living from the sale of their books alone, the concept of illustration changed. Now the aim was to arouse interest in a book by putting its ideas and stories before the public in a direct visual form. In short, illustration became a kind of picture writing; an art, that is to say, not so much concerned with Beauty as with communication of ideas. And so, even though there survived in it something of the old traditional close relationship between art and literature (*ut pictura poesis,* in the old formula), its appearance was another significant symptom of the gradual shift away from Beauty towards "realism" as the object of art. George Cruikshank in England and Gustave Doré in France are the outstanding representatives of its first phases.

Cruikshank, born in 1792, was Gillray's direct successor, taking over his business—and "business" is the correct term—in 1811. But after 1820, with the success of his illustrated *Life in London,* he gave up comic art in favor of book illustration—the first artist to make a living doing so. Cruikshank illustrated *Grimm's Fairy Tales* (1823), *Robinson Crusoe* (1831), *The Ingoldsby Legends,* and many others; but his greatest success was with the early work of Dickens: *Sketches by Boz* (1834); *Oliver Twist* (1836 page 107); *Pickwick Papers* (1838). The "Cruikshank style" of spidery line drawing passed into political cartooning, to influence Leech, Tenniel, and Nast; something of it is still discernible in the great 20th-century illustrations of children's books by Ernest Shepard (*Wind in the Willows,* the *Pooh* books, etc.). But by mid-century Cruikshank was aspiring to more. He essayed large blown-up versions of his illustrations and cartoons—like *The Runaway Knock* and *The Culprit* (*Naughty Boy in Church*), whose titles speak for themselves; he labored years over an enormous diatribe against drunkenness entitled *The Temple of Bacchus.* True, his paintings never received unqualified acclaim, and were soon forgotten; but the facts that such works could receive any acclaim at all, that they could be exhibited in Academy shows, that his *Bacchus* was acquired by the National Gallery (though now rolled up in the basement), would have been unimaginable fifty years earlier.

Gustave Doré's career followed a comparably significant pattern. Born in 1832, Doré too began as a precociously gifted cartoonist. At 15 he was publishing regularly in Philipon's *Journal pour Rire;* his *Histoire pittoresque, dramatique, et caricaturale de la Sainte-Russie* is still occasionally reproduced. Doré too then turned to illustration, making a great reputation in 1854 with *Illustrations of Rabelais,* and thenceforth going from triumph to triumph for over thirty years. His output was prodigious, for he drew straight onto the wood block or stone, never used models and hardly ever preliminary sketches; so was his range—from Tennyson to *Bluebeard,* from Cervantes to scenes of social realism in London, climaxed by the enormous success of illustrations for Dante's *Inferno* (page 109) (1861) and his illustrated Bible (1866), which more than one contemporary critic called "the grandest collection of religious pictures in the world." His income was even greater; between 1850 and 1870 he earned more than £280,000, making him the richest artist in France. And his reputation as an illustrator was lasting; as Lehmann-Haupt has said, "the agreeable terror of Doré has played a major role in the childhood memories of the last three generations." But, like Cruikshank, Doré was not satisfied to be a "mere illustrator"; he too tried for success as a "fine" artist, exhibiting regularly what amounted to blown-up versions of his illustrations in the Salons from 1854 through 1867. He met with similar rejection from the more perceptive critics, and in the end was so stung by an (entirely justifiable) attack on him as

14. *George Cruikshank: Title page to Charles Dickens's* Adventures of Oliver Twist, *1836.*

That Cruikshank, originally a cartoonist, could turn to professional book illustration and make a living at it is a significant indication of enormous social change—the rise of a middle class wealthy enough to buy books in quantity, leisured and literate enough to read them; but Cruikshank's later career is even more significant. Though the art he produced showed little change, its status did; by the 1840s he was exhibiting anecdotal illustrations like these, blown up to easel scale, at the Royal Academy.

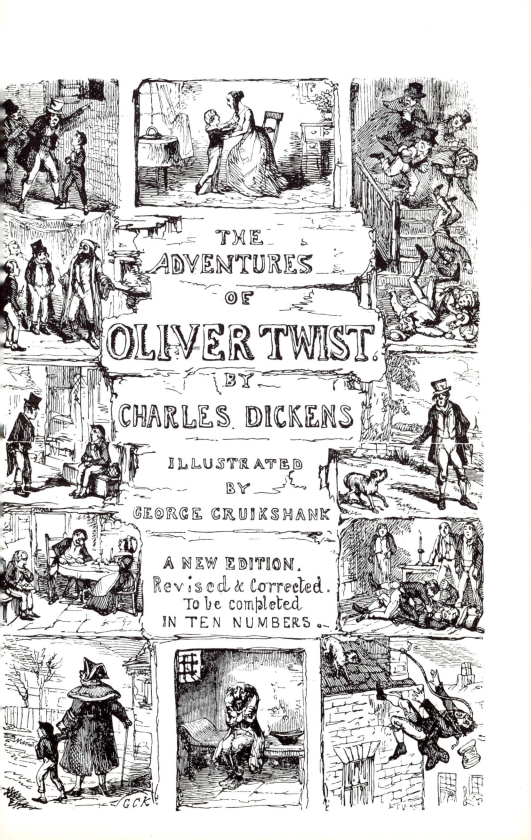

THE ADVENTURES OF OLIVER TWIST.

BY CHARLES DICKENS

ILLUSTRATED BY GEORGE CRUIKSHANK

A NEW EDITION.
Revised & Corrected.
To be completed
IN TEN NUMBERS.

lacking color sense that he refused ever to exhibit paintings in France again. But as in Cruikshank's case, the remarkable fact, given the kind of paintings Doré did, is that he had any success at all; yet in England his Doré Gallery at 35 New Bond Street was hugely popular and respected by many critics and throughout the 19th century he retained an immense and devoted following among the middle class everywhere. That Doré and Cruikshank failed to impress the best critics of the time is not surprising; what needs explaining is how anybody could have been impressed by anecdotal illustrations inflated to the dimensions of major oil paintings, why for a few decades in the middle of the 19th century the kind of art we unhesitatingly associate with cheap calendars could have been compared by so many people to the works of Rembrandt and Raphael and Michelangelo. The even partial and temporary elevation of painters like Cruikshank and Doré to the status of "great artists" is indicative of the tremendous economic and social changes going on in the mid-19th century.

What happened was actually very simple. Hogarth, Gillray, and Rowlandson had created an essentially new kind of art, an art intended for communication, not edification; an art concerned with Reality, not Beauty. But in their time it was still a middle- and lower-middle-class commodity; the upper-middle- and upper-class patrons who commissioned painting of consequence and dominated the academies maintained the traditional concept of what art was and did. Fifty years later the situation was very different. Now communication and Reality emerged as the actual—if never openly acknowledged—principles guiding the official taste of the ruling class; what had been an art for shopkeepers and tradesmen became, in dressed-up and grandiose form, the art of the

15. *Gustave Doré:* Dante and Virgil Crossing the River Styx, *from the illustrated edition of Dante's* Inferno *published by Doré, 1861.*

Like Cruikshank, Doré progressed from cartooning to book illustration to salon ambitions, thanks to change in patronage rather than any change in his art. Though he failed to win full recognition as a "serious" painter, his illustrations, and particularly his more ambitious parlor books like this, were of considerable significance in the evolution of 19th-century painting.

108

academies of England and France. It was this change in official patronage that made it possible for Cruikshank and Doré to pose, and by large numbers of people be accepted, as great artists. People whose parents or who even themselves had been lower-middle-class in 1800 now were sitting in the House of Lords and dictating the taste of England, and dominating the parliaments of France. And their taste was what had been lower- and middle-class taste fifty years before. It is in this way that we can see how the popular arts formed a background for the emergence of High Victorian academic painting—and for much else besides.

NOTES

Gillray's father was a Scottish soldier, invalided and pensioned at Chelsea. Like Hogarth, he was bound apprentice to a letter engraver, but soon ran away with a company of strolling players. On returning to London he studied briefly at the Royal Academy, and began his career engraving illustrations for Goldsmith's *Deserted Village*.

Unlike Hogarth, he had no connections with or interest in the intellectual life and society of his time; he wrote neither books nor pamphlets; remained unmarried; and for most of his life was employed exclusively by a printseller, Mrs. Humphrey, at whose shop his caricatures were sold. Gillray's plates were made in a combination of etching and engraving techniques, sometimes colored by hand; it is characteristic that even at the height of the classical craze he made very little use of classical allegory or literature; his audience was from first to last lower-middle-class.

His work is divided into two phases by the French Revolution and its aftermath. Until c. 1795 Gillray was pre-eminently a social caricaturist, one of the many who proliferated in the late 18th century and throve "like a caterpillar upon the green leaf of reputation." His chief target was the upper class and anything associated with upper-class pretensions: typical are *Old Wisdom Blinking at the Stars* (1782, satire on Johnson's criticisms of Milton [the great middle-class favorite] and others in his *Lives of the Poets*); *La Belle Assemblée* (1787); *Dido in Despair* (1790, representing Lady Hamilton as a grossly fat Dido wailing as her lover, Lord Nelson, sails away with his fleet from Carthage [Naples]), *Shakespeare Sacrificed, The Offering to Avarice* (1789, satire on London alderman Boydell, who made a fortune by commissioning Shakespearean prints for sale from leading artists); *A Peep at Christie's* (1797, showing Lord Derby and Miss Farren, the actress whom he married two months after the death of his first wife, looking at pictures in Christie's auction rooms). A particularly vulnerable target was George III and his family, assailed for the minor vices of stinginess (*A Simple Meal*) as well as the major ones (*The Vices: George III and his Family*). As Napoleon gained power and threatened England, Gillray's typically latent middle-class patriotism was aroused, and his later work is characterized by savage attacks on Napoleon, in the process of which he invented the character of "John Bull" for English virtue and "Little Boney" for French vice. In his early comments on the nature of the Revolution (*French Freedom and English Slavery*, 1792; *Pinnacle of Liberty*, 1793) he showed himself a much more acute observer of what was going on than many with higher intellectual pretensions—Wordsworth, for example. No longer a buffoon, George III becomes the personification of English power (e.g., *The Invasion of England*, 1803, representing "Little Boney" as Gulliver in Brobdingnag, a haggard Tom Thumb propelling a toy boat around a bathtub under the amused eyes of the giant English king). Napoleon's court, by contrast, is equated with Babylon's (*The Writing on the Wall*, 1803), and when in 1806 Gillray published *Her Former Profession* implying that Josephine, crowned a few months earlier, was in fact the whore of Babylon, Napoleon tried to take advantage of the Peace of Amiens then in effect to get Gillray jailed; he further ordered David, his court painter hard at work commemorating the coronation in *Le Sacré*, to produce cartoons in reply to Gillray's—which, needless to say, were hardly successful (cf. D. L. Dowd, *Pageant-Master of the Republic*, Lincoln, Nebr., 1951). Gillray carried on the fight against Napoleon until struck down by insanity in 1811; *A New Batch of Kings*, satirizing the concordat with the Papacy and Napoleon's nepotism, is perhaps the best known of the later works.

Illustrations and biographical material on Gillray and Rowlandson can be found in Cornelius Veth, *Comic Art in England* (London, c. 1929), G. Paston (pseud. E. M. Symonds), *Social Caricature in the 18th Century* (London, 1905); E. Fuchs, *Karikatur der Europaische Völker* (Berlin, 1901); Graham Everitt, *English Caricaturists of the 19th Century* (London, 1886).

Books on Rowlandson include those by Bernard Falk (London, 1949), F. G. Roe (Leigh-on-Sea, England, 1947), and Art Young (1938). On Cruikshank, the standard sources are G. W. Reid, *A Descriptive Catalogue of the Works of George Cruikshank* (London, 1871) and A. M Cohn, *A Bibliographical Catalogue of the Printed Works Illustrated by George Cruikshank* (London, 1914); see also Ruari McLean, *George Cruikshank, His Life and Work as a Book Illustrator* (1938); also Sacheverell Sitwell, *Narrative Pictures* (London, 1937).

For illustrations of Doré's principal works, see Edmond Ollier (ed.), *The Doré Gallery* (London, 1870). It is significant of Doré's English as contrasted to his French reputation that the two major biographies of him were brought out in English—one by Blanche Roosevelt (1886), the other by W. B. Jerrold (London, 1908). A good general study is Millicent Rose, *Gustave Doré* (London, 1946); see also H. Lehmann-Haupt, *The Terrible Gustave Doré* (1943).

2

"Reality" in High Victorian Academic Painting:

Sir David Wilkie (1785–1841)
Thomas Couture (1815–1879)
Adolphe William Bouguereau (1825–1905)

Steadily, inexorably, as the 19th century came on, a new upper class began to come into existence and take power. The Congress of Vienna, which was supposed to have saved Europe for the old order, and suppressed the wild-eyed rise of the "new men," did nothing of the kind; it could not, for this was a revolution not of force, or even of ideas, so much as of economics. As Hogarth had seen in the 18th century, and perceptively illustrated in the "Marriage Contract" scene of *Marriage à la Mode,* the basis of wealth was shifting from land to money, and all the old social patterns were changing. Finance was the new key to power; it was not the men who could command rolling acres and willing henchmen, but those who understood how money was made, who knew how to manipulate stocks and acquire companies and pyramid investments, who would control and rule the Victorian world. The Victorians had a word for these new-made men; they called them the *"bourgeoisie."* The term was derogatory; it brought to mind images of the money-grubbing, narrow-minded merchants who had brought glorious King Charles the Martyr to ruin. But they could not be ignored; for the future belonged to them. By the 1840s this was apparent to everybody, even the haughtiest of the old lords of England. As F. J. Klingender describes it,*

> When George Hudson [who had started life as a draper's assistant at York, and gradually obtained control over most of the north-eastern section of the British railway system] rigged the market to oblige the Duke of Wellington, whose sister had imprudently invested all her property in a bubble company, the aristocratic prejudice against "trade" had lost all meaning. Henceforth the moral subjection of the old ruling class to the bourgeoisie was complete; the ladies had perforce to admit the manufacturers' wives and daughters to their drawing rooms, and only the humble shopkeeper remained to smart beneath their haughty looks.

* *Art and the Industrial Revolution* (London, 1947).

112

And it was apparent to the painters, too. Already in the 1840s we find a keen critic like Thackeray observing that a new class of patrons was coming into existence, and commenting favorably on the amounts of money they were able to spend. Writing in *Fraser's Magazine* in 1845, he noted how much the industrialists and manufacturers were paying for Turner's paintings (his earlier, more "recognizable" ones, to be sure), in contrast to the paltry sums being paid by more exalted personages for the frescoes decorating the summer house in the grounds of Buckingham Palace: "What victims have these poor fellows [the Buckingham Palace painters] been of this awful patronage! Think of the greatest patronage in the world giving £40 for pictures worth £400—condescending to buy works from humble men who could not refuse, and paying for them below their value . . ."

But not all comments on the new patrons were so favorable—and they got worse. For the bourgeois was not at all the kind of patron the old aristocrat had been. This older patron, however unimaginative personally, however susceptible to cajolery and flattery, however he humiliated the artist (everyone remembers what Johnson said about the patron who "looks with unconcern on a man struggling for life in the water, and, when he has reached ground, encumbers him with help") still had a sense of responsibility for the cultural welfare of society. He was used to the idea of supporting painters and writers and musicians, commissioning them, attending their plays and concerts and exhibitions, and assuming social leadership generally.

For the artist, the new patrons' tendency to irresponsibility and indifference to things of the mind and the community was bad enough; but it was almost as bad, or even worse, when they did take an interest in him. For their taste was almost invariably and incredibly bad. How, indeed, could it have been otherwise? A sudden stroke of luck, a profitable business venture, and all at once obscure mechanics or shopkeepers or handworkers were elevated to positions of authority and prestige in matters cultural and aesthetic.

The older type of patron hung on, a last and faltering refuge for serious painters, until mid-century. But by the 1840s, there was no longer any doubt about it; the new bourgeois patron was going to be the man with whom the painter had to reckon; his tastes would determine the relationship between art and society. And every painter living through those years was faced with the same problem—what to do about it. Essentially, there were three choices open. He might refuse to have anything to do with the new class of patron. He might refuse to lower himself to the new standards or accept the new values in any way; insist on painting as he believed painting should be done, and take the consequences—which would certainly be poverty (if he had to live on his work), social neglect and contempt, but also great self-satisfaction. That is the line taken by the sort of painters represented by Courbet; that, as we shall see, is the main line to "modern" art. Or he might attempt a compromise. He might try to paint something resembling what "the people" want, but preserve his own integrity, infuse something of the older universal and expressive values into it. There are a variety of ways of doing this, and a good many painters who tried them; but in the end, as we shall see again, all of them proved futile. Or he could, finally, give the bourgeois what he wanted; he could acquiesce completely in the new patrons' tastes and standards, lower himself to their level, and accept their rewards, which were far from negligible—more munificent, in fact, than any earlier painters could ever have expected. This was the line of least resistance; this, human nature being what it is, was the line taken by most painters after 1840; this was the line that produced what we call generally

16A. *Sir David Wilkie:* The Blind Fiddler. *By courtesy of the Trustees of the Tate Gallery, London. 1806. See also 16B, Couture; 16C, Bouguereau.*

Against the background of taste fostered by the middle-class popular arts, the "Academic" painting of the 19th century becomes more explicable. It was not the result of some mysterious collapse of taste or technical deficiency, but the most obvious of several possible answers to the crisis in painting provoked by the social and economic upheavals of the time. Paintings like these were simply attempts to provide, as painters in every age before had done, what patrons and the public wanted. One unfortunate result was that these patrons' taste for jejune anecdotal subject matter obscured or nullified genuinely pictorial qualities: Wilkie's real abilities as a romantic painter, evident especially in the 1830s after he had seen Velasquez, Goya and Delacroix; Couture's classical command of composition and organization of elements; Bouguereau's extraordinary technical virtuosity, which still can excite admiration on first view.

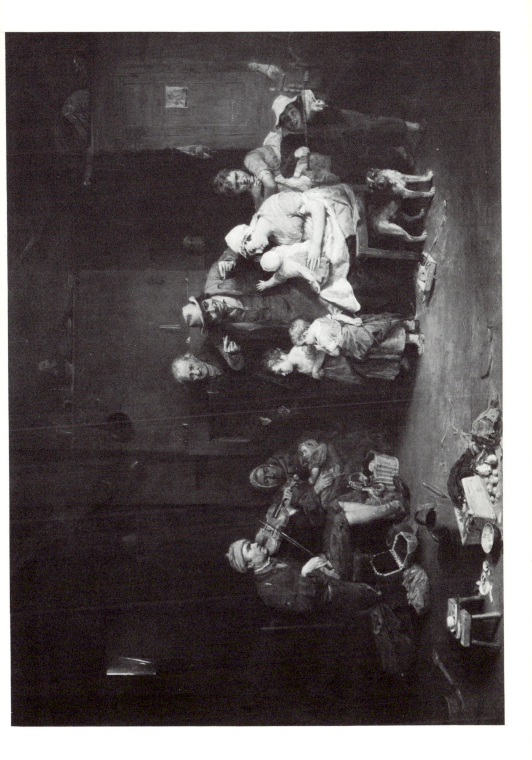

"Academic" painting, the characteristic painting of the High Victorian age.

The process began early in the century; by 1850, official academies—the Royal Academy in England, the Ecole des Beaux-Arts in France, the various official institutions in the German states—were already solidly "bourgeois." The new bourgeois patrons were financing them, buying the pictures they exhibited, setting the tone of their operations; and those painters who acceded most completely to the bourgeois taste were now dominating them. Of those painters, we can consider only a few here. That is only because there were so many of them, not at all because Academic painting is necessarily without interest, or the dull farce it is sometimes made out to be. Even though no one is likely to call it great art today, or attempt its revival, still Academic art did serve its time well, and as a cultural expression of the High Victorian age it is well worth more study than is usually given it. Let us here consider its evolution as represented by the paintings of three typical figures. First, Sir David Wilkie.

With Wilkie we meet at once the first problem in considering Academic 19th-century painting—its near-invisibility. As Maurice Grosser has noted in his excellent chapter on the subject in *The Painter's Eye,**

> We today have no idea how bad these pictures were. We have not seen them. The museums which once bought them or accepted them as gifts are ashamed to hang them, or even to admit that they still preserve them in their cellars. . . . Few students of 19th-century painting know them even as photographs. But what we all do know is that after Ingres, no painter we admire today belonged to an official academy. The living tradition of our painting is the tradition of revolt. . . . It is on this account that "academic painter" has come to mean "bad painter". . .

Seeing Wilkie's paintings is even more difficult for Americans, because so few American museums own one. His reputation went into decline before wealthy Americans started serious collecting, so that only acciden-

* (New York, 1954), "The Second Revolution."

16B. *Thomas Couture: working study for* Romans of the Decadence. *Providence, Museum of Art, Rhode Island School of Design. Based on a passage from Juvenal's* Satires, *VI, 292–293. c. 1846.*

tal and minor acquisitions are available for study. Yet reproductions are perhaps adequate to illustrate the qualities of paintings like *The Blind Fiddler* (page 115), *Blind Man's Buff,* or *News From Waterloo,* which ensured Wilkie's election as a full member of the Royal Academy in 1811, only six years after he had entered it as a student, and by 1830 had earned him a knighthood and the special post of Painter to the King.

To us it seems almost incredible that Wilkie's sentimental anecdotes of poor Scottish families and lower-class life generally could once have been ranked alongside the work of Delacroix, Goya, or Turner. Clearly, Early Victorians must have seen them in a different light from ours. So they did. For them, Wilkie's subjects were satisfactory examples of the noble form in noble action, and evoked appropriately "beautiful feelings." True, the action was not classical and was perhaps even a little petty; and the feelings hardly on the same plane of nobility with those engendered by the poetry of Wilkie's contemporary, Sir Walter Scott. But these faults were more than compensated for by a lofty "morality." Wilkie's paintings were "moral" in the same peculiarly Victorian and English sense which gave Dickens his great appeal; indeed, Wilkie's art affords many parallels to Dickens's. He exhibits the same love for the underdog, for the poor, the underprivileged. He has the same fondness for passages of vivid, proliferating, luxuriant description; the same aptness for seizing on the precise detail that will bring a situation most tellingly to mind; the *Blind Fiddler,* which made him famous, is a superbly Dickensian performance. And just as in Dickens's novels the plot tends to be buried under these mountains of detail, in the end becoming almost irrelevant to them, so to his contemporaries the main criticism of Wilkie's pictures was that they consisted too largely of masses of detail in which overall composition and unified visual organization was lost.

Here at the beginning of the 19th century the basic ingredients of Victorian Academic painting are already mixed: forms determined by the realism of the popular arts, especially illustration; feelings essentially romantic in character. In this sense Academic painting represents a perpetuation of the traditional theory of Beauty, modified in the direction

16C. *Adolphe William Bouguereau:* The Captive. *The Toledo (Ohio) Museum of Art, Gift of Sidney Spitzer. 1891.*

of popular realism; and as such it was understood and carried on throughout the century.

Thomas Couture's *Romans of the Decadence* (page 117), which at the Salon of 1847 enjoyed what more than one scholar has called "the greatest triumph known to art history," represents the mid-19th-century mixture of Academic ingredients. Where Wilkie's painting was more romantic than realistic, Couture strikes an almost exact balance. As in Wilkie's case, to judge the picture either by the standards of Beauty that motivated painting before it, or the Reality that came after, is to find little in it; but judged by the standards of its own day, *Romans of the Decadence* was a self-evidently perfect painting. It appealed to the same kind and level of taste as Wilkie's *Blind Fiddler*—a taste, that is, which has since reverted to the social stratum whence it came, and is now best recognized in 20th-century Hollywood "spectaculars" like *The Ten Commandments* or *The Fall of the Roman Empire*. Like these great modern money-makers, *Romans of the Decadence* was made to appeal to likings for an obvious story—one that everybody knew, or had at least heard of. There was the same vague flavor of "culture" about it, deriving from a degenerate romanticism ideally calculated to appeal to a half-educated audience. It had the same combination of meticulous attention to detail and "colossal" scale, easily and unthinkingly admired. Best of all, it. had the same sort of comfortable "moralizing," allowing one to wallow in vice and virtue simultaneously. It shows the evil consequences of riotous living, not necessarily to individuals (for whatever their future fate, the present for these Romans is certainly enjoyable) but to the State, preaches a sermon that everyone can appreciate, and gives one a warm feeling of concern for the welfare of mankind in general without any unpleasant personal implications.

In form, too, *Romans of the Decadence* perfectly satisfied the taste of its age. A working study like the one illustrated here obviously demands years of studying anatomy, underpainting, composition, life drawing, color theory, archaeological data, and classical literary texts in academy schoolrooms. Dozens, hundreds of preliminary drawings and sketches are boiled down into one intricately organized final distillation. It remained only for this 17″ × 26″ painting to be blown up ten times bigger to produce a perfect example of the "planned picture" towards which all Academic training was directed, and which could still be justified in terms of the traditional theory of Beauty. The result, in the eyes of its generation, was a definitive consummation of all the science, scholarship, and experience of past ages but yet, like the Picturesque Eclecticism in architecture of this same generation, a work of art with a style distinctly its own. An impressive performance; small wonder that Couture became for a time the most renowned painter of his day, and the most sought-after teacher. Small wonder, too, that from a studio where elements of Reality, of classicism in the old sense, and of romanticism were all tied into one neat package, should come painters as diverse as the old-line classicist Puvis de Chavannes, the anachronistically romantic Feuerbach, and the revolutionary mentor of Impressionism, Edouard Manet.

But when most people think of Academic painting today, what comes first to mind is generally something from the later 19th century like *The Captive* (page 119) by Adolphe William Bouguereau. By this time its realistic element had come to dominate romanticism almost entirely, so that to modern eyes Bouguereau's painting looks like nothing so much as typical exhibits in some amateur photography show. There is the same profuse redundancy, for Bouguereau inherited a habit of middle-class industry from his background in La Rochelle which drove him to complete a minimum of twenty major pictures a year, not counting portraits. There is the same sentimental realism in subject matter, which survives in amateur photography as nowhere else: variations on themes like "The Adventure of Life" (toddler meets doggy or kitty), "Heroism on Main Street" (the day Nussbaum's Department Store caught fire), and so forth. Above all, there is the same insistence on the most literal reproduction of things seen. Even today, when the perfection of color photography has put power to counterfeit natural appearances within easy reach of anyone and everyone, the consummate technical skill of Bouguereau's "invisible brush-stroke" still excites admiration at first view; what its effect must have been when the feat was less commonplace can be readily imagined from the honors heaped on Bouguereau: the *Prix de Rome;* gold medals; silver medals; membership in the Institute; Knight and then Officer of the Legion of Honor. . . .

Yet it is this very literalness, of course, which constitutes the crux of the whole damning case modern critics make against Victorian Academic painting. When you depict exactly what you see, all possibility of imaginative or allegorical re-creation of experience is out of the question. This means, put bluntly, that art is out of the question. The very word "art" implies some attempt to order or interpret the essentially formless and mindless physical world, something in some way distant and

121

different from flat actuality. It seems obvious that paintings like *The Captive* are no more than grandiosely painful commentaries on the classic pronouncement attributed to Sally Rand: "stripping without music ain't art"; that no matter what playful or romantic title he gives it, what Bouguereau puts before us is no more and no less than a naked girl-child who for reasons inexplicable in the context has wings tacked on her back and sits uncomfortably on a balustrade out in a garden, looking at a butterfly; that, in short, Academic painting "ain't art." It follows, presumably, that Couture and Bouguereau and the rest were not real "artists." But before dismissing Academic painters as beneath contempt and their work as fit only for barrooms or storage bins, there is another side to consider.

To begin with, it is obviously not true that people like Couture and Bouguereau were dead to formal values, that they had only a perfunctory interest in color and form and composition per se. Neither have even their worst enemies ever pretended that Academic painters were technically incompetent; indeed, some of them were among the most brilliant practitioners of the craft of painting who ever lived. Furthermore, if we use the term "artist" in its old social sense, we have to conclude that it was the Academicians who were the "real" artists, and their rivals, the rebels and noncompromisers, who were not. In painting what patrons wanted, the Academicians were only doing what Phidias and Raphael and Bernini and Reynolds and every other artist had done. Those who insisted on painting what and as they liked, who were striking out on a new course as independent critics of society, practitioners of "art" outside any fixed social context, were trying to become something "artists" had never been. If we say today that the Academicians were not "real" artists, that is primarily because our idea of what an artist should be and do has changed. And if what they produced no longer seems art to us, that is primarily because what and how their patrons required them to paint was different from earlier times, and from ours. It follows that its very failings as art make Academic painting all the more valuable as cultural expression, a manifestation of the kind of mind which dominated the Victorian age and so, inevitably, shaped our own.

In the financial system that governed 19th-century Europe, especially England and France, all values had come to be based on abstractions. It was a system built on paper. Men could make a great fortune in, say, iron or railroads or cotton mills, without knowing anything whatsoever about the technical processes of smelting iron, or how railroads operated, or the workings of a cotton gin. They gained control of these things, built a "kingdom" of this or that, by manipulating pieces of paper, by eying columns of figures in a stock market and guessing or maneuvering their movements. In the process all real distinction was lost between those values which rested on solid universal realities and those which were evanescent products of financial circumstance. It followed inevitably that when such men found themselves in the position of art patrons they could not appreciate the values inherent in the traditional theory of Beauty which depended on an assumption that objects possessed inherent, inalienable and universal properties of "beauty"; that there were certain forms and proportions and order which were always and everywhere superior to others; that there were certain categories of human emotions which were in and of themselves "noble" and "beautiful." What they admired in art and called "beautiful" were certain qualities—picturesqueness, sentiment, literal counterfeiting of specific Nature—which clearly, in retrospect, existed not in their art but in themselves. They projected into the paintings their Academicians made for them a set of emotional responses congenial to the particular temperamental climate of the High Victorian age. When that climate changed, as all such climates do, these qualities came to seem merely quaint, ridiculous, or meaningless.

Nevertheless, it is worth remembering that uncompromising insistence on physical fact, though it may have ruined Academic painting as a vehicle for genuine aesthetic or imaginative experience, is not in itself a bad thing. It was a habit of mind entirely characteristic and to a great extent the creation of what Mark Twain once proudly called "the plainest and sturdiest and infinitely greatest and worthiest of all the centuries the world has seen." * This same middle-class facing of the real physical world without fear, without delusion or superstition or preconception, made possible pasteurization, electricity, and anesthesia; it put Victorians (and ourselves as their heirs) in command of their world as no men had ever been before. And put at the service of a different sort of patron, modified to suit more universal kinds of subject matter, it could have become the basis for a new and vital kind of art to replace the moribund traditional theory of Beauty. To some extent, indeed, that is precisely what did happen, as we can see evidenced in diverse ways by the "creative illustrators," the Pre-Raphaelites, and the doctrinaire realists of the mid-19th century.

* *Life on the Mississippi* (1874), Ch. 38.

NOTES

One of the sanest and soundest expositions of the genuine deficiencies of Academic painting from the modern point of view is Maurice Grosser's chapter, "The Second Revolution," in *The Painter's Eye* (1954). A good example of the forlorn sort of guerilla warfare still being waged in the Academic cause is R. Ives Gammell, *The Twilight of Painting* (1946); unfortunately (as usually happens), he ruins whatever case can be made for it by carrying the argument too far. It may well be true that Bouguereau, Meissonier, or Landseer deserve more consideration than the present climate of opinion is disposed to give them, but that is very different from attempting to maintain that they were great painters. A sanely sympathetic view of Wilkie in particular and Academicians generally is provided by Stanley Cursiter, *Scottish Art* (London, 1949).

3

"Creative Illustration":

Honoré Daumier (1808–1879)
Winslow Homer (1836–1910)
Thomas Eakins (1844–1916)

In the mid-20th century, to call a painter an "illustrator" is almost as bad as to call him "Academic." Indeed, we so much dislike the whole concept of painting as dependent on literature or anything outside itself, that we feel any distinction between Academicians and illustrators is of no fundamental consequence.

Nevertheless there is a difference, and it is important. The root of Academic painting was in the old theory of Beauty—degenerate, to be sure, but still strong enough to saddle the Academician with vacuous subject matter which vitiated his forms. By contrast, the 19th-century art of illustration grew out of the realism of the early popular arts, and illustrators in consequence enjoyed a freedom of invention Academicians could never have. Crude though Cruikshank's spidery little vignettes may be, there is a life to them unmatched in the Academicians' polished performances. Because they suggest rather than describe, imagination can work on and in them with a freedom wholly denied by the precision of Academic detail; being quickly dashed off for the uses of a moment, without any pretensions to eternal stature, they achieve a spontaneity impossible in carefully planned Academic "machines." An illustrator like Cruikshank, in short, offered the Victorian public far more opportunity for genuine aesthetic experience than did Academic painters. And the same is true of Doré's drawings. Lehmann-Haupt is right when he says that the imagination of three generations was stirred by Doré; but he could have gone on to say that through Doré's borrowings from Delacroix, Michelangelo, and Greek sculpture the middle classes in England and France had their first real intimation of what art might be.

Furthermore, in contrast to the Academicians, who represented the last gasp of a dying tradition, Cruikshank and Doré were pioneers of a new movement. Whatever their shortcomings, they were at least trying to make a positive response to the great crisis in Western culture precipitated by the Industrial Revolution, to build a bridge over the abyss which separated the rising bourgeois classes from any appreciation of the great artistic tradition of the past. Because the "serious" painting of Cruikshank and Doré amounted to little more than blown-up oil versions of their commercial illustrations, we are able to ignore its social significance. We assume that popular arts and serious painting are necessarily and always antipathetic; we maintain that the popular arts acted like an opiate on people's minds, dulling and inhibiting them from appreciation of finer things; or we imagine that the popular arts are so inevitably restricted to things immediate and particular that illustrators necessarily cannot deal with universals. But when we turn to consider others in this generation—Daumier, Eakins, Homer—such preconceptions melt away. For although these are painters now counted among the 19th century's greatest, their careers are clearly and precisely in the Cruikshank-Doré pattern. All begin, that is, as commercial illustrators, and all develop their "serious" painting on this foundation. The only difference is that they have an ability to make this popular realism the basis of a genuine art, creative illustration of universal scope.

Daumier's *Third-class Carriage* (page 127) is a great and typical example. Its origin in the popular arts is clear—essentially it is a drawing, so thinly painted that the lined squares now show through. And what could be more particular and immediate than its starting point—an illustration of the interior of a French train of the early 1860s rolling into

125

Paris towards the end of a long trip? Daumier had satirized the new-fangled mode of transportation in cartoons often enough. Yet what could be more timeless and universal than the painting Daumier has made of it? In this unpromising material he has recognized the quality of universal human experience and made a timeless commentary on it.

From the beginning of time, men have had to travel. And from the beginning of time, they have found it painful; "travel" and "travail" are from the same root. This is a universal human condition and this is what Daumier depicts. Beyond and through his immediate subject—this group of lower- and lower-middle-class 19th-century Frenchmen—we see countless generations of human beings, past and present. More, we see ourselves. The experience Daumier illustrates is something all human beings know. The pleasures of starting out—the anticipation, the excitement, the packing and pressing, the bustle of departure—are now long behind. Now all talk is talked, all scenery seen, all food eaten. With clothes creased and sweaty, air thick and dry, it remains only to sit out the trip, hour after hour, mile after joggling mile. It remains only to numbly endure. And that is a sensation we all know. Even if we never traveled, we would know it, for travel is but an allegory of life. As the poets and philosophers and sages of all ages tell, life is a kind of journey, beginning, like this one, in hope and anticipation and interest, ending in dumb endurance. Ending in the sheer fact of existence; sooner or later

17A. *Honoré Daumier:* Third-class Carriage. *New York, The Metropolitan Museum of Art, Bequest of Mrs. H. O. Havemeyer, the H. O. Havemeyer Collection. c. 1862.* See also 17B, Homer; 17C, Eakins; 17D, Eakins.

That illustration, handled with proper breadth and universality, could be the basis for great and significant art, is abundantly demonstrated in works like these. This demonstration, however, went largely unnoticed; the first generation of bourgeois patrons was not yet ready to appreciate such subtleties, and by the time a more aesthetically refined upper-class generation had matured, it was too late. Revulsion against the banality of Academic "pretty pictures" had hardened into rejection of Beauty as a goal for painting altogether and a corresponding insistence on uncompromising Reality as the proper business of painters.

we all come to the state these people are in—simply existing. They do nothing, they say nothing, they see nothing; they simply *are*. Daumier, in short, illustrates life.

Between the heads in the rear compartment there is no correspondence. No more than an accidental chance of time and place brought them together; the same accident will disperse them forever at their journey's end. But in the foreground group there is a more fundamental unity. Although they neither look at nor speak to each other, they still belong together. The picture takes its structure, in fact, from this pyramid of grandmother in the center and a generation on each side—just as life in the West has always been built, not on transient groupings of business or sport or material interests, but from the love of mother and child, the training of the younger by the older generation. That this central composition is so strongly reminiscent of Renaissance altarpieces, of some Sacred Conversation, is no accident, for this image, like an icon, transcends particular moments of space and time. This is an illustration not of time but of eternity, of what the old writers meant by *ars longa, vita brevis*.

And Daumier achieves this monumental universality precisely because, and not in spite, of his training as an illustrator. It was in the course of making thousands of lithographs that he perfected that quick, loose, sketchy manner (reminiscent of Cruikshank's and Doré's) which, suggesting rather than describing, gives the imagination such room to work. This despised vehicle of popular art, suited for rapid reproduction and mass circulation, is what has taught him how to eliminate unnecessary detail; it is working with crayon on stone that has disciplined him to concentrate on the broad, essential masses in oil painting, so that his forms transcend particular circumstances to become the kind of monumental reductions of human experience to universal common denominators which Academicians tried and failed to realize with polished nudities, grandiose scale, and intricate compositional machines.

And because he was an illustrator, too, Daumier could remain that sort of artist, so rare in modern times, whose realism was oriented more towards people than towards art, who was a person first and a painter

17B. *Winslow Homer:* Eight Bells. *Andover, Mass., Addison Gallery of American Art. 1886.*

second. As a political commentator or social cartoonist, he has to see life as it is, not as the abstraction he might like it to be. He never can lose touch with the "common man" of his own age, and, in consequence, of any other. When in a political cartoon he dealt with taxation, law, skulduggery, or the problem of power, he was dealing with matters of quite as much concern in ancient Babylon and exotic Bali as in 19th-century France or 20th-century America—and he had to deal with them at the point where they most closely touched the life of the common man. That is why his *Uprising* (Washington, Phillips Gallery) is so different in spirit from Delacroix's *Liberty on the Barricade* and so much more effective. For Daumier sees, not in terms of literary symbolism and classical forms, but from the common point of view; he had probably never read any sociology, but from his deep awareness of people as individuals he knew that

> the mental universe of a revolutionary mob, as the nineteenth-century French sociologist, Gustave Le Bon, has pointed out, is a prelogical one, and the mob itself is not so much a social chaos as an archaic society, swept by intensive collective hates and fears, responding almost magically to charismatic leadership, displaying an ant-like capacity for spontaneous organization and endowed with an instinctual sense of strategy like that possessed by pack-hunting animals. These characteristics are not manifested by a normal political crowd, however indignant or agitated; they sometimes develop with eerie suddenness in the course of large-scale and prolonged civil disorders when the prestige of authority wears off in clashes and skirmishes with the rioters.*

Consequently, whereas Delacroix's *Barricade* is an attempt at universality which remains a period piece, Daumier's *Uprising* is a picture of all revolutions, everywhere.

Even Daumier's most topical cartoons show the same instinct for universality. Under the guise of satirizing bourgeois fashions and foibles in Victorian Paris, he poignantly exposes the sins that have afflicted the human race from the beginning of time—pride and envy, sloth and snobbery, pretension and folly, gossip and greed. And these simple yet

* Edmond Taylor, *The Fall of the Dynasties* (New York, 1963), p. 261.

17C. *Thomas Eakins:* The Swimming Hole. *Fort Worth (Texas) Art Center. 1883.*

all-comprehensive themes become the subject matter for Daumier's paintings. It is in this respect that Daumier reminds us strikingly of Shakespeare. Just as Shakespeare's great works are never merely plays, but always plays *about* something—*Macbeth* about ambition, *Lear* about renunciation, *Hamlet* about revenge, and so on—so Daumier never merely paints, he always paints *about* something which transcends immediate and local associations. An illustrator of the nature of mankind, he belongs in and carries forward the great classical Renaissance tradition of the western world.

As an illustrator, too, Daumier was preserved from the great 20th-century fallacy that universals can have any actual independent existence apart from particulars. He knew, because his living depended on it, that truth can be meaningful only in particular situations, that universals have validity only insofar as they are expressed by and embodied in specific events, people, and places. This has been the basic premise of all great universal art. Art that transcends its own period (classical, medieval, Baroque, whatever) knows neither stock figures nor pure "types." Insofar as Shylock was a stock type of 16th-century Jewish moneylender, he is of no more than historical interest to us; it is because Shakespeare knew how to present this stock type as a human being with individual feelings and personal passions that Shylock, and the *Merchant of Venice,* remain living works of art. Daumier's art lives for the same reason. In their lifetimes, Daumier and Doré both illustrated *Don Quixote,* for instance. Doré's was far more popular, because his Quixote was a kind of stock buffoon Victorian middle classes associated with the moribund hereditary aristocracy of the 19th century; but Daumier's has lasted, because like Shakespeare he saw the world in terms of people rather than types, and so understood instinctively how Don Quixote and Sancho Panza embody that warring union of body and soul, of lofty impossible aspiration and crass self-sufficiency, that exists and always has existed in all of us.

On such foundations a new kind of realistic art could have been built. But it was not; "realism" in Western art would mean something quite different in the years ahead. Indeed, by the time Daumier had his first

17D. *Thomas Eakins:* Robert M. Lindsay. *The Detroit Institute of Arts. 1900.*

exhibition in 1878, the mainstream of painting in France was flowing in another channel, away from illustration, towards quite another kind of Reality. Why this happened, we shall consider shortly. But before we do, we should look at a few more "illustrators," of whom some of the most outstanding were Americans.

Illustration being the art peculiarly associated with and created for the *bourgeoisie,* and America being beyond all comparison *the* bourgeois country of the 19th century, the art of illustration began earlier and flourished more vigorously in the United States than any other Western country; practically all the major names in American painting down to 1914 were illustrators in one sense or another. For almost as soon as the American provinces had developed to the point where patronage in the traditional manner was possible, the Revolution uprooted and disparaged the landed aristocracy. It spanned, in fact, little more than the genera-tions of Washington and Jefferson. The succeeding generations of Jacksons and Van Burens and Lincolns which shaped and epitomized the character of 19th-century America were extraordinary and outstanding in many ways, but not in aesthetic discrimination.

"Common men" predominated—"men of the people" who "knew what they liked." And what they liked was illustration; art that provided substitute images of people, places, and things that could be looked at when the originals were not available; that involved stories; that had the kind of practical usefulness both recent frontier experience and mercan-tile business attitudes taught them to admire. So whether in the form of "classical" painting by Vanderlyn or Trumbull, "romantic" painting by Allston or Quidor or Durand, reportorial prints by Currier & Ives, or John Rogers's tidy sculptural groups, illustration set the pace for and best represented the taste of most Americans, high and low alike, through most of the 19th century. Nowhere can the range of illustrative art be seen better than in American 19th-century painting generally; nowhere are its possibilities for greatness more apparent than in the art of Winslow Homer and Thomas Eakins. Their painting is a commentary on the problems and opportunities of creative illustration.

The basis of creative illustration is in the objective world. Thus Homer began as a Civil War illustrator, and Eakins with two years' anatomical study at Jefferson Medical College in Philadelphia; and though both painted with increasing looseness and freedom as time went on, they never lost the concept that painting is above all a faithful record of things seen and personally known. But fidelity to Nature never meant mechanical copying; it was not an end, but a means towards personal and cultural expression. Through their art we can realize better than in any other medium except Walt Whitman's poetry, perhaps, what "liberty" meant in 19th-century America. That "rugged individualism" at which a later generation nostalgically sneers is everywhere rampant in their paintings, from Homer's early *Prisoners from the Front* (so dramatic an exhibition of the civilian and volunteer character of the greatest of 19th-century wars) to Eakins's late *Cello Player,* playing alone at his own time and to his own inclination, with no voice pursuing, no clock hurrying, no compulsion niggling him; free from want, from care, from coercion; in those few decades when the older constraints of apprenticeship and rigid class structure have disintegrated and the new stratification by corporate wealth not yet solidified, enjoying a degree of liberty his ancestors could not have imagined and his descendants can only envy. And this kind of freedom could be enjoyed by painters too, of course. Painting in the lifetime of Eakins and Homer ranged all the way from the most servile eclecticism to the boldest experiments in pure form; never had painters been so free to experiment and create, and their own wide range of forms and subjects showed it.

But this freedom had its perils. Never before had society been so disparate; never before had it consisted so precariously of individuals each going his own way regardless of the rest. If it were possible to accomplish great things and rise swiftly from the bottom to the top, you could fall just as fast; if you could carve a great career for yourself in art, or business, or science, without family fortunes or connections behind you, it was also possible to be born in affluence and die unnoticed and alone. Never before had there been so few guideposts to direct an individual's development. Since everyone was free to go his own way, what discipline he needed he had to supply for himself. The result was not always happy. The hanging committee at the Philadelphia Centennial of 1876 who put Eakins's *Gross Clinic* among the medical exhibits rather than in the art gallery, for instance, was not entirely unreasonable. Eakins, insisting on his freedom to rely on his own observations rather than traditions taught in schools, to pursue his study of anatomy as if the painters of the 15th-century Renaissance had never existed, and to painfully relearn for himself what had long been known and long since built into a tradition, did often seem to be as much a scientist as an artist in the old sense.

Furthermore, a society that left painters free to paint as they liked also left them free to starve, and in many cases they came perilously close to doing so. Ideally, the illustrator represented a middle course for painters in the social crisis of 19th-century civilization. While Academicians catering to the new-rich were backing art into one tiny pocket of society, and the revolutionary "realists," working only to please themselves and their painterly friends, were trying to shut it up in another, illustrators were still performing a function that all elements in society had always accepted and recognized. By taking themes from everyday life and experience and raising them to the level of art, illustrators like Homer and Eakins and Daumier were carrying on the tradition of painters as men who could perceive beauties unsuspected by the common eye, who brought order and harmony out of what seemed to others mere dreary vistas of confused clichés. But in practice, unfortunately, creative illustration tended to satisfy nobody. Its kind of realism was too closely derived from the popular arts to please patrons who wanted to forget plebeian origins, yet developed too far beyond them for the masses generally to appreciate. At the same time the illustrators' concern for traditional Beauty made their work unacceptable to the uncompromising realists of advance-guard painting. In consequence, the creative illustrator found himself alienated from his society even more fundamentally than the doctrinaire advance-guard "rebel," for his alienation, being involuntary, was without even the satisfaction of martyrdom. This alienation is expressed by all the great creative illustrators, both in their characteristic choices of subject matter, and in the common pattern of their lives.

NOTES

Daumier was born at Marseilles in 1808, and began his career as a caricaturist, first (1830) with *La Caricature,* then with *Le Charivari* (1835 on), and made his living by this means throughout his life. He drew literally thousands of cartoons—lithographs and woodcuts—on every conceivable subject, single cuts and series (e.g., the *Robert Macaire* series, 1836–38 and 1840–41). Politics occupied him most at the beginning and at the end of his career (in 1832 he was imprisoned for six months for his *Gargantua* satire on Louis Philippe, while late commentaries on Louis Napoleon's foreign policy like *L'Empire, c'est la Paix* of 1871 anticipated in their broad handling of masses and symbolic characterization what came to be the accepted sort of 20th-century political cartoon); but his constant and favorite subject was the

19th-century *bourgeoisie* of France. He satirized every aspect of their lives and institutions—their habits (*Les Beaux Jours de la Vie; Tout ce qu'on voudra*), their morals (*Moeurs conjugales*), their cultural pretensions (*Les bas bleus; Histoire ancienne*), their character (*Croquis d'expression*), their love of inventions (railroads, daguerreotypes), their laws. But for all that, Daumier never forgot that the bourgeois was, after all, an individual with virtues as well as vices; through all his mockery ran a vein of profound human sympathy. It is essential to a good satirist that he not see too much, that he find the world black and white; precisely because Daumier was not a one-eyed purveyor of prejudice, because he did see the world in shades of gray, he was not remarkably successful in his profession. His cartoons never made him more than a pittance apiece, and in 1860 he was discharged by *Le Charivari* on grounds that the public had lost interest in his work. Throughout his life he had lived in the back streets of Paris almost totally unknown to the art world at large and selling his cartoons for only a few cents apiece; having no resources, he now might well have died from destitution. Fortunately, since he had begun painting (in 1848) his work had been attracting a small but fervent circle of admirers, among them some we now consider the leading painters of the age—Corot, Daubigny, Delacroix, and Courbet. They, especially Corot, now came to his aid, providing him with a home and eventually another job. They could not, however, get public or patrons at large to see in his paintings, with their thin paint and loose sketchy line, anything more than larger and somewhat more elaborate versions of his cartoons; no public exhibition of them was held until 1878, the year before his death, and until the 20th century Daumier the painter remained largely unknown.

Winslow Homer was born at Boston in 1836, and like Daumier, began his career as a lithographer, doing illustrations for the local *Ballou's Pictorial* (1847–59). From 1859 to 1876 he was a free-lance illustrator in New York, working mainly on wood blocks for *Harper's Weekly*. These media imposed on him, as on Daumier, a disciplined clarity of line, broad organization of light and dark masses, and succinct characterization. His first major painting, *Prisoners from the Front* (1866, New York, Metropolitan), one of several developed out of his wartime illustrations, was well received—primarily because of its timely subject matter, however; it was exhibited with the American show at the Paris Exposition of 1867. With this encouragement, Homer himself went to France in 1867–68 to study painting, but his background in the popular arts made him unsympathetic not only to Academic pretensions but also to Impressionism, the reigning advance-guard movement. As Dr. E. P. Richardson has put it:

> His long discipline in black-and-white made itself felt; instead of dissolving outline and form into a vibration of light and color, he developed luminosity within a construction of clear, firm outlines and

137

broad planes of light and dark. After he began to use water color
[1873] his treatment of outline became more fluid and subtle; but he
never lost the large, monumental quality of his early style in all his
later delicacy of nuance and aerial color.*

In consequence Homer, like Daumier, was never considered by his contemporaries either a great popular artist or a "real painter"; though never as utterly
destitute as Daumier, he too was unable to make a decent living, could not
even marry. Embittered, he went into self-imposed exile in 1881, first for two
years in bleak obscurity at Tynemouth in England, then until his death in
1910 at remote Prout's Neck on the Maine coast.

Essentially the same pattern characterizes the life of Thomas Eakins. Born
at Philadelphia in 1844, he began his career somewhat differently in that after
early training at the Pennsylvania Academy he went to Paris in 1866 for study
at the Ecole des Beaux-Arts. There, however, the influence of his American
background became apparent in his ignoring Impressionism and attaching
himself to that most anecdotal and factually literal of Academicians, Jean
Léon Gérôme; and on his return to Philadelphia he applied what he had
learned not to literary subjects but to illustrations of the lives and activities of
its people. Like Daumier and Homer, however, he soon found that upper-
class patrons thought such subject matter too common, while Parisian
training made his treatment of it too sophisticated for popular consumption;
the fate of his great *The Gross Clinic,* refused as an art exhibit and hung in
the medical section of the Centennial Exhibition, was symptomatic. And as
his technique became more and more literal under the stimulus of anatomical
studies at Jefferson Medical College and experiments in photography with
Eadweard Muybridge, it too drew increasing criticism for "vulgarity." At last,
when in furtherance of his principles he insisted on using nude male models in
drawing classes for women students at the Pennsylvania Academy, where he
had been teaching since 1876, he lost both his position (1886) and his
reputation as a serious painter; the last years of his life, to his death in 1916,
were spent in the same alienated obscurity as Daumier's and Homer's.

Consciously, creative illustrators characteristically worked as independents,
free spirits who chose themes at random interest. Unconsciously, however,
there runs through the art of all of them a persistent preoccupation with the
same two themes. First, the theme of alienation, expressed in a consistent
tendency to paint pictures having to do with people in some way out of touch
with society, in but not of it (like the painters themselves); second, and as a
corrective corollary, pictures having to do with those fundamental occupations and human relationships, most often found in lower-class life, on which
all social order and psychological security ultimately rest. In many cases the

* *Painting in America* (New York, 1956), p. 315.

two themes are combined in one picture; this often results in the greatest triumphs of creative illustration.

Typical themes expressing alienation in Daumier's work are his many paintings of *Don Quixote* (dating from the 1860s and probably inspired by Doré's *Quixote* illustrations which appeared in 1863); of people at the mercy of the law and lawyers (e.g., *Exhibits in Evidence,* Melbourne, National Gallery of Australia); of itinerant entertainers (e.g., *Street Singers,* Paris, Petit Palais; *Travelling Mountebanks,* Hartford, Wadsworth Atheneum); of introspective intellectuals (e.g., *The Print Collector,* Philadelphia; *Portrait of Corot,* New York, Metropolitan). Classics in this vein are the lonely and rejected Christ in *Ecce Homo* (1850, Essen, Germany, Folkwang), and *The Uprising* (c. 1860, Washington, Phillips) where he gives permanent form to a basic idea, expressed in many transient cartoons throughout his career (*Rue Transnonain,* 1834; *L'Empire, c'est la Paix,* 1871), that the common man's hopes for a better lot in life which ever and again find desperate voice in revolution, will never be realized—the most he can expect is possibly a change of masters, certainly misery for himself. The only enduring pleasures and stabilities in life are basic ones—recreation with old friends (*The Topers; The Chess Players,* Paris, Petit Palais); mothers nurturing their children; the family (e.g., Washington, Phillips); plays with the simple catharsis Aristotle advocated (*The Drama,* Munich). In Daumier's greatest works these two themes are combined: *Soup* (Louvre), and *The Third-class Carriage,* images of family solidarity amidst all the flux of circumstance, prescient of Steinbeck's *Grapes of Wrath; The Washerwoman* (Louvre), *The Butcher* (Cambridge, Fogg), *The Smith,* monumental figures whose significance transcends all generations and links past with future despite their present landless proletarian status; above all, illustrations of the artist in his traditional social role, bequeathing timeless Beauties from generation to generation (*The Painter and his Apprentice; Painter before his Easel*).

Winslow Homer expresses alienation in terms of man facing mindless Nature alone, as a sailor (*Fog Warning,* 1885, Boston; *Eight Bells* [page 129]), hunter (*Huntsman and Dogs,* 1891, Philadelphia), woodsman (*Adirondack Guide,* watercolor, 1894, Boston; *Adirondacks,* 1892, Cambridge, Fogg), or West Indies waterman (*Turtle Pound,* 1898, Brooklyn). He can make a poignant symbol of human life also out of the drama of Nature herself, as in *Winter Coast* (1890, Philadelphia) or *Northeaster* (1895, New York, Metropolitan); *The Fox Hunt* (1893, Philadelphia, Pennsylvania Academy) is a particularly striking example, with its fox floundering in the snow attacked by starving crows. This same sense for alienation makes him one of the greatest illustrators of the life of the Negro; here classic works combining the two images are *The Gulf Stream* (1899, New York, Metropolitan) and *After the Tornado, Bahamas* (1899, watercolor, Chicago).

Homer finds images of security in rural life and elemental dramas—*Haymaking* (1864, Columbus, Ohio), *Long Branch, New Jersey* (1869, Boston), *Children on a Fence* (1874, Williamstown, Mass.), *Boys in a Pasture* (1872, Boston), *The Campfire* (1881, New York, Metropolitan) *Snap the Whip* (1883, Youngstown, Ohio), *The Lifeline* (1884, Williamstown, Mass.), *The Herring Net* (1885, Chicago).

Eakins's images of alienation are most characteristically single figures standing out against a crowd—*The Gross Clinic* (1875, Philadelphia, Jefferson Medical College), where the surgeon becomes a symbol of the lone scientific pioneer amidst a crowd of ignorance and fear; the loneliness of the creative individual, as in *Benjamin Howard Rand* (1874, Philadelphia, Jefferson Medical College); *Crucifixion* (1880, Philadelphia); *The Pathetic Song* (1881, Washington, Corcoran); *Professor Henry A. Rowland* (1891, Andover, Mass.); *Robert M. Lindsay* (page 133). A classic example is *Salutat* (1890, Andover, Mass.), an illustration of boxing whose title, recalling Roman spectacles, implies the mood. Security is to be found in proficient self-sufficiency—*Max Schmitt in a Single Scull* (1871, New York, Metropolitan), *The Oarsmen* (1872, Philadelphia), *The Swimming Hole,* (page 131), *Pushing for Rail* (1874, New York, Metropolitan), and many others of sport generally. A classic is *The Agnew Clinic* (1889, Philadelphia, University of Pennsylvania) in which, by contrast with the earlier *Gross Clinic,* the physician is an accepted and integrated part of his surroundings. Pictures like *Miss Van Buren* (c. 1889–91, Washington, Phillips) or *Louis N. Kenton* (*The Thinker,* 1900, New York, Metropolitan) combine the two images and sum up Eakins's career.

Illustrations of Daumier's work may be found in Jean Adhémar's selection, *Drawings and Watercolors* (1954); of his paintings in Edward Fuchs, *Der Maler Daumier* (Munich, 1930), of his lithographs, W. Wartmann, *Honoré Daumier* (London, 1940). Other books on *Daumier* include those by M. Sadleir (London, 1924), Inez Ghirardelli (San Francisco, 1940), and Jacques Lassaigne (Paris, 1948).

Lloyd Goodrich's books on *Homer* (1944, 1951, 1959) are standard; see also Forbes Watson (1942) and M. B. Cowdrey (Northampton, Mass., 1951).

Books on *Eakins* include those by Lloyd Goodrich (1933), Roland McKinney (1942) and Fairfield Porter (1959). There are very perceptive analyses of Eakins and Homer in John McCoubrey, *American Tradition in Painting* (1963); a standard source reference for both is E. P. Richardson, *Painting in America* (1956).

II

"Realism"
as a Theory in Mid-19th-Century Painting

TO THE SUPERFICIAL EYE, THERE SEEMS LITTLE TO choose between what the mid-19th century called "realism," and "Academic" art or "illustration." All High Victorian painting looks pretty much alike to us—naturalistic in technique, literary and anecdotal in content. Not until the 1860s, in fact, does a change appear in the outward forms of painting marked enough to be obvious to everybody, and that is in what was technically called Impressionism, not realism. But in painting as in most other aspects of life, altered outward appearance is usually the last evidence and proof, rather than a symptom, of inner change. The changed forms of advance-guard painting after 1860 only manifested what had already been long under way, a shift in the fundamental goals and concepts of the art of painting itself. This shift was effected by the generation before, the generation of the Pre-Raphaelites in England, the Barbizon school and Courbet in France. The "realism" of these painters, who reached their maturity in the 1850s, provided the foundations on which Impressionism and all later "modern" painting was built.

They were a diverse lot, to be sure, sharing in fact only one common characteristic, but that was fundamental. All, in one way or another, represent a change of attitude—or better, perhaps, of direction. All, in one way or another, reject the principle of seeking for Beauty according to artificially set principles or ideal formulae; all propose instead to base their art on something more tangible, more "real." The Pre-Raphaelites propose to rejuvenate Academic standards by reviving what they think of as the truer forms of Raphael's time and earlier, to purify the effete religious painting of their day by returning to simple morality and historical fact. The Barbizon landscape painters propose to take landscape out of the planned-picture category, to paint direct from nature.

141

Millet and the "peasant painters" propose to replace the historical, classical, and other generally fictional characters who people Academic painting with those sturdy tillers of the soil on whom presumably all civilization ultimately depends. Courbet sees the painters of his time as "lackeys of the *bourgeoisie*" and proposes to restore the artist's ancient rights and privileges as an inspired seer and prophet, arbiter of social reality. All these painters, in short, represent a resistance—mild or violent as the case may be—to dominance of the *bourgeoisie* in matters cultural. They refuse either to conform, like the Academicians, or compromise, like the illustrators. They insist on their own standards; they will neither defend nor modify the old positions, but are bent on taking up entirely new ones.

Not that they themselves completely realize the full implication of what they are doing, of course; indeed, when they do realize it as often as not they repudiate it. Of all the Pre-Raphaelite painters only Rossetti and Hunt maintain any kind of consistent rebellion against the Academy; all the rest conform early and thoroughly. The Barbizon landscape painters soon tend to romanticize their "realistic" landscapes to the point of creating a quite unrealistic fairy-tale atmosphere; in inverse ratio to his growing popularity and prosperity, Millet's peasants begin to degenerate into stock figures from Ye Goode Olde Tyme, reflecting nothing of the 19th-century development of mass democracy, plutocracy, and the breakdown of old feudal patterns. Only Courbet seems to have been at all consciously aware that art cannot really be concerned with both Beauty and Reality at the same time, that ultimately you must choose to base your art on one or the other, and when you choose Reality you have fundamentally changed the nature of art; but even he shows considerable vacillation and inconsistency. In short, if ever a movement could be said to be a product of the "spirit of the time," the product of a hundred years of history, it was the realism of the 1850s. But consciously willed or not, it came. Reality, rather than Beauty, became the motivating principle. And with it begins what we call "modern" art.

1

The Pre-Raphaelites and "Moral Realism":

Dante Gabriel Rossetti (1828–1882)
Sir John Everett Millais (1829–1896)
Holman Hunt (1827–1910)
Ford Madox Brown (1821–1893)

Outwardly, there seemed to be considerable differences between creative illustrators and the young men who initiated the Pre-Raphaelite movement. Daumier, Eakins and their counterparts came from lower-middle-class backgrounds; their realism developed spontaneously out of roots in the popular arts. By contrast, the Pre-Raphaelites all belonged to the solidly bourgeois upper-middle class, and self-consciously proclaimed themselves concerned with the elevation and reform of "fine art." But precisely because the Pre-Raphaelites' background was so bourgeois, popular realism had a strong and consistent influence on their concept of painting, all the more because it was unconscious and quite unrecognized. Indeed, one of the main reasons why creative illustration failed to win critical acceptance in the 1870s was the very fact that the Pre-Raphaelites, having never understood what the source and rationale of their realism actually was, were unable to prevent a distortion and disintegration of their movement which cast lasting discredit on the whole concept of illustration as the basis for a new art, or any art at all.

The Pre-Raphaelite Brotherhood proper was founded in that great year of revolts against the old order, 1848, as an association of six painters and a sculptor, all barely out of their teens. Its leading figures were Dante Gabriel Rossetti, born in England of Italian parentage on both sides; William Holman Hunt, who proved to be most faithful of all to Pre-Raphaelite ideals and later gained fame for the extraordinary historical and archaeological realism of themes painted *in loco* on trips to Palestine; and John Everett Millais, a brilliant technician of good family who eventually attained great wealth, a baronetcy, and presidency of the Royal Academy. In succeeding years a number of other painters came into the Pre-Raphaelite orbit, chief among them Ford Madox Brown.

143

Older than the others, Brown had studied on the Continent and known the German "Nazarene" painters Cornelius and Overbeck in Rome, thus establishing a connection between the High Victorian Pre-Raphaelite movement in England and its Early Victorian romantic predecessors, the German Nazarenes and the French Lyonnais; he was in fact Rossetti's teacher. But the real champion and mentor of the group in its early days was John Ruskin, sometime defender of Turner and, thanks to the success of *Modern Painters,* now the leading critic of painting in England. The Pre-Raphaelite movement was made for Ruskin and he for it. He of all men most perfectly understood its basic concept of art as a vehicle for literary symbolism, and its basic objective of realism in religious painting. Unfortunately, since such concepts and objectives do not, to say the least, enjoy much favor today, Ruskin's reputation has suffered because of his connection with the movement; for many people it is hard to understand how the same man could have championed the bold loose *Slave Ship* (page 87) in 1843 and the tight, literal, literary painting of the Pre-Raphaelites only seven years later. Yet there is no mystery about it. In both cases Ruskin represented advance-guard awareness of the trend away from Beauty towards Reality as the goal of painting. But whereas we tend to think of Reality in terms of form— how a picture is painted—and so (mistakenly) admire Turner's late painting as a precursor of Impressionism, Ruskin consistently thought of Reality in terms of subject. He admired the forms of *The Slave Ship* only insofar as Turner had seemed to think them necessary to bring out the Reality of the subject and make the expression of cosmic decay more evocative; that he never really liked them is implied in his later giving the picture away. When he found this new group of painters dedicated to the same ideals of Reality in subject matter, but embodying them in precise and literal forms, he was all the more enthusiastic.

Literary symbolism is, if possible, even further out of critical favor than illustration today, which may or may not be a matter of transient fashion. Mid-Victorians in general were close enough to the classic traditions of the past (even while perverting, abridging, and abandoning them) to have no fear of the old formula "ut pictura poesis," and in the Pre-Raphaelite movement this Victorian conception of painting and poetry as sister arts reached its culmination. Just as Ruskin was given to complementing his writings with what to us seem niggling little water colors of fragmented landscapes and bits of buildings, so the Pre-Raphaelite painters believed it essential to complement their pictures with long descriptions in either prose or verse. They considered that painted image and written word were inseparable components, both indispensable to the Reality of an idea. Thus, to appreciate properly a painting like *Found* (page 149), we must not only look at the picture, we need to read the sonnet composed to accompany it:

> There is a budding morrow in midnight,
> So sang our Keats, our English nightingale.
> And here, as lamps across the bridge turn pale
> In London's smokeless resurrection-light,
> Dark breaks to dawn. But o'er the deadly blight
> Of Love, deflowered and sorrow of none avail,
> Which makes this man gasp and this woman quail,
> Can day from darkness ever again take flight?
> Ah! gave not these two hearts their mutual pledge
> Under one mantle sheltered 'neath the hedge
> In gloaming courtship? And, O God! to-day
> He only knows he holds her; —but what part
> Can life now take? She cries in her locked heart
> "Leave me—I do not know you—go away!"

Perfecting this concept of literary symbolism was the Pre-Raphaelites' first concern when the Brotherhood was organized; it is reflected in the illustrative character of their earliest paintings, particularly those by Millais, who, as the most technically and least literarily talented of the group, preferred to draw on ready-made themes like *Lorenzo and Isabella* (1848–49, Liverpool) or *The Huguenot* (1849–51, New York, Huntington Hartford). But literary symbolism was not an end in itself; as the name "Brotherhood" implied, the Pre-Raphaelites' ultimate goal was always to bring about a revival of religious art, through a new Reality of subject matter. Only as we understand that religious Reality was its end and literary symbolism its means can we appreciate the importance of the Pre-Raphaelite movement in art history, and its significance as a cultural expression of High Victorian England.

Certainly it was a propitious moment for reviving religious art. "The Church as she now stands," a despairing supporter of the Church of England had written in 1833, "no human power can save." And so indeed it had seemed, everywhere in Europe. Since the 1685–1715 "Crisis of European Conscience" so well described by Paul Hazard, all churches had been steadily, surely, swiftly declining in power and prestige, and men of "advanced" views everywhere had busied themselves with schemes for replacing them with more socially useful organizations. Freemasons' Lodges, Benthamite Societies, cults of Reason or Nationalism—almost anything would do, as long as there was no taint of

145

the supernatural about it. And art, as always, had reflected the situation. In 18th-century European art there seemed to have been nothing remotely rivaling the religious painting of Rembrandt, Bernini's sculpture, or Wren's church architecture. Its leading figures were artists like Reynolds who, for all their theoretical admiration of religious art per se, did as little of it as possible, and that tepidly. For a hundred years past, Catholic painting (generally speaking) had been dull, trivial, stereotyped; Protestant art, stultified by the Evangelicals' lack of interest on the one side and the hostility of philosophical rationalism on the other, as good as nonexistent.

But in the last few decades before 1850 a change in attitude was becoming apparent. In England the Oxford Movement, in Germany the Evangelicals, in France Catholic apologists like Châteaubriand, began to breathe new life into the ancient faith. As often as not, perhaps, eccentricity was mistaken for piety and romantic nostalgia for faith, but still there were significant manifestations of a new spirit. That spirit was soon reflected in the arts. Here and there architects began looking at Gothic buildings not simply as a source for lightly decorative "Gothick" motifs to relieve and set off classical severity but worthy of imitation in their own right, as vehicles for embodying "Christian" principles as opposed to "pagan" classicism. As early as the 1820s, too, little bands of fanatically devout painters began to work towards a comparable revival of medieval painting for similar ends—the Austrian Nazarenes in Rome, the "Lyonnais fellowship" centered at Lyons. By the 1830s and -40s a marked undercurrent of interest in religious themes was apparent both in the romantic classicism of Ingres and the orthodox romanticism of

18A. *Sir John Everett Millais:* Christ in the House of His Parents (The Carpenter's Shop). *By courtesy of the Trustees of the Tate Gallery, London. 1850. See also 18B, Rossetti; 18C, Brown.*

One of the most important but least appreciated experiments of the "revolutionary decades" in painting was the Pre-Raphaelite brotherhood, among the first conscious and deliberate attempts to establish Reality as the goal of painting. Its failure—falling into excesses of anecdotage on one side and medieval mysticism on the other—vitiated English painting for half a century and more.

146

Delacroix. It was all of these forces coming to focus in the Pre-Raphaelite Brotherhood which made it (however short-lived and however passingly acquainted either with painting before Raphael or with brotherhood) the single most important group movement in English painting of the 19th century.

Pre-Raphaelite painting was the exact counterpart to picturesque eclecticism in High Victorian architecture. Like such architectural contemporaries as William Butterfield or Alfred Waterhouse, the Pre-Raphaelite painters created a distinctive style based on elements borrowed from many diverse historical sources but so mixed and used as to be characteristic of no period but their own. From the preceding generation of Early Victorian romantics, the Pre-Raphaelites inherited that intense predilection for themes of necromancy and the romantically supernatural in literature—Dante, the Arthurian sagas, and so on—which in their early days seems so embarrassingly naïve, and in the later work of Rossetti and Burne-Jones, so sleezily sensual. From the Nazarenes and Lyonnais came their curious idea that Botticelli, Filippino Lippi, and other Quattrocento painters worked in a purer and more "Christian" style than Raphael and his followers. From Gothic Revivalists like Pugin and Newman they picked up that fabricated vision of the Middle Ages, that adulation for a golden age that never was and never could be, which gives so much of their work the same painfully artificial never-never-land quality that characterizes Pugin's treatises on church architecture and Newman's idea of a university. And it was ultimately from David's neoclassicism that they learned their conception of art as primarily a system of literary symbolism, that attitude to art as a thing to be read, something for the mind rather than the eye, which characterizes Victorian art throughout the century; they would have entirely agreed with Thomas Jefferson's proposal to give the professor of fine arts at the University of Virginia the chair of "Ideology." But what they made of all these borrowings was, like Picturesque Eclecticism in architecture, something new and distinctive. For unlike any of their predecessors, their ultimate objective was not Beauty, but Reality. Their goal was a new

18B. *Dante Gabriel Rossetti:* Found. *Wilmington, Delaware, Society of the Fine Arts, Samuel and Mary Bancroft Collection. Begun 1854, never entirely finished.*

kind of religious painting which would be realistic both in form and in subject matter.

Reality of form they proposed to achieve primarily by basing their art on what they considered the "pure" and "simple" forms of Italian painting before Raphael; and certainly some Quattrocento influence is evident in the Pre-Raphaelites' fondness for attenuated bodies, long sweeping robes, and Botticelli-type heads with languid eyes, long thick necks, heavy jaws and curly mouths. In practise, however, the most significant single eclectic source of Pre-Raphaelite form was probably 15th-century Flemish painting, evident not only in a general effect of jewellike precision (Millais's *Huguenot* in the Huntingdom Hartford Collection, New York, is a particularly good example) but in specific borrowings, such as the convex mirror from Van Eyck's *Arnolfini Wedding* which reappears in Brown's *Take Your Son, Sir* (1851, London, Tate). But the form of Pre-Raphaelite painting, like the massing and spatial composition of Picturesque Eclectic architecture, represents something much greater than the sum of its borrowed parts. It is a High Victorian manifestation of that characteristic English predilection for flat linear pattern which has found expression in every age of English history and in every medium—from Blake down through the limners of Georgian and Stuart times to Hilliard and Holbein, and thence through medieval rib vaultings and patterned brickwork and diaper-backgrounded illuminations to the herringbone stone walls of the Anglo-Saxons and the whole Celto-Germanic dynamic line tradition.

Pre-Raphaelite form could be so indigenous and so thoroughly English because it was more unself-consciously handled than Pre-Raphaelite subject matter. These painters were almost compulsively subject-oriented, overwhelmingly concerned with the overt "meaning" of art as opposed to inherent visual or structural qualities. Just as Pugin or Ruskin completely failed to see how an 18th-century classical church might express "religion" in its manifestation of man's God-given powers of reason and organization, and insisted that the outward shapes and details of a church must have a direct historical and literary connection with Christian dogma, so the Pre-Raphaelites began by thinking of

18C. *Ford Madox Brown:* Work. *Manchester (England), City Art Gallery. 1852–1865.*

"religious" painting as essentially a question of subject matter. If a painting represented Christ, or the Virgin Mary, or a scapegoat, or whatever, it was religious. If it represented a landscape, or 19th-century personages, presumably it was not. G. M. Young says of the intellectual life of mid-19th-century England:

> The age was learning, but it had not yet mastered, the lesson that truth lies not in the statement, but in the process; it had a childlike craving for certitude, as if the natural end of every refuted dogma was to be replaced by another dogma.*

That learning process is admirably exemplified by the Pre-Raphaelite movement, as we trace it through the 1850s.

It was in 1850 that the Pre-Raphaelites first exhibited as a group, and presented to the public their new concept of Reality in religious painting. In that exhibition Millais was represented by *Christ in the House of His Parents* (*The Carpenter's Shop,* page 147), Rossetti by *The Annunciation* (London), Hunt by *The Light of the World* (Oxford, Keble College), and Brown by *Christ Washing Peter's Feet* (London). In keeping with their ideal of reviving the old concept of the dedicated craftsmen who work not for fame but solely *ad majorem gloriam Dei,* the pictures were signed only "P. R. B."; all were intended to be in the same "realistic" style, and all dealt with the religious subject matter in a new "realistic" way. In practice, this meant ignoring theology as a useless complication, defining "realism" as physical, material, literal fact; and so producing slices of life in 1st-century Palestine archaeologically reconstructed in meticulous photographic detail.

The result was a great public outcry, led by no less a celebrity than Charles Dickens, and centered on Millais's *Christ:*

> In the foreground of the carpenter's shop is a hideous, wry-necked, blubbering, red-haired boy in a nightgown, who appears to have received a poke in the hand from the stick of another boy with whom he had been playing in an adjacent gutter [Millais was trying to suggest a prefiguration of the Crucifixion], and to be holding it up for the contemplation of a kneeling woman so horrible in her ugliness that (supposing it were possible for a human creature to exist for a moment with that dislocated throat) she would stand out from the rest of the company as a monster in the vilest cabaret in France, or the lowest gin-shop in England.

* *Early Victorian England* (London, 1934), Ch. XI.

Now we would be inclined to criticize the Pre-Raphaelites' explicitly religious painting too, I think, but not on the same grounds. As we see it, the real trouble is that the Pre-Raphaelites were in fact living in an age of growing doubt and reflecting it perfectly in their art. Pre-Raphaelite painting is a precise counterpart to poems like Tennyson's *In Memoriam,* which [,it has been said,] "gathered up all the doubts of Christianity, of providence, of immortality, which the advance of science had implanted in anxious minds. . . ." Like *In Memoriam,* Pre-Raphaelite painting is "one of the cardinal documents of the mid-Victorian mind, its ardent curiosity, its exquisite sensitiveness to nature, and, not less, perhaps, its unwillingness to quit, and its incapacity to follow, any chain of reasoning which seems likely to result in an unpleasant conclusion. In his highest mood, Tennyson sometimes speaks like an archangel assuring the universe that it will muddle through," and we could say exactly the same of the pre-Raphaelites. For their ignoring of theology was not entirely based on its being complicated or confusing; even more, it was because they only half believed it, or not at all. Being unable fully to believe in the Reality of a Divine Carpenter, Millais paints a domestic interior; unable to believe in the Reality of a Mother of God, Rossetti paints a frightened Victorian girl in a shift, obviously (and understandably) dismayed by the news just brought her; Hunt paints a kindly-faced Victorian gentleman in a nightshirt, who seems to have locked himself out of his house; Brown provides a preview of his own later concept of the "practical religion" of social service work.

This kind of failure was inherent in the Pre-Raphaelites' original premises. For if you want to start a new movement towards Reality in the physical, material sense, then, of all places, explicitly religious painting must seem the most unpromising to start. Of all kinds of art, religious painting is the one demanding the most imagination and flexibility in both thought and execution. Furthermore, since we don't and can't know what the historical Christ was really like, any attempt to paint that subject can only involve us in archaeological scene construction in the Hollywood sense, which will have nothing to do with Christian or any other religious experience. To their credit, the Pre-Raphaelites recognized their problem at once. They were not stupid; one experiment convinced them that Reality and explicitly religious painting could not be combined. They therefore decided to try obliquely religious painting—"realistic" examples of "moral behavior" in contemporary life inspired by Biblical precepts rather than Biblical scenes as such. Hunt, always

153

the most doctrinaire of the Brotherhood, showed the way with his *Hireling Shepherd* (1851, Manchester), an English rustic scene illustrating Christ's words about detecting false saviors, and *The Awakening Conscience* (1853, London, Sir Colin Anderson), to posterity at least a kind of Pre-Raphaelite classic, in which a kept woman starts up suddenly from her lover's lap "with [as Hunt explained in the usual verbal commentary] a startled holy resolve" to quit her sinful life; the immediate cause of her "recalling the memory of her childish home" is Thomas Moore's *Light Of Other Days,* which she and her paramour have been singing at the piano, but ultimately, of course, she is acting on the Biblical precepts learned there. To this same second stage of Pre-Raphaelite evolution belong Millais's *Ophelia* (1851–52, London, Tate) Brown's *Take Your Son, Sir* (begun 1851, unfinished; London, Tate) and Rossetti's *Found* (begun 1854, unfinished), expositions on the virtues of practical charity inspired (as we know in Rossetti's case at least from a note under his pen-and-ink sketch for the work) by Jeremiah 2:2: "I remember thee; the kindness of thy youth, the love of thy betrothal" and, incidentally, a good deal more meaningful at a time when a woman once "fallen" was liable to total rejection from society than it is now. In our eyes, such pictures seem at best funny, at worst horrible, and we congratulate ourselves on our superior perceptivity. But the Pre-Raphaelites were quite intelligent enough to find obliquely religious pictures inadequate, also. They did not make the same sharp distinction between genuine charitableness and mere sentimentality that we (perhaps mistakenly) think possible. Just as High Victorians cultivated picturesqueness in buildings at what seems to us the inexcusable expense of more purely architectural qualities as such, so the Pre-Raphaelites along with everyone else in their generation had an extravagant fondness for quaint and nostalgic images; even in so simple a picture as *Found* you have a whole roster of them (the old graveyard, the tear-jerking symbol of the calf in the net, the bridge of life leading out into the fog), and in many others a sloppy love of the picturesque is carried to the point of bathos. But they were acute enough to see that moralizing without a theological basis cannot escape having a good deal of cant about it; and they therefore began to abandon even obliquely religious subjects in favor of straightforward social commentary with a didactic intent.

In this spirit they created their most successful works. This was the inspiration for Millais's *Blind Girl* (1856, Birmingham), powerful both as an objective commentary on the landless proletariat and an implicit symbol of the human condition; and for Brown's *The Last of England* (1855, Birmingham), of which the same could be said. This was the inspiration, too, for *Work* (conceived 1852, completed 1865), Brown's finest and probably the most significant and successful of all Pre-Raphaelite works (page 151). Here at last was a genuinely religious painting, based on firm and fervent belief. For however shaky the High Victorians' orthodox creed had become, their faith in work was invincible. It was their heritage from many vital lines of descent: from the Evangelical Christian doctrine of work as a means toward salvation, springing from the Protestant priesthood of all believers; from the Calvinist concept of material prosperity as a mark of divine election; from the ubiquitous Victorian creed of progress; from the specific experience of the bourgeois class, which had risen in three centuries from the bottom of society to the top. Work was a theme endemic in Pre-Raphaelite thinking; in their first exhibition, both Millais's *Carpenter's Shop* and Brown's *Christ Washing Peter's Feet* had dealt with it. But Brown's great lunette was the definitive statement. The intangible resemblance of that picture to Raphael's *Disputa* is more than an accidental by-product of eclecticism; it is instinctive and inherent. Forming a central axis around which the whole composition turns are the chief cult images of the religion of work—laborers, or "navvies," who dig with spade and shovel. They embody the lowest common denominator of work, the kind of work that built the Pyramids and laid the Roman roads and expiated Adam's sins: "When Adam delved and Eve span, who was then the gentleman?" Surrounding them is "a cloud of witnesses," representing "all sorts of conditions of men"—beggars and ladies of the *bourgeoisie,* orphans and bankers and a hunchback waiter. Anchoring the composition, like the Church Fathers in the *Disputa,* stand the theologians of Work, social critic Thomas Carlyle and the Christian Socialist leader Reverend Frederick Denison Maurice, who, as Brown explains in his lengthy written counterpart to the picture, "seeming to be idle, work, and are the cause of well-ordained work in others." And forming a background to the whole is a contrast between Maurice's Christian Working Men's College on one side, dedicated to elevating the working class through education, and on the other, the useless and degrading kind of work performed by sandwich-board carriers hired to further the political ambitions of Bobus, the capitalist exploiter castigated by Carlyle. Set in a section of London instantly recognizable to every spectator, this is religious painting with precisely the same contemporary

155

immediacy as Flemish or Italian altarpieces of the 15th century, or medieval Books of the Hours; this is a true revival of the realism of religious painting before Raphael.

But Reality of this kind—neither romantic, nor medieval, nor explicitly Christian—was too far from what the original founders of the Pre-Raphaelite Brotherhood had had in mind. By 1854 the Brotherhood was already defunct as a formal organization. All its main figures began going separate and increasingly divergent ways. Each took, however, a few fragments from the original Pre-Raphaelite idea, and proceeded to exaggerate them in isolation. The end result of this process was to discredit the entire movement for generations. If you compared Millais's *Huguenot* of 1851 with the 1892 *Sweet Emma Morland* that hangs beside it in the Huntington Hartford Collection in New York, for instance, you could make a good case for Pre-Raphaelite painting being, after all, no more than glorified Academic illustration. When you looked at the later works of Holman Hunt, beginning with *The Scapegoat* (1856, Port Sunlight, England, Lady Lever), and saw how literally he interpreted Ruskin's "go to nature, rejecting nothing, selecting nothing, and scorning nothing," you could argue that even when they had painted things like *The Light of the World* or *Hireling Shepherd,* Pre-Raphaelites had never been more than unimaginative photographers without wits enough to choose suitable subjects. Brown's later works seemed to confirm what his earlier choice of subjects suggested, that Pre-Raphaelites were hopeless romantics, too; lacking all understanding of the economic realities of 19th-century life, they thought of "workers" in terms of the old "lower class" of the 18th century and earlier feudal times, who appear in the art of Hogarth and the Le Nains and the brothers Limburg, so that they dealt with romantic ghosts from a vanishing past instead of the proletariat of factory workers and miners who actually made the wheels of Victorian England go round. As for Rossetti, once freed of all disturbing contacts with logic and theology in the original Pre-Raphaelite discipline, he began dabbling and delving ever deeper in the erotic symbolism of pre-Adamite legendry (*Lady Lillith,* 1864, Wilmington, Delaware), luxuriating in Arthurian wizardry (*Wedding of St. George and the Princess Sabra,* 1857, and *How Sir Galahad, Sir Bors, & Sir Percival Were Fed with the Sangreal,* etc., 1864, London, Tate) and the Dante cycle (*Beata Beatrix,* 1863, London, Tate, original of six replicas); and he attempted to take the whole movement with him, using all his famous magnetic personality to convince the young Oxonians William Morris

156

and Edward Burne-Jones, and through them later generations, that the essence of Pre-Raphaelitism was and always had been its esoteric, literary, symbolic side. And to the very considerable extent that he succeeded, he managed to warp not only their promising talents, but the judgment of posterity as a whole. If we today identify Pre-Raphaelitism with a power cult based on occult mysticism, the slimy sensuality of Burne-Jones, or the degenerate bombast of George Frederick Watts, that is largely Rossetti's doing.

These disastrous late developments have effectively obscured all the really significant accomplishments and promise of the original Pre-Raphaelite movement. We forget how very advance-guard was its concern with Reality; how, long before Monet and Cézanne, Hunt and Hughes and Millais were braving every extreme of sun and rain and cold to face Nature with absolute honesty. We forget that the "happy worker" whom we meet in Pre-Raphaelite painting could be quite as much a Reality as the exploited proletarian. We ignore the incongruity of a generation which has made a cult of Renaissance and medieval and Baroque iconography having nothing but scornful mockery for the intricately symbolical iconography of *The Awakening Conscience* or *The Last of England*. We forget that the Pre-Raphaelites at least attempted to talk not only to other painters, but to society at large; and, like Tennyson and Arnold, to talk about big questions—of time and fate and morality and truth. In the disintegration of Pre-Raphaelitism the whole idea of objective Reality was discredited, and with it much of the historic tradition of art in Western civilization. Those who speak of "The Pre-Raphaelite Tragedy" are right. The later Pre-Raphaelite movement was a tragedy for painting in England, which from its mid-19th-century advance-guard leadership sank into febrile Late Victorian aesthetics, "fond of uttering platitudes in stained-glass attitudes." Thenceforth the history of the evolution of modern painting will be the history of painting in France.

NOTES

As founded in 1848, the Pre-Raphaelite Brotherhood included, besides Rossetti, Hunt, and Millais, four others whose contributions and interest remained minor—Frederick George Stephens (1828–1907), more significant as a scholarly and prolific art critic than as a painter; James Collinson

157

(1825–1881), a man of feeble talents and feebler conviction, twice converted to Roman Catholicism, twice re-converted to the Church of England, finally ending up as an anaemic genre painter; the writer and art critic William Michael Rossetti, Dante Gabriel's brother; and the sculptor Thomas Woolner. Some of the finest Pre-Raphaelite work was done, however, by painters who were not formally members of the founding group, but came into its orbit in various ways and times. Outstanding among them were Ford Madox Brown and Arthur Hughes (1830–1915), who for a time in the 1850s and early -60s produced some of the greatest Pre-Raphaelite pictures (*The Long Engagement,* 1859, Birmingham; *Home from the Sea,* 1857–63, Oxford, Ashmolean) and was also one of the greatest of Victorian book illustrators, working for Thomas Hughes (*Tom Brown's Schooldays,* 1857), George Macdonald (*The Princess and the Goblin, Curdie and the Princess,* etc.), and Christina Rossetti (*Sing-Song,* 1872). Others included William Bell Scott (1811–1890), whose *Iron and Coal* (c. 1860) is proof that the industrial worker was not always overlooked by Pre-Raphaelitism; John Brett (1830–1902) whose *Stonebreakers* (1858, Liverpool) makes an instructive contrast with Courbet's; Henry Alexander Bowler (1824–1903) who without formal connections painted one great Pre-Raphaelite picture, *The Doubt* (1856, London, Tate); and William Lindsay Windus of Liverpool (1823–1907), whose *Too Late* (1859, London, Tate) is a good example of Pre-Raphaelite influence outside London.

The most famous representatives of what is sometimes called the second phase of Pre-Raphaelitism, instigated by Rossetti in the mid-1850s following the breakup of the original Brotherhood in 1853, are William Morris (1834–1896), famous champion of medieval-inspired theories of socialism and handicrafts, and Edward Burne-Jones (1833–1898), famous in his lifetime for sentimentalized and veiledly erotic variations on Rossetti's mystical medieval themes; as the discoverer of Aubrey Beardsley, Burne-Jones is the link between Pre-Raphaelitism of the late 1850s and Art Nouveau in the 1890s. Other examples of late Pre-Raphaelite influence can be seen in the work of George Frederick Watts (1817–1904), whose *Hope, Love and Death,* and *Sir Galahad* combine the yearning sentiment of Rossetti with characteristically Pre-Raphaelite chins, necks, and love of intricate patterns in clinging drapery; Frederick Lord Leighton (1830–1896), of whose *Last Watch of Hero* or *Captive Andromache* the same can be said; Lawrence Alma-Tadema (1836–1912), whose *Reading From Homer* was once a treasure of the Philadelphia Museum and whose *At the Shrine of Venus* makes such an instructive comparison with Toulouse-Lautrec's *Au Salon;* and Albert Moore (1841–1893), whose *Summer's Night* is a decorative, fuzzy, and unpleasant combination of Rossetti's sensuality with Millais's literalism.

A competent scholarly introduction to the Pre-Raphaelite movement is provided by John Gere's catalogue for Robin Ironside's *Pre-Raphaelite*

Painters (London, 1948); see also John Gaunt, *The Pre-Raphaelite Tragedy* (London, 1942). To see how an old Pre-Raphaelite felt about the original concern of the movement for religious Reality, and its degeneration, it is worth reading Holman Hunt, *Pre-Raphaelitism and the Pre-Raphaelite Brotherhood* (London, 1905).

2

The Barbizon Painters and "Naturalism":

Jean François Millet (1814–1875)
Charles François Daubigny (1817–1878)
Rosa Bonheur (1822–1899)

At about the same time that the Pre-Raphaelite concept of Reality was developing in English painting, a comparable movement was going on in France, led by a similarly loose-knit group of painters known, from their common associations with the village of Barbizon in the "forest" of Fontainebleau, as the Barbizon school. Millet and Daubigny best represent the group's two main interests, peasant life and landscape painting; Rosa Bonheur, the wide appeal and popularization of its illustrative and anecdotal side.

Like the Pre-Raphaelites, the Barbizon painters were primarily in search of a new Reality to revitalize Academic painting. They conceived of it, however, not in literary or overtly religious terms, but as "naturalism." "Back to Nature" was their great principle. They looked for subjects in Fontainebleau, far from the "artificialities" of city life and the "corruptions" of formal society, painting homely figures of peasants instead of gods or heroes, rugged trees and rocks instead of picturesque mountains, muddy pools and rutted cart tracks instead of noble Italian vistas. But though their Reality was different from the Pre-Raphaelites', at first it met the same kind of shocked reaction. "This," snorted the distinguished Director of Fine Arts in France, "is the painting of men who don't change their linen, who want to intrude themselves upon gentlemen; this art offends and disgusts me." And certainly that reaction is understandable; it is easy to see how revolting a painting like Millet's

Goose Girl (page 163) would have looked to anyone trained to take Beauty for granted. Compare it, for example, to Ingres's *Odalisque* (page 35)—but the comparison is ridiculous! On the one hand, a composition of beautiful forms, arranged and balanced by Art; on the other, a "naturalistic" rendering of a naked peasant girl, artless and practically shapeless, gingerly slipping into a dirty pool along with the geese she is tending. Or contrast the beautiful sentiments evoked by Delacroix's panoramas of history or religion with what we feel when confronted by a pair of stolid Barbizon peasants in wooden shoes planting potatoes, some apelike rustic leaning on his hoe, two quarriers brawling in a pit! Nor did the Barbizon landscapes seem any better; the same repulsive Reality distinguished them too. Conservatives found it bad enough that Barbizon landscape should be ultimately inspired by Constable, whose new concepts had been such a sensation for the advance guard when first seen in 1823; but whereas Constable's pictures had at least preserved the old principles of planned and ordered Beauty, now the Barbizon painters seemed to be abandoning even that. In 1841 the invention of prepared oil paint in tubes had eliminated the old necessity for painters to mix and grind each day's colors in the studio; now it was possible to carry all the necessary equipment for making finished pictures on one's back, take it to a suitable spot, and work out of doors directly from Nature. The Barbizon painters were quick to see

19A. *Charles François Daubigny:* Morning on the Oise. *Collection of The Paine Art Center and Arboretum, Oshkosh, Wis. 1866.* See also 19B, Millet; 19C, Bonheur.

Two representative examples of the work of the Barbizon school. By realizing the new potentialities for outdoor painting afforded by the invention of paint in tubes, the Barbizon painters helped destroy the old tradition of studied selection and abstraction from Nature; by choosing subjects from everyday life, especially peasant life, they helped destroy the traditional concept of "noble forms"—compare this Goose Girl *with Ingres's* Odalisque *(page 35), for instance. But the Barbizon painters were not dedicated to doctrinaire Reality; essentially, their subject matter was romantic. They prepared ground for a new kind of painting, but did not themselves practice it.*

how this new method of working might result in greater Reality in landscape; and conservatives were equally quick to see that for all intents and purposes it meant abandoning the whole concept of the planned picture, and, into the bargain, most of the traditional process of arriving at beautiful forms by a process of reasoned selection and abstraction. To a considerable extent, the conservatives were right.

But not entirely. After the first shock, conservative critics soon came to the pleasant realization that Barbizon painting was not as wholeheartedly devoted to Reality as it seemed at first. It had a strong romantic streak. Like the Pre-Raphaelites, the Barbizon painters mistook for Reality what was in actuality an old, preindustrial, prescientific world, quite as remote from everyday experience as any romantic, or any bourgeois patron, might wish. Millet's *Man with a Hoe* might be ugly enough to inspire reformers like Edwin Markham, as late as 1915, to write indignant verse about the brutalizing effects of toil; but in Barbizon painting there was no hint of the major social fact of the 19th century, the rise of a revolutionary landless proletariat. Even in the major Barbizon painters there were no disquieting reminders of industrial unrest or festering tenements, while among its minor members like Constant Troyon or Jules Dupré the "happy peasant" theme became a banal cult. Likewise it soon became clear that the Reality of Barbizon landscape was even less uncompromising. Entirely free from chimneys or slag piles or beggars, Fontainebleau was not really a forest but a park. And though claiming to present Reality to the world, Barbizon painters remained satisfyingly innocent of the corollary that he who can perceive Reality where others cannot must be a superior and different kind of man; they continued to behave in the same docile way as those painters who were merely concerned with making the world more Beautiful.

Barbizon painting presented, indeed, not so much the facts of life as a sheltering buffer. One could feel up-to-date and "modernistic" while admiring them without being in the least "radical." Small wonder that a swell of popular favor for Barbizon painting soon began to set in. Already by the 1850s a scientific habit of thought was becoming predominant in both England and France. It was transforming the study

19B. *Jean François Millet:* The Goose Girl. *Baltimore, The Walters Art Gallery. 1863.*

162

of history and was beginning to transform everyday life with technological inventions. Sooner or later its insistence on facing Reality had to affect art. But most people, even those disposed to agree that the Academic tradition was raveling out, were unwilling to accept the kind of Reality represented by the young Pre-Raphaelites or Gustave Courbet; it had too many subversive implications, it was too closely associated with political or religious revolution for them to trust. In this situation, the Barbizon-school paintings, which were being unobtrusively produced through the 1830s and -40s, suddenly appeared as a revelation, solving all difficulties. Here was an art at once suitably up-to-date, properly "realistic," and yet perfectly safe. These parklike landscapes, with their lofty waving trees and gentle brooks, were not painted according to frigid classical formulae or with romantic exoticism, either; they were "modern" in the most proper sense.

No wonder, either, that the popularity of Barbizon painting lasted so long—from the 1850s through the Great War, in fact. Consistently throughout those years it came to be for French painters, and by extension for all sorts of painters in the range of Western middle-class tastes and standards, a well into which any painter, any collector could lower a pail knowing he would come up with something safe and salable. Theodore Rousseau's monumental, pantheistic sweeps of dell and glade; Daubigny's intimate studies by the riverside; Troyon's intelligent, orderly animals; the docile, pious, noble peasants of Dupré and Bonheur—all were eagerly bought, endlessly reproduced. No foreign school was so well known in the United States; Barbizon's stolid peasants, mighty rocks and towering oaks presented images of stability with the same appeal to the post-Civil-War generation as Richardsonian architecture. From the 1860s until the 20th Century American museums, classrooms and parlors were filled with prints of Millet's *Angelus* and *Gleaners;* picturesque French riverscapes and little stone bridges and rows of poplars

19C. *Rosa Bonheur:* The Horse Fair. *New York, The Metropolitan Museum of Art, Gift of Cornelius Vanderbilt. 1853–55. Typical of the many painters on the periphery of the Barbizon School was Rosa Bonheur, who attained great fame and popularity by romanticizing and idealizing Barbizon themes of peasant life.*

remained standard fare for calendars, advertisements, and jigsaw puzzles well into the 1920s.

And no wonder, finally, that when Barbizon painting did lose popularity, its eclipse was swift and near-total. Advance-guard painters by the 1870s had disowned the Barbizon men as insincere compromisers whose Reality was all surface and had passed on to sterner stuff. When at long last even middle-class taste was surfeited with picturesque peasants and placid frog ponds, there were no admirers left. Only recently have some slight signs of re-evaluation become apparent.

Yet whatever the current fashion in connoisseurship, there can be no doubt of the basic historical importance of the Barbizon painters to the evolution of painting in the 19th century. Romanticized though their peasant subject matter may have been, it at least prepared the ground for general acceptance of the idea that Reality might be a proper objective in painting. And although Barbizon painters never achieved that detachment from landscape which enabled Cézanne and Monet to refer to it simply as "the motif," they did effectively break away from the involvement with a landscape's "meaning" which still dogged Constable and Turner; the same stereotyping that left Barbizon painting open to popular vulgarization also left Barbizon painters free to concentrate more on realities of form. Without the Barbizon preliminary, there could have been neither Impressionism nor a Courbet.

NOTES

Insofar as the Barbizon painters constituted an organized school, its chief members were Millet, Daubigny, Theodore Rousseau (1812–1867), Jules Dupré (1811–1889), Constant Troyon (1813–1865), Charles Emile Jacque (1813–1894), and Narcisse Virgile Diaz de la Peña (1808–1876). Corot functioned as the patriarch of the group, and there were many "adherents," such as Rosa Bonheur, Jules Breton (1827–1906), and Henri Harpignies (1819–1916).

Millet was the most representative figure. Born of Norman peasant stock and trained at Cherbourg, he treated peasant themes with a minimum of romantic trappings (e.g., *The Quarriers,* 1846, Toledo, Ohio), and his first and most lasting fame rested on his "peasant subjects," beginning with *Haymakers Resting* (1849, Louvre) and *The Sower* (1850, Boston; 2nd version Philadelphia, Provident Trust) and reaching a climax in the late 1850s and early 1860s with such famous works as *The Gleaners* (c. 1856, Springfield, Mass.; 1857,

Louvre), *The Angelus* (1858–59, Louvre), *The Potato Planters* (1862, Boston), *Man with a Hoe* (1863) and *The Knitting Lesson* (1869, St. Louis). As his treatment of form became more monumental (reminiscent of and influential on Daumier) he became more interested in the medium of pastels, through which he achieved broader masses and less detail. From the late 1860s on he became more interested in landscape; typical examples are *The Rainbow* (c. 1868, Louvre), *Church at Gréville* (1871–74, Louvre; 2nd version Northampton, Mass., Smith College) and *Pasture in Normandy* (1871–74, Minneapolis). Through his friendship with William Morris Hunt (whose *portrait* he painted c. 1854, Northampton, Mass., Smith College) he became early and well known in the United States; the Boston Museum of Fine Arts has a large collection of his work in all media.

Daubigny's work was more largely confined to landscape; his particular importance, however, was as a symbol of the bridge formed by the Barbizon School between the Old and the New Painting in France. In his youth Daubigny was the pupil of Delaroche and friend of Meissonier—one of the leading Academic figures of later 19th-century French painting; they helped launch his reputation in woodcuts (1838), etchings, and graphic book and magazine illustrations, and it was as an illustrator that he was chiefly known in the 1840s. In the 1850s he made the acquaintance of Corot and gradually began to concentrate on painting, soon becoming a leader in painting direct from Nature in the open air. This led him directly into the path of Impressionism, and by the 1860s he was an inspiration for Pissarro and especially for Monet, whom he was able to help financially in the early 1870s thanks to the great success of his exhibit at the Universal Exhibition of 1867 in Paris; in 1872 he worked briefly with Cézanne at Auvers. Most major American museums have good examples of Daubigny's landscapes (page 161).

Rosa Bonheur was not technically a member of the Barbizon group. Essentially self-taught, she received some instruction from her father, who was a poor (in every sense of the word) painter. In 1849 she scored her first great success with *Plowing in the Nivernais* (Luxembourg) which was so popular that a companion piece was commissioned to hang next to it (*Haymaking in Auvergne*, 1855). She was particularly popular in the United States, her *Horse Fair* (page 165) being long considered one of the great treasures of the Metropolitan Museum, and as late as 1893 she scored a triumph at the Columbian Exposition in Chicago. In 1856 she bought a property at By, on the edge of the forest of Fontainebleau, and from then on she, like Troyon, tended to repeat herself endlessly; her great significance, however, is as a representative figure of Barbizon popularity and popularization.

Robert L. Herbert, *Barbizon Revisited* (Museum of Fine Arts, Boston,

167

1962), with its critical bibliography, has superseded most other writings on the Barbizon school, which reflect later 19th-century opinion, and is the standard reference. A good reference on Daubigny is the catalogue by Richard N. Gregg to *Charles François Daubigny at the Paine Art Center* (Oshkosh, Wis., 1964).

3

The "New Painting" in Theory and Practice:

Gustave Courbet (1819–1877)

The Studio is one of those rare instances of a single specific work of art that is absolutely indispensable for a proper understanding of its creator. Usually, the essentials of a given painter's ideas, style, and principles will be apparent in any good example of his work, but Courbet's case is different. Looking at the average Courbet, particularly the early ones, which range all the way from quasi-romantic and quasi-classical to Barbizon-type landscapes and Academic stage pieces, it would be hard to tell why he was so important, such a seminal figure in the history of painting. For in only a few works did Courbet express himself at all adequately; and completely, only in this one—*The Studio,* or, to give it its full title, *The Painter's Studio, a Real Allegory, Summarizing a Seven-year Phase of My Artistic Life.*

The Studio (page 171) was consciously intended as a demonstration of Courbet's theories on the nature of painting and the proper function of painters in society. A huge work, nearly 12 feet high and 20 feet long, it was painted for exhibition at the World's Fair of 1855 in Paris, which had for one of its themes French pre-eminence in the arts. An international jury rejected it, however, whereupon Courbet built at his own expense a "Pavilion of Realism" on the fair grounds and put *The Studio* and several others of his works (most notably *Burial at Ornans,* 1849) on display. Inevitably, perhaps, the Pavilion was a failure; neither the public nor many other painters liked or understood what they saw there. But *The Studio* nonetheless proved to be one of the pivotal paintings of the 19th century and a landmark in art history. For in this picture and the written statement accompanying it, Courbet made the

168

first great presentation of what we may call the New Painting. In it, painting's traditional concern with Beauty was directly and consciously repudiated. A new goal for artists was proclaimed. Henceforth, the artist's function was to discover and define for the world what Reality is. Henceforth, the painter was to be no longer a humble learner from Nature; no longer need he cater to the whims and pleasure of patrons. From now on, the painter could see himself as different from and superior to other men. He would be a leader, not a follower—the inspired seer whose vision penetrated ever deeper mysteries of being, whose mission it was to lead mankind to ever higher perceptions of truth.

Four centuries before *The Studio* was conceived, Leonardo da Vinci had set down some visionary and revolutionary thoughts on what painting really was, and what a painter's proper role in society should be. In an age when painters were generally considered no more than skilled artisans or clever craftsmen, trained as apprentices in the manner of chairmakers or goldsmiths or weavers, he had dared to proclaim, in the *Paragone,* that "Painting is philosophy. . . . Painting is poetry. . . . [If] music is composed of proportion, then I have used similar meanings in painting. . . . Truly this is a science and the legitimate issue of nature. . . ." Painting was all these things; the painter comprehended and surpassed all these other arts. His was a great and peculiar power: "If the painter wishes to see beauties that charm him, it lies in his power to create them; and if he wishes to see monstrosities that are frightful, he can be lord and God (creator) thereof. . . . In fact, whatever exists in the universe, in essence, in appearance, in the imagination, the painter has first in his mind and then in his hands." A lofty vision. But only in the free-ranging individualistic world of the 19th century could artists begin to believe that this ideal concept of their role could come true. Only in the 19th century could a poet declare, as Schiller did, that "the dignity of mankind is laid in thy hands," that the artist is "a king, living on the summits of mankind." And only in the 1850s could a work like Courbet's *Studio* have been painted.

In the center of the studio—the world—sits the Painter. On his easel is a landscape, on which he chooses to work at the moment. He may have made outdoor sketches for it, perhaps; but he need not refer to Nature to finish it—why should he? He is the master of Nature, not her servant, free to recombine her elements, change them, assemble them as he will. For it is his vision that in the end determines how Nature will look, and how other men will see her; not the other way around.

169

Over his shoulder, like the Muse who used to inspire painters in the old tradition of Beauty, bends a nude model—now the Muse of a new Reality. He is not painting her at the moment; she waits on his pleasure to proceed. And why not? He is the arbiter of human beauty. It is he who decides what Beauty shall be, or whether there shall be any at all; she depends on him. This is the consummation of all that Reynolds's theory had implied many decades ago. Beauty—once an absolute standard, then a matter of common agreement—is now something for the individual alone to determine; what he chooses to call Beauty is beautiful. Which is no more than to say that Beauty no longer exists, it is only part of the general question of Reality. And what Reality is, is for the painter to decide.

Around the throne of this king "living on the summits of mankind" are ranged all his subjects, the "beauties" or "monstrosities," whichever he may choose, that "lie in his power to create." All Courbet's favorite themes are here, in all their rich diversity (and given Courbet's theories, we begin to understand *why* they are so diverse, why no one painting reflects more than a facet of his achievement): the hunter with his dog and gun, the sombrero and guitar and dagger of romantic imagery, an artist's manikin suggesting at once a crucifixion and an academic drawing cast, and so on. Round the painter's throne, too, are ranged all the sister arts that painting encompasses and leads, in the person of their representatives who were Courbet's friends and sounding boards—Baudelaire the poet, Proudhon the social philosopher, Promayet the musician, Champfleury the novelist and critic.

20. *Gustave Courbet:* The Studio (The Painter's Studio, a Real Allegory, Summarizing a Seven-year Phase of My Artistic Life). *Paris, Louvre. 1855.*

Courbet first of the 19th-century painters set forth without equivocation the theory and practice of a new kind of painting based on Reality; this is the great document of it. Taking the position that it was hopeless to try and educate the upper-class bourgeois patrons to true aesthetic values, and despicable to conform to the ones they had, Courbet declared that painting should be for painters alone to determine, and patrons and public alike should be obliged to follow their, and especially his, lead.

170

Besides these obvious symbols, *The Studio* is crowded with other figures, representatives of "all sorts and conditions of men," much as they crowded around Christ in Rembrandt's *Christ Healing the Sick,* which Courbet had discovered at Amsterdam in 1847. All social classes are here—laborer, merchant (a Jewish secondhand dealer), prostitute, actor, priest, lovers, connoisseur, patron (Bruyas). All ages of men are represented—infancy in the suckling child, youth in the lovers, old age, and death. Humbly, reverently they stand in the painter's presence. Why? Simply because he happens to have a knack of counterfeiting natural appearances? Of course not. Something much profounder than that compels their admiration. They seek him out because, like Christ, he gives them what no one else can. He gives them insight into the nature of Reality. From him they can learn what Reality is, what is real and what is not. He, the painter, does not merely show them the world; he, in the most literal sense, makes them see the world as they do.

That is where the three most important figures in the allegory come in: the cat playing in the foreground, the child looking up at the easel, and the small crouched figure drawing on the floor.

Of all creatures, man is the only one who makes his environment fit him, who has any true power to choose and mold the kind of world he lives in. And of all men, the painter is most concerned with making the choice and doing the molding; for it is through art that men's perception of the world is ordered, and what they will recognize as Reality is determined. To know and understand this, says Courbet, is to be an intelligent being. Not to know or understand it is to be an animal. So the cat, completely absorbed in play, is the only being in the studio entirely unconcerned with the painter and unaffected by what he does.

In deliberate and dramatic contrast to the cat stands the little boy. He gazes at the painter and his work with rapt attention, even adoration; he is experiencing that awful awareness of the peculiar magical power of art which moved the world in earlier, wiser times. With childish intuition he senses what future generations will come to see, that Courbet's realism has restored the true and original function of art. In Courbet, the "coarse, vulgar, proletarian painter," he recognizes the same power of determining what Reality shall be on which in times past pharaohs and emperors, priests and primitive chieftains all depended for their authority. Upon the artist's godlike works, "creations" in the literal sense—in towering stone, or painted relief, in pyramids and temples and rostra, on

172

the walls of caves and teepees—rested the immemorial civilization of Egypt, the stability of imperial Rome, the tribal organization of primitive man everywhere. And what the artist was before—seer, prophet, arbiter of truth—he can be again. What now only a child, with innocent and unclouded intuition, can grasp, will one day be recognized by everybody. Everybody will one day regard a painter with the deference Courbet makes Bruyas show him in *Bonjour, Monsieur Courbet*—greet him hat in hand, pleased, proud, and flattered that a painter should deign to address him. That is Courbet's great claim. Arrogant, presumptuous, preposterous as this may have been, behind all the bluff and bluster lay (perhaps only half understood by Courbet himself) historical truth and, even more, psychological insight. And on this claim rests much of the structure of modern art.

This brings us to the third major figure in the allegory, the small scribbler on the floor. He is producing a primitive, childish drawing. Why? Is this, as some would have it, an indication of Courbet's precocious awareness of the worth of child art? Is this some deliberate intimation of the vogue for "primitivism" that would sweep over French painting thirty or forty years after *The Studio?* Hardly. Courbet had an intuitive understanding of the nature of primitive art. He grasped the essential principle of it, the idea that the primitive artist is concerned neither with Beauty nor with communication, but with creating Reality. He understood, however vaguely, that this was the secret of the power of art in ancient times. But it was as yet too soon for him to realize fully that style and content go together in primitive as in all other forms of art; it would take another couple of generations before all the implications of the artist's role in *The Studio* could be worked out and implemented. In all probability, he meant to demonstrate by this scrawler, working away on his crude drawing without reference to the master at the easel, the worthlessness of attempts to express ideas without proper technical training, how futile it is for artists to attempt to discover Reality on their own.

For there is no evidence, either in Courbet's art or in his life, that he had reached any conviction that the Reality painters determine and create should be their own. Reality for him, as for most other people in his generation (illustrators, Barbizon painters, historians, scientists, Pre-Raphaelites) was the very opposite of the subjective thing it would be in later times. It demanded, instead, a scrupulous attention to material, physical, objective form: "Show me an angel and I'll paint one" was the

173

essence of their attitude. Like his contemporaries, Courbet conceived realism in subject matter to mean painting what you saw in the world, literally, without subterfuge or self-delusion. Realism in form meant essentially Ruskin's (possibly misunderstood) formula of going direct to Nature, "rejecting nothing, selecting nothing, and scorning nothing." In these basic positions he was no more "advanced" than anybody else in the 1850s.

Where he was more advanced, however—and this is his real significance—was in consistent logic. Essentially a theoretician, he took steps towards working out the principles of realism to logical conclusions that left his contemporaries behind. In subject matter, he was the first painter to be consciously and systematically aware of the importance of the new proletarian class the Industrial Revolution had created. Where other realists still painted peasants and similar survivors of the preindustrial class structure, hired day laborers and working-class women began to appear in Courbet's pictures (obvious examples are *The Stonebreakers, Burial at Ornans,* and *Two Girls on the Banks of the Seine,* 1856, Paris, Petit Palais). And the violent antagonism his pictures provoked was not simply (as in the case of early Barbizon or Pre-Raphaelite works) because the subjects were thought vulgar, but even more because his critics believed (correctly) that they expressed a Marxist conviction that the proletariat was the only "real" class, all other human subjects being destined to disappear. Courbet's was a realism with social and political implications his contemporaries were reluctant to perceive.

The same was true of his "realistic" form. Courbet came to understand better and sooner than they did what going direct to Nature in the photographic sense actually involved. He saw that, taken literally and completely, it meant turning the painter into a cameralike device for recording light. It meant recognizing that all we actually see are impressions of light, in different colors and shapes. Any translation of these impressions into ideas (as of trees or apples, houses or horses, pots or posteriors) takes place in the mind. It is a matter of mental selection, combination, and interpretation; the eye has nothing to do with the process. Therefore, the painter who wants to be entirely realistic in the camera sense must abjure any and all interpretation and selection. He should try, however impossible it may be to succeed completely, the human mind being what it is, to paint the way a photograph is made, by recording impressions of light; no less, and no more. Already by 1860 Courbet had pushed his realism to this point. In his later landscapes,

174

particularly, for all that his subjects were "primeval realities" such as rocks, forest, seas, we can see that he was already in essentials what the 1870s would call an Impressionist.

That this concept of the artist as a mechanical, impartial observer is quite incompatible with the artist as an inspired seer, prophet, interpreter and determinant of Reality to men seems very obvious to us. Either the painter is a master who imposes himself and his ideas on Nature, or he is subservient to Nature, and lets Nature impose itself on him; you can't have it both ways. And we wonder that the contradiction was not obvious to Courbet also. We wonder that he could not see how defining "worker" in Marxist terms involved imposing his own view of Reality on the world; how the artificial side-view rigidity of his stonebreaker involved a personal comment on mechanical labor. But he evidently remained quite unaware of it. So, by and large, were the Impressionists who followed him; indeed, Impressionism as a movement foundered on this very rock, as we shall see. Not until the great post-Impressionists— Cézanne, Gauguin, Van Gogh—shifted the basis of the search for Reality from objective study to subjective interpretation was the dichotomy resolved. Courbet and the Impressionists were misled by the unchallenged basic assumption of their age, that Reality must be objective. This was the age when Realpolitik began, when Ranke's concept of a flatly objective history was developed, when Darwin could work out a theory of evolution in the full confidence that he could and had removed himself from his own system. It was an age that took for granted what seems to us the curious notion (but we need not feel superior—later generations will surely find many of our unconscious assumptions equally amusing and astonishing) that total objectivity is possible, that the human mind can contemplate the world with complete impartiality. Therefore, for Courbet and the Impressionists it seemed a normal and natural assumption that recording Nature exactly was the same thing as interpreting and dominating it. And if we now have come to see that recording Reality is one thing and meaningfully interpreting it another, so that the contradiction hidden from them is self-evident to us, we should at least remember that their first trial-and-error experiments into the nature of Reality made our wisdom possible.

Courbet's, we think now, was a simple doctrine; simple-minded, even. But that very apparent simplicity was its greatest recommendation to the younger painters who followed him. When they considered the endless centuries of wrangling over the nature of Beauty with no apparent result, shifting the goal of painting to Reality seemed a blessed release from darkness into light, from tortuous dialectic and medieval sophistries to plain and straightforward purposes. Only later would they realize how endless were the wranglings the search for Reality entailed, how infinite were the frontiers to which painting was now committed. That realization was left for Courbet's successors, in the next two generations, the Impressionists.

NOTES

Gustave Courbet's first training in art was from local teachers in Ornans (where he was born in 1819), and Besançon. In 1840 he came to Paris, determined to become a painter, and largely educated himself by studying in the Louvre—first the Venetians, later (significantly) Velasquez, Hals, and Rembrandt. Equally significantly, the first two pictures he had accepted in the Salon (1844 and 1845) were self portraits (*Courbet with his Black Dog,* 1842, Paris, Petit Palais; *Le Guitarrero,* 1844, New York, private collection); they were the first of a long series, which included such famous examples as *Portrait of the Author,* also called *The Man with the Pipe* (1846, Montpellier, Musée Fabre) and *The Cellist* (1847, Stockholm, National Museum). These and other works were essentially romantic in feeling, however. Not until 1849 did the deliberate development of his "realism" begin. In that year he painted *The Stonebreakers* (formerly Dresden, burnt 1945), and began *Burial at Ornans* (Louvre). These works, and *The Peasants of Flagey Returning from the Fair* (1850, Besançon) caused an uproar when exhibited at the Salon of 1850, and to meet his critics Courbet began consciously formulating the principles of Reality in art, and working out its social and political implications. In this endeavor he had the implicit and explicit help of thinkers and writers in other fields. From the theory of Saint-Simon and his followers, and from Jacques Louis David's example, came his concept of art as an agent for social reform, assisting and inspiring a social revolution which would bring about an ideal future society in which art would satisfy man's moral needs in the same direct way industry provided his physical necessities (of which Malraux's concept of art as 20th-century religion is a distant descendant). Champfleury, early champion of Reality in literature, probably helped him write the manifesto in his 1855 catalogue. His longer statement, published in the *Courrier du Dimanche* for December 25, 1861, was probably inspired by Proudhon, who in 1862 published a treatise *On the Principles of Art and Its Social Destiny.* But it was in his pictures, properly enough, that he explored the full implications of Reality in art—in social commentary (*Village Maidens Distributing Alms,* 1851, New York, Metropolitan; *Two Girls on the Banks*

176

of the Seine, 1856, Paris, Petit Palais; *Toilette de la Mariée,* 1860, Northampton, Smith College); in "shocking the *bourgeoisie*" with portraits of his mistresses (*The Spanish Lady,* 1855, Philadelphia Museum; *Sleeping Blonde,* 1857, Paris, private collection) and assorted unsavory characters (*Mère Gregoire,* c. 1860, Chicago; *Sleep,* 1866, Paris, Petit Palais; *Woman with a Parrot,* 1866, New York, Metropolitan), and above all by stating the painter's claim to be a philosopher-king of men in pictures (*The Studio,* 1855; *Fortune Saluting Genius,* otherwise known as *The Encounter* or *Bonjour, Monsieur Courbet,* 1854, Montpellier, Musée Fabre). By the late 1860s his doctrines had triumphed among the advance guard; he was acclaimed by them everywhere, and his one-man shows at the Rond-Point du Pont d'Alma in Paris in 1867, and later at LeHarve, Ghent, and Bensançon enjoyed huge success. Having no further need to propagandize his ideology, he now began to concentrate on his formal developments in the direction of Impressionism, the sequence of which may be traced in such works as *The Source of the Loue* (c. 1850, Buffalo), *Portrait of Max Buchon* (1854, Vevey, a portrait astonishingly like Manet's in the 60s), *The Quarry* (1857, Boston), *Willows and Brook* (1862, Philadelphia), *The Gour de Conches* (1864, Besançon), *Deer in Covert* (1866, Louvre), *Deer in the Forest* (1868, Minneapolis), *The Waves* (1869, Philadelphia), *The Sea* (1869, Caen), and *Head of a Pig* (1869, Paris, Jacques Guérin).

In 1871, unfortunately, Courbet put his ideals into practice by joining the Paris Commune, and was implicated in the destruction of the Vendôme Column; arrested, he was jailed for six months (*Gustave Courbet in Sainte-Pélagie Prison,* 1871, Ornans), and in 1873 fled to Switzerland to escape condemnatory proceedings. There he continued to paint landscapes and still lifes, pushing forward experiments with Impressionistic form (e.g., *Mixed Flowers in a Bowl,* 1872, Boston) until his death in 1877.

From the 1930s on, recognition of Courbet's place in the history of modern painting has been increasingly warm; exhibitions and publications are numerous. Among the best-known are Gerstle Mack, *Courbet* (1951), the two dozen bulletins of the *Société des Amis de Gustave Courbet* published since 1947, and the catalogue of the Gustave Courbet exhibition of 1959 at Philadelphia and Boston (H. Clifford, ed., with essay by René Huyghe).

On Courbet's theories, see C. E. Gauss, "The Realism of Courbet," *Aesthetic Theories of the French Artists,* ch. 2 (Baltimore, 1949); for a critical analysis of *The Studio,* Werner Hofmann, *The Earthly Paradise* (1961).

III

Impressionism

FOR MANY PEOPLE, THE HISTORY OF "MODERN ART" begins with Impressionism. And it is true that Impressionism did mark a turning point. One reason is that the twenty years of its heyday, from 1865 to 1885, coincided with the establishment of mass education in all advanced industrial countries and, in consequence, the maturity of the popular arts. Each new specialized kind of popular art that developed—comics, advertising, wood-block illustration, simplified techniques for portrait and reportorial photography—cut another huge slice from what had been throughout history bread-and-butter work for painters proper and narrowed their function and social usefulness. Portrait painters, history painters, creative illustrators all found their traditional provinces eroded and themselves facing technological unemployment. Some (Samuel F. B. Morse is a good American example) recognized what was happening very early and explicitly "retrained" themselves in new media and social functions; others, most notably the later Academicians, implicitly did the same thing. The famous episode of Millais's *Bubbles* being "sullied" by its use, *mutis mutandis,* in a Pears' Soap advertisement was one striking example of the popular turn his art was taking, the fantastic commercial success of prints made from his *Boyhood of Raleigh* or *Yeoman of the Guard,* another.

But there was a minority which reacted by beginning a "retreat from the public" which paralleled the "retreat from patrons" which had set in during the 1840s; they turned inward on the art of painting itself, as if to fence off a preserve from further popular invasions. Inevitably, the result was a trend towards subjectivity and a "retreat from likeness." So it happened that Impressionism is the first appearance of a kind of painting whose outward form is obviously and inescapably different from what had gone before—in which the paint exists in its own right, as palpable strokes and spots, and not simply as a "medium" through which you perceive something else.

178

Impressionism as a theory of painting, too, has a new and "modern" character. While some concern for Beauty remains, it is quite plain that Impressionist painters are primarily looking for something else. And in their search, the characteristic tendency of 20th-century advance-guard painting to split into various schools and "isms" first becomes apparent. We can in fact distinguish at least three more or less definite types of Impressionism: brush-stroke Impressionism, with Manet as its chief early exponent; pointillistic Impressionism, as exemplified by Pissarro, Monet, and most exhaustively by Seurat; and in contrast to the predominantly formal interests of these two, social Impressionism, best represented by Renoir, Degas, and Toulouse-Lautrec. Typically "modern," again, is the Impressionists' preoccupation with the theoretical side of painting, with means more than ends. They think of art, and treat it, in a new and "scientific" spirit. And so with them begins the prevalent 20th-century concept of art as, according to its friends, an esoteric, specialized field of knowledge like theoretical physics or chemistry or mathematics, unintelligible without years of study—or alternatively, according to its enemies, as a kind of magnificent and continuing fraud on the public, a great hoax on the world (as Swift saw science, for instance, in Laputa).

But with all this, however, Impressionism is still not modern painting. For it lacks the one essential element—a subjective concept of Reality. For the Impressionists, Reality was still objective; they sought for it outside themselves. Their art was still ultimately dependent, as art had been in the Renaissance, in the Middle Ages, in classical Greece, on the external world. That this was incompatible with the painter's new claims to dominate and determine what was real, we have seen. Sooner or later the Impressionists had to come to realize it, too. But when they did, they would cease to be Impressionists; and then modern art in the true sense could begin.

NOTES

The hard core of the Impressionist movement, insofar as it was an organized movement at all, consisted of the group that met at the Cafe Guerbois in the late 1860s and early 1870s, principally Manet, Pissarro, Monet, Renoir, and Degas. However, as a force or climate of opinion in painting, Impressionism ran over three generations. There was first the generation born in the 1820s and -30s, whose chief representatives were

179

Manet, Pissarro, Degas, Johan Barthold Jongkind (1819–1891), Eugène Boudin (1824–1898), and Adolphe Joseph Thomas Monticelli (1824–1886). Characteristic works by Jongkind like *The Drawbridge* (Philadelphia) or Boudin's *Fair in Brittany* (Washington, Corcoran), show the influence of the Barbizon School on this generation; Boudin was also famous for seascapes (*Beach at Trouville,* Philadelphia), which influenced Monet, whose first teacher he was. Monticelli's ultimate inspiration was in the romanticism of Delacroix; he was a pupil of Delaroche, and developed a highly personal kind of broken and quasi-pointillistic brushwork. These men, for all their differences, shared a common awareness of the problem of Reality in form, though none pushed it as far as their slightly younger contemporaries Manet, Pissarro, and Degas.

Following them was a group born in the 1840s. Besides the leading figures of Monet and Renoir, it included Alfred Sisley (1839–1899), who was chiefly influenced by Monet (e.g., *Snow at Louveciennes,* Washington, Phillips); Armand Guillaumin (1841–1927) who was one of the few exhibitors in the first Impressionist show of 1874 to appear in the last of 1886; and three painters of wealthy families who demonstrate that some at least of the *bourgeoisie* understood at the time how perfect an expression of the world view of liberal capitalism Impressionist painting could be—Jean-Frédéric Bazille (1841–1870), early friend and patron of the group as well as a significant painter in his own right, whose death in the Franco-Prussian war was a severe setback for the Impressionists' hopes of broad recognition; Berthe Morisot (1841–1895), student of Corot and sister-in-law of Manet, granddaughter of the 18th-century painter Fragonard; and the American Mary Cassatt (1845–1926), daughter of the president of the Pennsylvania Railroad and great admirer of Degas.

Finally there was a group born around 1860, whose diversity is represented in its two leading figures, Seurat and Toulouse-Lautrec; to it belonged Paul Signac (1863–1935), and Henri Edmond Cross (1856–1910). The best broad account of the whole Impressionist movement is John Rewald, *History of Impressionism* (Museum of Modern Art, revised, 1961).

1

The Impressionist Vision:

Edouard Manet (1832–1883)
Camille Pissarro (1830–1903)

In the year 1874 a number of painters who had been working in Paris in loose association since the 1860s came together to put on an exhibition under the title of "The Anonymous Society of Painters and Sculptors." To describe what they saw there, critics coined a new word—Impressionism. It was no compliment, however. As one of them put it: "We have seen an exhibition by these *Impressionalists* . . . M. Manet is among those who maintain that in painting one can and ought to be satisfied with the *impression.* . . . [They] appear to have declared war on beauty."

Insofar as these painters were not concerned with Beauty in the traditional sense their critics were right, of course. Emile Zola, exemplar of the new "realism" in literature and Manet's great companion, spoke for the Impressionists when he declared flatly,

> . . . Beauty is no longer an absolute, a preposterous universal standard. Beauty is identical with life itself. . . . Beauty lives within us, not outside us. What do I care for philosophical abstraction, for an ideal perfection conjured up by a small group of men! What interests me as a man is mankind, the source of my life.*

But there was nothing particularly new in that. Zola's conclusion had been inherent and inevitable in the logic of Reynolds's theory of Beauty long ago; once say that Beauty is not absolute, but dependent on agreement of the "generality of mankind," and sooner or later you must proceed to "Beauty is what a majority of mankind thinks it is," thence to "what some people think it is" and finally to "Beauty is what I think it is," at which point Beauty and Reality become indistinguishable. And indeed by the later 1860s Reality was being generally accepted, however unintelligently or unwillingly, by more and more critics of painting in France; the first major premise of the great revolution in theory that had begun in the 1840s—that Reality of subject matter to which illustrators, the Pre-Raphaelite painters, the Barbizon school, and finally Courbet had

* Quoted in G. H. Hamilton, *Manet and His Critics* (New Haven, 1954), p. 92.

181

each in their differing ways contributed—had been largely conceded. But the revolution was far from complete. However intellectually willing critics might be to accept the theory of Reality in painting, emotionally they were quite unprepared for the changes in the outward form of painting that Reality inevitably entailed. That was what so furiously dismayed them about Impressionist painting.

Traditionally, painting had begun with line drawing. In this preliminary drawing, the painter tried to bring out what he knew of the permanent, tactile qualities of objects existing in space—solid forms that could be touched or walked around. Only after establishing this basic form did he touch in whatever incidental appearances of light and color affected the form he was representing. This was Ingres's method, for example; and, though he made more of the painterly qualities of the finished picture, Delacroix's; it was still Daumier's and, except for his later works, Courbet's. But that was not at all how these Impressionists approached representation. For them Reality did not involve a drawing; it did not even mean working for a photographic likeness, as with Courbet. It meant "seeing like a camera"; and that was something entirely new. For the camera "knows" nothing of what is before it. It has no experience, no memory, none of the powers of selection or abstraction inherent in drawing. It simply records areas of light—full-tones, half-tones, shadows, in (if it could) varying hues and intensities. This process the Impressionists had set themselves to emulate. They knew, of course, that it was physiologically impossible for human beings to achieve objectivity comparable to the camera's, but they hoped to approximate it by using premixed paint in tubes, introduced by the Barbizon school, to speed the physical process of painting to a point where they could at least try to set down directly the impressions of light that struck their eyes; no more, and no less.

They did so in various ways. One, developed principally though not exclusively by Edouard Manet, was to establish the lights, half-lights, and shadows of a given object—a hand, say, or a sleeve—with broad stripes of paint, so applied as to follow its shape; often, the ridge of paint piled up by the brush as it followed the form established a kind of linear outline in itself. This we can call brush-stroke Impressionism. Others, of whom Pissarro is the earliest example, chose to set down impressions of light as smaller strokes, hooks, commas, or dots of paint; this we could loosely call pointillistic Impressionism. It may have been affected by early experiments in color photography, in which as early as 1862 plates were covered with tiny grains soaked in solutions reacting to different primary colors, with a resulting mass of colored spots somewhat resembling a pointillistic canvas. Photography certainly influenced this technique in the direction of greater spontaneity in composition. But to most critics distinctions between kinds of Impressionism seemed idle. As far as they were concerned, all Impressionist canvases were confused masses of paint.

The first brunt of the attack fell on Edouard Manet in the early 1860s, largely because he appeared as a follower of Courbet. The critics found this very strange. Certainly Manet's subject matter had a good deal in common with Courbet's, insofar as he seemed to be intent, like Courbet, on "shocking" accepted standards of taste with "crude" and "vulgarly common" Reality in subject matter: a *Dead Christ* who looked, one writer said, like "the Poor Miner Rescued from a Coal Mine, executed for Renan"; a naked courtesan on a bed, called *Olympia;* a licentious orgy entitled *Luncheon on the Grass.* But between the form of Courbet's works and these "unfinished" paintings by Manet there was, clearly, no comparison. Courbet, particularly now in his later works, was beginning to use a palette knife more and more freely, to be sure—to lay on paint (particularly in the rocks and foliage of his backgrounds) in large patches and dabs, so that you were aware of it as paint. But his main figures were still "finished," not with the completely invisible brush stroke of polished Academicians like Bouguereau or Couture, perhaps, but still carefully enough. But this Manet—instead of having the light strike his figures from one side or the other, so that it casts shadows to accentuate the forms, he poses them as if he were taking a photograph, with the light source directly behind him, so that the forms are illuminated head-on. That is why the surfaces seem so harsh and flat, with shadows clinging only around the edges; these shadows, furthermore, are painted in great loose brush strokes outlining the form as in a drawing. Indeed, the whole painting looks more like a rough brush-drawing than a "proper" work of art.

And his background, too; it is no more than a few broad areas of flat paint, loosely brushed in, as if it were a photographer's backdrop. We have no objection to a painting looking like a photograph (M. Courbet has convinced us on that point) but surely no photograph ever looked like this? How could the perpetrator of these loose daubings ever think himself a follower of the Master of Ornans?

Edouard Manet's concepts of what photography involved, and how it was related to painting, were indeed very different from Courbet's, partly because of their difference in age. By the time Daguerre's invention had become common knowledge, in the 1850s (it was first made public in 1839), Courbet was a mature painter; his generation could do little more than react to the product. But Manet's generation (he was born in 1832) grew up with photography as an accepted part of everyday experience. He had an opportunity to reflect on the nature of the process involved. And the problem it posed—what "seeing like a camera" really involved—was for Manet first and last the fundamental question in painting.

Manet's preoccupation with this problem was further stimulated by the general revival of interest in Spanish and Dutch painting also characteristic of his generation. Whereas in 1781 Reynolds had visited Holland and pontificated that Rembrandt's *Night Watch* was much overrated, now, under the influence of the pervasive picturesqueness characteristic of mid-19th-century romantic painting and architecture alike, Rembrandt's luminous composition and loose brushwork suddenly came back into favor, and a new genius was discovered in Frans Hals. So fervently was Hals admired that from almost total obscurity at the beginning of the 19th century he came to be ranked next Rembrandt at its end. At the same time Spanish painting was being comparably re-evaluated; and on Manet the influence of Velasquez was even greater than that of Hals. Towards the end of the 18th century an extraordinary number of accounts of travels in Spain had begun to appear (at least two in Italian and two in French, and half a dozen in English) inspired by the decay and inaccessibility of the country which made it romantically remote; the Napoleonic wars inspired further interest. But it was only in the 1840s, when the Carlist troubles in Spain ended and travelers could visit Madrid more or less freely and report on the collections there, that Spanish painting was effectively rediscovered, and Velasquez in particular recog-

21A. *Edouard Manet:* The Old Musician. *Washington, National Gallery, Chester Dale Collection. c. 1862.*

A typical example of the optical focus Manet learned from studying Velasquez, this picture may possibly have been inspired by Los Borrachos *in the Prado.* See also 21B, Pissarro.

nized as a great master. Courbet had been interested in him, but it was on the succeeding generation that Velasquez had the real effect. To Manet, particularly, he came as a revelation. Manet knew Velasquez' paintings first in the Louvre, then through Goya's etched set of Velasquez subjects, finally on his own 1865 trip to Spain. It seemed to him that here, in these neglected masterpieces, relegated to attics and bathrooms, the Old Master had solved a problem he was only beginning to formulate. These old kings and queens of Spain, these court dwarfs and ladies in waiting who had sat to Velasquez two hundred years before—they were far more alive than Academic portraits finished the day before yesterday, more "real" than photographs. How had this old master achieved such astonishing immediacy?

If you analyzed Velasquez' paintings, you realized that their secret was representing things, not as the camera's eye sees them, but as the human eye sees them. Evidently there was a difference. When we look at a given scene, we don't take in every detail of foreground and background in the same sharp focus, as a 19th-century time-exposed photographic plate would. The only object we see in sharp focus is the one on which our eye rests at the moment; everything else gets progressively more out of focus, the farther away it is. That is how Velasquez painted: one thing in tight literal detail, everything else painted more and more loosely, until at the edges of the picture—the edge of vision, that is—cuffs and hands or backgrounds or furniture are simply suggested by rough strokes of the brush. When we stand before one of his pictures, then, and look at the center of interest, we at once see the whole scene as he did. We see the

21B. *Camille Pissarro:* Boulevard des Italiens, Morning Sunlight. *Washington, National Gallery, Chester Dale Collection. 1897.*

To represent things "as the camera sees them" is not the same as "photographic reality"—that was the first great discovery made by those who, following Courbet's precepts, tried to achieve a "scientific" Reality of form. Manet in seeking immediacy of effect like Velasquez and Hals, Claude Monet in seeking instantaneous time through sequences of pointillistic studies, Pissarro in seeking the spontaneity of camera composition, all learn and demonstrate that the human eye and the camera "see" differently.

186

scene through his eyes, and we occupy his same instant of time.

Manet was typical of his High Victorian generation in that he had no interest in reviving Velasquez' painting as such. Like his contemporary, the architect Henry Hobson Richardson, he was a true creative eclectic. Just as Richardson had no interest in reproducing Romanesque churches as such, but only in deriving from them elements and ideas to use in new and original creations of his own, so Manet was uninterested in *why* Velasquez had painted as he did. When he studied Velasquez' great masterpiece *The Ladies in Waiting,* he did not realize that by organizing the whole complex picture in terms of an optical focus originating in the King's own eye, Velasquez with subtle brilliance was flattering royal absolutism by implying that the whole world is ordered by the eye and brain of the monarch; even if he had known, he would not have cared. All that mattered to him was a revelation of a new kind of vision for painters of his own generation. Painting as we see—that, he thought, is the secret of Reality. That is why Velasquez' paintings are so much more immediate than even a great realist's like Courbet. Courbet still painted each of the main objects in his picture with approximately the same degree of careful detail; the result was manifestly an assemblage of images seen at different times—*The Village Maidens* (1851, New York, Metropolitan) is a particularly painful example. But Velasquez painted in terms of a single quick impression; he painted a scene as you would take it in at one glance. Velasquez', not Courbet's, is our normal mode of vision. Think how the descriptions of an escaped bank robber vary from witness to witness, for example; or how when suddenly called on, we find we can't recall the details of some object we have passed every day for weeks, and you will soon be convinced that we do not normally see with the detailed objectivity of a camera. Velasquez, in short, is more realistic; and if we once accept Reality as the goal of painting, Velasquez, not Courbet, is the model to follow. The artist should produce, not detailed descriptions, but Impressions. And with that logic, a new phase in the history of painting could begin.

Not that Manet, Pissarro, or the other Impressionists had any intention of repudiating the photographic image. Quite the contrary. They were trying to perfect the kind of vision it represented. They were trying to be more scientific, not less. This appears most evidently, perhaps, in their attitude to composition, and especially in the spontaneous composition first perfected by Pissarro.

In the 1860s and -70s, the "art" of photography (as opposed to the purely mechanical process) was still largely thought of in terms of traditional painting. Early photographers, imitating the practice of Academic painters, composed their pictures in relation to a frame. You started with this given area in mind; into it, you fitted your various figures and forms, each neatly and completely rendered, in a preallotted space. The frame set the limits within which action could proceed; it was literally the "framework of reference" on which the positioning and interrelationship of everything in the picture depended. Manet was still composing in this traditional manner well into the 1860s; but first Pissarro, and then Impressionists generally from the 1870s on, discarded this kind of planned picture for a "candid view." He proposed to set down simply what appeared before his eye—figures, background, everything moving in and out of his line of vision. The frame no longer determines the composition; it is nothing more than an arbitrary limit to what can be seen. This, the Impressionists argued, was true photographic vision. We do not see the world as David showed it in *The Oath of the Horatii* (page 21), or even as Courbet showed it in *The Studio* (page 171), arranged as on a little stage, with the action taking place parallel to a picture plane and the spectator looking on from some point outside; the picture plane is determined by our eye, not a frame. We should paint as we see; the spectator should interpret for himself the impressions we set down in paint, just as he interprets for himself the impressions of light in nature, or on a photographic plate.

All of which was easy enough to understand once you knew the theory. Once you knew what the Impressionists were trying to do, it was clear why their pictures looked the way they did. But if you failed to grasp the principle, you could make nothing of the product. It was like seeing a formula in physics, or a complicated electronic device; without technical knowledge, the thing was useless and meaningless. And that is by no means an idle comparison. For the Impressionists were trying to investigate the nature of Reality in their field just as physical scientists might investigate it in theirs. Like scientists, they were primarily interested in perfecting the means; the end, what might be done with any resultant product, was of no great concern. And if this aspect of Impressionism made even its own practitioners occasionally uneasy, how much more baffling it seemed to contemporary critics! In it they sensed—sometimes precisely, sometimes only by intuition—the beginnings of an entirely new relationship between painters and their public.

Ever since primeval bards had chanted to assembled tribesmen, or

189

cavemen decorated grotto shrines, it had been taken for granted that art existed in some way to serve the public. Even the early realists conceded that much; Millais spoke not only as a respected Academician, but for Pre-Raphaelites and Barbizon school painters, when he told Holman Hunt, who was preparing material for his *Pre-Raphaelitism and the Pre-Raphaelite Brotherhood,*

> You argue that if I paint for the passing fashions of the day my reputation some centuries hence will not be what my powers would secure for me if I did more ambitious work. I don't agree, A painter must work for the taste of his own day . . .*

But beginning with Manet, the Impressionists introduced a very different attitude. Approaching any and all subjects with the same kind of scientific objectivity, they seemed to consider problems in representation as ends in themselves. Their idea of an "interesting picture" was one that interested the painter as a problem; whether or not it interested anybody else hardly mattered. This is the peculiar significance of the fact that every one of Manet's major works in the early 1860s was obviously based on earlier precedents: *The Surprised Nymph* (1861, Buenos Aires) on Rembrandt's *Susannah; Luncheon on the Grass* (1863, Louvre) on Giorgione's *Pastoral Concert* and Raimondi's engraving of Raphael's *Judgment of Paris; The Dead Christ* (1864, New York, Metropolitan) from Mantegna's *Two Angels at the Tomb of Christ* in Copenhagen; *Olympia* (1863–65) from Titian's *Venus of Urbino.* Oswald Spengler in *The Decline of the West* cited these borrowings as evidence for a basic cultural change in Western civilization during the 19th century, but he completely missed the point. It was not that creative originality was in decay, but that for the first time artists began addressing themselves primarily to other painters rather than to the public. These are didactic pictures, but they are primarily intended to teach, not the public, but other painters how to paint. In each case Manet takes a "standard" theme in the old theory of Beauty, and interprets it in terms of the new Reality, not only as to content, but also as to form. He tells other painters what to see, and how to see it. If the public understands, well and good; if not, the public be damned. It is the public's obligation to understand the painter, not vice versa. It is up to him to lead, up to them to follow.

Such an attitude clearly had immense ramifications. And it was these

* Quoted in John Gaunt, *The Pre-Raphaelite Tragedy* (London, 1942).

ramifications which most bothered the many contemporary critics who, as Professors Hamilton and Sloan have admirably demonstrated, understood what Manet and his followers were doing. Contrary to popular notions, they were often quite sympathetic to Impressionist painting; but already by the late 1860s it was becoming apparent that the more painters made themselves into scientists, working on their own specialized problems in the field of picture-making, the more unintelligible to everyone but themselves their works must inevitably become. Furthermore, the more complicated Manet made his theory of vision, the simpler the technical side of painting became. Discarding all the old academic formulae, rules, and guides as hindrances to the new vision, he was already producing paintings that seemed incomprehensible daubs to the uninitiated; and clearly this was only the beginning. Where would it end? In painters working only to please themselves, to solve their own problems? How then would they justify their existence? Scientists, if they chose, could point to all sorts of tangible marvels resulting from their abstruse cogitations—labor-saving machines, better food, better clothes. But the painter had nothing comparable to offer. He could not claim to be filling the world with Beauty, for he had abjured that end. And if in fact his goal of giving the world a truer picture of itself resulted in a meaningful expression of the ideals, aspirations, and beliefs of his age, that was accidental, incidental, and of no immediate consequence anyway. It seemed clear that, carried to any logical conclusion, Impressionist theory must change the fundamental nature of painting itself. Certainly it involved an immediate change in the traditional relationship between the painter and his subject matter; that became apparent in the 1870s.

NOTES

Manet's formal painting career began in Couture's studio, but he seems to have relied largely on himself and his eye for basic ideas. His early evolution can be traced through copies of Delacroix (*Barque of Dante,* 1854, New York, Metropolitan), Velasquez (1855), Brouwer in the manner of Couture (*Absinthe Drinker,* 1858–59), and *Portrait of the Artist's Parents* (1861) in the manner of Courbet—his first accepted in the Salon. In the early 1860s his maturity of style was signalized by *Concert in the Tuileries* (1860–62, London), and consummated in a series of didactic pictures (cited in this text) which included *Olympia* and *Luncheon on the Grass;* his chief inspiration is evident in the large number of "Spanish pictures" from this time—e.g.,

Spanish Singer (1860, New York, Metropolitan), *Victorine Meurend* [his model for *Olympia, Luncheon,* and *The Fifer*] *in the Costume of an Espada* (1862, New York, Metropolitan), *Ballet Espagnol* (1862, Washington, Phillips), *Bull Fight* (1864, New York, Frick), *The Dead Toreador* (1863–64, Washington). This series, significantly enough, ended after Manet's visit to Spain in 1865. *The Fifer* (1865–66, Louvre) shows Velasquez' influence combined with a new interest, Japanese prints; by the time of his one-man show at the 1867 Paris Exhibition his style was fully mature, and Manet became the champion of advance-guard painting in Paris. To the next decade belong *Execution of Emperor Maximilian* (1867, Mannheim), *Luncheon in the Studio* (1868, Munich), *Portrait of Emile Zola* (1868, Louvre), *The Balcony* (1869, Louvre). Manet's trip to Holland and his admiration for Hals is commemorated in *Le Bon Bock* (1872, Louvre); his stay at Argenteuil in 1874, painting in the open with Monet, by *Monet in His Boat* (1874, Munich), *Sailing* (c. 1874, New York, Metropolitan), and *Boating at Argenteuil* (1874, Tournai). Whether or not at this time he became aware of the inherent contradictions in doctrinaire Impressionism, in fact he began from this time on to turn more and more to social commentary and portraiture, the process marked by *Portrait of Stéphane Mallarmé* (1876, Louvre), *Le Skating* (1877, Cambridge, Fogg), *Nana* (1877, Hamburg), *Faure as Hamlet* (1877, Essen), *Portrait of Lina Campineau* (1878, Kansas City, Nelson), *At the Café* (1878, Baltimore, Walters), *Portrait of George Moore* (1879, New York, Metropolitan), *Portrait of Antonin Proust* (1880, Toledo), and climaxed by *Bar at the Folies Bergères* (1881, London, Courtauld). At this point he became ill and died in 1883 at the age of 51.

Camille Pissarro was born in the Danish West Indies (St. Thomas, now U. S. Virgin Islands), but from 1855 on was resident in France. His style matured in the 1860s, but almost all his early paintings were lost when his house in Louveciennes was occupied by the invading Germans in 1870. In 1874 he took part in the first Impressionist exhibition and exhibited in every subsequent one including the last of 1886. The most consistent of all the Impressionists, he was also influential on all of them; working in the open air in all media, he had an enormous production which is represented in almost every museum of consequence in the world.

Besides standard accounts of Manet and Pissarro in John Rewald, *History of Impressionism,* there are books on *Manet* by John Richardson (1958), K. Martin (*Watercolors and Pastels,* London, 1958), G. H. Hamilton (*Manet and his Critics,* New Haven, 1954), S. L. Faison (1953), Georges Bataille (1955), Robert Rey (1938), and Paul Colin (Paris, 1932). See also L. R. Pissarro and L. Venturi, *Camille Pissarro, son art et son oeuvre* (Paris, 1939).

2

The Impressionist Painter versus His Subject:

Claude Monet (1840–1926)
Georges Seurat (1859–1891)

When most people think of Impressionist painting, it is pointillism—painting in small dots or "points" of color—that comes to mind first. And when they talk of Impressionist theory, they usually mean the principle of optical mixture—setting small dots of different hues together so that from a distance they mix in the eye to produce a blend of the original intensity, instead of the lowered intensity resulting from mixing pigments. Thus Monet is sometimes called the greatest of the Impressionists, and Seurat a "Neo-Impressionist" who attempted to revive the pure theory, while Manet is hardly an Impressionist at all. Be that as it may (and it may be purely academic) certainly it is true that in the work of Monet and Seurat we have the best illustration of the central tenet of Impressionism, the idea of "objectivity," of the painter's being "only an eye." They more than the rest abjured the whole idea of the painter being an interpreter of Nature; if they painted in small dots it was not, in theory, to help anyone gain greater insight into the Reality of Nature, but simply because in that way they could approximate more exactly the natural scale of light intensity. And thereby in their work they raised the fundamental questions of Impressionism in most acute form: what was the effect of this imitation, this intensive study of the physical properties of vision, on the traditional relationship of painters with their subject matter? Could painters in fact achieve anything like the degree of mechanical detachment from their subjects which such objectivity required? And was it worth achieving?

Their model was the camera. The camera as they first knew it made a picture in a few minutes; later, in a split second. It captured everything before it not only in relation to a single point in space, but at a single instant in time. But even with the advantage of premixed paint in tin tubes that were available from the mid-19th century on, no painter could produce a picture that fast. By abandoning the old planned picture, by working without preparatory sketches and applying their paint directly to

193

the canvas, the Impressionists might do a picture in a matter of hours or even minutes, instead of the days and weeks that used to be customary; but even a few minutes was too long. For the human eye is so constructed that it moves incessantly; and every time it does, ever so slightly, the relationship of every object to every other object in its line of vision is altered.

The human eye can never be stopped long enough to fix a uniform spatial relationship among all the objects it sees, as the Greeks and Romans, who tried it for centuries, discovered; not until Alberti's 15th-century invention of the templet and measured box freed painters from dependence on their own eyes, got them outside their work, were painters able to perfect even one-point linear perspective. As for total unity of time—"instantaneity," as Monet called it—that is even more difficult. For just as the human eye ranges over space, so the mind is forever ranging through time, incessantly remembering, incessantly influencing what the eye sees by what it knows to be there. To make the eye behave like a lens, transmitting sensations of light without any commentary from an interpreting, understanding mind, might seem an obvious impossibility. But the early Impressionists were nothing if not courageous; they would "do the difficult instantly; the impossible will take a little longer."

So by the 1890s we find Monet pushing past the already complex Impressionism practiced by Manet and Pissarro towards just this sort of experiment in instantaneity. He sets up a number of easels before some apparently chance subject—haystacks, poplar trees, a cathedral façade—and tries to "get a true impression of a certain aspect of nature and not a composite picture." Originally he thinks he will need only two canvases, one for cloudy and another for sunny skies; gradually he increases the number to a dozen, to fifteen, and more. From one to another easel he rushes, as the sun goes round the sky, as white light gives place to green, as red light reflects into blue shadows and then onto yellow hay ("Only an eye, but what an eye!" as Cézanne said of him) snapping what he presumes will be oil-painted photographs, impartial records of nature casually seen and candidly reported. But were they photographs in oil? Were they objective and impersonal records? Nothing of the sort. They came closer to the true scale of natural light than anything painted before, perhaps; but beyond that, they turned out to be almost as highly personal a record of what one individual, Claude Monet, saw on a given day in 1890, as if he had deliberately tried to set it down. It is not so much that the paintings have Monet's personal "style," his own peculiar way of applying paint to canvas, his own "handwriting"; even more, it is that, while in theory he and all Impressionist painters were supposed to be entirely neutral about their choice of subject matter, recording anything that afforded interesting enough impressions of light, in practice he limits himself to a relatively few favorite themes. And almost all of them have this one thing conspicuously in common: they represent, or have obvious associations with the idea of, transience, impermanence, the passing moment. His favorite still life is a bouquet in full bloom—another day, and the flowers will droop and die. His favorite seascape is the cliff at Etretat, with its natural arch cut through by erosion; sometime (who knows? it might be any moment) wind and wave will complete their work and the rock will collapse. He likes to paint snow scenes, a subject of some permanence in Labrador or Vermont, perhaps, but an affair of hours or a day in France. Railroad stations attract him; not the impressive stone façades of stations proper, with their monumental pretensions, but train sheds, which, with their billowing, dissolving clouds of smoke and steam and hurrying dots of travelers, are of all human structures the most suggestive of man's ephemeral voyaging through life. And what subjects are chosen for most intensive study? Poplars—of all trees the most shimmering, the most constantly in movement, the fastest growing and the soonest decaying. Rouen Cathedral—symbol (for his tough-minded generation, which included Zola and Clemenceau and distrusted anything not demonstrable by direct experience) of the passage of time, of an institution once great and now crumbling under the republican tide of the times, as inexorably doomed to be swept away as the Etretat rock. Haystacks (page 197)—the very substance the ancient Psalmist took to epitomize the fragility of human life: "As for man, his days are as grass . . ." Waterlilies—fragile, floating emanations of a few rare hours and moments.

Now it takes no great psychological insight to explain this kind of predilection. Impressionism by definition is committed to depicting the world as it appears from instant to instant. If you were the sort of person who enjoyed contemplating the traditional, stable, and permanent elements of human life, Impressionism as a theory would hardly appeal to you. Only people who found the transience of human life exciting to think on, who were prepared to accept and delight in the thought of time rushing onward in a succession of tantalizing moments, would be tempted to become pioneers of a movement like Impressionist painting. Such a

195

person would inevitably and naturally be drawn to certain given categories of subject matter. However Monet and other Impressionists might
believe they were indifferent to what they painted, in the end their choice
would prove almost as personal, almost as selective, as any demanded
by the traditional theory of Beauty. It is a dichotomy that runs through
Impressionist painting generally, and Monet's in particular, from beginning to end. So, for example, those critics who see in the form of
Monet's late *Waterlilies* intimations of Abstract Expressionism are probably right; but these paintings remain intimations, because their explicit
content belongs to another era and tradition entirely.

To the succeeding generation of advance-guard painters born around
1860 it seemed obvious that Monet and his contemporaries had failed to
be completely objective, or anything like it. Many of them drew the
inference that the New Reality in painting must be subjective; but there
was a minority who felt that the solution was a more rigid adherence to
the fundamental doctrines of Impressionism. To these Neo-Impression-
ists, it seemed that the lesson to be learned from Monet's example was
that instantaneity, like linear perspective in the Renaissance, could only
be achieved by means of a machine. Very well, they say; a machine we

22. *Claude Monet:* The Haystack. *Springfield, Mass., The Museum of
Fine Arts, James Philip Gray Collection. Dated 1893. Monet's first
series of fifteen studies of this theme was exhibited in 1891.*

*Painters trying to follow Courbet soon find an inherent contradiction
in his teachings and example. They cannot simultaneously achieve total
objectivity of vision—be "only an eye"—and play the role of inspired
interpreters of Reality that he envisioned. Thus, however much they
may profess objective indifference to subject matter, Impressionists generally and Monet in particular show a marked predilection for themes
which suggest transience—haystacks, railroad stations, eroding cliffs,
shimmering light on water. In so doing they change the nature of
painting still further. Not only is there no longer even a vestigial interest in eternalizing the Beautiful—ars longa, vita brevis—there is no
longer any question of a permanent Reality underlying the world of appearances. Reality is the world of transient appearances, an affair of
passing moment—vita longa, ars brevis.*

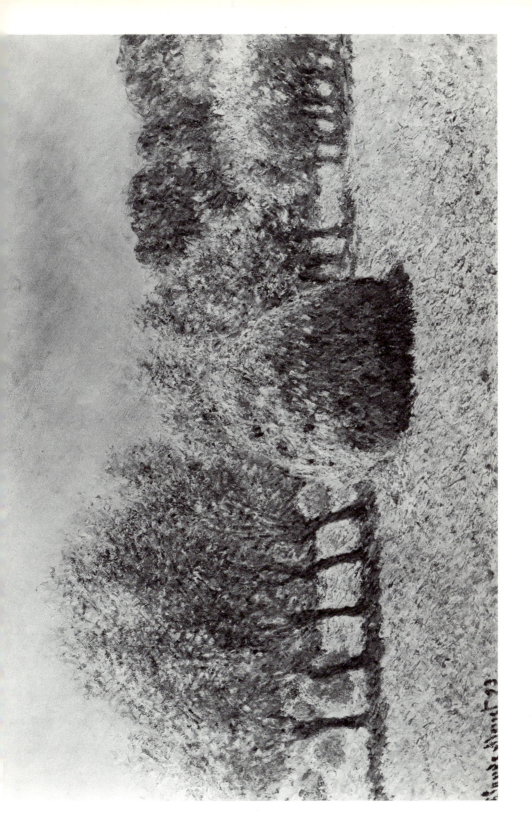

shall construct. A dozen younger painters—Angrand, Dubois-Pillet, Cross—begin to work on the problem. Georges Seurat's solution is the one we best remember. Every dot the same size; every tone coldly calculated; a precisely predetermined number of dots per square inch of canvas. Here is his published formula:

Esthetic

Art is Harmony. Harmony is the analogy of contrary and of similar elements of *tone,* of *color* and of *line,* considered according to their dominants and under the influence of light, in gay, calm, or sad combinations. The contraries are:

For *tone,* a more (luminous (lighter shade against a darker

For *color,* the complementaries, i.e., a certain red opposed to its complementary, &c. (red-green; orange-blue; yellow-violet).

For *line,* those forming a right angle.

Gaiety of *tone* is given by the luminous dominant; of *color,* by the warm dominant; of *line,* by lines above the horizontal. . . .

Technique

Taking for granted the phenomena of the duration of a light impression on the retina [here a new influence from photography perhaps—early experiments with motion pictures]: a synthesis follows as a result. The means of expression is the optical mixture of tones and colors (both of local color and of the illuminating color—sun, oil lamp, gas lamp, &c.) i.e., of the lights and their reactions (shadows) according to the laws of contrast, gradation and irradiation . . .

And so on. With this formula, the painter need not stand out in the sun or rain, like Pissarro, or try to capture by his own breakneck dexterity the fugitive effects of passing moments. Once he has made his studies on the spot, established his mood and subject, he can run it off with cool mechanical precision in the studio. Up on his ladder, far into the night, Seurat can work by artificial light, constructing his objective machine— dot,dot,dot, dab,dab,dab. The result, as we see it in works like *La Grande Jatte* (page 201), is certainly astonishing. But the astonishment is not so much at what it is, as what it is not.

La Grande Jatte is not, to begin with, an objective record of Nature, or anything like it. It hardly looks like Manet's or Pissarro's earlier kind of Impressionism at all. And there is certainly nothing of a casual, candid, or accidental glimpse of life about it, nothing impartial or impersonal in style or subject matter. Instead, what we have is a systematically organized, mathematically calculated arrangement of forms—arbitrarily full-front or full-side figures spaced methodically along a grid, obviously manifesting the highly selective eye and sensitive interpreting mind of one particular individual, Georges Seurat. And furthermore, we are aware, as we have never been before, of the picture *as* a picture—of the canvas and the paint as entities in themselves, quite apart from what they represent. This is hardly the expected consummation of Impressionist theory; it looks more like its opposite, its negation, a denouement instead of a climax. Whatever happened?

Simply that Seurat did for Impressionist theory what David had done for Reynolds's theory of a Grand Style a hundred years before. He relentlessly, methodically, systematically pushed its basic premises to their logical conclusion. And with a similar result; he destroyed what he set out to perfect. Pissarro, with the intuition for theory of first-generation Impressionists, was quite acute enough to see this. In 1885, while Seurat was still working on the *Grande Jatte,* Pissarro met him, was at once taken with his revival of the pure Impressionist theory, and wrote his friends that he was adopting "divisionism." But in 1888 he wrote a friend that "having tried this theory," he realized that it was a "diametrically opposed esthetic," and proposed to return to the older "Impression of life." Unfortunately that could not be done. Impressionism after the *Grande Jatte* could never be the same again. Once and for all Seurat had exposed the inherent incompatibility of the two basic principles bequeathed Impressionism by Courbet: the artist is to achieve impartial, impersonal, scientific objectivity, and he is to be the godlike creator who controls and decides Reality. By operating at one and the same time on the assumption that painters should completely dominate the objective world, and that they should be entirely passive recorders of it, Seurat demonstrated that the basic principles of Impressionism were not merely incompatible, they were precise opposites. That he did so was a remarkable *tour de force,* but the result was not Impressionism. It was another kind of painting entirely—or more exactly, contained the germs of two.

Impressionist painting, like all other painting before it, involved two distinct operations. First, the making of marks on a flat surface. And second, the arranging of these marks in such a way as to bring to mind physical images or abstract ideas like thirst, or social classes, or Beauty. Self-evidently, these two operations can never be given equal weight; one must serve the other. Traditionally, form—marks on the surface—had been considered only the means; content—the ideas these marks brought to mind—was the painter's proper end. But the emphasis on scientific objectivity in Impressionist theory made subject matter of secondary importance, encouraged painters to concentrate on the means. Once that happened, sooner or later the actual paint surface was bound to become the dominant element in their pictures. Thus the first thing that Seurat's painting brings to mind is not a Sunday afternoon on Grande Jatte Island, or anything else in the physical universe; it is a surface covered with dots of paint. The picture surface, the paint, *is* the picture. That something like this would happen sooner or later was inevitable; all Seurat did was to speed the process. He destroyed the balance earlier Impressionists had maintained, ·making manifest in his work what in theirs had been only inherent, creating in the *Grande Jatte* the first embodiment of the modern dogma that "a picture is not a window."

But he did something else. He also pushed to a new extreme the other and opposite premise of Impressionist theory: that the painter must organize the world in terms of his personal, individual vision. It is beside the point that he may well have done so unwittingly and indirectly, by constructing a mechanical formula into which he fitted his personal observations, or that he was entirely sincere in declaring, "They see poetry in what I have done. No, I apply my methods and that is all there is to it." Willingly or not, Seurat did mold Nature according to his own

23. *Georges Seurat:* A Sunday Afternoon on the Island of La Grande Jatte. *Chicago, The Art Institute, Helen Birch Bartlett Memorial Collection. The final outcome of 30 studies in oil and 27 preparatory drawings, it was painted over the years 1884–1886.*

In this work pointillism is used not to depict the world with photographic actuality, but as a contrived device to accentuate the total artificiality of even a Sunday afternoon's recreation. Here the inherent contradiction between objective "realism" of photographic form and subjective "realism" of content comes into the open, and clearly demands a choice. In effect, the social Impressionists have already decided the issue, simply by exposing it. It remains for the Post-Impressionists to abandon all pretense at objective form, and concentrate on developing an art whose Reality will be subjective in form and content alike.

200

particular vision. Grande Jatte Island in Seurat's picture is something it never was before. He made it a creation, extension, and expression of his own personality. The *Grande Jatte* is not a transcription of Nature; it is Seurat's personal commentary (however unconscious) on the state of man in his world, on the state of culture in late 19th-century France. Choosing a typically Impressionist subject of middle-class leisure activities made possible by the new wealth created by bourgeois capitalism, he makes it a vehicle to express what he considers is the Reality beneath the leisured veneer—a rigidly mechanical world whose every moment, whether at work or play, is governed by a stylized code of behavior which fixes a stereotyped pose and mandatory response for every situation, from wandering in a public park to viewing exhibitions of painting. Seurat was driven by the force of his own logic to demonstrate what Courbet had failed to realize: if a painter is to command Reality, he must abandon all pretense at an objective, photographic form; the premises of the New Reality in painting must be subjective.

With Seurat the function of Impressionism as a bridge between the old theory of Beauty and the New Painting with Reality as its goal was accomplished; its vital role in the evolution of painting was over. There remains only to view it historically, as the great cultural expression of life in the heyday of 19th-century bourgeois capitalism.

NOTES

Monet's career falls into three distinct phases. The first begins when he met Boudin in his home town of LeHavre in 1856, and learned from him to admire more the fresh instantaneous Reality of a sketch than studied pictures laboriously constructed by traditional processes of selection and abstraction. In 1859 he went to Paris, and in the succeeding decade developed Boudin's precepts into a systematic pointillistic impressionism, much influenced by Pissarro, whom he had first met in 1860. Typical landmarks in this process are the Boudin-influenced *LeHavre: Boats leaving Harbor* (c. 1865, Farmington, Conn., Hill-Stead Museum); *Portrait of Camille* (1866, Bremen); large figural compositions inspired by Courbet's and Manet's example: *The Picnic* (1866, Moscow, Pushkin, a small version of a huge uncompleted canvas); *The Luncheon* (1868, Frankfurt, Staedel); *The Beach at Sainte-Adresse* (1867, Chicago); *The Seine at Bougival* (1869, Manchester, N. H.); *La Grenouillère* (1869, New York, Metropolitan); *Beach at Trouville* (1870, Hartford, Wadsworth Atheneum).

By 1870 or 1871, when he went to London to escape the Franco-Prussian War, his early style was mature; in 1872 he painted *Impression: Sunrise* (Paris, Marmottan), which gave a name to the group which exhibited together in 1874, and for the next twenty years he devoted himself to refining the principles of Impressionism, becoming the classic exemplar of the movement. At first he lived in great poverty at a succession of places—Argenteuil, Vetheuil, Poissy, Etretat, but by the time he settled at Giverney in 1883 he was becoming established, and in 1890 he bought a house there and began to create his famous water garden, marking the termination of his second phase. His immense output over this period may be conveniently summarized in terms of characteristic subjects embodying the concept of transience, on which he concentrated, such as snow scenes (*Snow at Argenteuil*, c. 1875, Boston; *Winter in Vetheuil*, c. 1880, Buffalo); bridges and railroad stations (e.g., *Saint-Lazare Station*, 1877, Cambridge, Fogg, one of a series begun in 1876 and carried on into 1878); flowers (*Poppies*, 1873, Louvre; *Gladioli*, c. 1873, Detroit; *Sunflowers*, 1881, New York, Metropolitan; *Poppy Field near Giverney*, 1885, Boston); water effects (*Pool at Argenteuil*, 1874, Providence, Rhode Island School of Design); the cliff at Etretat (e.g., 1883, New York, Metropolitan).

Monet's discovery of the heightened color of southern France, commemorated in such works as *Cape Martin, near Menton* (1884, Boston) and *Old Fort at Antibes* (1888, Boston), in conjunction with the growing acceptance of Impressionism generally and his own painting in particular, which made experimental works more easily salable, is reflected in his final phase beginning c. 1890. It is marked by an ever-increasing propensity for experimentation with effects of pure color and light. To it belong the famous series of studies of poplars and haystacks (both begun 1890–91), and Rouen Cathedral (1892–95); of atmospheric effects in London (e.g., *Waterloo Bridge*, 1903, Washington) and Venice (1908–12, e.g., Brooklyn, Chicago); and of waterlilies, which, beginning in 1901 and continuing to his death, became the great preoccupation of his later life. Its climax came in the series commissioned for the state at Clemenceau's suggestion, painted 1916–26, installed in oval rooms of the Orangerie in the Tuileries and dedicated 1927— "the Sistine Chapel of Impressionism."

Among the many studies of Monet, that by William C. Seitz, *Monet* (1961), with bibliography, is definitive.

Seurat's short life is remarkable for its single-minded devotion to the theory of painting. The first three years of his active career (1880–83) he dedicated to perfecting expression in black-and-white drawings. 1883–84 was a period of transition when, under the influence of Signac, he turned his attention to color generally, and pointillistic theory in particular; the last seven years of his life (1884–91) he spent working out the full implications of it. To them belong, besides a few studies of landscape, especially harbors (e.g., *Port-en-Bessin,* 1888, Saint Louis; *Bridge at Courbevoie,* 1885–86, London, Courtauld), the major "demonstration pieces" on which his fame rests—*The Baignade* (1884, London, Tate) and *Grande Jatte* (1885, Chicago; study in Cambridge, Fogg); *Les Poseuses* (1887–88, Philadelphia, McIlhenny; Merion, Pa., Barnes); *Le Chahut* (1889, Otterlo, Kröller-Müller; studies in London, Courtauld, and Buffalo); *La Parade* (1889, New York, Clark) and *Le Cirque* (1890–91, Louvre, unfinished).

Books on Seurat include those by R. H. Wilenski (London, 1949), André Lhote (Paris, 1948), G. Seligman (*Drawings,* 1947), and D. C. Rich, *Seurat and the Evolution of "La Grande Jatte"* (1935); standard is J. Rewald, *Georges Seurat* (London, 1949).

3

Impressionism as Cultural Expression:

Auguste Renoir (1841–1919)
Edgar Degas (1834–1917)
Henri de Toulouse-Lautrec (1864–1901)

Any rigid classification of the major Impressionists would be nonsense. All were committed to the new principle of cameralike vision; all had to cope with the resultant problem of being at one and the same time "only an eye" and a "form-giver"; and in all of their works an expression of the culture of their age is inherent. But they showed varying degrees of interest in these diverse aspects of Impressionist painting. To some, like Pissarro and Manet, formulating the new vision tended to be a satisfying end in itself. Others, like Monet and Seurat, were more concerned with exploring the relationships of Impressionist form to Impressionist subject matter. For still others, however, Impressionist vision and form were never more than means to an end; these were the "social Impressionists," of whom Renoir, Degas, and Toulouse-Lautrec are the outstanding examples.

Least doctrinaire of them all, closest to the traditional concept of what painters were and did, was Renoir. Undoubtedly much of the difference between him and more orthodox Impressionists is explicable in terms of his (for an Impressionist) unusual background and training. Of lower-class and hence more conservative origins, his early vision and taste were shaped by painting loose and filmy decoration on chinaware in a porcelain factory. Never a systematic brush-stroke or pointillistic Impressionist, and with no intention of turning himself into any machine for recording light, Renoir's chief interest in form was always the sensual quality of paint itself, almost as it had been for the Venetians or for Delacroix. For formal experimentation in itself he had little use; his subject matter was never an excuse for disquisitions on form but was his prime interest. Indeed, except that his subjects were spontaneously taken from ordinary life around him, they were hardly realistic in Courbet's (or our) sense at all. For while what he painted may not have always been drawn from the traditional categories of "beautiful objects," certainly they did arouse a traditional kind of "beautiful feelings"—which explains, of course, why both in his own lifetime and later Renoir was the most widely popular of all the Impressionist painters.

Renoir's was a world of people boating, playing games, making music, bathing; of couples dancing, skating, talking around lunch tables, a world full of the joy of leisured living, of people engaged in the pursuit of happiness; a world peculiarly characteristic of the free-ranging individualism of the High Victorian age at its apogee between 1850 and 1885. Something like it appears in the genre paintings of 17th-century Holland, or in the popular arts of Hogarth and Rowlandson; but never before had people enjoyed themselves with such abandon, such spontaneity, or so consistently as they do in Renoir's pictures of the late 1860s, 1870s, and early -80s.

There had never been an age like Renoir's. For the first time in history, it had become possible for great masses of people, born poor, to attain a degree of leisure only men born to wealth and station had formerly enjoyed. More and more, the middle classes were coming into possession of what has always been the greatest thing money can buy—free time, time to do what you like without being pushed around by anybody. They had created a new civilization based on commerce and industry; now they were beginning to take advantage of the standard of living and new leisure it made possible. The feckless vulgarity of Edwardian times, the fatuous dream of parasitic and paralytic idleness that made *rentier* capitalism the scorn and shame of civilized men in the 1920s and -30s were still in the future; Renoir's *bourgeoisie* played with the healthy vigor of people who have not yet forgotten what work means.

And he was just the man to immortalize this moment in time. His brand of Impressionism, free alike of stiff Academic formulae and the chilling mechanics of formal divisionist theory, let his brush sparkle untrammeled across the canvas, sometimes in dots, sometimes in strokes, sometimes in smears, as mood or moment suited, catching the shimmer of sunlight and flicker of shade, the glint of glass, the sheen of hair, the bloom of skin. It is the kind of painting you can almost hear—long skirts rustle, music tinkles distantly, a babble of light conversation floats over everything. Renoir's life, too, seemed to fit the part. Among all the painters of his time he had the reputation of the great hedonist, the happy-go-lucky extrovert, who even towards the end of his life, when he was crippled and had to paint with brushes strapped to his wrists, could say that his goal was to "make the flesh on my canvas live and quiver."

Whether or not Renoir was in fact the happy man legend makes out, there is no need to attribute his choice of subjects solely to personal temperament. Not only was the Impressionist doctrine of impersonal objectivity strongest in his generation, so that his friend Monet could paint the serene and rippling *River* of 1868, now in Chicago, at a moment when his finances were so desperate and critical attacks on him so merciless that he was on the point of suicide; the old concept of Beauty as the painter's goal survived in him most strongly of all the Impressionists. He is indeed an early example of what will become a recurrent phenomenon in the New Painting—the artist who reverts from the pursuit of Reality to the older theory of Beauty, who knows intellectually that Reality is the approved goal of the advance-guard movement, but emotionally cannot help being pulled back to more traditional goals and standards. This penchant in Renoir shows up in many ways. Not only does he ignore Courbet's dogma that only the working classes are "real," and paint happy middle-class people instead, he also has no objection to showing upper-class bourgeois subjects in a favorable light. But perhaps the clearest indication of his deviation from the Impressionist line is his preoccupation with the nude. Much has been made of this in relation to his allegedly passionate temperament; but the fact seems self-evident that he was interested in it for basically the same reason that Botticelli or Giorgione or Tintoretto were interested in it—as *the* supremely beautiful form, the vehicle for expressing an ideal world. Similarly, his often-expressed wish to paint "classical" pictures, particularly after his trip to Italy in 1882, did not imply an interest in classical mythology or history, and only incidentally classical form as such; it implied an interest in Beauty as an objective in painting, as embodied in the timeless theme of the nude. Renoir's means of expressing this theme were different—Impressionist brush stroke, and plays on light and color —and consequently the specific forms, particularly his late "strawberry sundae" nudes, often seem more like parodies than reincarnations of classicism, but his end was the same. In terms of the evolution of a New Painting, this is retrogression, if you like; but it did provide proof that one way to make form and content agree was to return to the older and more traditional concept of Beauty. That, however, was not how history would go; Renoir's fellow social Impressionists, Degas and Toulouse-Lautrec, were already demonstrating another and in the long run more promising solution.

Degas and Toulouse-Lautrec agreed with Renoir in insisting on the importance of subject matter and so rejecting Impressionist form as an end in itself; like him, they tended to use whichever of the formal means of Impressionism (pointillism, sketchy brush stroke, spontaneous composition) best served the ends of the moment. Where they differed from him, however, and moved in the mainstream of advance-guard development, was that Reality, and not Beauty, primarily and always dictated the content of their pictures.

Degas's uncompromising Reality was dramatized in the first major work he exhibited, *The Bellelli Family* of 1859—a group portrait of his uncle, aunt, and two young cousins. Instead of idealizing the figures or making the family relationship appear "beautiful" as the conventions of Beauty demanded, Degas not only showed his aunt and cousins in all their homeliness, but went out of his way to display marital discord within the family, by seating the uncle with his back to the spectator, and isolating him by strong compositional verticals from the unified pyramidal group formed by the mother and daughters. The real state of affairs within the family was further brought out by such subtle compositional devices as contrasting a fussy broken-up background behind the uncle with broad and simple forms behind the aunt, and by placing the older daughter, whose allegiance was torn between father and mother, in such a way that her figure broke out of the maternal pyramid and by look and gesture moved towards the father's side. Degas's *Bellelli Family*, in short, displayed a precocious mastery of traditional Renaissance techniques. Like Masaccio in the Brancacci Chapel, like Leonardo in the *Last Supper,* like Velasquez in *The Lances,* he so organized compositional forms as to make the content self-evident, "showing the state of the soul through the gestures of the body." But whereas the Old Masters used their mastery of composition to further the traditional ends of painting, spiritual Beauty and "beautiful feelings," Degas used his to present Reality. Four years after Courbet's *Studio,* Degas already embodied the new concept of the painter as a seer, who points out truth to the world. And paralleling Manet's didactic pictures of the early 1860s, Degas in the same years was painting a series of "historical" pictures with the same ultimate purpose—"realistic" versions of traditional themes. *The Miseries of the City of Orleans* in 1865 is typical. Nothing of Pugin's or Delacroix's or Morris's romantic idealization of the Middle Ages here; this is the Reality of that epoch as sober history lays it bare; cruelty, violence, dirt, suffering, and stark privation.

As he matured, Degas mellowed and became increasingly interested in Impressionist technical effects as such; in his later works, particularly after he began to concentrate on pastels, there is an undeniable concern for Beauty of color and composition, and considerable interest in pure pictorial elements (surface and texture) for their own sake. But the primary orientation towards Reality is unaltered. Never does Degas merely study light, merely play with textural effects, or merely record life as it passes before him. In every case a commentary on the Reality of the human condition is involved. This commentary is achieved in two ways: explicitly, by the kind of subjects he chooses to paint, and implicitly, in the way he paints them.

Three themes particularly interested him—horseracing, musicians, and the ballet. But if we compare his expressions of these themes with comparable subjects by Renoir, an immense difference is apparent. Where Renoir's is a world of spontaneous gaiety and carefree amusement, Degas paints organized, commercial entertainment; contrived, forced routine; regimentation and discipline. When Degas paints musicians, he occasionally deals with individual and personal satisfactions comparable to those enjoyed by Renoir's young ladies amusing themselves for an hour at the piano or Eakins's *Cellist* playing for his own pleasure—*Degas's Father Listening to Lorenzo Pagans* (1869–72, Boston) is an example. But his consistent theme, like Seurat's, is the professional whose living depends on doing precisely what he is told. One slip, one missed rest, one deviation from the precise phrasing set out by some composer long since dead, and the poor devil will be out looking for another job. The same terrible tension is found at the racetrack. Beneath the bright surface of gaily waving crowds and colorful jockeys there is no playfulness, only the bitter business of fortunes at stake and broken reputations. Least of all is there anything carefree about Degas's depictions of the ballet. When the company moves out before the footlights, its kaleidoscopic pattern of gossamer skirts and flying feet makes a lightly entrancing picture, no doubt; but that is not the picture Degas customarily chooses to see and show. He shows us instead the practice bar, the endless rehearsals, the aching feet, the sweat-stained clothes. What he paints is not the joyous abandon of spontaneous creativity, but robots drilling to execute maneuvers passed down through a chain of command extending back for centuries (page 213). He points out with fearful clarity what in the final polished performance is often hidden—that of all arts the ballet is the most mechanized, that of all artists the ballet dancer is the least free, the perfect symbol of a rigidly organized society.

In these pictures Degas makes his point, as he had in *The Bellelli Family,* primarily through composition; but the type of composition changes. In his earliest works he still used the formal balanced grouping learned at the Ecole des Beaux-Arts; now he makes himself one of the first great masters of spontaneous composition, of the fragmentary "slice of life." The inspiration comes, of course, from Impressionist experiments in cameralike vision; but unlike Pissarro (say), Degas does not use the new vision experimentally. For him it always remains a means to an end, a way of implicitly commenting on the human condition. In every characteristic picture the human figure is intruded upon, chopped up by, subordinated to, the artifacts he has created. In *The Cotton Merchants* (1873, Cambridge, Fogg), for instance, a huge bale angles into the foreground of the picture and pushes into background insignificance the ostensible subjects of the picture. In *The Milliners' Shop* (c. 1882, Chicago) hats and hat racks completely dominate the milliner herself. Perhaps the most obvious example is Degas's handling of the nude as compared to Renoir's. No "female form divine," here; simply one more element in the total composition of a picture, of no more and no less significance than any other. Where Renoir's nudes dominate their surroundings in statuesque majesty, Degas's melt into them; the figures of his bathers, climbing awkwardly and unobtrusively in and out of bathtubs, having their hair dried, and so on, are no longer the most beautiful of all possible objects, but mere providers of interesting contrasts in tone and texture with towels and basins, everywhere broken into and hidden by bits of furniture, curtains, servants bearing teacups, and the like. So are the bodies of Degas's dancers; as for their faces, they are of no more importance than their skirts or slippers, or the stage floor, or the windows and chairs. All Impressionist painters tend, if they follow their own theory of form at all consistently, to obliterate individual personality, subsuming it among effects of light. *Bar at the Folies Bergères, Bastille Day on the Rue de Berne,* or *Le Skating* are typical examples in Manet's work; but Degas does it most consistently and consummately. And in retrospect, the significance is obvious.

On the immediate and practical level, what happened to the human figure in Impressionist painting of the 1870s and later was a parallel to what was happening to the middle class, whose creation and expression Impressionism basically was. When that movement began in the 1850s and -60s, Victorian individualism was at its full high tide. The final vestiges of the social stratification of the 18th century were vanishing, and as they did, individual freedom of expression seemed possible to a degree

24A. *Auguste Renoir:* The Luncheon of the Boating Party. *Washington, The Phillips Collection. 1881.* See also 24B, Degas; 24C, Toulouse-Lautrec.

Recognizing the inherent impasse in Courbet's concept of Reality, many Impressionists frankly abandon attempts at objectivity, take from Impressionist form whichever elements suit them (spontaneous composition, textural surface effects, etc.), and concentrate on the artist's role as social commentator. In retrospect we see in these "social Impressionists" collectively the great expression of liberal bourgeois society at its most luxuriant. In almost the traditional search for Beauty, Renoir records the pleasures of leisure made possible by the progress of industrial capitalism—boating on the river, dancing in the park, and so forth. These are the themes also of Degas, Toulouse-Lautrec, and Seurat—ballet, concerts, jockeys, circuses; but in the way they represent these subjects, the price paid for this new wealth and leisure is made evident—mechanical, robot-like figures, forced into conformity by the pressures of an increasingly organized society, robbed of all individuality, a social system which instead of "loving people and using things" does the opposite. Of this theme, the most powerful representations are Toulouse-Lautrec's brothel scenes.

unheard-of before: "Of all the decades in our history," said G. M. Young of *Victorian England,** "a wise man would choose the 1850s to be young in"; and the same was true all over Europe. But by the later 1870s, many in this generation were beginning to sense that the years of their youth had not been the beginnings of some new era of ever-widening personal freedom; but a time of transition between one kind of restriction and another. The same industrial system that had destroyed the rigid pattern of older societies imposed a pattern of its own. Great trusts began to appear, which it took no supernatural perspicacity to see ultimately pushing small entrepreneurs to the wall. A growing cult of patriotic nation-worship encouraged governments to extend their powers in all directions. Conscription, taxation, regulations of all kinds weighed more heavily on the individual with every passing year, and there was no end in sight. The young man of 1880 faced a very different world from the one his grandfather knew in 1850. Not that all young men—or many people—were consciously aware what had happened: the change was so gradual, so subtle, that most people went on reciting the old creeds of individualism with conviction. Only after the Great War shattered all complacency did the form of the new world shaped and ruled by big business, big government, big labor, big everything, become apparent to the mass of the people. Only in the 1920s did people begin fully to understand what the social Impressionists had been saying; and then they seemed not so much sensitive renderers of the passing scene—much less passive recorders—as the prophets and seers Courbet had urged painters to become.

But as cultural expression, the treatment of human figures in social Impressionist painting had far broader implications; it was part of a wholesale shift in man's thinking about himself in the world, a displacement of man from his old central position in the universe to which every field of human knowledge had been contributing since 1750. It began in history, perhaps, with books like Gibbon's *Decline and Fall of the Roman Empire,* which unmistakably implied (whatever the intentions of the author may have been) that there is an inexorable tide of destiny in

* *Op. cit.*

24B. *Edgar Degas:* Ecole de Danse. *Washington. In the W. A. Clark Collection of The Corcoran Gallery of Art. c. 1880.*

all human affairs which no human ingenuity can forestall and no individual foresight resist. Then there was astronomy, which put man on a tiny, dark, remote planet which had been formed by the chance collision of two insignificant stars, round one of which he circles forever, far from the center even of his own galaxy. Or the economics of Adam Smith, which suggested that human happiness was dependent on possession of good soils, navigable rivers, or useful minerals, and forever at the mercy of time, tide, and the excessive breeding which man was as helpless as any other creature in Nature to prevent. While geologists were implying that terrestrial history had begun long before man ever appeared, physicists were suggesting that it would probably end long after he had vanished; he was merely one of its passing incidents. And now Darwinism made man (or was believed to have made him) the same sort of blind end product of atoms and genes rearranging themselves as trees or turtles or dragonflies. To people at all inclined to credit the theories of science, the old concept of the human form as a specially significant part of Creation, or of the human mind as possessing any special powers of organization and interpretation, seemed unreal. The comforting thought that it was their minds, after all, which were responsible for this interpretation, rarely occurred. Impressionists of all painters were the most susceptible to scientific attitudes, Impressionism having been built to a large extent on a claim to scientific habits of mind. No wonder, then, that this new image of man as simply another part of Nature appears first in Impressionist painting.

So the social Impressionists fit human forms into their pictures as casually as the stage properties painters in the older tradition used to throw in as ballast around the corners of theirs; they cut off arms, legs, or heads by the frame or intervening objects; they make no attempt to organize pictures around whatever human figures are in it. They make no attempt, indeed, to focus the spectator's eye on any object; they let it wander undirected around the picture, stopping or starting where it will. The painter makes no comment and gives no direction. And that, again, is in the spirit of the age. Once upon a time the world had been organized by divine command, and medieval painters tried to show

24C. *Henri de Toulouse-Lautrec:* The Sofa. *New York, The Metropolitan Museum of Art, Rogers Fund. 1894.*

everything *sub specie aeternitatis;* later it was man who gave it purpose and meaning, and Renaissance painters took him for their frame of reference. Now there is no principle of organization; man wanders through life as he does over these pictures, simply meeting one damn thing after another damn thing.

That in these circumstances formal perspective begins to disappear from painting is no surprise. For perspective as Renaissance painters had used it was above all the expression of man's mind controlling the world, the concept that man could and should put everything into a personally intelligible framework of reference. Once deny man that role, and perspective becomes as pointless as it was in the Levantine or Far Eastern worlds, where no systematically intelligible relationship of cause and effect was postulated, where there was no predictable sequence of events, where everything happened according to some inscrutable Fate or Tao or the Will of God, and history was seen as an interminable series of fragmentary episodes whose pattern could never be comprehensible to mortal men. Hence the curious resemblance of the social Impressionists' compositions to Persian and Turkish miniatures they had never seen; hence their great enthusiasm for Japanese prints which they consciously admired for pure line, form and pattern, and unconsciously because they were beginning to share the view of a world no longer under man's control. As yet the social Impressionists were not entirely aware of their own motivations, but the Impressionist generation immediately following Degas is already conscious that, in a world where human intelligence no longer guides and commands, the other great Renaissance concept—the unique value of individual personality—necessarily becomes meaningless; Reality demands that it, along with perspective, should disappear from painting. Of this development, the great representative is Toulouse-Lautrec.

Lautrec was a devoted admirer of Degas and showed it in the sincerest form, by choosing much the same sort of mechanized occupations as subjects, and painting them with the same eclectically Impressionist techniques and compositional devices. But the spirit of his social commentary is subtly different. It is possible to read sympathy into even the most biting of Degas's commentaries; not so, Lautrec's. His view of life is harsh, cruel, remorseless. The many pictures—or often sketches —Lautrec made of the night-club life he frequented show these characteristic qualities very well. The people he depicts here are not individuals with personalities of their own; they are not even people whose personalities are suppressed by routine. They are not people at all, but things, moving in fixed behavioral grooves, like birds in migration or bees building a honeycomb. Usually their hopelessly depersonalized condition is implicit in the composition, which cuts off and breaks up heads and bodies and faces even more savagely than in Degas's work; in the color—unnaturally green faces, yellow skin, red hair, and harsh color combinations everywhere; or in gestures and attitudes—rigid habitués sitting with glazed eye while "entertainment takes place" before them, dancers whose gaiety is all the more chillingly forced, whose routines are all the more fearfully stereotyped, because they, unlike Degas's ballerinas, are supposed to be performing freely and spontaneously. Sometimes it is explicit, as in the portraits of clowns and singers, like Yvette Guilbert or Jane Avril, where the synthetic character of the personality manufactured for them by mask and exotic costume is made so heartlessly evident, or even more in works like *Jane Avril Leaving the Moulin Rouge,* in which we see the "star" reduced to her original nameless self— a forlorn undistinguished body floating aimlessly through the world, borne along on a mass of pointillistic dots, symbol of human rootlessness and despair, of man adrift in a hostile universe.

You can see Lautrec's characteristic qualities even better in his circus themes. In them there is nothing of the innocent acts of earlier times, strolling performers at country fairs; compared to Lautrec, the performers of Watteau and Daumier were figures of majesty. For he makes of the circus a power symbol—behind these acts which make such elegant designs there stands the ringmaster with his whip, and the paymaster with his power, who force acrobat and rider to ever more unnatural feats that only crippling death can end. But it was in the brothel that Lautrec found his great and ultimate symbols of the human condition.

Of all Toulouse-Lautrec's pictures, his brothel scenes are perhaps the most famous; certainly they are the most significant. What was it that attracted him to this subject? Not any erotic implications, that is sure; nothing could be less pornographic than the blowzy, lumpy, ruined fragments of humanity he painted (page 215). Rather it was the fact that they were ruined, that they had, as the Victorians saw it, practically lost their membership in the human race, that their personality had been destroyed, that they were valueless as individuals. For what Toulouse-Lautrec, like all advance-guard painters, wanted to show was Reality, and here, in this subject, he thought to show the Reality of the human condition. These whores are no longer people; they are things to be used

217

and discarded, like tin cans or old theatre tickets. Which is really no more than a particularly dramatic way of saying what is implied in Seurat's or Degas's handling of the human figure in their paintings—that between man and the rest of the physical universe, between people and things, there is no real difference.

Toulouse-Lautrec, his critics said, was a wicked and immoral man, a perverted exhibitionist who flaunted sin in the public's face. But from his point of view, that made no sense. Sin has been succinctly defined as "loving things and using people." If you don't recognize any difference between people and things, sin is only a word; you may be guilty of error, but that is something else. Again, immorality implies opposing or breaking some accepted code of behavior. But "things" can have no code of behavior. You cannot call an animal immoral; it is *a*moral. And that is the state of affairs here. The concept of man as developed by social Impressionists like Degas, Seurat, and Toulouse-Lautrec cannot properly be called antihumanism; it is *a*human. In Lautrec's case there can be no doubt at all. More than one writer has suggested that had it not been for the childhood accidents to his legs which left him a dwarf, he might well have passed his life as a country gentleman, pursuing the avocations of the aristocracy to which he belonged; be that as it may, it surely takes no deep insight into psychology to see how his deformity affected his view of the world. Small wonder that as he grew into manhood he saw the world in terms of his own alienation; that the Reality he painted would be the harsh bitterness he knew. Lautrec was among the first to make the content of his art fully subjective; in this sense he belongs among the great Post-Impressionists who brought the New Painting to maturity.

NOTES

Renoir's divergence from orthodox Impressionism began when he was apprenticed to a porcelain manufacturer in his native Limoges, and set to decorate chinaware with copies of 18th-century Rococo paintings, their fragile forms enhanced by the characteristic softness of the medium. He then fell successively under the influence of Delacroix, and of photographic literalism; by 1870, when he painted *Bather with Griffon* (São Paolo, Brazil), a "realistic" version of a classical Venus type, he was imitating Courbet. Becoming friends with Monet, he initiated his long series of leisure-time themes in a distinctive variant of pointillistic form; to the 1870s and early

1880s belong his most popular works. Typical examples are *Moulin de la Galette* (1876, Louvre); *The Swing* (1876, Louvre); *The Loge* (c. 1876, Louvre); *Madame Charpentier and Her Daughters* (1878, New York, Metropolitan); *Boating Party at Chatou* (1879, Washington); *Luncheon of the Boating Party* (page 211); *Dance at Bougival* (1833, Boston).

In the course of the 1880s, he, like Monet, found himself progressively free of financial worries and able to experiment with form. His main preoccupation was to give "realistic" expression to classical themes; thus the large *Bathers* of 1884–87 is a reinterpretation of a late 17th-century relief by François Giraudon at Versailles, *Two Girls at the Piano* (1892, Louvre) might be related to Renaissance idealizations of music, and his many late bathers (e.g., *Three Bathers,* Cleveland; *Judgment of Paris,* Philadelphia, McIlhenny; *Seated Bather,* Cambridge, Fogg) to the classical tradition of Beauty generally. The many Renoirs from all periods in the Barnes Foundation at Merion, Pa., are illustrated (along with others) in A. C. Barnes and V. de Mazia, *The Art of Renoir* (Philadelphia, 1944). Other books on Renoir include those by D. Rouart (1954), P. Haesaerts (sculpture, 1948), J. Rewald, ed. (drawings, 1946), M. S. Fox (1952), and Germain Bazin (1939). M. Drucker, *Renoir* (1949) has a full bibliography to that date.

Degas's career began with his entry into the Ecole des Beaux-Arts in 1855, studying with a pupil of Ingres. In *The Bellelli Family,* which he exhibited in 1859, he demonstrated both how well he had mastered traditional classical form, and how far he would depart from classical content in the interests of Reality. The implications of Reality were further explored in his series of legendary and mythological subjects beginning with *Spartan Boys and Girls Exercising* (1860, London) and ending with *The Miseries of the City of Orléans* (1865, Louvre). From 1865 on he began associating with the Impressionists, whose influence was reflected in formal experimentation with texture and spontaneous composition (e.g., *Woman with Chrysanthemums,* 1865, New York, Metropolitan) and content drawn from everyday life; his continuing interest in horseracing and ballet themes begins at this time (e.g., *A Carriage at the Races,* 1870–73, Boston; *Races at Longchamp,* c. 1873–75, Boston; first ballet themes c. 1872–73). From October 1872 to April 1873 he visited with relatives in New Orleans, and a definite trend towards social commentary sets in soon thereafter, represented by *The Cotton Office, New Orleans* (1873, Pau); *The Cotton Merchants* (1873, Cambridge, Fogg); *Interior: The Viol,* illustrating a scene from Zola's *Madeleine Férat* (1874, Philadelphia); *Absinthe* (1876, Louvre); *Cafe Singers* (1876–77, Washington, Corcoran); *Singer with Glove* (1878, Cambridge, Fogg).

During the 1880s he was particularly interested in experiments and innovation in media—*peinture a l'essence* (oil paint thinned with turpentine and blotted), superimposed layers of pastel, gouache, egg tempera, many

219

kinds of etching and aquatint; he also did more than seventy works of sculpture in wax, from which bronze casts have been made. As his eyesight began to fail pastel became his favorite medium; by 1898 he was almost blind. Books on Degas include those by P. A. Lemoisne (Paris, 1954), Georges de Traz (François Fosca, 1954), E. Hüttinger (1960), P. Cabanne (1958), D. C. Rich (1951), C. Mauclair (1945), and J. Meier-Graefe (1923). On Degas's sculpture, J. Rewald (1956); on his portraits, J. S. Boggs (Berkeley, 1962).

Toulouse-Lautrec was born in 1864, into the old aristocracy of the Midi; the accidents that crippled him occurred when he was fourteen or fifteen. In 1882 he began his serious study of art in Paris, and by 1885 had a studio in Montmartre, where he soon began frequenting nightclubs—especially the Moulin de la Galette and the Moulin Rouge, making paintings, sketches, and posters of the activities and personalities there: among them singer and song-writer Aristide Bruant, dancers La Goulue and Jane Avril, singers Yvette Guilbert, May Belfort, and May Milton, and celebrated habitués like Maxime Dethomas. His first exhibitions were at the Salon des Independants in 1889 and with Les Vingt in Brussels, and in 1891 his first posters brought him immediate recognition. His first color prints were made in 1892, and his first one-man show was held in 1893. In 1895 he made the first of several visits to England, where he came to know Aubrey Beardsley and Oscar Wilde. By 1898 his health was beginning to break down, and he died from dissipation in 1901. He worked prolifically in many media; typical examples are to be found in most museums—e.g., *Ring Master* and *The Moulin Rouge* (Chicago), *Monsieur Boileau au Café* (Cleveland), *Yvette Guilbert Taking a Curtain-call* (Providence, Rhode Island School of Design), *La Goulue Entering the Moulin Rouge* (New York, Museum of Modern Art). Books on Toulouse-Lautrec include those by M. Joyant (2 vols., Paris, 1926), G. Jedlicka (Paris, 1929), Gerstle Mack (1938), Francis Jourdain (1951), Douglas Cooper (1952), R. Wilenski (London, 1955), Hanspeter Landolt (Drawings and Sketches, 1955).

Significant parallels and comparisons in literature to social Impressionism in painting are provided in Chapters 19 and 20 of Erich Auerbach, *Mimesis* (Princeton, 1953).

IV

Impressionism
as an International Style

BY THE MID-1880S, THE TRIUMPH OF IMPRESSIONISM IN French painting seemed assured. Only louts still laughed at it; and if the majority still preferred Bouguereau over Monet, a growing minority appreciated (if not always entirely understood) Impressionism enough to support its older practitioners financially. Most significantly, the rising generation was coming to take Reality for granted as the goal of art, even though not always explicitly conscious of the fact. As a result, Impressionism by the 1890s had become what the Attic Greek language had become in Antiquity—a koine, a common international language of form spreading far beyond its place of origin to serve all sorts of people for all sorts of purposes. And just as in that process Attic Greek soon lost all its original subtle nuances and graces in foreign mouths, so now Impressionist techniques, divorced from the rationale which had originally inspired them and used often for ends antipathetic to it, were rapidly altered—transformed, subsumed, vulgarized, distorted, as circumstances determined. All at once, it seemed, anything like a central tradition in European painting disappeared, and in its place came a bewildering succession of conflicting new movements and moribund old ones, chaotic new theories, blind searchings for new foundations.

In retrospect, however, we can see that there were two distinct and divergent lines of development. On the one hand, there was a small number of painters whom we now recognize as *the* great Post-Impressionists, chief among them Cézanne, Van Gogh, and Gauguin; taking from Impressionism its central and basic idea of the search for Reality, they realized that for painters this could only be interpreted subjectively, and proceeded to develop an appropriate formal structure for the purpose. On the other was a much larger and much more immediately successful number of painters who tacitly or explicitly rejected Reality as

221

an end, but took from Impressionism such technical means as loose brush stroke, high-keyed palette, or patterned picture surface, and used them to rejuvenate the old tradition of Beauty. Within this group were wide differences of class and motivation; it included what we may identify, very broadly, as Academic Impressionism, Impressionistic Symbolism, Popular Impressionism, Aesthetic Impressionism, and, as a kind of summation of them all, Art Nouveau.

1

Academic Impressionism:

John Singer Sargent (1856–1925)

By the late 19th century the social upheaval precipitated by the Industrial Revolution was visibly subsiding. A class structure based on the wealth of industrial capitalism was firmly established. In contrast to the fluid situation of half a century earlier, most of the upper class now had a generation or two of wealth and social position behind them, and while still far from ready or able to assume the older aristocracy's traditional role of cultural leadership, were rapidly dropping their earlier middle-class outlook and values. The taste for anecdotage and literal naturalism in painting, inherited from the realism of early popular arts, was fading; and as it did, more and more of the upper class were able to appreciate and willing to patronize what only a couple of decades before they would have called the "daubings" of brush-stroke or pointillistic Impressionism.

Among the first to capitalize on the new situation was John Singer Sargent. Sargent was to Manet rather what Doré had been to Delacroix —a great adapter, who made advance-guard concepts and techniques palatable to a wide audience by compromising old and new. He sensed that by the 1880s the chief objection to brush-stroke Impressionism was not the technique but the subject matter, or, more specifically, Manet's "scientific" indifference to subject; furthermore, he realized that in portraiture brush-stroke Impressionism had many advantages. Once upon a time, to have a portrait of oneself was a mark of solid bourgeois success in life, but now, with the advance of photography, to have a likeness to pass down for the admiration of posterity was no longer a rare accomplishment. Anyone with a few dollars or francs could have a portrait on his wall, a likeness as good as the invisible-brush-stroke portraits of the old Academic masters. But a painting done in the distinctive brush-stroke style of Manet was quite a different matter. That was really and obviously a painting; that cost money. Sargent, raised in a wealthy cosmopolitan society, seized the opportunity. He also had the ability to make the most of it; no one, however ill-disposed to all Sargent stood for socially or in the history of art, can fail to respond to the sparkle and brilliance of his flashing brushwork that so brilliantly depicts the notables of late 19th-century and Edwardian society. Indeed, Sargent's deft paint handling rivaled and on occasion surpassed Manet's; and when combined with a comparable mastery of Manet's kind of casual and spontaneous composition, could result in breath-taking exhibitions of virtuosity, in likenesses of astonishing immediacy.

But though their means are the same, they pursue very different ends. Except in Sargent's earliest works and some of his sketches, he shows nothing of Manet's uncompromising search for Reality. His brush-stroke Impressionism is used to create images of sage and dignified financiers, serene matrons of means, *nouveaux-riches* striking the poses of 18th-century English aristocrats—portraits which remind us not of Manet, but of Titian, Bernini, Van Dyck, and above all, Reynolds and Gainsborough. "Historians tell us Alexander the Great was low and mean in appearance; the painter ought not so to represent him"—Reynolds's classical formula for idealizing the lords and ladies of 18th-century England is Sargent's guide in painting the plutocracy of the Edwardian age. However fashionably realistic his technique, Sargent's objective is idealized Beauty. As Reynolds made Mrs. Siddons a modern counterpart of the Delphic Sibyl of the Sistine Ceiling, so Sargent makes the daughters of Sir Percy Wyndham (1899, New York, Metropolitan) reincarnations of Phidian goddesses on the pediment of the Parthenon. And, of course, he enjoys the same success. More, indeed; for, like the "revival of the Revivals" going on in architecture at the same time, Sargent's kind of respectable Impressionism, satisfyingly up-to-date in form, safely conservative in content, perfectly suited the psychological needs of a new upper class, still uncertain of its perquisites and position, for an art which could be patronized in the traditional way without risking any exposure of its still shaky taste. No wonder, then, that

223

Sargent was only one of dozens of painters—from Academicians to peripheral members of the Impressionist movement—to work for this vast new market.

If Academic Impressionism can be said to have had a founder, a good candidate for that distinction would be Franz Xaver Winterhalter (1806–1873) of Bavaria, who perpetuated the 18th-century Grand Style of portraiture far into the 19th, and in his later works at least intimated how it might incorporate the new Impressionist brush stroke; but the leading figures in it all belonged to the generation born around 1860. Anders Zorn (1860–1920) from Mora in Sweden, famous for buxom Swedish nudes, for peasant scenes à la Barbizon, and for translating the mannerisms of brush-stroke Impressionism into etching with a result rather like the pen-and-ink style of C. D. Gibson; Joaquín Sorolla y Bastida (1863–1923) from Valencia; Sir John Lavery (1856–1941), Walter Sickert (1860–1942), and Augustus John (1878–1961) from England—they all were part of an international school comparable to the one that flourished when the popes lived at Avignon half a millennium before. And like that medieval International Style, Academic Impressionism was the sophisticated expression of a sunset era, the last glow of a social order soon to collapse. Its inherent contradiction between traditional ends and revolutionary means, between the old goal of Beauty and the techniques of the new realism, is an exact counterpart to the inherent contradictions within European civilization during the decades before the

25. *John Singer Sargent:* Lady Warwick and Her Son. *Worcester (Mass.) Art Museum. 1901.*

By the end of the 19th century an Academic Impressionism, depending on Impressionist techniques generally and Manet's brush stroke in particular, had become an accepted manner of painting for the upper classes. Sargent was one of its most typical representatives; in his portraits are perfectly mirrored the values and outlook of Edwardian society. Comparing his work with Manet's, however, it becomes obvious that he has only taken over the surface characteristics of Impressionism, not the rationale which inspired it. His goal is still Beauty; he idealizes his subjects quite in the spirit of Reynolds, making rich men look noble, peasants picturesque, and the like.

Great War—between systems of government originating in smaller, compacter, technologically simpler preindustrial times, and the ever more complicated and explosively destructive forces being generated by urbanization, rapid technological advances, irredentist nationalism. On more levels than one, Academic Impressionism was the mirror of those leaders of the old order who, in Edmond Taylor's expressive image from *The Fall of the Dynasties,** rode helplessly like engineers on a runaway train, desperately pulling knobs and levers, calling on all the old formulae of government, only to find them useless in controlling the catastrophic march of events.

NOTES

Sargent was born in 1856 in Florence; his parents, of Boston and Philadelphia origins, had permanently retired to live in Europe. He studied in Rome, in Florence, and in Paris at the studio of Carolus Duran; made his first visit to the United States, to establish his citizenship, in 1876. In 1883 he established a studio in Paris with (among others) his counterpart the Italian Giovanni Boldini (1845–1931); in 1885, at Whistler's suggestion, he moved to London and made Whistler's old studio permanent headquarters. His trips to the United States, and especially to Boston, became increasingly frequent, however, particularly after making the acquaintance of Mrs. Jack Gardner in 1886, and securing the first of his large commissions for murals at the Boston Public Library (1890, finally completed 1925). Among the better known of his works are *El Jaleo* (1881, Boston, Fenway), and *Mrs. Jack Gardner* (1888, Boston, Fenway); *Madame X* (*Mrs. Pierre Gautreau*, 1883, New York, Metropolitan—the painting which precipitated his leaving Paris); *The Wyndham Sisters* (1899, New York, Metropolitan); *Robert Louis Stevenson* (1884, Cincinnati, Taft); *The Boit Children* (1882, Boston). A useful reference is David McKibbin, *Sargent's Boston* (1956, Boston, Museum of Fine Arts).

* *Op. cit.*

2

Impressionism in the Popular Arts:

Wilhelm Busch (1832–1908)
Charles Dana Gibson (1867–1944)

It was inevitable that Academic Impressionism should influence the popular arts pervasively and soon. In this development the work of Wilhelm Busch in the Munich humor magazine *Fliegende Blätter* (page 229) was of outstanding importance. As a serious painter, Busch shared the typical interests of his time in instantaneous effects; as a cartoonist, his experiments in the 1860s and -70s with various means of achieving greater vividness of effect resulted in a new convention for suggesting movement—a series of broken lines extending outwards from the edge of a "moving" object (really a shorthand abbreviation of the kind of sequence of overlapping images produced by multiple photographic exposures). By the 1890s Busch's invention had become standard practice among popular artists, and was eagerly seized on by creators of the new comic strips, where vivid indications of action were essential. Curiously enough, essentially the same convention made a great sensation when adopted in advance-guard circles a few years later. The Futurists in particular made much of it; and paintings like Giacomo Balla's *Dog on Leash* (1912, New York, A. Conger Goodyear) or *Swifts: Paths of Movement* (page 322) were hailed as brilliant innovations in a new field, with little if any apparent awareness of the fact that in this instance the popular arts were influencing advance-guard painting rather than vice versa.

By the 1870s, approximately, the popular arts had reached maturity; from then on, their several functions in society had been fairly well defined. There was an upper-class popular art, concerned with sophisticated commentary on political and social foibles, which characteristically appeared in magazines like Busch's *Fliegende Blätter, Punch* in England, *Charivari* in France, *Judge* and the old *Life* in America; a middle-class popular art, dedicated to information and persuasion, represented best by the arts of illustration, political cartooning, and advertising; and a lower-class popular art whose purpose was primarily entertainment. Academic

Impressionism influenced them all to varying degrees. Upper-class popular art, directed to an educated class, had correspondingly advanced forms; in the work of leading upper-class cartoonists of the 1890s and 1900s like Caran D'Ache and Max Beerbohm in England or Charles Dana Gibson in America (facing page)—and, of course, Busch—you could recognize plentiful borrowings and influences from Manet, Degas, and Toulouse-Lautrec. The middle-class public was not so ready to accept the new techniques (Thomas Nast, for instance, though contemporary with Wilhelm Busch, had no impressionistic elements in his style of political cartooning), and they only became common in middle-class

26A. *Wilhelm Busch:* Finale Furioso, *from* Der Virtuos, *in* Fliegende Blätter, *Munich, 1865.*

26B. *Charles Dana Gibson:* The Greatest Game in the World—His Move. Collier's Magazine, *1901.*

26C. *E. C. Segar:* Popeye and Toar, *two boxes from* Thimble Theatre, *November 21, 1935.*

Though abandoned by the most advance-guard painters in the 1880s, Impressionist techniques early became and long remained a lingua franca for Western art on other social and intellectual levels. Thus, in the popular arts, Wilhelm Busch was experimenting with time-space conventions as early as the 1860s; by 1900 C. D. Gibson (among others) had developed a distinctive kind of pen-and-ink Impressionism for illustration and cartooning; and in comic strips, Impressionist conventions have been standard since c. 1910. Here E. C. Segar (1891–1938) uses a whole battery of them to dramatize the exploits of his folk hero, Popeye. Popeye as Segar conceived the character was the American Hercules; immortal, indestructible, champion of the weak and the underdog, tangible symbol of the virtues and values of his society, he came of no ordinary parentage, matured precociously, had a son but no wife. The long suspense sequences in Thimble Theatre *from 1932–38, some of them running a year in length, were American folk epics; a far cry from the infantile stereotypes* Popeye *became in later hands, they deserve republication.*

popular arts during the 1910–1920 decade—compare, for example, the Manetlike technique of James Montgomery Flagg's illustrations with the still very 19th-century Academic anecdotage of Howard Pyle at the turn of the century. As for the lower-class popular arts, they remained substantially uninfluenced by Impressionistic techniques until the 1920s. Early motion pictures were almost invariably composed in terms of the boxlike stage convention of Academic anecdotal painting; as late as 1916, D. W. Griffith was "pioneering" in the kind of casual spontaneous angle-composition made common by Degas and Monet in the 1870s. And though Busch's space-time convention for suggesting movement, derived from his Impressionistic studies, was adopted early by comic-strip cartoonists, it was stylized and perpetuated without significant change (as often happens in quasi-folk arts) for decades; only with the development of "suspense strips" in the 1930s—*Tarzan* being the first—did techniques comparable to Gibson's or Flagg's graphic impressionism become common in lower-class arts. In compensation, of course, Impressionism still remains the dominant technical vehicle in the popular arts to this day.

NOTES

On Busch, see Fritz M. Novotny, *Wilhelm Busch als Zeichner und Maler* (Vienna, 1949); for illustrations of his work, O. Nöldeke, *Busch: Samtliche Werke* (Munich, 1943) and *Albums* (Munich, 1955; Freiburg, 1955, by H., A., and O. Nöldeke). On Gibson, Fairfax Downey, *Portrait of an Era as drawn by C. D. Gibson* (1936); on comics, Coulton Waugh, *The Comics* (1947). Alexander Dorner, in *The Way Beyond Art* (1947, p. 121), has discussed to what extent Busch (and so the popular arts) anticipated by nearly fifty years Futurist depiction of a Reality of movement.

3

Impressionistic Symbolism:

Gustave Moreau (1824–1898)
Odilon Redon (1840–1916)
The Nabis

> The weakness of M. Manet and of all those who, like him, want to limit themselves to the literal reproduction of reality, is to sacrifice man and his thought to good brush work, to the brilliant handling of a detail. . . . As a result their figures lack . . . intimate and inner life. . . . It is on this point that true artists find themselves in decided opposition to paltry and restricted research. Although they recognize the necessity for a basis of *seen* reality, to them true art lies in a reality that is *felt*.

So Odilon Redon, a young painter of Bordeaux, commented in a letter to *La Gironde* criticizing the Salon of 1868.* Here he defined the rationale of what later would come to be known as the Symbolist movement in late 19th-century painting—a reassertion of the primacy of imagination over naturalistic realism. Redon's analysis was extraordinarily perceptive, foreseeing the inner contradictions between concepts of the artist as creator and as mechanical eye on which Impressionism later foundered. It was also paradoxical; precisely that loose Impressionistic brushwork which Redon deprecated became the means whereby the Symbolists could pursue their visions free of the technical restrictions of academic discipline.

You could see this development plainly in the work of the earliest exemplar and *de facto* founder of the Symbolist movement, Gustave Moreau. Moreau's first important picture was *Oedipus and the Sphinx,* exhibited in 1864 (New York, Metropolitan), which invited obvious comparison with a painting by Ingres of the same subject sixty years earlier (1808, Louvre). In forms and technique, Moreau followed Ingres's classical tradition; in content, however, the emphasis was quite different. Where Ingres had represented a statuesque figure standing

* Quoted by J. Rewald in catalogue to the Redon-Moreau-Bresdin exhibition, (New York, Museum of Modern Art, 1961), pp. 19–20.

with one foot on a rock in balanced colloquy with the Sphinx opposite, Moreau depicted the Sphinx clinging to Oedipus's waist and staring directly into the hero's eyes, so that the two figures were in effect fused into a symbol of that eternal wrestling with the mysteries of life which goes on relentlessly within the soul of every individual. For such a mystic interpretation classical forms were totally unsuitable, of course; and Moreau was quite aware of the resulting bizarre incongruity of content with form. To resolve it became the central problem of his life. Throughout his later years, the content of Moreau's art remained extraordinarily consistent. Classical subjects of Europa, Prometheus, Galatea, Hercules, Leda, Semele; Biblical subjects of Salomé (facing page), the Angel of Death, Delilah, the meditative David, Jacob wrestling with the Angel; medieval subjects of the Temptation of Saint Anthony, the woman with the unicorn, the Satanic Decameron, the Fables of Lafontaine—they were all variants of a single theme, the inner warfare of reason with imagination, duty with passion, logic with intuition. In this content is the vital difference between Moreau's Symbolism and the romanticism of Delacroix's generation which, at first sight, it resembles. In paintings like Delacroix's *Dante and Virgil* or *The Capture of Weislingen* (page 83), "beautiful feelings" are evoked by external objects and events, but in Moreau's works they are evoked by a subjective drama of which external objects or events are only symbols. This being so, there is no point in any literal description of these external things; and as Moreau comes steadily to realize that fact, there is a corresponding change in the forms of his art. Classical composition is gradually abandoned, sharp line is dissolved, defined color areas are broken up into stretches of broken Impressionistic brushwork, until finally in his latest works Moreau paints so freely and loosely that 20th-century Expressionists could claim him for a spiritual ancestor. Where Delacroix evokes the spectator's response primarily by what he paints and only secondarily by

27A. *Gustave Moreau:* Salomé Dancing before Herod. *New York, The Gallery of Modern Art including The Huntington Hartford Collection. 1876.* See also 27B, Redon.

A typical work of Moreau's middle period, it is looser and more painterly in form than· in the 1860s, but still a mass of elaborate extrinsic symbols.

how (color, brushwork, and so on), with Moreau it is the other way around.

A comparable pattern is apparent in the work of Moreau's admirer and follower, Odilon Redon. A younger man and consequently always freer of academic disciplines, Redon's content was correspondingly less literal and anecdotal than Moreau's, and he used Impressionistic techniques from the first. Where Moreau's Symbolism was elaborately iconographic, Redon's was allusive: classical subjects—one-eyed Cyclops (facing page), Phaetons, Andromedas—vaguely suggest the supernatural powers and mysteries of life without describing them; fantasies on death; winged heads; weeping spiders; eyes in the forest; plant forms of all kinds evocative of the secrets of the universe. In form, Redon progressed from obvious derivations from pointillism to free masses of paint which formed and reformed like clouds over his canvas.

It remained for the Nabis to complete the final dissolution of Impressionistic form, however. This short-lived organization of young painters, formed in 1888, defunct ten years later, and ostentatiously named after the Hebrew *Nebiim* ("prophets"), affected Moreau's and Redon's kind of abstruse symbolic content with a self-conscious directness and pomposity quite foreign to the older masters; they proclaimed themselves, on the strength of their manifestoes, "bound together by the mystic cords of understanding and the condition of being closer to the truth than others." And in the same self-conscious manner, they pushed the implications of Impressionistic form to an ultimate conclusion: the one statement for which the Nabis are chiefly remembered today was Maurice

27B. *Odilon Redon:* Cyclops. *Lithograph. Collection, The Museum of Modern Art, New York, Gift of Victor S. Riesenfeld. 1883.*

According to a theory popular in occult circles at the end of the 19th century, the Cyclops legend recalled the existence of a "median eye," an organ of mystic perception now reduced to a rudimentary pineal gland; Adolf Hitler, among others, was fascinated by the power implications of this idea.

Concurrently with Academic and Aesthetic Impressionism, Impressionistic means were being made into a vehicle for creating expressive images symbolic of moods and emotions and the imaginative life of the mind by Symbolic Impressionists like Moreau and Redon.

Denis's "Any painting, before being a battle steed, a nude woman, or some anecdote, is essentially a flat surface covered with colors arranged in a certain order." Such a premise was always inherent in Impressionist theory, of course; but in carrying it to such an extreme the Nabis distorted the original rationale of Impressionism even more completely in their way than did the Academic Impressionists in theirs.

NOTES

Moreau's public image was first established at the Salon of 1867, where he exhibited a *Salomé* and *Hercules and the Lernean Hydra* (Chicago, Richard L. Feigen), both of them much clearer in their symbolism than most later work—the *Hercules* no burly adventurer, but the archetype of sensitive artist-poet, with an almost androgynous body, combating Philistine hostility; the *Salomé* obviously exhibiting the idea of man's reason conquered by his passions. A majority of Moreau's works are conserved in the Musée Gustave Moreau, Paris; in America, besides the large *Salomé* in the Huntington Hartford Gallery of Modern Art, New York, the Fogg Art Museum in Cambridge has *The Sirens* of c. 1880 and *David Meditating* of 1878. Dating Moreau's works is difficult because, as his first biographer Ary Renan wrote in *Gustave Moreau* (Paris, 1900), Moreau carried "obsessions" on certain themes for years and was constantly reworking his canvases. R. van Holten, *L'Art fantastique de Gustave Moreau* (Paris, 1960) contains the most complete list of Moreau's work; in English, see Dore Ashton, "Gustave Moreau" in the catalogue to the Redon-Moreau-Bresdin exhibition at the Museum of Modern Art, 1961.

This catalogue also contains a definitive essay on Redon by John Rewald. Redon's significance in the advance-guard movement is clear from such statements as "The future belongs to a subjective world," and his development of a content—especially fantastic vegetable forms—of no fixed meaning. There are many drawings and lithographs by Redon in American collections; typical of his paintings of flowers is *The Large Green Vase* in Boston and *The Apparition* of c. 1910 in the Princeton University Art Museum.

The Nabis are well described in John Rewald, *History of Post-Impressionism* (1956). Redon and Gauguin provided the chief inspiration for its two spokesmen, Maurice Denis (1870–1943) and Paul Sérusier (1863–1927). It is typical of the loose-knit Nabi group that Pierre Bonnard (1867–1947) and Edouard Vuillard (1868–1940) were associated with it even though differing from Denis and Sérusier in frankly favoring Impressionist ends and means, and having little interest in symbolic expression.

4

Aesthetic Impressionism:

James McNeill Whistler (1834–1903)
Pierre Bonnard (1867–1947)

James McNeill Whistler should have been the man to introduce the New Reality to American painting. Born, bred, and well-connected in the United States, he came to Paris in 1855, at just the right moment to meet and understand the leaders of the advance-guard movement in painting—Courbet, Manet, Degas. Whistler was one of the first to appreciate the true significance of the Japanese prints which had begun to appear in the West after Japan's centuries of isolation ended in the 1850s, and to see that such works, whose subject matter was generally unknown or without much meaning even when it was ascertainable, forced people to think and see entirely in terms of pictorial qualities, of line and pattern and color; to adapt them as demonstrations of the principle that Reality in painting is intrinsic, not a matter of copying anything outside itself. Furthermore, Whistler was highly articulate; in his letters and writings he reiterated his ideas that painting should be appreciated like music, for itself alone, without the support of any extraneous associative ideas; that therefore the subject matter of pictures was immaterial, and counter-feiting the outward appearances of things no proper business of painters; that inasmuch as painters are the only competent judges of what is or is not Reality in art, "laymen" have no business talking about painting at all. Acting on his own theories, he steadily dissolved his subjects into masses of nondescriptive color entitled "symphonies," "nocturnes," and the like, until by the 1870s he was producing canvases consisting substantially of great areas of paint only vaguely suggesting natural forms. The net effect was curiously reminiscent of the late works of Turner; but John Ruskin, Turner's great champion in earlier years, was perceptive enough to see that however similar Whistler's ultimate prod-uct, the process by which he arrived at it involved quite different, and to him fraudulently wrong, premises. Thereupon Ruskin publicly accused Whistler of being a "coxcomb" bent on making a mockery of art by "flinging a pot of paint in the public's face." Whistler sued, and technically won the well-publicized case; but the court's contemptuous

237

award of only a farthing's damages neatly manifested its real verdict.

Retrospective writers have commonly maintained that in this case the public demonstrated its usual stupidity and blindness; or explained the reaction in America particularly by the extraneous and fortuitous circumstance that John Ruskin happened to be Whistler's adversary; for Ruskin's sociological writings had almost Biblical authority for precisely those progressives of the 1870s and 1880s who might have been expected to be the most ardent partisans of new movements generally, and especially of a "persecuted radical." Yet the public judgment on Whistler was not wholly wrong. For the fact is that there was an undesirable element of deceit in Whistler's presentation of "modern painting."

However inarticulately, people recognized that Whistler was appropriating the poses and trappings of the artist as social seer and critic without accepting the corresponding integrity of purpose the New Reality demanded. Whistler was in fact a compromiser, not of the same kind, but of the same order, as the Academic Impressionists. For all his dissolution of Thames riverscapes into nondescriptive "symphonies" and nocturnes" of color expanses punctuated with spots and streaks, for all the aesthetic delicacy of his etchings, for all his egregious insistence that the portrait of his mother was a mere *Arrangement in Grey and Black,* and his portrait of Thomas Carlyle merely *Arrangement in Grey and Black No. 2,* they remained "beautiful" in the old sense nonetheless, and Whistler knew it. His ultimate intention was not to present truth or realism but to provide an aesthetic experience; he was using Impressionistic means and the Impressionists' advance-guard prestige for a fundamentally romantic end. In this sense, Ruskin was right; compared to

28A. *James McNeill Whistler:* Caprice in Purple and Gold: The Golden Screen. *Washington, Smithsonian Institution, Freer Gallery of Art. 1864.* See also 28B, Bonnard.

An early and later example of Aesthetic Impressionism, using Impressionist clichés of brushwork, surface patterns, and textures to create an art dedicated not to Reality, but to the pure "art for art's sake" which came to be so typical of the aesthetic intellectual of the 1880s and -90s.

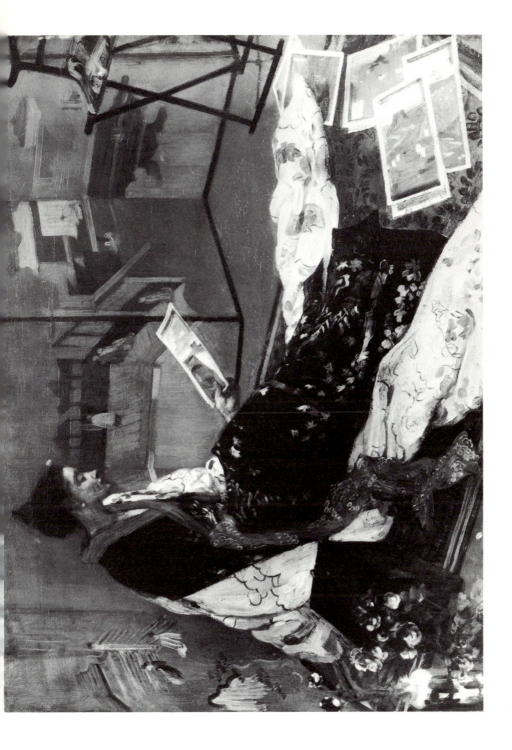

Turner, Whistler confused ends and means with flagrant and conscious dishonesty. That Whistler should be best known to the 20th-century American public not as a fearless leader of the modern movement, but as the creator of one of the most saccharine images of Mother's Day, is paradoxical, perhaps, but hardly unfair.

Much more honest, and so fundamentally much more significant, was the Aesthetic Impressionism of Pierre Bonnard. Like Whistler, Bonnard used Impressionistic means for the end of aesthetic effect rather than any presentation of Reality as such; but he had no illusions about what he was doing, and consequently achieved it much more effectively. No flourish of trumpets, but the sale of a poster he had designed to advertise champagne in 1889, persuaded Bonnard's father to agree to his son's switching from the study of law to painting; and this unpretentious beginning was symptomatic of Bonnard's whole future career. Though the poster attracted and had definite influence on Toulouse-Lautrec (he became a friend of Bonnard's in consequence) and though Bonnard was associated with the original Nabis group, he had no aspirations to the status of a great or godlike creator, and soon drifted away. By the early 1900s Bonnard had developed a quiet sort of painting which he perfected and refined with extraordinary consistency over the next four decades. He painted simple, unobtrusive subjects (luncheon tables [facing page]), small street scenes, inconsequential people doing inconsequential things) with a correspondingly simple and unobtrusive emphasis on the appeal of paint surfaces and textural qualities: "If there exists such a thing as the exquisiteness of banality," as Rewald once put it neatly, "that was exactly what Bonnard discovered." In short, Bonnard isolated and brought to perfection that strain within the Impressionist movement which represented the old artistic goal of providing pure visual pleasure—a narrowly restricted concept of painting, to be sure, but one far from contemptible.

28B. *Pierre Bonnard:* The Luncheon Table. *The Baltimore Museum of Art, Cone Collection. c. 1900.*

NOTES

Born in Andover, Massachusetts, Whistler attended West Point and worked as a Navy cartographer (where he learned the technique of etching) before going to Paris in 1855. In 1859 he moved to London. Demonstrating a competent command of the new painting idiom with works like *The White Girl* (portrait of Jo Heffernan, 1862, Washington), he became a self-appointed champion of the new aesthetic, but a quarrel over the decoration of a London house in 1876 (the Peacock Room, Washington, Freer) and his lawsuit in 1878 with Ruskin over criticism of his *Nocturne in Black and Gold* (1877, Detroit) ruined him financially, and to recoup himself he went to Venice (1879–80) to make a series of etchings, which were well received by connoisseurs, but never re-established his reputation as a pioneering figure in painting. (Boston has a large collection of them.) Typical examples of Whistler's painting in American collections are *Portrait of Theodore Duret* and *Cremorne Gardens No. 2* in the Metropolitan, New York; *The White Girl No. 4*, and *Nocturne in Blue and Silver* in the Fogg, Cambridge; *Grand Canal, Venice* in Philadelphia and *Base of the Tower, Venice*, pastel in Andover; by far his best-known work is *Arrangement in Grey and Black No. 1* ("Whistler's Mother," 1871, Louvre, on loan to the Metropolitan, New York). *Arrangement in Grey and Black No. 2: Thomas Carlyle* is in the Glasgow Art Gallery and Museum. A particularly good study of Whistler is Denys Sutton, *Nocturne* (Philadelphia, 1964).

After a brief brush with the Nabis in 1889–91, Pierre Bonnard settled down to evolve an aesthetically decorative variant of Impressionism which he maintained with extraordinary consistency to the end of his life. Some typical examples are in the Phillips, Washington: *Movement in the Street* (1900), *The Open Window* (1921), *Woman with Dog* (1922), *The Riviera* (1923). In the Museum of Modern Art are *The Luncheon* (c. 1927) and *The Breakfast Room* (1930–31); others are *Landscape of the Midi* (c. 1930, Northampton, Smith College), *Dinner Table and Garden* (1934, New York, Guggenheim), *Still-Life, Lunch* (1940, Chicago). John Rewald, *Pierre Bonnard* (Museum of Modern Art, 1948) is a standard reference.

242

5

Art Nouveau

Henry Russell Hitchcock once explained "by a humble culinary analogy" why "no amount of analysis can wholly explain how Art Nouveau came into being":

> If you wish to describe the taste of curry, it does not help very much to know the ingredients. The flavor of curry is like the flavor of curry; and Art Nouveau has a similar idiosyncratic identity: the whole is certainly something different from the sum of its parts.*

That is to say, Art Nouveau was less a consistent and coherent movement, like the Impressionism or Barbizon school painting to which painters dedicated all or most of their lives, than a wave of taste which caught the mood of a transient moment at the end of the 19th century, touched a great number of artists of all kinds for a few years, then petered out as quickly and spontaneously as it had appeared. The principles of Art Nouveau were never consistently or specifically formulated. It had no one particular source. It was concentrated in no definable center. In its own time, it did not even have a single generally accepted name. English writers, thinking of it as French, called it "Art Nouveau"; Italians called it the *stile inglese;* in France and Germany it was most often simply "modern": *le style moderne, Modernismo, Jugendstil;* it also went under a series of lively descriptive nicknames, as the Italian *stile floreale,* the Belgian *paling stijl* (eel style), the French *style nouille* (noodle style), the German *Bandwurmstil* (tapeworm style). Art Nouveau was in fact a consummation, a summary, a terminal manifestation of all those diverse trends of art and thought which constituted the legacy of Impressionism. Elements and ideas from Academic, Symbolic, and Aesthetic Impressionism were all combined in Art Nouveau, given a distinctive and climactic form.

Art Nouveau had the international and cosmopolitan character of Academic Impressionism. In Belgium, which the Brussels group *Les Vingt,* formed in 1884, had made a center of the modern movement, Art Nouveau was represented by (among others) Henri Van de Velde, later

---

* "Art Nouveau Architecture," Peter Selz and Mildred Constantine, eds., *Art Nouveau* (New York, Museum of Modern Art, 1959), pp. 125, 151.

famous as creator of the first entirely Art Nouveau architecture; in France, by the posters of Toulouse-Lautrec and the paintings of Paul Gauguin and his follower Emile Bernard; in Britain, by the late work of Burne-Jones, by Aubrey Beardsley, and by Charles Rennie Mackintosh; in the Netherlands by Jan Toorop and Thorn Prikker; in Switzerland by Ferdinand Hodler; in Austria by Gustav Klimt; in Norway by the young Edvard Munch; and so on. Like Academic Impressionism, Art Nouveau was essentially created for and by the new wealth accumulated by the late 19th-century upper class; Art Nouveau architecture particularly exemplified this characteristic, with the conspicuous waste and lavish cost of its entirely hand-crafted buildings. And in the same way, Art Nouveau was always closely related to the popular arts; illustrators and popular decorators appropriated its ideas from the beginning, and well into the 1920s its sinuous lines and flat planes could be recognized in middle-class mass-market advertising arts, fashion design, and especially children's books.

All the leading exponents of Art Nouveau were influenced to a greater or lesser extent by the ideas of the Symbolist movement, some in a rather *détente* and essentially playful way (compare, for example, Beardsley's *Salomé* [facing page] with Moreau's); others with an embarrassingly

29A. *Aubrey Beardsley:* Salomé and Jokanaan (*John the Baptist*). *Illustration, drawn about 1895, for Oscar Wilde's* Salomé, *which implied an erotic attachment of Salomé for John the Baptist. See also 29B, Munch.*

All the diverse movements engendered by Impressionism were gathered up at the end of the century and woven into the texture of the short-lived international Art Nouveau or Jugendstil. For most young painters, of whom Edvard Munch is typical, Art Nouveau was a phase, a vehicle by which they were introduced to the means and ends of 20th-century Reality in art. Beardsley, however, was an Art Nouveau artist from beginning to end of his short career. His work epitomizes Art Nouveau: sinuous linear patterns, flat color (or none), predilection for highly esoteric symbolism, self-consciously decadent sensualism in theme; patronage of wealthy upper-class aesthetes; close association with the popular arts of book illustration and interior decoration.

serious sensualism, like the sleazy and painfully worked out allusions to sin, sex, and suffering in the paintings of Klimt or Hodler; still others with overtones of Freudian psychology, like Edvard Munch's dire Nordic introspections.

Equally if not more obvious was the relationship of Art Nouveau to Aesthetic Impressionism. The genesis of Art Nouveau was in the decorative arts, essentially understood in the applied Victorian sense: "I believe," as the Glasgow designer Jessie Newbery once put it with touching directness, "in everything being beautiful, pleasant, and if need be, useful." Art Nouveau painters generally were inordinately concerned with effects of line, pattern and texture per se; if any one principle could be called basic for them, it was "art for art's sake."

Most significantly of all, however, Art Nouveau summarized the essential sterility of all the late 19th-century movements of which it was composed. Art Nouveau dramatized, as no single narrower movement could, to what an inevitable dead end Impressionistic techniques must come, once the basic rationale of Impressionism was abandoned and its roots in objective Reality cut off; to later painting it contributed hardly more than a heritage of artful attitudes. The vital aspects of Impressionism were left for Cézanne, Van Gogh and Gauguin to develop; to them we now turn.

NOTES

A great many books have been published within recent years dealing with *fin de siècle* movements in general; among the more authoritative are John Rewald, *Post-Impressionism* (1956); Emil Langui, *Gateway to the Twentieth Century* (with Jean Cassou and Nikolaus Pevsner, 1962); Nikolaus Pevsner, *Pioneers of Modern Design from William Morris to Walter Gropius* (1949), and Robert Schmutzler, *Art Nouveau: Jugendstil* (Stuttgart, 1962). Catalogues of Museum of Modern Art exhibitions dealing with individuals and the period generally include *Art Nouveau* (1959), *Pierre Bonnard* (1948), and *Redon-Moreau-Bresdin* (1961).

29B. *Edvard Munch:* The Cry. *Lithograph. Washington, National Gallery, Rosenwald Collection. 1895.*

246

V

Post-Impressionism:
Old Pioneers of the New Painting

OUTWARDLY, THE THREE PRIME MOVERS IN THE NEW Painting of the 20th century had little in common. It would be hard to find three men as different in temperament as Paul Cézanne, devoutly Catholic son of a stolid Provençal banker; Vincent Van Gogh, neurotic ex-evangelical missionary from a Dutch manse; and Paul Gauguin, former stockbroker whose ancesters included Peruvian viceroys and socialist agitators. Neither did they have any great sympathy for or understanding of each other's work. All they shared—but it was fundamental—were new systematically subjective principles of painting, and a pattern of development those principles forced on them.

Significantly, none of the three was a "natural" painter. In contrast to artists like Raphael or Rembrandt or Michelangelo or Bernini, whose talent was innate and precociously evident, theirs was consciously developed and matured relatively late in life. Because of their basically subjective approach, all three worked out pictorial forms dependent on primitive principles of representation (conventions determined by what the mind knows is there rather than what the eye sees) and tended to use painting for ends usually associated with other disciplines—religion, anthropology, psychology, pure science. Their basic subjectivity made them indefatigable self-portraitists. In succeeding generations, they were basically misunderstood, the general public especially admiring them for what they themselves would have considered all the wrong reasons, for "beauties" of design and texture, decorative qualities, "interesting" or "appealing" subject matter, which for them were only secondary concerns. Of decisive significance, all three were even more misunderstood in their own time. Not only did they have to face the same conservative public hostility that the Impressionists had met, but they had to meet the opposition of "moderns" as well. Impressionism ruled the advance-guard Paris scene in the 1880s, and any "modern" in serious disagreement with it could hardly survive there. To escape critics who thought their departures from Impressionism went too far, and called their subjectivism in particular a farce and perversion of modern painting, all three felt forced to withdraw from Paris and isolate themselves from society at large.

This withdrawal was both physical and in spirit. Physically, they went to remote places—Cézanne to Aix-en-Provence, Van Gogh to Arles, Gauguin to the South Seas. Their spiritual withdrawal was even more extreme. Explicitly, it was apparent in the forms of their painting, which by conventional standards "distorted" nature more and more, became "meaningless" to all but an enlightened few—which few consisted in the beginning, to all intents and purposes, of themselves alone. Implicitly, it was apparent in their concept of the painter's social role and responsibilities. Historically (or at least since the Renaissance) the poetic and imaginative side of painting had made its practitioners always seem somewhat "different" from other people, as Rudolf and Margot Wittkower have so brilliantly described in *Born Under Saturn* (London, 1963); but generally speaking, painters until around 1850 were considered, and considered themselves, *of* rather than merely *in* society. With the shift from Beauty to Reality as the goal of painting, the gulf between painters and public began to widen; but as long as Reality remained objective, the gulf was still bridgeable—a cultural lag more than a chasm. Now, however, the three great Post-Impressionists leave painting "for the people" to Academic Impressionists who revert to the old goal of Beauty, or to popular artists who revert to the even older goal of Communication; they concentrate on Realities created essentially and primarily for themselves. And as events were to prove, in withdrawing from society the Post-Impressionists took Painting with them. In their art the historical process of separation of painters from their public was consummated, and a fundamentally new relationship was begun.

1

"Significant Form":
Paul Cézanne (1839–1906)

According to the old Socratic theory of knowledge, we are born with all essential knowledge, and what we call an individual's evolution and development is simply his coming to realize and suitably express that which he has always known. Paul Cézanne professed to believe in something like this theory; whether or not this was the basis for his work, certainly his career is one long commentary on it. From beginning to end, Cézanne was obsessed by a single goal, what critics in later years would call "significant form." When first we meet him as a young man, he already has all the goals and principles of his mature art so fixed that the rest of his life consists essentially of the struggle to identify and express them, continuing to the day he died.

Cézanne first became known in Paris during the 1860s as practitioner of a "savage" or "brute" style, which to most people, even sensitive critics, seemed at best clumsy and heavy-handed, at worst simply incompetent. In this manner he executed what seemed equally heavy-handed and jejune themes—portraits of his father in patriarchal poses, of his uncle as a monk, scenes of murder, rape, orgies. In retrospect, these works are interesting as representing the beginnings of Cézanne's lifetime search for ultimate values. As unerringly (and perhaps as unconsciously) as Impressionists chose themes implying transience, Cézanne's themes embodied ideas of permanence—the traditional father symbol of social stability and discipline; the monk's costume, symbol of institutions enduring through the ages ("Weak in life as I am," Cézanne once said later, "I think it best to put my faith in Rome"); the elemental forces and passions underlying all history. As unerringly (and perhaps again as unconsciously) as the Impressionists employed open compositional arrangements to break up solid forms, Cézanne emphasized solidity by closed compositions—Renaissancelike pyramids and axial balances. He painted his father once in straight profile, as Courbet had painted his Stonebreaker, and again full front, immobile as the statue of a Pharaoh. And quite deliberately, through masses of paint brushed on in lumps and ridges or piled up with a palette knife, he tried to simulate the effects of solid form, as if trying to carve in paint.

As intimations of things to come, we can appreciate Cézanne's early "savage style" paintings; in themselves, it is difficult not to think them incompetent. Certainly most of Cézanne's contemporaries thought so; even the Impressionists seemed to welcome his contributions to their exhibitions as a means of deflecting the critics' fire; with so many adjectives expended on Cézanne, fewer were left to hurl at the rest. And it would seem that Cézanne himself eventually came around to this opinion. At any rate, he began abandoning this early manner by the early 1870s and, like all serious painters of that decade, moved into the Impressionists' orbit.

Impressionism taught Cézanne a good deal. He learned to lighten his colors, to use fresh primaries instead of muddy mixtures. From Impressionist example, too, he developed a technique of small squarish superimposed brush-strokes which he used for the rest of his career. But he never became an Impressionist. He continued his entirely un-Impressionistic search for painting that would be "solid, like the museums' "; to this end, he studied Old Masters in the Louvre (his copy of Titian's *Pietà* is a famous example), trying to get beneath precisely those superficialities of surface light and texture which most appealed to Impressionists, and discover the basic forms on which, he felt, the Old Masters' enduring significance depended—almost as Reynolds had advised. Indeed, there is more than one coincidence between Reynolds's precepts and Cézanne's practice; but Cézanne went far beyond Reynolds's generalization of form. Already he was isolating something like the basic geometric shapes—cubes, cylinders, cones—of which he was later quoted (or misquoted) as saying that all Nature was composed. Whereas for Reynolds generalized forms were means to the end of Ideal Beauty, for Cézanne they were ends in themselves, possessing a significance for which he was prepared to sacrifice everything else.

Paris in the 1870s was no place to promulgate ideas like these. From conservatives in their anecdotage he could expect no sympathy; neither could he find much hearing among the Impressionists, to whose basic principles he was flatly opposed. In the circumstances, there was nothing to do but leave Paris and go home. There, in the seclusion of his father's estate at Aix-en-Provence, broken only by the odd trip to Paris or a visit from painter friends, Cézanne brought his principles to mature expression.

In Cézanne's painting the scientific approach always implicit in

Impressionism became explicit and paramount. In his studio he searched for the fundamentally real, the ultimately significant form, as scientists searched for truth in their laboratories. And the progress of his investigations repeated, in a curious but unmistakable way, the pattern of development in scientific research over the course of 19th-century history.

Cézanne's painting falls into three more or less distinct and successive phases or fields: still life, landscape, and human figures. Not that at any given time he concentrated on one of these fields to the exclusion of others; but there is a certain sequence in his dominant interest. From c. 1870 to c. 1885 still life was of special concern; from c. 1880 to c. 1895, landscape; from c. 1885 to his death in 1906, figure painting. Roughly the same pattern is discernible (with the same qualification) in the history of 19th-century science. In the early part of the century, scientific advances were most striking in geology and allied questions of fossil formation and the date of creation; by the middle of the century, in biology and questions of evolution and the origin of species; at its end, in psychology and related fields. The coincidence is not fortuitous. In each case the sequence is determined by the increasingly difficult character of the relationship between the investigator and what he is studying.

Between the geologist and his rocks or shells, as between the still-life painter and his bottles or bowls, no personal relationships intrude; the investigation can be entirely objective. No extraneous prejudice need warp the scientist's judgment, or color interpretations of his findings. In such circumstances, unequivocal success is possible. In biology, as in landscape painting, the situation is more complicated. Man the scientist lives among, with, or on the other forms of life he studies, just as man the painter lives in the landscape he paints. By and large, however, this relationship remains essentially impersonal; impartiality, if not complete objectivity, can be achieved. But in psychology, as in Cézanne's figure painting, it cannot. Darwin's findings affect his idea of what he is, but what he is does not necessarily affect them; not so with Freud or Ellis. Since what they study are beings like themselves, they cannot help beginning their investigations with certain subjective assumptions and preconceptions which inevitably color their findings, however objectively arrived at. In any scientific investigation, it is an axiomatic fact that the more objectivity, the greater chance for success. And this axiom Cézanne's painting illustrates very well.

Cézanne's command of significant form was first and best established in still life. In his "savage style" phase, even while landscape and figures were still clumsy and gauche, he was creating masterpieces of still life like the little *Black Clock* of c. 1870. Here he seems at last to have consciously realized what in other themes he only sensed; ignoring or minimizing Beauty and romantic associations, he concentrates on things ultimately significant. At this stage, that primarily means subject matter; he assembles a collection of objects with particularly stable chemical composition—ebony, glass, china, shell, porcelain—the kind of permanent records of civilization an archaeologist might find on some sea floor a thousand years hence. Form remains auxiliary to content; basically following his heavy "savage" manner, it is carved in paint by brute brushwork. A strong note of lemon yellow in the center, and the treatment of the tablecloth, presage changes to come, however; ten years later, with Impressionist experience as a catalyst, Cézanne achieves mature expression in still life. By the early 1880s he has subordinated content to forms whose solidity is no longer a physical matter of crude masses of paint, but created by a number of subtle visual devices empirically worked out. Disciplined patterns of contrast are developed on the principle that "warm" colors advance towards a spectator's eye, "cool" colors recede from it. The "deceptions" of linear perspective, whereby distant objects seem smaller than near ones when they may not be so in fact, or parallel lines seem to converge when in fact they remain as far apart as ever, are systematically eliminated and disguised (as children and "primitives" of all kinds generally do—and for the same reasons) by composing in terms of a parallel frontal picture-plane at which the eye is kept by over-all textural uniformity. True physical properties and true spatial relationships are suggested by what seems the "primitive" principle of additive composition (i.e., adding together characteristic views of an object as the mind knows it to be to make a composite image—the round top shape and the cylindrical side shape of a cup), but which in fact was probably an attempt to represent how we "really" see around objects with two eyes, instead of the one-eyed view established by Renaissance convention. In the later 1880s and -90s significant form presents no more problems in still life; Cézanne's later still lifes are undertaken in the spirit of a scientist developing the ramifications of a basic discovery already achieved, working in the sheer joy of mastery.

It took Cézanne somewhat longer to perfect the representation of landscape on comparable principles, and he was not as completely successful. One of the reasons is suggested in a perceptive article by Dr. Jonas S. Friedenwald on "Knowledge of Space Perception and the Portrayal of Depth in Painting": *

> Suppose you close one eye and look at a neighbouring table. Try to estimate the distance from the near to the far side of the table. After you have made the estimate consider for a moment how you reached your conclusion. Perhaps you said to yourself: "I noticed when I came in that the table is round. The distance near to far is the same as that right to left." Perhaps you said: "People are all of about the same size. Those on the far side of the table look smaller than those on the near side. They must therefore be farther away."
>
> Now open your other eye and you will find that you have a direct unequivocal apprehension of the table's size and shape. You do not need any indirect argument or guide to your apprehension. The size and shape, so to speak, jump directly into your consciousness. This is what I mean by the enrichment in space perception through binocular vision. *If you repeat this same experiment looking at a more distant object, say a hundred feet or more away, you will find little or no difference between your monocular and binocular impressions. Binocular vision enriches the space locally, not generally* [italics mine].

In landscape painting, that is to say, significant form had to be established in three planes, not just one; perspective illusions of size diminishing with distance and convergence of parallel lines could hardly be ignored if the theme were to remain intelligible. Cézanne long resisted the necessary compromise. At first, in the landscape settings for early figural compositions like *The Pond* or *The Picnic* in the 1860s, he treated figures and landscape alike as if they were part of a single still life set in a foreground plane. In "Impressionist" landscapes of the early 1870s (e.g., *The Suicide's House* in the Louvre, or the *View of Auvers* in the Art Institute, Chicago) he still tried to keep to a single plane, pulling the background in and pushing the foreground back; the result, in effect, was an enormous outdoor still life set in a near-middleground. By the mid-1880s, however, in landscapes like the *View of L'Estaque* in Chicago or the *House in Provence* at the John Herron Art Institute in Indianapolis, he has succeeded in establishing a firm middleground and distance, largely through the use of advancing and receding masses of color. And in the later 1880s he successfully incorporates a foreground plane also, tying the three together by a subtle framework of horizontal, vertical, and

* *College Art Journal,* Vol. XV, No. 2 (1956).

diagonal compositional lines, creating a kind of isometric perspective rather like Japanese prints; outstanding examples are his studies of *Mont-Sainte-Victoire* at the Metropolitan in New York, the Courtauld in London, the Phillips in Washington, or the *Chestnut Trees at Jas de Bouffan* (page 257) at the Minneapolis Institute of Arts.

By the early 1890s, then, Cézanne was able to express significant form in landscape almost as effectively as in still life. Thenceforth in this field too he could paint with a new freedom, spontaneity and pleasure; his later landscape themes have an almost romantic or lyrical quality. But it was not—could not be—as completely assured a mastery; significant form in landscape necessarily had to be somewhat more subjective, and consequently somewhat less entirely convincing, simply because the painter could never be as detached from landscape as from still life. This larger subjective element is perhaps most evident in comparative subject matter. By the late 1880s Cézanne's choice of still life had become as completely free of subjective or unconscious limitations as is humanly possible; whereas in the beginning he had needed to choose objects extraneously associated with permanence (ebony and china and shell) now he is so sure of his vision that he will make images of eternity out of flowering plants and sprouting vegetables, plaster casts and ripening fruit. Not so in landscape; here Cézanne's range of subjects remained much more limited by subjective considerations almost to the end. Mountains—"the eternal hills"; rocks—"rock of ages"; pines—*"du grünst nicht nur im Sommerzeit, nein auch in Winter . . ."*; stone houses of the peasantry, timeless and styleless folk architecture, unchanging from generation to generation; these are his chosen themes, obvious and overt symbols of permanence every one of them, repeated over and over again. By so much is the significant form that Cézanne discovers in landscape less universal and absolute, more his personal creation, than in his still life.

Even more obvious is the personal and subjective element in Cézanne's figure paintings. As an orthodox Christian, considering the human form in some sense divine, this was for Cézanne *the* subject; he once commented on the impossibility of truly painting a figure of Christ, as too close to the "final absolute." This was probably Cézanne's most unrealized motif. Certainly it was the one in which the differences between him and the Impressionists were sharpest and most irreconcilable. They painted people—individuals in individual situations, at particular times: dancing, loving, playing, eating. Cézanne painted types. When he was young, his most characteristic figures were symbols of a vaguely romantic sort—of rage, of lust, of authority and power, those elementary states of mind from which all "higher" ambitions and aspirations finally spring. In maturity, his most characteristic subjects were peasants and servants, lower-class folk generally. Changeless, ageless, faceless, they are destined to outlive all the changing, temporal, individual civilizations and cultures built on their labor, and so Cézanne paints them—sometimes sitting motionless with cards or a rosary in their hands, oftener just sitting or standing immobile, doing nothing, gazing at nothing, simply existing like the statues on medieval cathedrals. Since he himself was so far from being a peasant, he could be reasonably objective about human beings of this kind, study them to some extent like pots or pine trees. But portraits and nude studies were something else again.

Theoretically, Cézanne considered realization of significant form in the human figure to be a technical problem like any other. Theoretically, painters should study it in the same coldly objective spirit as landscape or still life. And superficially, he would seem to have succeeded. He can paint Mme. Cézanne's body as stiffly immobile as the coffee pot beside her; he can spend as much time on Gustave Geoffroy's shirt front as on his face. Nobody looking at portraits like these or the great *Bathers* (page 259) in Philadelphia, on which Cézanne worked over his last half-dozen years, would think of denying that they are successful as paintings, magnificent compositions. But they are magnificent as still lifes or landscapes, hardly as figure paintings; and in Cézanne's own frame of

30A. *Paul Cézanne:* Chestnut Trees at Jas de Bouffan. *The Minneapolis Institute of Arts, William Hood Dunwoody Fund. 1885–87.* See also 30B, Cézanne.

In isolation at Aix-en-Provence, Cézanne applied means derived from Impressionism to the entirely un-Impressionistic end of discovering permanent Realities underlying precisely those transient appearances which for the Impressionists had constituted visual Reality and been their chief concern. In this typical work he deliberately avoids perspective recession (as an "unreal" illusion), creates space by advancing and receding color masses, and eliminates all but the most permanent elements in the landscape—mountain, leafless trees, stone walls.

reference they must be considered failures. For is this really significant human form? Surely the essence, the basic Reality of humanity, is precisely that it is something different from and more than rocks or pots or pines. Surely it is obvious that just as inescapable preconceptions and assumptions hampered the objectivity of psychologists more than geologists or biologists, so Cézanne's studies of significant human form were vitally affected by his congenital inability to get along with people, his shyness, his loneliness, his social gaucherie, his general failure to establish more than a bare minimum of successful human relationships. Surely it is obvious that Cézanne's architectonic and rigidly formalized presentation of the female nude, the fact that his *Bathers* are sexless as the trees above them, does not represent the final successful outcome of years of cool reasoned objective research so much as a reflection of the curious misogyny for which he was notorious. The figure paintings of a man pathologically unable to stay in the same room with a nude female model can hardly represent the same kind of cool detached analysis as his studies of rocks and trees.

Cézanne's portraits and nude studies raise the fundamental question of his objectivity generally. Cézanne believed that he was objective; in his isolated "laboratory," the "hermit of Aix" considered he was perfecting an artistic vehicle for a concept of Reality which would probably find its closest formulation in the writings of Plotinus: "Nature . . . , the spectacle which the *Pater Omnipotens Aeterne Deus* spreads before our eyes," Cézanne said once, was "the true and immense study to be undertaken." All his life a devout churchgoer, he seemed to believe he had a mission to restore a medieval sense of Reality to art. Taking from the world generally and the human figure in particular everything originating in the transitory world of impressionistic sense, stripping Man

30B. *Paul Cézanne:* The Bathers. *Philadelphia Museum of Art, Wilstach Collection. 1898–1905.*

Discarding the Impressionists' lingering interest in "beautiful objects," Cézanne works in the spirit of a scientist conducting impersonal experiments, for whom the conclusion—discovery of Truth—is everything, the experimental apparatus (particular pictures) no more than incidental by-products, discardable evidence.

to his essence, he would make an image of eternal Reality in a temporal world. But as an old man, finally achieving recognition, he expressed doubts of his success: "If they organize my triumph, do not believe in it; if they try to create a school in my name, tell them they have never understood me, nor cared what I have done." Objectivity can only be achieved by the artist stepping somehow outside his own work; a classic example is the problem of linear perspective in Renaissance painting, impossible to achieve empirically, neatly solved by constructing space in a little box with strings on a template which artists could study from the outside. Did Cézanne build any such machine (metaphorically speaking) to study his significant form? Not at all; his method was as empirical as Van Eyck's perspective. Essentially, whatever he himself may have believed, Cézanne's significant form was not the discovery of some pre-existing absolute, in the classic sense of Renaissance tradition; it was the creation of his own mind. Like early psychologists, he tended to find in Nature what he already believed was there.

One indication of Cézanne's subjectivity is the extraordinary importance he put on his own head. Few painters have done so many self-portraits; and while it is possible to say the reason was mere convenience —he was his own most readily available model—that is hardly more plausible than to explain some egotist's filling a house with portraits and busts of himself on grounds of pure love of art. Another is implicit in the kind of forms he developed. Basically, Cézanne represented the world as primitives, savages, children do, painting what he knew was there rather than what his eye saw, imposing his preconceived ideas of Reality on Nature before him. That is why in the last analysis Cézanne's art did not resemble the classical art of a Poussin or a Claude or even a Reynolds, why he was instead "the primitive of a new art." His was not the old, absolute, universal Reality which the classical mind derived from Nature, but a New Reality imposed on Nature by himself.

Not only the forms, but the rationale of Cézanne's art involved a return to that primitive state in which the artist determines what Reality is by a process best described as collective solipsism.

> No two persons perceive the outside world in exactly the same way. But for purposes of mutual comprehension, we accept certain conventions about the nature of the world around us. These conventions are the result of collective solipsism, imposed on us as children. The child asks his parents, "Why is the grass green?" We reply, "Because it is." The question actually means, "Does everyone see grass the same color I

do?" Now, we know, and the Impressionists demonstrated it to us again, that grass sometimes appears white, yellow, blue, brown; but we reply to the child, "Yes, for practical purposes, we accept the fact that grass is green." We discipline the child, we impose Reality on him.

Similarly, in the childhood of the race, among prehistoric men and savages, the multitudinous concepts of Reality as various individuals see it are reduced to formulae which are impressed upon all. It is a necessary process if society and social intercourse are to come into being. And the art of the primitive mind is the prime vehicle by which this Reality is made comprehensible.*

By the same token, Cézanne's art, though subjective, is not nonobjective.

So Cézanne consummated Courbet's work. Courbet had told painters they should show Reality to men; Cézanne demonstrated how to do it. No wonder that, despite his warning, "they" promptly proceeded to "found a school" in his name. But not in his name alone. For Cézanne was not the only man in his generation to seize the truth that if painters were to define Reality it would have to be in subjective terms. He was not the only painter to think of rejuvenating society by imposing new concepts of Reality in art. Of Van Gogh and Gauguin's work he knew only imperfectly; yet with different forms and other motivations, they too were pursuing the same end.

NOTES

Paul Cézanne was born at Aix-en-Provence in 1839, son of a small capitalist and local magnate—the power symbol of several early pictures. His first trip to Paris to study painting, in 1861 at the Ecole des Beaux-Arts, soon ended in failure and retreat back to Aix—a pattern repeated a good many times over the next ten years. A "savage style" of heavy brush- and palette-knife work, dark colors, and quasi-romantic subject matter was characteristic of his painting in this period. In the years 1873–78 he came into the orbit of Impressionism, contributing in 1874 to the first Impressionist Exhibition. Though his manner of painting changed, his purposes did not, and his work still met little but derision. In 1878 he retired to L'Estaque on the Gulf of Marseilles, and henceforth spent more and more of his time isolated in the South, especially at his father's summer place, which he later inherited, the Jas de Bouffan near Aix. The mature expression developed in these years was

* Alan Gowans, "A-Humanism, Primitivism, and the Art of the Future," *College Art Journal,* Vol. XI, No. 2 (1952).

first introduced to the general public at a one-man show at Ambroise Vollard's in 1895, which marked the end of this period. Thereafter to the end of his life Cézanne exhibited more frequently—at the Centennial of 1900; in Brussels and at the Independents in 1901; and in 1904 an entire room at the Salon d'Automne was devoted to his work. Cézanne died in October, 1906, as the result of being caught in a rainstorm while painting out of doors.

Considering his work somewhat in the spirit of laboratory experiments, less valuable in themselves than as means to an end, Cézanne rarely dated his pictures, and their exact chronology is largely a matter of inference and deduction on the basis of stylistic development. Most books follow the dating suggested in Lionello Venturi's catalogue, *Cézanne, son art, son oeuvre* (Paris, 1936, 2 vols.).

Typical of Cézanne's early work, to 1870, are family portraits (*The Artist's Father,* 1860–63, Philadelphia; *The Artist's Father Reading L'Evènement*—in which Zola's first articles on Manet had appeared—c. 1866; *The Man in the Blue Cap,* 1865–67, New York, Metropolitan; *Uncle Dominic as a Monk,* c. 1866, New York, Haupt Collection) and representations of elemental moods—*The Rape, The Orgy, The Murder* (São Paolo, Brazil). Of his "impressionistic" period, examples are *The House of the Hanged Man* (1873–74, Louvre); *View of Auvers* (c. 1874, Chicago); *A Dessert* (1873–77, Philadelphia, Tyson Collection).

Cézanne's increasing command over still life can be traced in such works as *The Black Clock* (c. 1870); *Still Life* (c. 1883, Cambridge, Fogg); *Still-Life with Peppermint Bottle* (1890–94, Washington); *Tulips and Apples* (1890–94). Famous examples of mature still lifes can be found in many other American museums, as well as in Europe.

The evolution of Cézanne's landscape can be seen in successive versions of characteristic themes like the *View of L'Estaque* (1883–85, New York, Metropolitan; c. 1886, Chicago), *Mont-Sainte-Victoire* (c. 1885–87, Washington, Phillips; c. 1885–87, London, Courtauld; c. 1898, Baltimore; c. 1904–06, Philadelphia, Tyson), pines and rocks (c. 1885, New York, Modern; c. 1892, São Paolo, Brazil; *At Fontainebleau,* c. 1894–95, New York, Metropolitan).

Typical portraits would include those of Boyer (*Man in a Straw Hat,* c. 1870–71, New York, Metropolitan); *Victor Choquet Seated* (c. 1877, Columbus, Ohio); *Madame Cézanne in a Red Easy-Chair* (c. 1877, Boston); *Louis Guillaume* (c. 1879–82, Washington); *Gustave Geoffroy* (c. 1895, Paris, Lecomte); *Vallier* (1906, Paris, Rosenberg). Typical nude studies are the *Bacchanal* (*Lutte d'Amour,* 1875–80, New York, Harriman); *Male Bather* (c. 1885–87, New York, Modern); *The Bathers.* The theme of *Card Players* is represented (among other places) in the Louvre, in Washington, and in the Clark Collection, New York (early 1890s).

262

Typical self-portraits are those in the Kunstmuseum, Bern (1879–82), Tate, London (1879–82), Winterthur (c. 1882), Cézanne Family Collection, Paris (with palette, 1885–87), and Boston (with beret, c. 1890).

Among the better-known critical studies are Roger Fry, *Cézanne, A Study of His Development* (1927); Fritz Novotny, *Cézanne und das Ende der wissenschaftlichen Perspektive* (Vienna, 1938); Meyer Schapiro, *Paul Cézanne* (1952). Biographical works include those by Gerstle Mack (1935), Bernard Dorival (1948), and Maurice Raynal (1956).

2

"Expressionism":

Vincent Van Gogh (1853–1890)

For the 20th century, Vincent Van Gogh has become one of the great romantic figures of history. His tragic career has been the theme of melodramatic books and even more melodramatic movies. Cheap prints of his sunflowers, his views of Arles, his grain fields and his bridges are sold in dime stores and distributed by popular magazines, decorate dormitories, apartments, executive suites and split-level ranch houses. Of all "modern" painters, he is perhaps the best-known. Yet of all "modern" painters he was perhaps the least-known in life; and by the general public at least he remains one of the most totally misunderstood.

Part of Van Gogh's fame derives from the circumstances of his life. He is the archetype of the Tragic Hero doomed and tortured by Fate—a Hamlet among painters. Everybody knows the general outlines of his story. His troubled, moody, pious youth in a Calvinist manse in Holland. His successive failures—at selling art, at school teaching, in love; the fiasco of his evangelical work among miners in the Borinage; his attempt to redeem the prostitute Christine through love. Finally his taking up painting as a kind of religious therapy; his desperately clumsy attempts to master technique; his furious output concentrated in a half-dozen years, rising to a fantastic crescendo in the last year and a half; his madness, suicide, and belated recognition. Yet the significance of this biography is that it explains not what he painted, but why he painted. Even more than in the case of Cézanne or Gauguin, it is clear that for

Van Gogh painting was an activity substituting for something else. Superficially, of course, for medical therapy; Van Gogh is the great precedent for modern usage of painting in psychiatric research. But in a deeper sense, Van Gogh's painting was a substitute for religious experience. It was for him a medium of transcending the limitations and frustrations of earthly life, "a means of grace and a hope of glory." From that, everything else about it stems.

To understand Van Gogh's art we need to remember, first of all, that he was raised a devout Calvinist Protestant. Against this background the intensely personal character of his painting becomes intelligible; he belonged to a tradition which maintained that progress and salvation depended on the efforts and improvement of individuals, not on institutions. Even more, it meant that Van Gogh was imbued with a peculiar way of looking at work. Long ago and far away in 17th-century New England, Mistress Ann Bradstreet, the Puritan poetess, expressed the essence of that attitude:

> There is no object that we see, no action that we doe, no good that we injoy, no evill that we feele or fear, but we may make some spiritual advantage of it all.

Most people tend to think there is a "religious" art, which has to do by function or subject matter with ecclesiological matters, and a "secular" art which does not, just as there are some buildings which are "churches" specially consecrated for religious purposes and some which are not, or a special class of "clergy" concerned with religious offices in contrast to the great mass of "laymen" whose concern is with everyday work. Not so the evangelical Protestant For him, such a distinction was invidious and unreal. You are not saved, you do not attain eternal life, by what you do in the way of charitable works or church attendance or "religious duties." You are saved by what you are, by the kind of person you make yourself. It is not what you do, no matter how spiritually motivated or ethically elevated, that counts, but the spirit in which you live and do your day-by-day work.

With this belief bred into him it was easy for Van Gogh to switch from attempts to save the world through evangelism in the coal pits or through schoolteaching, to saving it through art. Art in itself was only important as a means to such an end. Painting could become the "sacred vocation" denied him when he failed his entrance examinations to theological school; painting would be his means of bringing people to truths about themselves and about the nature of life. With such a goal, it is hardly surprising that Vincent should have proved as mediocre and dissatisfied a student at art school in Antwerp as Blake had been in London some eighty years before. What these men wanted from art no orthodox teacher of painting could understand; and so Van Gogh, like Blake before him, had to find his own technique, his own subjects and language, simply because no one could supply them.

Van Gogh's first models—inevitably, given his narrow cultural outlook and turn of mind—were the "peasant painters" of the mid-19th century: Millet and the Barbizon painters in general, and their Dutch followers— Mauve, Maris, and Israels in particular. Their precedent justified his choice of themes from peasant life; their example determined the heavy lines and somber colors with which he first painted. But from the beginning Van Gogh was no servile imitator. There was nothing romantically remote or picturesque about Van Gogh's peasants, nothing didactic or doctrinaire about his presentation of laborers. What interested him was precisely that intensely prosaic existence which made them, as he conceived, dearest of all humanity to God. Not quaint old-fashioned customs and faith, but the total sanctity of life and work was his theme. An old woman pulling up carrots, or ragged children trundling faggots, were more sacred subjects than saccharine Madonnas and Christ Children painted for sleek bourgeois congregations, cushioned by money against life. Van Gogh's masterpieces of this first phase are the *Man at the Loom* of 1884 (Kröller-Müller, Otterlo; variant studies and drawings) and *The Potato Eaters* (page 267) of 1885. This weaver is counterpart to those Baroque monks and hermits painted by Zurbaran and Ribera two centuries before, descendant of Rembrandt's melancholy genre portraits and Biblical themes; all of them live in isolated worlds of their own, totally absorbed in and by the symbols of salvation that surround them—relics, books, and beads in the one case, mundane artifacts in the other. And in *The Potato Eaters* we can recognize a sacramental picture in the sense Mistress Ann Bradstreet, John Bunyan, or any other in the evangelical Protestant tradition would have understood it. These are transcendental images. Above this altar table shines a sanctuary lamp; around it sit, as in early Christian times, the simple people of God, partaking of their solemn *agape,* dipping their hands into the common dish, all in the somber colors befitting "the priesthood of all believers."

On such a note culminated the first phase of Van Gogh's painting. A complex of considerations—social, financial, personal, and not least the rapid erosion of his formal Christian belief—put an end to it and impelled him to Paris, in March of 1886. Like Cézanne before him, and for fundamentally the same reasons, Van Gogh found Paris intolerable. The Impressionism he found reigning there fascinated him but repelled him even more. From Impressionism he learned, like Cézanne, a new brush stroke and a heightened sense for color; but like Cézanne, he could never accept its premises. Painting for Van Gogh could never be simply a set of formal technical problems, or a vehicle for commenting on life. Painting for him was life itself, a sacred obligation he had undertaken. He was not concerned with capturing the transient moment; his concern was with eternity, the ultimate meaning of life. And so, like Cézanne, he felt forced to leave Paris and work out his art and his salvation in isolation. His choice, for reasons of health as well as theme—he thought it would offer visions of color and line most like the Japanese prints he adored—fell on remote Arles in Provence. There, in a brief space of fifteen-odd months, he brought to maturity a new concept of painting.

Outwardly, Van Gogh's painting in Provence looks very different from his earlier art. Dull ochres, greens, and blacks vanish in a blaze of color, primaries are squeezed directly from tubes to canvas, applied in vibrant unadulterated contrasts. Emotional effect, more than naturalistic description, increasingly determines them—harsh and evil, lush and tranquil, vividly buoyant. And as command over his medium is realized, his Germanic heritage becomes irresistibly evident. In Van Gogh's brushwork the dynamic line of Carolingian and Ottonian illumination, of late German Gothic sculpture, of Dürer's engravings and Rembrandt's etchings, comes to life again; he draws in paint, vigorously outlining objects, filling spaces between with linear textural patterns that have a life of their own, convey subjective moods and instincts quite apart from anything

31A. *Vincent Van Gogh:* The Potato Eaters. *Amsterdam, Municipal Museum, V. W. Van Gogh Collection. 1885.* See also 31B, Van Gogh.

Van Gogh began painting when his ambitions for the Protestant ministry were frustrated, and at first his goal was "preaching continued by other means." Climax of this phase is The Potato Eaters—*the painting of a sacrament performed through the "priesthood of all believers."*

they happen objectively to represent. His subject matter changes outwardly, too. Overtly didactic descriptions of peasant life are given up;
now his themes are symbols, sometimes consciously chosen and sometimes not, of his compulsive preoccupation with Life and Death. Sowers
and reapers: seven paintings and twenty-two drawings of *The Sower,*
mostly based on reproductions of Millet's *Sower,* which Van Gogh had
seen; *The Reaper* painted over and over again, especially at Saint-Rémy,
and specifically identified as an "image of death" to Theo (letter 604).
Bridges of all kinds, from quaint drawbridges reminiscent of Oud
Holland to ugly products of 19th-century iron foundries, and people
walking over them; with Addison, Van Gogh sees them

> . . . standing in the Midst of the Tide. The Bridge . . . is human
> Life. . . . Multitudes of People passing over it . . . and a black
> Cloud hanging on each End of it. . . . innumerable trapdoors lay
> concealed in the Bridge . . . set very thick at the Entrance of the
> Bridge, so that Throngs of People no sooner broke through the Cloud,
> but many fell into them. They grew thinner towards the Middle, but
> multiplied and lay closer towards the end of the Arches that were
> entire. . . . Alas, said I, Man was made in vain! How is he given alway
> to Misery and Mortality! tortured in Life, and swallowed up in
> Death . . .*

But for Van Gogh it is increasingly difficult to see, with Addison, the
Blessed Islands below the bridge, and to conclude, "Does Life appear
miserable, that gives thee Opportunities of earning such a Reward? Is

* "Vision of Mirzah," *Spectator,* No. 159.

31B. *Vincent Van Gogh:* Bedroom at Arles. *Chicago, The Art Institute,
Helen Birch Bartlett Memorial Collection. 1888.*

*In isolation at Arles, Van Gogh develops Impressionistic techniques
into a distinctive medium of subjective expression, using the objective
world merely as a springboard from which to project personal Realities
of mood, feeling, and aspiration. Where painting for Cézanne had been
a kind of scientific research, Van Gogh makes it a kind of therapeutic
religious experience, a medium for transcending the limitations and
frustrations of life, "a means of grace and a hope of glory."*

Death to be feared, that will convey thee to so happy an Existence? Think not Man was made in vain, who has such an Eternity reserved for him." Nor can he believe in any foreseeable end to those roads that for him symbolize the journey to that far country from whose bourne no traveler returns, lined with cypresses which for centuries have been associated with burial, reminding us that in the midst of life we are in death. He sees flamelike trees lining Les Aliscamps, the old Roman cemetery at Arles, towering over the sarcophagi like fires from hell; and behind them again, factory chimneys, symbols of hell in his Industrial Age. In compensation, sunflowers and iris become symbols for him of the life-giving sun, of female fertility; and in a velvet night sky he sometimes tries to see stars blazing like souls of the righteous in the hand of God.

But intrinsically, Van Gogh's painting remains unchanged. Technical maturity means for him, as for Cézanne, no new direction or goal, only that the goal held from the first can be more perfectly and more powerfully realized. His art remains as it always had been, a personal religious expression; but now it moves farther from the objective world, takes on the quality of icons, becomes a medium for transcending material things, of mystic vision. Aldous Huxley, in *The Doors of Perception,* once described how under the influence of mescalin he perceived in a "little nosegay" on his desk

> . . . what Adam had seen on the morning of his creation—the miracle, moment by moment, of naked existence.
>
> "Is it agreeable?" somebody asked (. . . recorded on a dictating machine). "Neither agreeable nor disagreeable," I answered. "It just *is.*"
>
> *Istigkeit*—wasn't that the word Meister Eckhart liked to use? "Is-ness." The being of Platonic philosophy. . . . a bunch of flowers shining with their own inner light and all but quivering under the pressure of the significance with which they were charged. . . .*

This realm that Huxley entered through drugs Van Gogh was more and more coming to inhabit as a matter of course, and developing the ability to record; no better description of the effect of one of Van Gogh's great flower paintings could be found, surely, except possibly in Van Gogh's own letters:

> If we study Japanese art, you see a man who is understanding, wise, philosophic, and intelligent, who spends his time how? In studying the distance between the earth and the moon? No. In studying the policy of Bismarck? No. He studies a single blade of grass.

* (New York, 1954), pp. 16–18.

But this blade of grass leads him to draw every plant, and then the seasons, the wide aspects of the countryside, then animals, then the human figure. So he passes his life, and life is too short to do the whole. . . . [September 1888]

It is this quality of personal mystical experience that makes a roomful of Van Gogh paintings so extraordinarily overpowering. We feel not merely in the presence, but inside the mind and spirit, of this man long dead. We stand in his lonely room, colored by his moods, surrounded by belongings—his chair, his pipe, his shoes—holy relics like the lamp and dish of *The Potato Eaters*. We follow him to the little provincial café where he takes his relaxation, and see through his eyes, with harshly broken line and screaming color, its full stark sordidness; we feel it, as he does, a kind of *via crucis,* a place where the wine of pleasure turns vinegar and mortifies the flesh. His eating places, his sleeping places, his walking places, his painting places, all serve as shrines to himself.

In these last months Van Gogh consummates the substitution of painting for conventional religion. Through art he aspires to that immortality he once sought and despaired of in orthodox Christianity. Color, always symbolically emotional, now takes on an almost liturgical significance for him. In the several paintings of his room, for instance, it shifts from penitential to festival with his moods; in his café its harsh starkness frankly evokes the atmosphere of hell. And the more Van Gogh seeks immortality in art, the more he becomes his own symbol, his own subject, his own reason for painting.

His perspective is affected by this increasingly obsessive self-orientation. Whereas in orthodox Renaissance painting parallel lines recede to a vanishing point fixed according to formulae methodically and dispassionately arrived at, in Van Gogh's later paintings his perspective is fixed by his will. As Cézanne developed advancing and recessive color, so Van Gogh develops a system of converging and intersecting planes that rush towards or compulsively recede from him; it is as if he sets the whole world moving in relation to himself. In the last year of his life he develops this empirical perspective into an expressive vehicle of enormous power. In his paintings of the corridor or cloister of the Saint-Rémy asylum, for instance, it creates nightmarish stage sets in which tiny figures scuttle frantically about trying to find a way out of a world which has no fixed limits, no points from which to take a bearing; in his last work, the glowing cornfields rush forward towards us like some great fatal comber sweeping in and cresting above a hapless, terrified swimmer.

271

Also at Saint-Rémy, Van Gogh develops copying of earlier art into a compulsively personal expression. He takes the *Diggers,* which Millet had romantically represented as the great stable peasant foundation of society, and transforms them into symbols of life's fever at its most fitful, a writhing mass of high color, nervous brush strokes, dynamic outlines; visual counterpart to the great Protestant hymn "Work, for the Night Is Coming." Especially effective is Van Gogh's version of *The Prison Yard* from Gustave Doré's series of London life; in Van Gogh's fevered hands the old illustrator's descriptions become moving symbols of the endless meaningless round of human existence, crushed and tortured by the compulsively contracting perspective of towering prison walls. Doré's was the objective expression of a romantic and a reformer in touch with the world outside; but Van Gogh never was a romantic, and now he no longer paints, as when he depicted *The Potato Eaters,* with the explicit idea of helping mankind to better its lot. Now he paints symbols of mankind primarily meaningful to himself; significantly, in the foreground prisoner we recognize a portrait of Van Gogh himself. *The Prison Yard* reminds us of nothing so much as Goya's *City on a Hill,* inasmuch as only with wings can men escape from these prisons of frustration in which the discrepancy between their aspirations and their limitations has shut them; no exit is visible. But whereas Goya in an earlier age painted men with wings, soaring about his City, Van Gogh does not. For him painting itself was the wings that could enable man to transcend "the prison of this death."

In short, Van Gogh rejects, like Cézanne, the old objective principle of starting from the outside, accepting the world as it is and working from that; instead, he insists on making the world over to conform with the patterns of his mind. A comparable self-deception resulted; but whereas realization of the gulf between what is and what was hoped for meant only disappointment for Cézanne, for Van Gogh it meant madness. Comparing photographs of Cézanne's motifs with his paintings of them is a revelation of aesthetic method; but in Van Gogh's case it is the revelation of a mind going to pieces under inner pressure. In actuality, the olive groves of Provence stretch out in orderly serene rows; in Van Gogh's paintings, they heave, roll and shake like the Teutonic Evangelists of the Ebbo Gospels—ground quaking, sky shivering, not to express a divine visitation or in response to dynamic line patterns but as the convulsive effusion of a painter's tortured mind. In the crucible of this brain, the rolling wheatfields of Auvers and the crows soaring over them become omens of doom, of overwhelming helplessness and lonely struggle. The whole outside world becomes a springboard from which to project an inner world; all creation is one great self-portrait.

Van Gogh was one of the great painters of self-portraits in history. In their prolific number, he resembles his contemporaries Cézanne and Gauguin; in the use he made of them for self-analysis, he resembles his great Protestant and Germanic predecessors Rembrandt and Albrecht Dürer—painting himself at all stages, times and seasons, as young and intense, eager and determined, ill, dispirited, demented. But he is subjective to a degree none of them ever were. He is not content to paint himself as himself; he painted every one and everything else as himself, too. From the faces of an old Provençal peasant, or Dr. Gachet at Auvers, or the postman Roulin, the same intense eyes stare fixedly out, set in the same curiously shaped skull, framed by the same stiff hair; sometimes it would be hard to tell without titles who is Van Gogh and who is not. Often it seems to have been hard for Van Gogh; in his later work he seems to revert to the attitude of a child who is interested in the external world only insofar as it relates to himself. Like Cézanne, he denies validity to the objective world, fashions a world in his own image. But he goes further; in his world he is the Creator, by Whom and for Whom all things are made:

> In life and in painting too I can very well dispense with God, but as a man acquainted with suffering, I can't do without something greater than myself, which is my very life: the power to create.

To outward appearance Van Gogh has come a long way indeed from the humble sacramental art of his earlier years. But not in fact; for what we have here is really a transmutation of the Calvinist doctrine of the total depravity of man. Man trusting in his own powers is sure to be damned, the old dominies had taught, for man has in fact no powers to help himself; his strength comes from outside. But for Van Gogh there is no longer any outside; he has left the objective world, including an objective God, far behind him. Damned then he was; helpless, with no resources, suicide his only solution.

And along with his life, he took art in the old sense. In ages hitherto, art had been justified and determined by some concept, though it varied in detail, that there was an ultimate reality in the objective physical world. In Van Gogh's painting this concept is abandoned. For him, as for the Early Christian artists who transformed the art of Antiquity, the external world was only a means to the end of realizing inner and eternal verities. It follows that there is no longer any compelling reason for painters to pay attention to it at all. Soon enough Van Gogh's successors will find, like Byzantine iconoclasts, that the external world is a positive hindrance to them; not merely a convenient illusion, but an obstacle, to be eliminated. From Van Gogh's Expressionism to Kandinsky's nonobjectivism and the Abstract Expressionism that followed him are short steps indeed.

NOTES

Vincent Van Gogh was born at Groot Zundert in the Dutch Brabant in 1853. From 1869 to 1876 he worked for the Goupil Art Gallery, successively in The Hague, Brussels, London (1873) and Paris (1875); in this period occurred his infatuation with his London landlady's daughter, Ursula Loyer, who refused to take him seriously. From 1876 to 1879 Van Gogh was preoccupied with orthodox religion. Leaving the Goupil Gallery on grounds of disgust with its necessary dishonesty, he attempted schoolteaching in England and failed, returned to Holland late in 1876 and, after a few months clerking in a Dordrecht bookshop, went to Amsterdam to study for entrance examinations to theological college, which he also failed (July 1878). Refusing to give up, he gained an appointment as lay evangelist to miners in the Borinage, living near Mons and as temporary pastor at Wasmes. Self-imposed privations broke his health, however, and in July 1879 he was forced to quit. That fall Pastor Pietersen, an amateur water-colorist, encouraged his latent interest in painting as a means of taking his mind off his troubles, and in the summer of 1880 Van Gogh wrote an impassioned letter to his younger brother Theo, who was working for Goupil's in Paris, announcing his determination to become a painter.

For the next five years Van Gogh studied and painted peripatetically in the Borinage, in Holland, and Antwerp; then, in March 1886, made a sudden decision to go to Paris.

Van Gogh stayed in Paris almost two years. He studied at Cormon's studio, met some of the Impressionists and became acquainted with their work. But while accepting many of the Impressionists' means, he could not accept the ends of the movement, and in February 1888 left for Arles.

Van Gogh's object in going to Arles was to paint himself back to mental health, and a not too well-defined idea of founding a quasi-religious artists' colony. Neither was successful. Gauguin's famous visit with him (October–December 1888) was the only tangible realization of the colony, and it was a traumatic fiasco. And by May 1889 his mental health had deteriorated so far that he committed himself to the asylum at nearby Saint-

Rémy; thenceforth fits of manic depression were recurrent. In January 1890 the first appreciation of Van Gogh's painting was published, by Albert Aurier in *Le Mercure de France,* and in March the first and only one of his pictures sold during his lifetime was bought, from the Brussels exhibition of *Les Vingt.* It was too late. Though he had worked with frantic fertility—more than 150 pictures belong to his last few months—in his own eyes Van Gogh' was a confirmed failure, a permanent charge on his brother's charity. In May he returned to Paris, then went to live with Dr. Gachet in Auvers, where in July 1890 he attempted suicide. Even this was a failure; after shooting himself he was able to get up and walk home. Two days later, however, he died of his wound.

The largest single collections of Van Gogh's work are those of Vincent Willem Van Gogh in Amsterdam and the Kröller-Müller State Museum in Otterlo. For example, most of the drawings from Van Gogh's first (c. 1880–c. 86) period, such as *Miners, The Borinage* (1880), *Old Man in Despair* (c. 1883) and *The Loom* (1884), are at Otterlo; *The Potato Eaters* and *Self-Portrait* (at Neunen or Antwerp) are in Amsterdam. In American collections, representative works of his two years in Paris (1886–88) include *Factories at Clichy* (Saint Louis); *Old Shoes* (Cambridge, Fogg; and also Baltimore); *Montmartre* (Chicago). Of his Arles period (February 1888–May 1890), examples in America include such landscapes as *Starry Night* (New York, Modern), *Public Gardens at Arles* (Washington, Phillips), *The Road Menders* (Cleveland), *Orchard, Springtime* (New York, Payson), *Rain* (Philadelphia, McIlhenny), *Bridge at Trinquetaille* (New York, Kramarsky), *Landscape with Olive Trees* (New York, John Hay Whitney). Still lifes and interiors from the Arles period include *The Night Café* (New York, Clark); *Sunflowers* (Philadelphia, Tyson), *Irises* (New York, Payson), and *Bedroom at Arles* (page 269). Representative portraits include *La Mousmé* (Washington), *L'Arlésienne* (*Madame Ginoux;* New York, Metropolitan); and in Boston, *Roulin the Postman* and *La Berceuse* (*Madame Roulin*). Van Gogh's *Self-Portrait* with bandaged ear is in the Block Collection, Chicago; with palette, in John Hay Whitney's, New York; with cropped hair, in the Fogg, Cambridge. Representative of Van Gogh's last period (May–July 1890) are *Houses at Auvers* (Boston), *Stairway at Auvers* (Saint Louis) and *Mademoiselle Ravoux* (San Francisco).

Among the many useful books on Van Gogh are the studies by Charles Estienne (1953) and Meyer Schapiro (1950); Douglas Cooper, *Drawings and Watercolours* (1955), and, of course, John Rewald, *Post-Impressionism* (1954). Particularly significant source material is *Complete Letters,* tr. by Johanna Van Gogh-Bonger and E. de Dood; re-ed. by Mrs. R. Amussen et al., with drawings (1958). A *catalogue raisonné* of Van Gogh's works is provided in Frank Elgar, *Van Gogh* (1958).

3

"Primitivism":
Paul Gauguin (1848–1903)

Perhaps the most typical of all Paul Gauguin's self-portraits—and he, like Van Gogh and Cézanne, painted himself extraordinarily often—is the one in the National Gallery, Washington (page 285). Not that it is more attractive than others; all Gauguin's paintings are eye-catchingly decorative, with their distinctive combinations of large flat areas of bright color and sinuously linear patterns. Its significance is in the painter's unequivocal presentation of himself as a new and different sort of being. Here, holding between his fingers the revered uraeus serpent, ancient sign of ineffable wisdom and absolute power, is the artist as King and Seer; but even more deliberately, here is the artist as God. Haloed by a Holy Spirit, featured like Christ, he stands a second creator in Eden, able to give or withhold that paradisial fruit behind him which can teach men to become as gods knowing good and evil.

Put so baldly, it sounds blasphemous, or silly, or both; surely, we say, it must be a joke. And most people, then and now, have considered it one—a spoof, Gauguin laughing at himself. But Gauguin was not the type to laugh at himself. No one ever took himself more seriously than the man who wrote to de Rotonchamp, "I am not ridiculous, I cannot be ridiculous, for I am two things that cannot be ridiculous: a child and a savage."

The plain fact is—a fact recognized in Camille Pissarro's often quoted letter to his son describing "how shamelessly Gauguin behaved in order to get himself elected (that is the word) a 'man of genius' "—that for Gauguin painting was above all a means of making himself famous and important. Technically, he was far from a genius; we know, his friends knew, and even Gauguin himself was aware that his contributions to the art of painting were nothing compared to Cézanne's or Degas's or Courbet's. In form and content Gauguin's art was a potpourri of borrowings, chiefly from Pissarro and Degas, with a dash of Symbolism and Van Gogh's expressionism thrown in. He could disguise that as a joke, ironically castigating himself as "born of Cézanne, of Van Gogh, of [Emile] Bernard . . . what a clever pasticheur I am!" But the fact

276

that such talent as he had lay in the direction of decorative color patterns, line, and texture, was obvious even to so otherwise obtuse a critic as the *Athenaeum* reviewer who noted, apropos of the famous Post-Impressionist show Roger Fry organized at the Grafton Galleries in London in 1910, that Gauguin

> painted South Sea Islanders and made decorations not unsuitable for our own houses. His confreres [Cézanne and Van Gogh] painted subjects in a manner fit for the huts of savages.

Such comments (for this was neither the first nor the last) always infuriated Gauguin. To be thought of as a decorator was the last thing he wanted, no matter how salable it made his pictures. His ambition—or, better, his compulsion—was to be known as a profound thinker, a leader of men. With his technical gifts as mediocre as they were, only on these grounds could he justify his life to himself and to the world.

Even more obviously than Cézanne or Van Gogh, Gauguin differed from great painters in the old tradition in that he was anything but a precocious genius. When we first meet him in Paris he is a prosperous ex-stockbroker, a man in his thirties, with a Danish wife and six children abandoned in Copenhagen, who is trying to turn what has been a Sunday-afternoon avocation for painting into a full-time profession. And we may be sure he feels something of a guilty conscience; throughout the rest of his life we always sense, never very far below the surface, an impulse to self-justification. Whatever he has done he does only, he proclaims, because he is a truly great man who owes it to the world not to let his genius lie fallow; at all costs he must maintain the pose of the inspired artist whose superiority to ordinary mortals justifies all departures from ordinary codes and conventions. Defiantly, compulsively, he flaunts the banner of Courbet, wraps himself in it, makes it his armor. No doubts of the doctrine can ever be entertained. The Impressionists compromised Courbet's concept of the divine artist-creator by attempting to combine with it the idea of the painter as a follower and impartial recorder of Nature; Gauguin will have none of that. Borrower of Impressionist techniques he may be, but their objectivity he entirely rejects; he will be, he must be, the Creator consciously able and determined to make a world in his own image.

Now if you want to get the reputation of a great and original thinker but have no obviously great or original talents, what is the most promising way to go about it? Eccentricity of behavior, of course; you wear bizarre costumes, you break conventional codes, but that is too easy and not enough. One of the surest ways, experience has shown, is to cultivate religion, or, more precisely, religiosity. You can become a professed "seeker" after "religious experience." And this Gauguin did with great success. The times, to be sure, were right for it. However much both sides might deny it, the fierce mid-19th-century battle of Darwinists with believers in Biblical revelation had in fact completed the long erosion of orthodox convictions which the 17th-century Wars of Religion and 18th-century rationalism had begun. Churches might continue to profess the old doctrines, but they did so with new, softer, more relativistic interpretations; the old certitude, the old black-and-white authority, were gone. And in their place came, paradoxically enough, a furious resurgence of all those old superstitions which the Age of Reason had apparently crushed forever. Necromancy, racialist folklore, spiritualism, fetishism—they all reappeared, but under new auspices. What 18th-century rationalists had considered atavistic survivals of primitive and prehistoric cultural patterns among the lowest classes of the population were revived by a new class of intellectuals as serious fields for "scientific" research. Sir James G. Frazer, for one, spent a lifetime collecting and collating in his *Golden Bough* those very legends of primitive fertility rites and myths of creation which intellectuals three or four generations before had tried to stamp into oblivion. And work like his, popularized by the new fast presses of the late 19th century, triggered off and sustained a whole constellation of cults and coteries dedicated to more or less occult speculation among the vast and growing world of subscholarship which mass education was bringing into being. In such a setting, a man of Gauguin's pretensions could flourish.

It was easy to pick up the language of the new occult scholarship and proclaim that if we are not to become the kind of automatons revealed in the social Impressionism of Degas and Lautrec, we must get back to those "realities" intuitively known to primitive peoples which our overcivilized culture is ignoring and destroying. They alone can save us; and it is through the medium of art that they can be best recovered. Art must be brought back to its "primitive" roots, not only for its own rejuvenation, but that the world may be saved through art. This was the burden of Gauguin's message; and suiting his actions to the word, he ostentatiously abandoned the effete and overcivilized world of the late 19th century in a series of dramatic and successively more remote self-imposed exiles.

The story unfolds like a fantastic parody of *The Pilgrim's Progress*.

We see Gauguin first a prosperous stockbroker in Paris, the bourgeois City of Destruction (1871–83). But increasingly he begins to go about crying *what shall I do to be saved?* and in due course the Word comes to him. He sees what must be done; clutching the Word to his bosom, he forsakes wife and children to set out on his pilgrimage to the Celestial City—first stop, Rouen (1883), where he confidently hopes to earn a living as a full-time painter without difficulty. Disillusionment is speedy, and he falls into his Slough of Despond; everywhere the true vision of the artist's mission has been perverted, everywhere the Word goes misunderstood. It is hard enough to be scorned and censured by his wife's relatives in Copenhagen, where he goes to live after the Rouen fiasco; far worse is it to find himself regarded by the established Impressionists on his return to Paris alone as a tiresome braggart and callow opportunist (1883–86). Nevertheless he struggles on, and eventually finds his Interpreter's House—the little village of Pont-Aven in Brittany, where a group of faithful admirers and believers gathers to strengthen his sense of mission. On a brief visit to Martinique (1887), his vision is confirmed by his first really primitive "experience," albeit not an entirely satisfactory one, since this place is both too civilized for salvation and too primitive for Gauguin's civilization-sapped constitution.

On his return to Paris (1888) he slips, like Christian, into a Pleasant Arbor. On the strength of his pseudo-anthropological and sociological studies of primitive cultures, his fame spreads enough to make Gauguin the center of a small cult; but in the end this Arbor proves for him, as for Christian, a moment of retrogression. Word of his achievements reaches Arles, where poor Vincent Van Gogh is so industriously and so desperately working to sublimate frustrated religious impulses into painting; thinking Gauguin a kindred soul to himself, he eventually persuades Theo to finance the new seer's trip south to see him and make the little yellow house in Arles center of a religiously "real" movement in art (October 1888). Seduced momentarily by the prospect of free accommodation, Gauguin comes to Arles; but to his dismay it soon appears Van Gogh thinks of art as a divine end in itself, not merely a means to create godlike artists; like Christian, Gauguin has been lulled into losing the Word. Leaving the shattered Dutchman to pick up the pieces of his life and person alone, Gauguin hastens back to Paris to return to the Way (December 1888).

His reward is the Palace Beautiful—a stay in Brittany (first at Pont-Aven, then at LePouldu in Finistère, 1889–90). Here he experiences his first real success as titular leader of his own art movement—"syntheti-cism"—and head of a coterie of worshipful admirers, including paying patrons. Here he paints the first truly mature statements of his new religion, among them *Bonjour, Monsieur Gauguin* (Museum of Modern Art, Prague; a curious tribute to the Prophet's painting, *Bonjour, Monsieur Courbet,* which Gauguin and Van Gogh had seen together at the Fabre Museum of Courbet's work in Montpellier), *The Yellow Cross* (Buffalo) and *Jacob Wrestling with the Angel* (*Vision after the Sermon,* Edinburgh).

In the latter two, he celebrates vestiges of that "true" religion which has survived from pagan times among the Celtic peasantry of this remote corner of Europe. He shows his followers how, whereas degenerate orthodoxy would have us believe that supernatural realities are absolute and outside man's control, in fact it is the other way round: New Testament stories of Christ on the Cross and Old Testament legends of the god of Abraham, Isaac, and Jacob are real only insofar as peasants like these believe in them. Such, he maintains, was the religion of Ancient Egypt, where Pharaoh owed his godlike powers to his people's faith in them. Solipsistic faith like this moves mountains without miracle. And, of most importance, in a world resting on this kind of Reality, the painter is unchallengeably prime mover. Just as it was on the carvers and painters who made his images that Pharaoh's power ultimately depended, so in the new age to come the artist will recover his ancient power and glory. Already Gauguin hints at what such a Creator can do for his people, when he immortalizes the innkeeper Marie Henry, or invests Meyer de Haan, his new-found patron, with the awesome wisdom of mages and lohans in the portrait *Nirvana* (c. 1890, Hartford, Wadsworth Atheneum).

At the end of 1890 Gauguin returns to Paris, determined to press on to the primeval Zion, which he now decides is to be found in Tahiti. First, however, he must go through his valley of Humiliation and vanquish his Apollyon. Despite what he thinks of as his swelling fame, the returns from a sale of pictures arranged by his admirers prove disappointingly small. And he has to withstand his wife's last reproachful efforts to lure him back to bourgeois Destruction, which he does with the usual arguments that it would be doing mankind a disservice for him

> . . . to abandon the prize for the shadow, and the shadow is the role of an employee. If I were employed at 2,000 or 4,000 francs [a month], the price of your brothers, what would there be to reproach me with?

Nothing. I wanted, in spite of the conviction that my conscience gave me, to consult others (men who also count) to know if I were doing my duty. All were of the same opinion, that my business is my art, it is my stock-in-trade, the future of my children, it is the honour of the name that I have given them. Consequently, I work for my art which is nothing (pecuniarily) at the moment (times are difficult), but which I can divine for the future. It's a long process, you all say, but what am I to do? I am the first to suffer. I can assure you that if the people who know said that I had no talent and that I am lazy, I would have abandoned the game long ago.

The Celestial City is in fact in sight, and nothing can deter him:

May the day come, and soon, when I shall go and bury myself in the woods of an island in Oceania, live there joyfully and calmly with my art . . . far from this European struggle for money.

In this deadly struggle no weapon, least of all hypocrisy, is neglected:

You are wrong when you say that our two lives are broken. Yours is delivered of all its shackles. Surrounded by your family and by your children, your days pass . . . flattered, respected, loved. Your genius has been remunerated. . . .

And so Apollyon is thrust aside, defeated forever; in April 1891 Gauguin sets out for Tahiti where, he expects, "I shall be able, in the silence of the lovely tropical nights, to listen to the soft murmuring music of the movements of my heart in loving harmony with the mysterious beings who surround me. True at last, without money troubles, I shall be able to love, sing, and die."

Now for a time the Way runs straight before him. After a brief and unpleasant brush with colonial civilization at the capital town of Papeete he settles in the interior, finds a *vahine,* Tehura, through whom "I have all the enjoyments of a free, animal, and human life," by means of letters and canvases expounds his doctrine to Faithful and Talkative friends, and confirms himself in his mission. Now appear before his eyes, in living Reality, those primitive archetypes he had known from books and photographs, and had been deceived by a wicked and doomed civilization into imagining long dead. In *Ia Orana Maria ("Ave Maria")*, a Tahitian mother and child are presented gifts in a ceremony recalling at once Javanese temple ritual and the Christian story of the Visit of the Magi (New York, Metropolitan, 1891). *Te aa no Areois ("The Queen of the Areois")* sits with full-front torso and side-view legs like some Egyptian tomb figure reincarnate (1892, New York, Paley). In *Ta Matete* (*"The Market"*) (Basel), the hierarchical dignity of an Egyptian frieze is reinforced by an emphasis on simple primary colors of the sort old Roman Pliny attributed to the revered Polygnotos, father of Greek painting. In *Manao Tupapau* (*"The Spirit of the Dead Watching"*) (New York, Conger Goodyear), a plump nude in a typical Rococo pose is now reimbued with the old power of the naked female body to evoke awareness of the mysterious powers and occult forces of life. This is Gauguin's first great creative period, and when in August 1893 he returns to Paris to recover his health, and collects an inheritance from an uncle, he enters upon that "delicate plain called Ease, where" he goes "with much content":

> Gauguin was for a time, at least, a figure, and he determined to make the most of the moment. He dressed in a way that was well calculated to shock those *imbéciles* who could not understand his latest paintings. He wore a long blue frock coat with buttons of mother-of-pearl over a blue Russian shirt bordered with yellow and green embroidery . . . He had a large grey felt hat with a sky-blue ribbon, white gloves and walking stick, the handle of which he had surmounted with a blister-pearl and carved into the form of a male and female figure in an intimate embrace. He wore the special Breton sabots that he had carved and decorated himself. . . . He had moved into a new studio . . . in the rue Vercingétorix. . . . the entrance . . . had . . . a warning in Tahitian, *te faruru,* which informed his visitors that his studio was an abode of love. . . .*

But alas, the "plain [called Ease] was but narrow," and "quickly got over." Gauguin has yet to meet Giant Despair and Doubting Castle. In the summer of 1894, during a visit to Pont-Aven, Gauguin gets into a street fight and has his ankle broken; Javanese Annah deserts and robs him; he promptly contracts syphilis from a streetwalker. Crass practical trials threaten to break his spirit; but suddenly, " 'What a fool,' quoth he, 'am I thus to lie in a stinking dungeon, when I may as well walk at liberty. I have a key in my bosom called Promise . . .' " "I have made a final resolution, which is to return to Oceania for always." In February 1895 he does so.

Back in Tahiti, the Delectable Mountains soon come into view. Now at last it is vouchsafed the pilgrim to discover direct and tangible and final evidence of that faith which in *The Golden Bough* had been mere

---

* Robert Burnett, *The Life of Paul Gauguin* (New York, 1939).

abstruse deduction, to proclaim to unbelievers with the conclusive conviction of personal experience that what in the bourgeois City of Destruction were considered its "highest" forms of art and civilization were in fact no more than effete and decadent reflections of archetypal primitive Realities. Some might sneer that Gauguin was no better than Mark Twain's "innocents abroad," that he found on Tahiti only what he brought there and had prepared himself to find; no matter. At least and at last Gauguin has no doubts. Here in a primitive world with primitive vocabulary he re-creates the greatest masterpieces, truer than the originals. He has already transfigured Raphael's *Transfiguration* into *Mahana No Atua ("The Day of the God")* (1894, Chicago); now he re-creates the classical Venus, *Te Arii Vahine,* (1896), *Woman with Mangoes,* (1899, New York, Metropolitan); Greek horsemen, *The White Horse* (Louvre); the Christian Nativity, *Maternity on the Seaside* (c. 1899, Leningrad); and he climaxes them all with a primitive "academic machine" inspired by Puvis de Chavannes—*Whence Come We? What Are We? Whither Go We?* (page 287), which he regards as his masterpiece: "a philosophic work, comparable to the Gospel." Yet obstacles still find him; Little-Faith, the Flatterer, Ignorance try his spirit, and in January 1898 he attempts suicide by taking arsenic, succeeding only, however, in further damaging his already deteriorating body. In April 1898 comes his encounter with the Enchanted Ground, thoughts of Temporary and Turnback, as his remittances from Paris are delayed. A friend tempts him with the suggestion that he give up and go back to stockbroking, and he apparently can think of no better excuse than his being "an old man of fifty" unable to cope with "Jewish youths" in the banking business; he even sinks to taking a job as clerk with the government in Papeete.

But Beulah land—*nave nave fenua, noa noa* ("the delectable world, the fragrant world")—lies just ahead. By January 1899 enough money has arrived to clear his debts. In February 1899 his *vahine* gives birth to a boy, almost white: "lovely, like everything adulterous," Gauguin exults. He works with the infant in his studio, but he feels no bourgeois care for it: "Children do not bother me, for I 'abandon them.'" He can even couch his strongest compulsion in joking language: He can so work, for "I am a first-class bounder who has abandoned his wife and his children." His pilgrimage is nearly done; in 1901 he leaves Tahiti, as being too civilized for him now, for Hiva-Hoa in the Marquesas, where he indulges one last joyful defiance of Beelzebub, incarnate in the bourgeois colonial authorities, and in May 1903 triumphantly crosses the River, realizing that ambition which he had expressed when Stéphane Mallarmé died in 1898, that "I, who now love painting only—neither wife, nor children," should be "another who has died a martyr to art."

Of the three great Post-Impressionists whose lives and work completed the half-century-long transformation of the concept of what paintings do and what painters are, Paul Gauguin was by far the most immediately influential. At first it seems hard to understand why.

In every respect but one, Gauguin was manifestly the weakest artist of the three. Lacking either the determined persistence of Cézanne or the fierce dedication of Van Gogh, his technique never rose to the level of their mature competence. As for his basic ideas and procedure, they were so obviously fallible that more than a century earlier Samuel Johnson had succinctly cut them down to size, when Boswell, on September 30, 1769,

> attempted to argue for the superior happiness of the savage life, upon the usual fanciful topics. JOHNSON: "Sir, there can be nothing more false. The savages have no bodily advantages beyond those of civilized men. They have not better health; and as to care or mental uneasiness, they are not above it, but below it, like bears. No, Sir; you are not to talk such paradox: let me have no more on 't. It cannot entertain, far less can it instruct. Lord Monboddo, one of your Scotch judges, talked a great deal of such nonsense. I suffered *him;* but I will not suffer *you.*"
>
> BOSWELL: "But, Sir, does not Rousseau talk such nonsense?" JOHNSON: "True, Sir, but Rousseau *knows* he is talking nonsense, and laughs at the world for staring at him." BOSWELL: "How so, Sir?" JOHNSON: "Why, Sir, a man who talks nonsense so well, must know that he is

32A. *Paul Gauguin:* Self-Portrait with Halo. *Washington, National Gallery of Art, Chester Dale Collection. 1889.* See also 32B, Gauguin.

In semi-isolation in Brittany, and total isolation in the South Seas, Gauguin consummated the Social Impressionists' practice and Courbet's principles of the painter as a savior of society, basing his technique on the one and his behavior on the other. There is nothing accidental in the resemblance of this self-portrait (and several others) to conventional pictures of Christ.

284

talking nonsense. But I am *afraid* [chuckling and laughing] Monboddo does *not* know that he is talking nonsense." BOSWELL: "Is it wrong then, Sir, to affect singularity, in order to make people stare?" JOHNSON: "Yes, if you do it by propagating error: and indeed, it is wrong in any way. There is in human nature a general inclination to make people stare; and every wise man has to cure himself of it, and does cure himself. If you wish to make people stare by doing better than others, why, make them stare till they stare their eyes out. But consider how easy it is to make people stare, by being absurd. I may do it by going into a drawing-room without my shoes."

But in one respect Gauguin was outstanding. He had a genius for self-dramatization that Cézanne and Van Gogh entirely lacked. Whatever he did was done in a blaze of notoriety. Furthermore, he was articulate. Whereas a claim to godlike creativity was merely implicit in Cézanne's or Van Gogh's creation of subjective Realities, Gauguin made it explicit, flamboyant, unmistakable. Consequently he was able to bring the New Art and the New Artist to critical and public attention as the other two never could. Gauguin's death in 1903 marked the culmination of the transitional period from Old to New Painting, of a conscious search for Reality of a kind and along the lines he had made so ostentatiously plain.

32B. *Paul Gauguin:* Whence Come We? What Are We? Whither Go We? *Courtesy, Museum of Fine Arts, Boston. 1897–98.*

Much more conscious of himself as a "great painter" than either Cézanne or Van Gogh, Gauguin was in fact shallower than either. But possibly just because of this, Gauguin was the most immediately influential of the Post-Impressionists. His idea that the roots of Reality are to be sought in primitive and unspoiled communities of peasants and savages had irresistible appeal to a generation of intellectuals fascinated by Frazer's Golden Bough, Havelock Ellis, *and Freudian insistence on the pre-eminent importance of childhood experience. At the same time, his bright colors and sweeping patterns, supposedly manifesting "primitive" sensibilities though in fact derived from the sophistications of Art Nouveau, were equally appealing to all the diverse people who vaguely felt that somehow paintings ought to be pleasing to look at as well as "realistic."*

NOTES

Noteworthy among critical monographs on Gauguin are those by Robert Burnett, *The Life of Paul Gauguin* (1939), from which most quotations here are taken, and Charles Estienne, *Gauguin* (1953). Extensive information and documentation on Gauguin's life until 1893 is contained in John Rewald, *Post-Impressionism from Van Gogh to Gauguin* (Museum of Modern Art, New York, 1956). Gauguin's writings and letters have been extensively published: e.g., *Noa-Noa* (O. F. Theis translation, 1927), and *Letters to his Wife and Friends* (Cleveland, 1949).

THE 20th-CENTURY SEARCH FOR REALITY

I

"Classic Modern Art"

1900–1920

BY THE OPENING OF THE 20TH CENTURY, THE "FIFTY years' revolution in painting" was over. Among the advance guard at least, its basic principles were firmly established. Now it could be taken for granted that art was concerned with Reality, not Beauty. Now it could be taken for granted that the true artist's function was not to beautify life, but to reveal its truths. And now as the smoke of battle cleared, the older warriors seemed all at once to move off the field. Those of the great original Impressionists not already dead retired into inactivity or the status of classics. Van Gogh died in 1889 and Seurat in 1891; Toulouse-Lautrec in 1901, Gauguin in 1903, Cézanne in 1906. For a moment there were many followers but no real leaders; and, freed alike from any need to establish or defend basic positions and from any really dominant personality, the rising generation of advance-guard painters began to fan out in all directions over the newly won terrain. The immediate result was an immense proliferation of small new movements in painting, not only in Paris, but also in Milan, Moscow, Dresden, Munich, Vienna. Accompanying his admirable 1951 exhibition entitled *Climax: 1913,* Sidney Janis prepared a chart which dramatically illustrated what had happened by a great black peak, representing the steady multiplication of new ideas and movements which rose sharply to crest in 1913, just before the Great War.

Analyzing all these movements in detail would require, and has already elicited, many books. Substantially, however, through all their diverse manifestations there runs the same basic motivation, the same new concept and expression of Reality. And one figure in retrospect summarizes them all. For, to paraphrase Churchill's *Gathering Storm,* "into the gaping void which had been opened up" in the artistic life of Paris, "after a pause there strode a . . . ferocious genius" from

291

across the border—Pablo Picasso. To understand him is in a sense to understand all the rest.

1

Eclectic Man and Apocalyptic Symbol:
The Early Picasso (*1881–1908*)

What made Picasso leader of the modern movement after 1900? Or in other words, of what did his genius consist? Not primarily technical skill, though of this he had plenty, for technical skill was not what the hour demanded. Nor yet originality; it would be difficult to prove that Picasso originated any ideas. Essentially, it was a combination of compelling personality and extraordinary ability to synthesize both techniques and ideas. To this day Picasso's powerful personality can still put people under its spell, as witness what Alfred Werner in the *Saturday Review* called the "appallingly unselective . . . campaign biography" of *Picasso: His Life and Times* by Roland Penrose, "a trusting, uncritical worshipper," who "from a reverent distance . . . watches his god work." And when to this was added a genius for picking ideas from the ambient air, success was inevitable.

If there is one old master to whom Picasso may be best compared, it is Raphael Sanzio, "Prince of Painters" in the High Renaissance. Not, of course, because of any resemblance in the forms of their respective art; but because not since Raphael had any painter so decisively seized the leadership of painting in his time at such an early age, and because both did it in much the same way—through an uncanny gift for sensing the trends of advance-guard taste a moment before others, and riding just ahead of them on each successive wave. As the young Raphael learned from, absorbed, and reinterpreted Perugino, Leonardo, and Michelangelo in turn, yet never entirely understood or surpassed any of them, so by the time he was twenty-five Picasso had absorbed and recapitulated, like an embryo, the whole historical development of painting in the last half of the 19th century.

By 1900 Picasso had covered as much artistic ground as he could in his native Spain. From a mastery of mid-Victorian literal and Academic realism inherited from his father he had progressed to experimentation in the Art Nouveau idiom—predominantly its English version, going back via Beardsley and Burne-Jones, as known from magazines, to Pre-Raphaelite sources—which was then the advance-guard movement in provincial Barcelona.

And the instant he arrives in Paris, in October 1900, he begins casting about in every direction, sniffing to pick up the most promising trail. He finds that the Art Nouveau wave on which he arrived from Spain has already crested in the world art capital. Instantly he gives it up and jumps on its successor, the vogue for Toulouse-Lautrec. A flurry of youthful pictures ape those dyspeptic commentaries on amorality and social degeneration which have just captured the advance-guard imagination. But characteristically, he varies them just enough to avoid being labeled a Lautrec follower—particularly after he is accused of being one by a reviewer of his first Paris show, at Vollard's in June 1901. Sometimes he adds a dash of "terrible Spanish ferocity" from the tradition of Ribera and Valdés Leal (and more directly, by imitating the work of Isidore Nonell, an older Spanish contemporary who lived from 1872 to 1911 and lent Picasso a studio). Sometimes he adopts an exaggeratedly crude pointillism for expressive effect. Sometimes he affects a cold linearism and flat color areas in the mood of Degas. And then, as he picks up the main current of French painting, Lautrec's influence is abruptly subsumed in successive waves of ideas from the three great Post-Impressionists, beginning towards the end of 1901.

First, a brief encounter with Van Gogh. Picasso has as little empathy with tortured as with timid souls. But he can appreciate the value of Van Gogh's implicit demonstration that genius justifies turning the world inside out to use as a vehicle for expressing the greatness of a painter's inner life, and the appeal of Van Gogh's dramatic slashes of paint; a few bites, and that much of Van Gogh, at least, is digested. Next it is Gauguin's and the Symbolists' turn. Here are more congenial spirits. To see in the painter a godlike creator who vouchsafes men oracular wisdom couched in archetypal primitive forms—that lesson Pablo Picasso hardly needs to be taught. It is Gauguin and his followers who primarily inspire the forms of Picasso's "blue" paintings beginning in 1902, on into the "pink" period of 1905. But, of course, he copies Gauguin at an even more discreet remove than he copied Lautrec, disguising his borrowings in many ways. He carefully chooses different prototypes; if Gauguin's primitive models came from Britanny or Polynesia, Picasso will draw on Negro Africa or Ancient Egypt for his.

293

Furthermore, he mixes them up so that, while the Symbolist inspiration for a painting like *Life* (1903, Cleveland) is patent, it is not provable from the forms, which may or may not owe something indiscriminately to archaic Greek *kouroi,* Iberian sculpture, El Greco, or African idols. And where Gauguin used riotously primitive colors, Picasso, though imitating his brush stroke, deliberately affected monochromatic arrangements.

By the end of 1905 this vein is about worked out; Gauguin can provide no more nutriment. A countereddy against the prevailing drift towards primitivism becomes apparent. Picasso is sensitive to such things, as always, and his large *Acrobat Group,* the major work of 1905 (Washington), shows it. But this kind of cool stability goes against the grain, and will not last. The next shift is signaled by a landscape painted at Gosol in the summer of 1906 and based with what for Picasso was extraordinary obviousness on Cézanne (New York, Springold). Among the *cognoscenti* of Paris, a trickle of interest in Cézanne had been growing ever since his reintroduction at Vollard's show of 1905; but at this moment he was still far from widely known. Few could have predicted that with Cézanne's death in October, and the large retrospective show of 1907, that trickle would suddenly become a flood of adulation strong enough to put three Cézannes in the Louvre by 1912. Yet Picasso, with his uncanny sense for timing, was one of the few. His "blue" and "pink" periods end with the same abruptness with which Raphael's style changed when he added the last figures to the "School of Athens" in the Vatican Stanze. Picasso has met his Michelangelo. And for a moment it looks as if he, like Raphael, has bitten off more than he could chew.

Only for a moment. Where Cézanne, after a lifetime of study, had tentatively declared that he thought he was beginning to realize what he had in mind, Picasso soon proclaims that he not only understands Cézanne's goals perfectly, but is able to realize them. The trick is to fuse Cézanne's "significant form" with Gauguin's "primitivism." On the basis of a chance remark by the Master about all nature being composed of cylinders, cones, and cubes, you reduce the subtleties of "significant form" to a trite system of lines, angles, and quasi-geometrical shapes, which you proceed to identify with the kind of stark planes and sharp angles characteristic of primitive arts in the South Seas or Negro Africa. You are then in a position to maintain that the Reality of form which Cézanne so long and so painfully sought to distill direct from Nature has already been revealed through primeval intuition in the arts of primitive men. It follows that all the perceptive modern painter need do is to develop these primitive revelations to a formal conclusion. The thing was easy; how easy, Picasso showed in a sequence of pictures from late 1906 and 1907. *Portrait of Gertrude Stein* (New York, Modern) in which a body posed in the manner of Lautrec and painted in the manner of Cézanne has the impassive and impersonal face of an African mask. *A Woman Combing Her Hair* (Chicago, Marx), whose classically modeled lower torso slowly congeals into primitively rigid shapes, culminating in a masklike face, as if the whole evolution of classical art from archaic column-figure to Polyclitus and Alkamenes were reversed in one painting. Standing nude figures (e.g., *Two Nudes,* Pittsburgh, Thompson) in which in late 1908 take on the forms and attributes of archaic column-figures. And then, to sum it all up, the *Demoiselles d'Avignon* (page 299) in the spring of 1907. Here, repainting an earlier brothel scene imitating Toulouse-Lautrec, Picasso begins with an archaic column-figure on the left, and proceeds through a series of four other figures to produce a disquisition on formal structural analysis climaxed on the right by a figure broken up into dissociated geometric elements evocative of African idols. This brings him to 1908.

In the fall of 1908, Georges Braque's exhibition at the Salon d'Automne breaks away from dependence on primitive inspiration in favor of more purely intellectual and quasi-scientific dissections of form. Art critic Louis Vauxcelles christens the idea "Cubism." Picasso hesitates not an instant. Without breaking stride, he turns into a cubist. Cubism proves the perfect vehicle for him. On it he rides to fame and fortune. And through that fame and fortune, his attitudes to art and his concept of the artist become widely accepted as characteristic of modern art in general. Before considering Cubism, then, it is worth considering what these attitudes and views were.

Picasso in those early years never wrote much; but his art spoke for him. In it were discernible three constant and constantly related principles. And, all his admirers' talk of inexhaustible fertility and unpredictable creativity to the contrary, this small stock of basic ideas was all he ever had; he never varied from the fundamental outlook on life established in these early years, however much his later modes of expressing it changed. These principles are simple to summarize. First, a conviction that the true artist is and must be alienated from society, and indeed from civilization at large—"alone and unafraid, in a world he never made." Second, corollary to the first, a conviction that the true Reality which this artist must ever seek is not to be found in or derived from Nature; that it consists of ideas, created by and dwelling in the realm of the mind generally, and the painter's mind in particular. And third, corollary to the other two, that the artist's immediate (though not necessarily ultimate) function in society is to attack, tear down, destroy the false Reality of this tangible world here and now, so that the other, truer, intangible Reality which now can be known only through the painter's and the mystic's inspired intuition, may one day stand freely forth revealed to all. These principles are manifest both in Picasso's early art and in his early life.

Picasso in his early Paris years was a lonely young man, living among other lonely young men in colonies of exiles, predominantly Spaniards and Jews. But this exile was self-imposed. Had he chosen, he could easily have made a career for himself in Spain, unlike some of his acquaintances, who were real exiles with nowhere else to go. His attitude, and indeed his whole appearance in these years (the wide staring eyes, the cowlick over the forehead) is curiously reminiscent of another voluntary exile who at this very same time was living the life of a tramp in the doss houses of Vienna, likewise dreaming of fame and power to be achieved through art. Picasso cultivated and reveled in this pose of desperate alienation from these earliest days when he helped publish *Arte Joven* in Madrid, dedicated to social outcasts, to the time when, for all the fame and fortune heaped upon him, he remained as aloof, as unknowable, as egocentric, as ever. And in his early art, see how he represents himself—now as an Egyptian; now as the tormented young

33. *Pablo Picasso:* The Blind Man. *Cambridge, The Fogg Art Museum, Harvard University, Maurice Wertheim Collection. 1903.*

Often compared to Raphael for precocious leadership of his time in art, Picasso is also comparable to Raphael in eclectic ability to appropriate and exploit the accomplishments and ideas of predecessors, without fully digesting or overtly imitating them. So in an early work like this there is evidence of the successive absorption of ideas and techniques from Art Nouveau, Degas, Toulouse-Lautrec, Gauguin, and Van Gogh, but insofar as there are specific borrowings, the Douanier Rousseau had real method in his madness when he told Picasso, "We are the greatest painters of our time, you in the Egyptian style, I in the modern."

man oppressed by present, past and future *Life;* now as Harlequin set stonily apart from the world of life and gaiety around him. His favorite themes are social outcasts—families of clowns and acrobats, forever homeless, forever on the move; blind beggars; beings mentally, spiritually, physically deformed. True, most of them are drawn from Toulouse-Lautrec; but significantly he changes them from people to symbols of alienation, by composing them in closed instead of open forms, making them cower helplessly unrelated to the space around.

To realize how consistently Picasso's Reality is set in the realm of generalized ideas rather than derived from tangible, specific particularities, compare his handling of themes like *Maternity* (1903, Cambridge, Fogg) or harlequins or prostitutes with Daumier's, or with Toulouse-Lautrec's. There are universal truths in Daumier—that is the secret of his enduring appeal to generation after generation, but always contained within a framework of specific individual experience, Daumier brings the cosmic down to earth, personalizes it, makes it meaningful to individuals in the great humanistic tradition of the Renaissance. By contrast, Picasso begins and ends with dehumanized abstractions. His monochromatic schemes of blues or pinks have the effect of dissolving all immediacy, all particularities, in one timeless spaceless nowhere. For Picasso's "maternity" we can have none of the personal identification we feel with Daumier's mother and child in the *Third-class Carriage* (page 127); this maternity in general, abstracted from any particular mother or any particular baby, can never be anything but intangible and remote. And from this conviction that Reality is an abstraction, not of this world, Picasso has never varied. It has informed both his art and his life from

34. *Pablo Picasso:* Les Demoiselles d'Avignon. *Collection, The Museum of Modern Art, New York, Lillie P. Bliss Bequest. 1907.*

In 1906 influence from Cézanne became predominant in Picasso's work; but, characteristically, he combined it with ideas derived from Gauguin's "primitivism" and Van Gogh's "expressionism." By 1907 he had arrived at the fusion represented in this famous disquisition on formal picture-making that heralds his Cubist phase.

beginning to end. People have professed surprise at Picasso's partiality for international Communism; but the attachment is entirely logical. A mind already predisposed towards fundamental abstract Realities finds it easy, if not indeed necessary, to disguise the tangible physical facts of millions of murdered men, women and children as some remote "liquidation of undesirable elements," to subsume military conquest, subversion, treachery, and assassination under the abstraction of "world revolution" or "the peace campaign."

"How he does hate the human race! How he enjoys pushing its face!" So a perceptive critic described the young Picasso's compulsive delight in distorted bodies, faces broken into fragmented facets, congealing in undifferentiated spatial planes like frost on a window. And that, too, has never changed, though nowadays the sport has become such a matter of commonplace clichés that its old shock value is largely gone.

Superficially, this manifest urge to attack and destroy can be explained in simple contemporary terms, as the expression of a fashionable mood of disillusionment with science prevalent among certain groups of intellectuals at the beginning of the 20th century. A feeling was beginning to spread abroad that the great advances in technical thought and method over the preceding few decades were not, as had been confidently expected, resulting in a progressive elimination of things unknown. Quite the opposite; huge areas of ignorance, unsuspected before, were being revealed. Instead of a world more and more firmly under man's control, everything now seemed infinitely more mysterious and complex than ever. Science was literally dissolving the solid ground on which men stood, showing that rocks and tables and grass and water were all seething masses of molecules pursuing haphazard courses at incomprehensible speeds, microcosms within microcosms. Wassily Kandinsky, who as a forty-year-old painter ranked as a man of great wisdom among the youthful groups he frequented, was fond of recounting how the news of Rutherford and Soddy's discovery in 1904 that atoms could be divided came as a

> terrific impact, comparable to that of the end of the world . . . All things became flimsy, with no strength or certainty. I would hardly have been surprised if the stones had risen in the air and disappeared. To me, science had been destroyed. In its place—a mere delusion, guesswork . . .*

* Quoted in H. Rebay, *In Memory of Wassily Kandinsky* (New York, 1945), p. 49.

It was the 20th-century version of the *Sorrows of Werther*. Full of self-pity, these representatives of "the generation that grew to manhood about 1900," as Georges Lemaître describes it, found

> reality everywhere breaking up into elusive impalpable fragments. The intellectual conceptions which for centuries had been man's stay and support in hours of doubt and trial, now suddenly collapsed. Then began in many eager young men an impatient desire to clear away that wreckage . . . a spontaneous impulse to escape from the conventional, the artificial, and to. . . . return to a preintellectual state, to a primitivism akin to that of the Negroes of Central Africa—a stage of development in which intellect had not yet had a chance to draw an interpretative veil between the core of reality and man's sentient being.*

This is the intellectual background of the evolution of Picasso's forms in the years 1905–7. It helps to explain how he was able to foist a "primitive" interpretation on Cézanne's "significant form," and more significantly, why so many people were willing to accept what in retrospect seems a patently jejune synthesis.

A key monument in this development is the *Boy with a Horse,* which Picasso painted in 1905 as one study for a projected larger picture to be entitled *The Watering Place* (New York, Paley). As an ambitious statement about man's relationship to Nature, using the old Renaissance symbol of Man and Horse, Picasso's picture is curiously comparable, in its very different way, to the similarly ambitious and similarly unfinished *Adoration of the Magi* painted almost four hundred years earlier by that precocious harbinger of those artistic claims to godlike creatorship, Leonardo da Vinci (c. 1481, Florence, Uffizi). As Leonardo had used it in the background of the *Adoration* and in the Colleoni statue he helped Verrocchio design for Venice, Man and Horse had symbolized the triumphant command of human reason—i.e., science, the medieval "ratio"—over brute nature. True, in his later Sforza and Trivulzio variants on the theme, Leonardo had introduced the figure of a fallen foe beneath the horse's hoofs to emphasize that the powers of science in practice inevitably meant the power of a few men over many, using science-tamed Nature as an instrument; but still for him, as for all men in the historic Western tradition from Romanesque times to the late 19th century, science was the tool wherewith man puts the world into

* *From Cubism to Surrealism in French Literature* (Cambridge, Mass., 1947), p. 55.

purposeful order, whose power the artist showed forth by organizing a subject full of historical and mythological and allegorical complexities into measured and meaningful human sequences. For Picasso, science means the opposite. That the *Boy with a Horse* appeared at approximately the same moment as Einstein's theory of relativity is undoubtedly no more than a coincidence; but Picasso did not have to know specifically how the new physics was dissolving the old stable world of Newtonian cause and effect into a flux of time-space relationships and forces to sense that science no longer meant any measured and experimental confirmation of common sense. So, where Leonardo's concern was to make figures solider through subtler chiaroscuro, more meaningfully related to human experience through increasingly correct and expressive anatomy, and the whole more orderly through systematically proportioned and defined compositional planes, Picasso's was the reverse. His was no Renaissance man sitting confidently astride a controlled Nature, this, but a boy, whose pose deliberately recalls the stiff *kouroi* of those times before classical Greek insight learned to interpret and relate the world to individual minds and bodies; a figure floating in a vast unformed space with no fixed point of orientation; a figure who goes through the motions of leading the horse but in fact has nothing to lead him with—symbol of the plight of a humanity which goes on acting as if it were still in command whereas in fact Nature has somehow slipped out of control.

And now, if you believe that you can no longer rely on Reason or Science to give the world meaning, what is there left? Only to "clear away the wreckage" and free that atavistic instinct, that mystic extrasensory perception, on which primitive societies relied in the days before Reason and Science ever developed. So from the *Boy with a Horse* we go straight into the sequence of primitivizing pictures of which the *Woman Combing her Hair* is representative, which culminates in the *Demoiselles d'Avignon* of 1907, and thence to Cubism. In this development is a parallel to the burst of interest in psychic research characteristic of these years, with all its overtones of witch doctors inciting the spirits of the dead, and revivals of what in homo sapiens is the vestigial remnants of that extrasensory communication used by bees, ants, and lower forms of life; and in it, too, is a premonition of that primitivization of whole societies so well analyzed by Toynbee, manifested alike in the barbarization of the proletariat and the revival of primitive practices of slavery, the extension of individual guilt and punishment to entire families, clans, and races which within a few decades would be condoned and admired by people who considered themselves intellectuals and enlightened.

It is obvious that Picasso's principles, so early formulated and so consistently held, involve much more than the local reaction of some small group of early 20th-century intellectuals to a particular set of early 20th-century conditions. As a symbol and symptom, Picasso can be seen in a much wider historical perspective. This cultivated alienation, this passion for abstract Reality, this compulsive attack on Reason, all make him the supreme 20th-century representative of that antirational strain in European civilization which Lawrence Brown in *The Might of the West* analyzes as a constant counterpoint to the mainstream of historic Western life and thought:

> In the 13th century this view of life was called Joachimism. It has since been called many names, millenarianism, utopianism, socialism, international communism, for its outward program has always been in the style of its age. But under these shifts of fashion and intellectual formulae it has been one restless movement driven by the same powerful emotion. It has always been built on the same structural core: a passionate distaste for the kingdoms of this world and a mystical certainty that these wicked kingdoms will soon be replaced through the operations of powers that are not of this world. Whether these powers are given the name "God" or the name "science" [or "Art"] has been a difference of time, not of quality. The believers in each age have simply used the word current in their time for the mightiest power they could imagine.*

* (New York, 1963), p. 397.

303

NOTES

For data on Picasso's early career I have drawn chiefly on Phoebe Poole and Anthony Blunt, *Picasso: The Formative Years* (1962); Alfred H. Barr, Jr., *Picasso: Fifty Years of His Art,* and *Picasso: 75th Anniversary Exhibition* (Museum of Modern Art, 1957), and Roland Penrose, *Portrait of Picasso* (Museum of Modern Art, 1946). Quotations from Kandinsky in H. Rebay, *In Memory of Wassily Kandinsky* (1945, p. 49); from Lawrence Brown, *The Might of the West* (1963, p. 397); from Georges Lemaître, *From Cubism to Surrealism in French Literature* (Cambridge, Mass., 1947, p. 55).

Besides works cited in this chapter, any list of major early works by Picasso in American collections would include the following examples. Of his early phase: *Le Moulin de la Galette* (autumn 1900, New York, Thannhauser); of Toulouse-Lautrec influence: *Old Woman* (1901, Philadelphia); *The Blue Room* (1901, Washington, Phillips); of Van Gogh influence: *Self-Portrait* (1901, New York, John Hay Whitney); of the "blue" and "pink" periods, 1902–5: *Blind Man's Meal* (1903, New York, Metropolitan); *Maternity* (Cambridge, Fogg); *Blind Guitar Player* (1903, Chicago); *Woman with Crow* (1904, Toledo, Ohio); *Boy with Pipe* (New York, John Hay Whitney); *Circus Family* (1905, watercolor, Baltimore); *Woman with Fan* (1905, New York, Harriman).

2

Classical and Romantic Reality in the New Painting:

Cubism, Expressionism, and Futurism, 1907–1914

To the casually art-minded public of Europe, the developments in painting during the dozen years before 1914 seemed unbelievable. All the previous shocks administered by the "moderns" were nothing compared to what was now going on. All of a sudden small intense bands of painters seemed to spring up, not only in Paris but in cities all over Western Europe, viciously quarreling among themselves, but all agreeing that artists were superior to ordinary mortals and exempt from social conventions, and that painting no longer had any concern with making pictures of things. Subject matter in the old sense was not simply "distorted," it completely disappeared, leaving canvases covered with what to the uninitiated seemed mere smears, blotches, stripings of paint. Compared to the work of these Cubists, Futurists, Suprematists, Wild Beasts, Vorticists, Spiritualists, and the rest, what had been advance-guard painting in 1900 looked in retrospect reassuringly tame, conventional, even conservative. It was as if the traditional art of painting had suddenly been destroyed in a great explosion, leaving the scene littered with unidentifiable fragments.

But what was happening came as no surprise to those comparative few who knew how the art of painting had been evolving over the previous half century. It was in fact an entirely logical development. Once accept the premises that Reality is the painter's proper business and that true Reality must be subjective, and some such climax in abstraction and nonobjectivity becomes inevitable. In the New Painting as in the Old, form follows the function of content; change the inherent concept of what painting is, and a change in outward form is inevitable.

Furthermore, just as in the traditional theory of painting two concepts of Beauty had been recognized as equally legitimate goals—beautiful forms and beautiful feelings—so now it is apparent that beneath all the superficial differences of competing groups and "isms," two similarly basic and complementary concepts of Reality have emerged among painters in the new tradition. The one holds that Reality in painting is a matter of forms—shapes, lines, and colors in themselves; most representative of this concept is Cubism in its several variants. For the other, Reality is in the realm of elemental feelings and emotions which pure color, pure line, and pattern evoke; broadly, this concept is best embodied in Expressionism.

Superficially, Cubism and Expressionism seem quite separate movements in origin, evolution, and rationale, having in common only their peripheral offspring, Futurism. Cubism proper, successor to the classical tradition of form, was a short-lived and close-knit movement. Essentially confined to a small set of painters working in Paris, it appeared in mature form in 1908, reached a climax about 1912, by 1914 was already visibly disintegrating, and by the 1920s had broken up. Like the traditional bride's costume (appropriately enough for a movement that represented at once the climax of a long growth to maturity and the beginning of a new phase of life) its theory was systematically built out of something old (Cézanne's significant form), something borrowed (Gauguin's primitivism, taken over by Picasso and his circle and applied in African, Iberian, archaic Greek and other contexts), something blue (the concept of ahumanistic abstract Reality exemplified in Picasso's "blue" period), and something new (science replacing the old measurable

35A. *Pablo Picasso:* Portrait of Kahnweiler. *Chicago, The Art Institute, Gift of Mrs. Gilbert W. Chapman. c. 1910. See also 35B, Picasso.*

Two stages in the act of Creation—decomposing the visible world into its fundamental elements through analytical Cubism, then using those elements to build a new synthetic world of the painter's own. In The Eye of Man *(p. 145), Selden Rodman writes, "There is no greater aesthetic virtue in painting a table as the eye sees it than in so disguising its nature that its reality is lost; the thing is to paint a table in such a way that the spectator sees it, feels it, and knows it for the first time, and in so apprehending it receives some insight into his relation to it and its relation to the world." Were such criticism applied to this* Table, *however, it would miss the point; for this art is not the falsehood condemned by Plato as twice removed from Reality—a copy of a copy of an Idea—this is its own Reality, the Original Idea in the mind of the Creator.*

common-sense Reality with a complex of shifting primordial atoms whose counterpart it was the serious artist's duty to evoke). Expressionism, successor to the romantic tradition, was by contrast international, diverse, and long-lived.

The "Fauve" group in Paris, led by Henri Matisse and Georges Rouault, which first exhibited at the Salon d'Automne of 1905, was only one of several similar groups elsewhere, which in retrospect appear equally or more important; most notably The Bridge (Die Brücke) founded in Dresden in 1904, and The Blue Rider (Der Blaue Reiter) which developed in Munich a half-dozen years later. There were in addition individual Expressionists of all nationalities; the Norwegian Edvard Munch, the Austrian Kokoschka, the Russians Soutine and Kandinsky, the Swiss Paul Klee, the Germans Modersohn-Becker and Nolde, and many more. Expressionism developed somewhat earlier than Cubism, and remained viable far longer; certainly through the 1930s, and it is far from moribund yet. Its theory is likewise much more amorphous; though the influence of Van Gogh's life and practice was seminal, his was only one of all sorts of diverse elements that Expressionism incorporated in different ways, places, and times—Symbolism, medieval German illumination, Neo-Impressionism, primitivism, to cite only a few.

Yet in the last analysis, these differences turn out to be peripheral and far less important than the common core of similarities. Fundamentally Cubism, Expressionism, and their variants all manifested the same broad concept of what art is, were motivated by the same premises and impulses, and expressed the same view of the ultimate nature of Reality. The proof of it is to be seen in the pattern of evolution common to both Cubism and Expressionism. Though precise means and motives vary, both begin with a conviction that painting must be, first, a weapon to attack and destroy existing concepts of Reality, and second, a vehicle for establishing a New Reality which, though again precise formulations differ, both agree must not be "of this world." And there follows in each case a split between those who want to "reform" the old concept and uses

35B. *Pablo Picasso:* Table. *Northampton, Mass., Smith College Museum of Art. 1922.*

of painting, and those who want to change the nature of painting completely.

The Cubists, in their attack on the Old Reality, proudly claimed to be "scientific." Starting with the kind of additive images made by children and primitive peoples—composites of many different characteristic aspects of the same object—they went on to break Reality into pure abstract particles, creating fluid sequences of elements perceived in time, rather than static compositions. By 1912 this first, Analytical, phase of Cubism had reached a climax. All particular forms, even color, vanished from advanced Cubist canvases. Now the Cubists found themselves in the intoxicating position of God before Creation, in Plato's primeval world of undifferentiated archetypes. And now they could indeed take on the role Courbet and Leonardo had foreseen for artists. Now they could build a new world of their own out of these atoms. The result was the second or "synthetic" phase of Cubism. To uninitiated eyes, Synthetic Cubism seemed to mark a re-emergence of recognizable images; the musicians and still lifes that succeeded violins and bottles and human beings splintered into atoms were, to be sure, hardly anything like photographic images but still they were recognizable to the extent of having upsides and downsides, color and pattern with some apparent association with the tangible exterior world. But the resemblance was specious; these were not images in the old sense. In fact, Synthetic Cubist paintings were something quite new in the world, in every sense. Always before, even in Analytic Cubism, the act of painting had involved three elements—an external world, a painter who perceived that world, and a painting which, however selected and abstracted in form, was derived from it. Always before, the Reality of the external world existed before the painter selected or abstracted from it; should the painting be destroyed, that original Reality would go on existing. But no longer. Now there were only two elements—the painter, and his painting. Synthetic Cubist painters recognized no original external Reality at all. They supplied the "natural" elements themselves, from their analytically created atoms, and from actual bits and pieces of paper or wood or string pasted onto their canvases in collage. The result was a creation *ex nihilo;* as God made the world out of primordial chaos, so the painters made theirs. Before a Synthetic Cubist canvas came into existence there had been Nothing; should it be destroyed, there would be Nothing again. The painting is its own Reality—a Reality truly "not of this world." The painter has created and lived in a genuine new world of his own.

310

Expressionists in many countries arrived at the same end by different means. Expressionist rejection of traditional objective Reality was more emotional than intellectual, and primarily inspired by the sudden availability of historic art of all kinds through photography, new methods of reproduction and mass distribution, and improved communications all over the world. Frenchmen, following Gauguin's lead, began to find the stark arts brought into Paris from remote corners of the new French Empire, like Dahomey, Tchad, or Tahiti, preferable to what seemed the tame and sickly oversophistication of Academic painting, Impressionism, or Art Nouveau alike. Germans, smarting under the paradox of belonging to a nation which since 1871 had been unquestionably the greatest military and economic power in the world but somehow in matters cultural seemed more and more dependent on despised and defeated France, thought one solution might be a return to the raw and powerful creations of earlier Germanies. Art history aided and was in turn stimulated by the new German nationalism; Wilhelm Worringer's analyses of "Germanic characteristics" in *Abstraktion und Einfühlung* (1908) and *Formprobleme der Gotik* (1912) seemed to provide particularly apt blueprints for reconstituting a truly German art. German art history rediscovered Byzantine mosaics and Coptic frescoes as historical expressions, too; and the many Russian painters wandering around Germany began to explore the possibilities of expressing themselves and their culture by reviving what they learned to consider the "spiritual" qualities of these arts. Italians likewise compared the present sad state of their national arts with the glorious creations of earlier times, and decided too much polish and too much refinement were smothering "primitive" and "intuitive" powers; "Burn the museums!" the Futurists roared. In short, Expressionists everywhere felt rather than analyzed the "death" of traditional art, and by this different route arrived at the same conclusion as the Cubists, that the carcass had to be cut up and cremated in order to clear the ground for a new and vital Reality. Their methods, however, were as spontaneous and intuitive as their theory; and so it happened that whereas Cubism developed in systematic stages, Expressionism seemed to burst out all at once in many places.

French Expressionism—Fauvism—is typical. As late as 1904 Henri Matisse is still using color and form in a basically Impressionist way; his *Luxe, Calme, et Volupté* of that year is still conceived in basic terms of Signac's Neo-Impressionist formulae. Then suddenly revelation bursts in on him. He sees color not as a means to an end, but as an end in itself. Much as Delacroix in the old romantic tradition had deliberately evoked "beautiful feelings" through painterly effects, so now Matisse begins deliberately applying color in such a way that it could not possibly be interpreted descriptively. In a portrait of his wife exhibited at the Salon d'Automne in 1905 (Copenhagen) he splits the face in two with a broad stroke of green which riveted attention on the color and the stroke in its own right. A year or so later he produced his *Blue Nude* (Baltimore), in which color and brush stroke deliberately fight an independent battle with, rather than serve, the subject matter and sense. Then he climaxes French Expressionism with his *Joy of Life* (c. 1907), in which a ring of nude dancing figures, obviously drawn from classical imagery, are treated so broadly and with such distortion that no one could possibly miss the point—that the expression of joy is made not through associations with any classical Arcadias, but purely through the play of bright color and lively pattern. "What I am after," he writes in *La Grande Revue* for December 1908, "is expression. Composition is the art of arranging in a decorative manner the various elements at the painter's disposal for the expression of feelings." Georges Rouault followed a comparable path with his series of variants on Toulouse-Lautrec's circus and prostitute themes; however, Rouault's expression of the horror of a world without God was made not through secondhand ideas associated with social outcasts, but directly, through heavy clashing colors and stark black lines. For their pains, Matisse, Rouault and their friends were dubbed *les Fauves,* "Wild Beasts."

In Germany the same thing was happening. Individuals like Munch and Kokoschka and Nolde, groups like Die Brücke and Der Blaue Reiter,

36A. *Henri Matisse:* Joy of Life. *Merion, Pa., The Barnes Foundation. c. 1907.* See also 36B, Kirchner.

French and German Expressionism contrasted. In both pictures, line, color, and texture are used as expressive elements in their own right; but whereas for Matisse they are ends in themselves, for Kirchner they are what they were for Van Gogh—means to an end, enhancing the power of a subjective and symbolic image of the painter's inner state, specifically his fears that the War would in some physical or psychological way destroy his ability to create.

all began working out the principle inherent in Van Gogh's art: for true painters external subject matter could never be more than a vehicle for expressing inner Realities of personal or national feelings. To make their point, they painted blue cabins and purple cows, forests composed of strident stripes of paint, human figures twisted, floating, with yellow faces; as occasion demanded they adapted to their purposes dynamic early medieval patterns of line, cubistic geometric forms, sinuous Art Nouveau curves, bold Van-Goghian brushwork, masses of Impressionistic paint. Inexorably, they moved in their differing ways towards the same consummation as Cubism—elimination of subject matter in the old sense. For the conclusion was inescapable: if what you paint is less important than how you paint it, if expressiveness is essentially a matter of line and color and form independent of what these lines and colors and forms may happen to represent, then why represent anything? If the external world can never be more than an intermediary, why retain any vestige of it? It only gets in the way. Let the canvas itself be the intermediary. So by 1913 Expressionist paintings were becoming, or had become, simply pieces of canvas covered with colored lines, splotches, and patches of paint. Their goal was, as Franz Marc put it, "to dissolve the entire system of our partial sensation, to show an earthly Being that dwells behind everything." The phrasing is typically fuzzy, but the intent is clear enough. Paintings are no longer of significance in themselves, they are only means to an end. Precisely what that end was varied from Expressionist to Expressionist. For some, it might be a mystical experience, like Marc's pantheistic emanations of identity with the whole created universe, or Kandinsky's "spiritualism" in the literal séance-medium-ectoplasm-Madame-Blavatsky sense, or Rouault's evocation of the worthlessness of a sinful godless world. For others, like Dufy, or Matisse, or some of Die Brücke painters, it might be more hedonistic, a reveling in the pleasurable visual impact of color and line and pattern. But in the end, the Reality achieved by Expressionism was of the same sort achieved by Cubism—nontangible, nonmaterial, unprovable by normal senses, "not of this world."

36B. *Ernst Ludwig Kirchner:* Self-Portrait as a Soldier. *Oberlin, Ohio, Allen Memorial Art Museum, Oberlin College, Charles F. Olney Fund. 1915.*

But this was an end which far from all Cubists or Expressionists were fully prepared to accept. In fact, there was a decided split in both camps between those completely dedicated to the New Reality, and those who sought some compromise with the older tradition.

In Cubism, the two parties diverged distinctly. On the one hand was the native French group led by Georges Braque and Jean Metzinger, and including Roger de La Fresnaye, Albert Gleizes, André Lhote, Robert Delaunay, and Henri Le Fauconnier. Theirs was a (relatively speaking) cool and intellectual approach. It was Braque who first developed the Cubist idea, and, by common consent, Metzinger's portrait of Guillaume Apollinaire in 1910 which marked its first full maturity. Apollinaire, who also basically belonged to this group, wrote the definitive formulation of Cubist theory for the Cubist show in Brussels in 1911. Claiming mathematical premises, proud of their descent from classical French tradition through Cézanne, given to analytical "decomposition" of classic works by Raphael and Leonardo, willing to accept as Cubists "instinctive" painters uninterested in mystical or metaphysical proclivities but simply painting in a more thoroughly abstract manner than before, this group has been aptly described by Lemaître as "haunted by the existence of concrete, tangible shapes." Essentially they conceived of the analytical process as a temporary withdrawal from the classical tradition which, once having been consummated in complete abstraction, would serve as the basis for reconstituting the art of painting on a more solid foundation. Following the climax of 1913, these men accepted Synthetic Cubism hesitantly, some halfheartedly, some not at all. Braque, for example, who had begun painting as a commercial decorator's assistant, by the 1920s, had in essence reverted to using Cubism merely as the

37. *Georges Rouault:* The Old King. *Pittsburgh, Museum of Art, Carnegie Institute. 1937.*

Religious Expressionism, French style. Pure paint used to evoke images of sin, suffering, and redemption and create a "modern religious art." Traditional overtones are very strong, however; in a work like this we are reminded of Rouault's contemporary, the California architect Bernard Maybeck, whose approach to church architecture was "to put myself in the boots of a fellow living in the twelfth century."

formal vocabulary for a decorative art of design, to the goal of Beauty in the old sense; Roger de La Fresnaye returned to classical painting in every sense of the word. On the other hand, there was the group led by Picasso, predominantly composed of Spaniards and Jews, including Juan Gris, Louis Marcoussis, and Franz Kupka. Their attack on the common-sense world was carried out in a mood of apocalyptic exaltation and finality; they conceived Cubism not as a means of reconstituting painting as the Western world had known it, but of destroying it forever. They entertained no doubts about the validity of the new world Synthetic Cubism created; that they had divined true Reality they knew with the mystical certainty of a Saint Paul or a Karl Marx. And even though the early 20th century failed to share their vision, so that they had to cut their canvas to fit the blindness of the times, they never entirely lost it, and passed it down to Dadaists, Surrealists, and Abstract Expressionists of later generations.

Expressionists split along the same lines. Matisse, Rouault, Nolde, Kirchner, Munch, all were concerned with "feelings" in almost the traditional romantic way. When you compare Matisse's *Blue Nude* of 1907 with Picasso's *Demoiselles d'Avignon* of the same year, you might think both equally bent on the destruction of traditional form; but nothing could be further from Picasso's goal than Matisse's

> What I dream of is an art of balance, of purity and serenity devoid of troubling or depressing subject-matter, an art which might be for every mental worker, be he businessman or writer, like an appeasing influence, like a mental soother, something like a good armchair in which to rest from Physical fatigue.

Or again, Turner or Friedrich might well have subscribed to Emil Nolde's

> Behind walls lives the artist, rarely in flight, often in his snail's shell. He loves the rarest and most profound natural occurrences, but also the bright, the ordinary reality, moving clouds and blooming, growing flowers, the living creatures. Unknowing creatures are his friends. He sees not much, but other men see nothing.*

Der Blaue Reiter, painters like Marc and Schmidt-Rottluff, Jawlensky and Kandinsky, are the Expressionistic counterparts of Picasso and Picabia. When Marc, for instance, weaves his images of the "one-ness

* A. Ritchie, ed., *German Art of the Twentieth Century* (New York, Museum of Modern Art, 1957).

within nature's fabric," we are irresistibly reminded of Meister Eckhardt's "pulse of God" and all that Rhenish Nordic mysticism which in the 15th century was branded a Christian heresy, a fundamental divergence from that insistence on the reality and importance of this present world which the Western church has always maintained.

Fundamentally, then, Cubism and Expressionism were not antithetical but complementary, both facets of a single concept of the function of

38. *Karl Schmidt-Rottluff:* The Road to Emmaus. *Woodcut. Philadelphia Museum of Art. 1918.*

•

Religious Expressionism, German style. Like Rouault, the German Expressionist tries to revive a religious spirit of earlier ages of art by distilling their starker essences.

319

art in life. Even before the War, their identity was evident in the considerable comings and goings between Cubist and Expressionist camps. Perhaps the best example is their joint progeny, Futurism, derived almost equally from both of them. And this may be the chief reason for the revival of interest in Futurism half a century later; its significance seems greater now than it did then.

Futurism as a movement sums up the state of advance-guard painting in its climactic years from 1900 until the Great War, much as Picasso summarizes the status of the advance-guard painter. Futurism was officially launched by the littérateur Marinetti in 1908, first comprehensively exhibited in 1912, and moribund shortly after the outbreak of the Great War. It embodied almost every significant trend in advance-guard painting of those years. Like German Expressionism, it involved a self-conscious nationalistic riposte to the artistic hegemony of France. Like Cubism, it employed a pseudoscientific rationale to fragment the objective world into atomic elements. Like Fauvism, it evoked purely sensory responses through line and color and planes per se. Like all their advance-guard contemporaries, the Futurists demanded the destruction of conventional Reality and its replacement by something nontangible and immeasurable.

Superficially, however, Futurism seemed more positive than other movements. Its announced goals were, in theory, "intuitive intimation of an ideal order" and "realistic emotion"; in practice, the establishment and expression of speed, force, violence, as Realities in their own right, and a revitalization of decadent Italian life by emphasis on such Realities, drawn from battleships and automobiles and locomotives. And at first sight such 20th-century expressions of the old Western awareness of Reality as a process, of dynamic perpetuation of human institutions, seem much more in the Western tradition than the Nirvana of Kandinsky or the nihilism of Picasso.

A good case for the Futurists could be made on this basis; but that is not really what is at issue in evaluating advance-guard painting in the early 20th century. The issue—and it is the peculiar importance of Futurism to present it unmistakably—is whether such objectives are proper for painting at all. If we seriously want to know about the Reality of dynamics, we go to a physicist or a mathematician, not a painter. It is not the Reality that is questionable, but whether painting is the proper medium for embodying it. Futurism demonstrated how complete the gulf between painters and public had become. To the generation which

39. *Franz Marc:* The Antelope. *Providence, Museum of Art, Rhode Island School of Design. Watercolor.*

In their own time, the protagonists of German Expressionism had nothing like the prestige and influence of the School of Paris. Yet in retrospect they are at least equally significant. They also typify facets of German national character which helped bring on the War of 1914–18, not only in the nationalistic enthusiasm of their attempts to revive the echtdeutsch *spirit of earlier German art, but even more in their penchant for a kind of literate mysticism. Of this, Marc's animals are famous examples—no flesh-and-blood beasts these, but symbols of a pantheistic life-spirit evoked in color, line, and pattern, moving inexorably towards pure abstraction. Such mystic fervor was all too easily transferable to other, less esoteric causes and ends.*

321

40A. *Giacomo Balla:* Swifts: Paths of Movement plus Dynamic Sequences. *Collection, The Museum of Modern Art, New York. 1913.*

40B. *Marcel Duchamp:* Nude Descending a Staircase (No. 2). *Philadelphia Museum of Art, Arensberg Collection. 1912.*

Two characteristic examples of Italian Futurism, combining an Expressionist Reality of force, movement, and inner life with a basically Cubist vocabulary. In Balla's studies of swifts in flight, the tenets of Futurism were particularly well realized; Duchamp's Nude *was the sensation of the Armory Show of 1913, which for all practical purposes introduced the New Painting to the United States.*

322

NU DESCENDANT UN ESCALIER

attacked Manet's paintings with umbrellas there succeeded a generation which only a need to feel *au courant* kept from yawning before formal disquisitions by Balla or Severini which proved that "the experience of continuous movement generated by the painting finds eventually a kind of resolution." If you are not a painter, you can eavesdrop only so long on a conversation in which Expressionists talk only to Cubists, and Cubists talk only to God, or at most refer to the world outside their own in terms of asides and allusions. So when we turn to the history of painting since the Great War, we have to consider it in another setting.

NOTES

Scholarly studies and picture books on this period are voluminous, and so are examples of Cubist, Expressionist, and Futurist paintings in American collections; to attempt an enumeration of them would be tedious.

Among the more noteworthy studies of Cubism as a movement are Christopher Gray, *Cubist Aesthetic Theories* (Baltimore, 1953), John Golding, *Cubism: A History and an Analysis* (1959), and Guy Habasque, *Cubism* (1959), all well illustrated.

In mature form—an intellectual analysis of form without the "primitivistic" element derived from Gauguin—Cubism was first developed by Georges Braque (b. 1882) in the summer of 1908; Henri Matisse described these pictures to critic Louis Vauxcelles as made "avec des petits cubes," and Vauxcelles coined the name "Cubism." Cubism was soon taken up by a crowd of painters, including Picasso; Juan Gris (1887–1927), Jean Metzinger (1883–1956) and Albert Gleizes (1881–1953), who together wrote *Du Cubisme* in 1912; Roger de La Fresnaye (1885–1925); Francis Picabia (1879–1953); Louis Marcoussis (1883–1941); Henri Le Fauconnier (1881–1946); André Lhote (1885–1962); Fernand Léger (1881–1955), Robert Delaunay (1885–1941) and Marcel Duchamp (1887–   ) who were particularly influential on Futurism.

The name "Fauves" was applied to a group of painters interested in pursuing the general principle of expressing emotion directly through sharp color and flat pattern, who chanced to exhibit together in a room at the 1905 Salon d'Automne in Paris alongside a small reproduction of a Donatello sculpture, so that an adverse critic wittily remarked on Donatello's presence "au milieu des Fauves" (wild beasts). Best-known of these exhibitors were Henri Matisse (1869–1954); André Derain (1880–1954); Georges Rouault (1871–1958); Maurice Vlaminck (1876–1958); and Raoul Dufy

(1877–1953), who exhibited with the group in 1906. Never closely or formally associated, these painters soon went different ways. An exhibition of Near Eastern art which Matisse saw at Munich in 1910 set his course definitively towards an art of decorative flat patterns built around arabesques, flower motifs, and bright colors set off by thin lines and contours. Rouault, who, like Matisse, had studied with and been deeply influenced by Gustave Moreau, never strayed far from a Moreaulike repertoire of religious themes (especially the Passion), dreary landscapes and flower pieces, all executed in a distinctive thickly impasted style. In the 1920s Vlaminck, Dufy, and Derain watered down their Fauvism to create decorative pictures very popular with timid connoisseurs and tourists who wanted "modernistic" but not "modern" paintings.

Among the many books on Fauvism are those by Jean Leymarie (1959), Georges Duthuit (1950), and John Rewald's introduction to the Fauvist exhibition at the Museum of Modern Art in 1952. On Matisse alone there are books by Roger Fry (1930), A. H. Barr (1951), Gaston Diehl (1958), J. Lassaigne (1959), and Raymond Escholier (1960).

Any list of the main figures in German Expressionism would include Edvard Munch (1863–1944) and Lovis Corinth (1858–1925), who afforded significant links between the older forms of Art Nouveau, late Impressionism, Symbolism, and the newer Expressionist movements in Germany; Paula Modersohn-Becker (1876–1907), who attempted to fuse Gauguin's primitivism with medieval Germanic traditions, in particular Romanesque sculptural forms and Netherlandish "primitivism"; Oskar Kokoschka (1886–   ), who developed a highly personal variant of Van Gogh's manner; Emil Nolde (1867–1956), who developed a comparably personal expression of Biblical, figurative, and landscape themes; and Christian Rohlfs (1849–1938), oldest of the group, who slowly worked his way through a succession of traditional and early modern modes of painting to perfect a highly personal expression that earned him the title of "grand old man" of German Expressionism.

The first "school" of German Expressionism was Die Brücke, founded at Dresden in 1904 as a "bridge" to link "young and fermenting elements" in German art, with Ernst Kirchner (1880–1938), Karl Schmidt-Rottluff (1884–   ), Erich Heckel (1883–   ), and later Max Pechstein (1881–1955) as its chief figures; it broke up in 1913.

More important, because more consistent and thoroughgoing, was Der Blaue Reiter, founded at Munich in 1911 as an offshoot of the New Artists Association by Franz Marc (1880–1916) and Wassily Kandinsky (1866–1944), and dedicated to the proposition enunciated in Otto Fischer's *The New Picture* that "Color is a means of expression that speaks directly to the soul . . . Things are not things alone if they are an expression of the soul." Kandinsky published its manifesto, "On the Spiritual in Art," in 1912.

Other members were August Macke (1887–1914), Paul Klee (1879–1940) and Alexei von Jawlensky (1864–1941). A standard reference in English is Peter Selz, *German Expressionist Painting* (Berkeley, 1957).

The leading Italian Futurists were Giacomo Balla (1871–1958), Carlo Carra (1881–), Umberto Boccioni (1882–1916), Gino Severini (1883–), Luigi Russolo (1885–1947) and the architect Antonio Sant 'Elia (1888–1916). The two leading studies on the movement are by R. T. Clough, *Futurism* (rev. 1961) and J. C. Taylor, *Futurism* (Museum of Modern Art, 1961).

II

"Modern Art"
as Cultural Expression
1920-1940

AMONG THE WARS WHICH FITZGERALD'S "LOST GENERA-
tion" found had all been fought by 1919 was the battle of "modern"
versus "traditional" art. For the wave of disillusionment with all things
and ideas Victorian that came in with the 1920s transformed "modern
art" from the esoteric embattled cult of some few relatively unknown
individuals into a fashionable mass movement. In consequence, however, "modern art" came to have a different kind of cultural importance.
As an underground movement largely ignored by the great mass of
people, it had been dominated by a few major figures in each generation
who had step by step transformed the basic concept of what painters are
and do in society; its history, by and large, had been their history. Now
this history broadens out, and must be considered in terms of representative rather than seminal figures; that is, instead of a history of art, it
increasingly becomes a cultural expression, a comment on and a tangible
embodiment of the basic ideas molding civilization, to which a great
many painters contribute, but which is dominated by none.

The first of these expressions was the reaction to that calamity for
Western civilization which is still very properly called the Great War.

1

Collapse of the Old Order:

Cultural Aftermath of the Great War

"The Limpid Wind of Momentary Sensation": Dada, 1916–1921

"Because of what it did to Europe in the human sense," wrote Edmond Taylor in *The Fall of the Dynasties,** "the 1914 war remains the cruelest trauma in Western history since the Wars of Religion." It called into question all the historic traditions and supporting ideas of Western civilization, and found many of them wanting. The romantic attitude, backbone of the whole Victorian aesthetic over the past hundred years, to all intents and purposes collapsed completely; even that basic confidence in Reason which had governed Europe for a thousand years was momentarily shaken. All the various antirational movements of the later 19th and early 20th centuries, from the serious and systematic attacks of Cubists and Symbolists to the macabre painted fantasies of James Ensor in Belgium and the gruesome whimsy of early films like Georges Lumières' *Doctor's Dilemma,* were strengthened by the spectacle of the great nations of the Western world tearing each other to pieces in a struggle that seemed to have no purpose, no meaning, and no end. What to most people before the War had seemed no more than the harmless aberrations of a few fanatics or cranks now seemed, for a while at least, to be theories worth taking seriously. For a few years immediately after the War, arts of nihilism and nonsense perfectly suited the prevailing intellectual mood. These were the years of Dada.

What is Dada? the Dadaists demanded of themselves and the world:

DADA MEANS NOTHING [screamed a 1918 manifesto by the Roumanian Tristan Tzara, who in 1916 had invented the word in the Cabaret Voltaire in Zurich]. Abolition of logic, which is the dance of those impotent to create: Dada; abolition of memory: Dada; abolition of archaeology: Dada; abolition of prophets: Dada; abolition of the future:

* *Op. cit.*

328

Dada; absolute and unquestionable faith in every god that is the immediate product of spontaneity: Dada; . . . .We recognize no theory. We have enough cubist and futurist academies: laboratories of formal ideas. . . . The new artist protests: he no longer paints (symbolic and illusionist reproduction) but creates—directly in stone, wood, iron, tin, boulders—locomotive organisms capable of being turned in all directions by the limpid wind of momentary sensation.*

Confident in the spirit of their age, the Dadaists bestrode the ruins of a world, rejoicing. Nevertheless, Dada was by no means all farce. As cultural expression, it was enormously significant. Only in a world temporarily deranged could the Dadaists have flourished, called conferences to read from telephone books, held exhibitions in and of public urinals, even temporarily convinced a public that there was some deep symbolism in displays of obscenities usually found furtively scribbled on the piers of bridges or the walls of lavatories.

It was even more significant in the unconscious way it presaged the unfolding pattern of European culture between the wars. As surely as in the fumbling compromises at Versailles, the seeds of World War II were evident in the differences between Dada as manifested in its main center, Paris, and in Germany.

Dada in Paris inherited the spirit of the nihilistic wing of Cubism. Its leading figures were predominantly non-French—i.e., deracinated people: the Roumanian Tzara, the American Man Ray, the Alsatian Hans (or Jean) Arp, the German Max Ernst, the Italian De Chirico. At first its predominant mood was one of reveling in futility, a confirmation of prewar irrationality: typical examples are De Chirico's *Seer,* a stuffed dummy propped up in a crazy world facing a blackboard covered with meaningless figures; Ernst's *Graminious Bicycle,* the meaningless title for a meaningless conglomeration of bacterialike forms, symbolizing the meaninglessness of a world accidentally generated by haphazard chemical reactions in some primordial slime; Arp's *Figures Arranged on Three Planes Like Writing,* defying any claim that art is an orderly activity.

Dada in Germany, by contrast, was much more of a positive protest. Its leading figures were Germans, many of them highly sensitive, sincere, intelligent, and patriotic, who were appalled at what was happening to their native land, and spoke out against it through Dada. Such was poet Richard Huelsenbeck, spokesman of the movement, whose "final manifesto" in 1949 emphasized that Dada had "both destructive and construc-

* Robert Motherwell, ed., *The Dada Painters and Poets: An Anthology* (New York, 1951), pp. 81, 77, 78, respectively.

tive sides," the latter being a "mission to expose the unspiritual, . . . in its own symbolic language." Such was George Grosz, whose Dadaist attacks on the social structure of the Kaiser's Germany was a jumping-off point for the "social protest" movement in German painting of the 1920s. Such, above all, was Kurt Schwitters of Hannover. Through the gutters of this starving, drab, defeated German city, Schwitters wandered, stuffing his pockets with old street-car transfers, stubs of theatre tickets, wrappers, string, torn newspapers, returning home to paste them together into what he called "Merz" pictures. Originally, these collages seemed typical Dada nothingness: "the word 'Merz' had no meaning when I formed it," Schwitters wrote. "Now, it has the meaning which I gave it." For though Merz was madness, there was method in it. What is it, Schwitters seemed to be saying, that civilizations bequeath to posterity in the end? Their works of art. Athens we know from the Parthenon and Phidias, Rome from the Colosseum and the Arch of Constantine, the Renaissance from the Sistine Ceiling and the Stanza della Segnatura. And what has Imperial Germany bequeathed to civilization? Mountains of trash, heaps of rubbish. The implication and impetus to action is veiled but unmistakable.

In Dada you see the shape of the 1920s. On one side of the Rhine, irresponsibility, lethargy, hopelessness. Passion, anger, festering disgust on the ·other. As yet that resentment and disgust remains formless, unfocused in the arts of Huelsenbeck or Grosz or Schwitters. But soon enough a focus and channel for it will be found.

41A. *Max Ernst:* Trophy, Hypertrophied. *Collection, The Museum of Modern Art, New York, Gift of Tristan Tzara. 1919.* See also 41B, Schwitters.

Most immediate manifestation in painting of the cultural and spiritual disillusionment and loss of nerve occasioned by the Great War was the nihilistic art which proliferated for half-a-dozen years after 1917, and went under the generic name of Dada. Representative of it in France was Ernst's intimations of a world composed of mindless molecules; in Germany, Schwitters's commemorating the achievements of civilization in collages of trash.

330

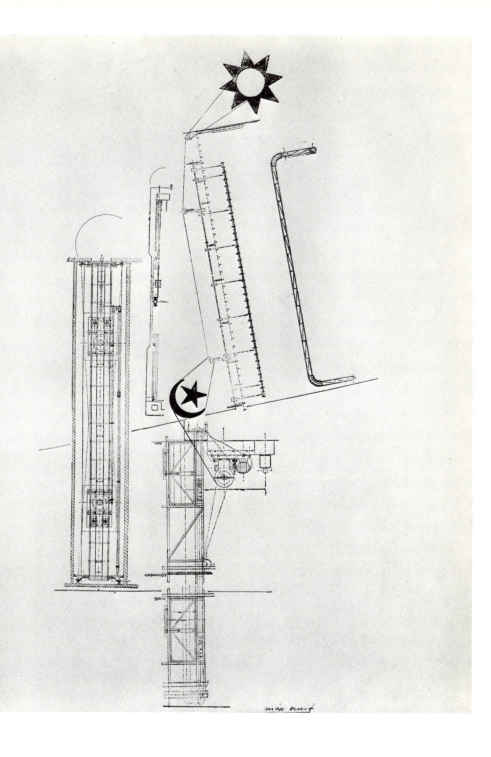

max ernst

NOTES

Among the chief figures of the original Dada group which assembled in Zurich in the course of the War were the Roumanians Tristan Tzara and Marcel Janko; Hugo Ball, Richard Huelsenbeck and Hans Richter from Germany; and Hans Arp from Alsace. Its first public appearance was as a cabaret entertainment, in February 1916; in March 1916 the Galerie Dada was opened, and in July 1917 the first number of the magazine *Dada* appeared; the first of many books appeared soon after; and in early 1918, a film. A comparable group of refugees from the War began assembling in New York in 1915; it included Francis Picabia and Marcel Duchamp, found a patron in Walter Arensberg, and exhibited at the gallery of photographer Alfred Steiglitz. A third Dada group developed in Berlin in 1918, led by Huelsenbeck, who had returned from Zurich, and including George Grosz and Raoul Hausmann. After the war little Dada groups crystallized in various places around given individuals—in Cologne around Arp and Max Ernst, in Hannover around Kurt Schwitters; but soon German Dada was swept up in the broader Social Protest movement of the 1920s. In Paris Dada lasted longer, its final phase dominated by André Breton, Louis Aragon, and Paul Eluard. Then it in turn dissolved into a successor movement, in its case Surrealism, from around 1922 on.

Among the many books on Dada are A. H. Barr, *Fantastic Art: Dada, Surrealism* (Museum of Modern Art, 1936); Robert Motherwell, *The Dada Painters and Poets: An Anthology* (1951), which contains a detailed bibliography; Marcel Jean and Arpad Mezei, *The History of Surrealist Painting* (London, 1959).

41B. *Kurt Schwitters:* Kynast-fest. *Northampton, Mass., Smith College Museum of Art. 1919.*

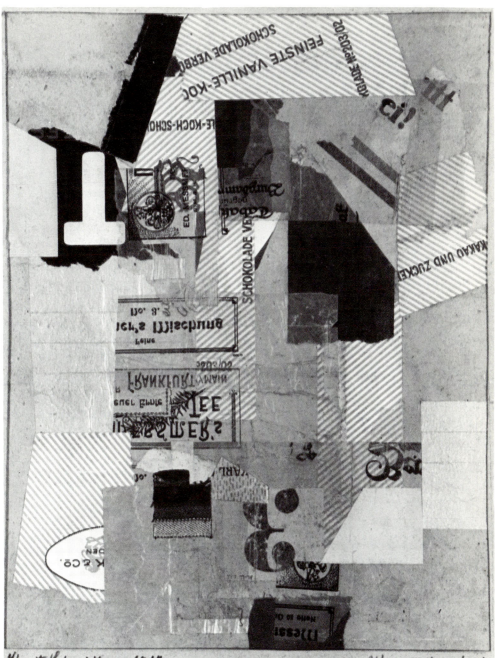

Kurt Schwitters 1919   Kynast – felt

THE AGE OF IRRESPONSIBILITY: PARIS IN THE 1920S

The twenties [wrote George Orwell] were the golden age of the *rentier-*intellectual, a period of irresponsibility such as the world had never before seen. The war was over, the new totalitarian states had not yet arisen, moral and religious tabus of all descriptions had vanished, and the cash was rolling in. "Disillusionment" was all the fashion. Everyone with a safe £500 a year turned highbrow and began training himself in Taedium Vitae. It was an age of eagles and crumpets, facile despairs, backyard Hamlets, cheap return tickets to the end of the night.*

And painting, as always, mirrored its age. Paris in the 1920s seethed and swarmed with painters of all descriptions, from anywhere and everywhere. Some were serious and competent; some were serious and incompetent; some were competent but frivolous; some were plain charlatans, deceiving themselves and others. And in the prevailing atmosphere of challenge to all set values, when "style" was everything and yet no one could define what "style" was, it was hard to tell which was which. Reputations fluctuated madly. Chance or whim would suddenly elevate an unknown to the rank of a great master, then as

* "Inside the Whale," *Inside the Whale and Other Essays* (London, 1940).

42A. *Amedeo Modigliani:* Nude. *New York, The Solomon R. Guggenheim Museum Collection. 1917.* See also 42B, Picasso; 42C, Dufy; 42D, Utrillo.

In France the 1920s were the decade of irresponsibility, when all "causes" were unfashionable, and the achievements of three decades of pioneers in painting became the clichés of a fragile and frivolous art reminiscent of Rococo painting before 1789. Minor figures like Modigliani, Dufy, and Utrillo briefly attained the popular reputation of great masters, ringing what were in effect parodies on the forms of Cézanne, Van Gogh, Gauguin, and Matisse. Picasso, sensitive as ever to the climate of the times, surpassed all others, parodying his earlier self with kaleidoscopic inventiveness and shifts of style not merely from year to year, but from picture to picture.

suddenly relegate him to *vieux-jeu* obscurity, whence in time perhaps yet another chance or whim might move some museum director or dealer or thesis writer in a later postwar age to rescue him. In this decade there was no one discernible advance-guard trend, as there had been before; but there was certainly an advance-guard mood—a common denominator which might be best called a spirit of elegant futility. That, for instance, is what painters otherwise as diverse as Maurice de Vlaminck, Maurice Utrillo, Amedeo Modigliani and Fernand Léger have in common. For all the superficial differences between Utrillo's low-keyed streetscapes of Paris suburbs in the manner of Monet and the stormy brushwork of Vlaminck's vaguely Van-Goghish landscapes, between Modigliani's attenuated nudes with their Cézannesque orange and blue-gray color schemes and masklike faces *à la* Picasso's "blue" period, and the Cubistic stylizations of Léger's odalisques and quasi-genre compositions, they are at bottom all the same, ringing what are in effect parodies on the now near-classic styles of the great Impressionist and Post-Impressionist masters. Even more perfectly representative of the period were Marie Laurencin and Raoul Dufy. That Marie Laurencin could ever have been thought a significant painter is in itself a commentary on the age; yet there was a time when her feeble pastiches of Cubism-cum-Fauvism-cum-Renoirish-Academic decoration were seriously discussed by critics. Dufy's elevation to major rank is less surprising. Light, tinkly, delicately high-brow in theme, and in form tinctured with remembrances of Fauvism past (for implausible as it seemed in the 1920s and -30s, this tame sketcher of fashionable hunts, horseraces and boudoirs had once been one of the "Wild Men") Dufy's painting was the precise counterpart to those upper-class situation comedies which gave rise to the bittersweet joke that the Great War had been fought "to make the world safe for Noel Coward."

Most buoyant of all the floaters in this babbling brook was Picasso. Nature had formed him to take advantage of the "celebrity cult" developing in those years. With his sure instinct for publicity and innate talent for serving the climate of his times, he soon made himself the first

42B. *Pablo Picasso:* The Bather. *Hartford, Wadsworth Atheneum. 1922. Painted about the same time as the* Table *(page 309).*

and still the greatest of painter celebrities, ranking with the stars of Hollywood and café society. Matisse was his only possible rival; but Matisse was not in the same league with the Spaniard, who made front-page news with his amours and his aphorisms, but above all with his incessant shiftings of style, not merely from year to year or season to season, but from picture to picture. Sometimes he professed "classical" moments, commemorated in female nudes of allegedly Venetian idyllic inspiration, and males that echoed Cézanne's studies. Then again he would play variants on Synthetic Cubism, fusing geometric abstractions with the increasingly popular decorative manner Matisse went on perfecting throughout this decade, or intimate a return to Naturalism. Or he would toy with recollected Futurism, or pseudoscientific time-space sequences. And down the stream after him bobbed a horde of small-fry imitators, hoping to find revealed in one or the next unpredictable bend and eddy Picasso's secret of popular success, never suspecting it to lie precisely in Picasso's genius for capturing the spirit of a society already, as Churchill later phrased it,

> decided only to be undecided, resolved to be irresolute, adamant for drift, solid for fluidity, all-powerful to be impotent . . . preparing . . . months and years . . . for the locusts to eat.*

Some who seriously study Picasso's work of the 1920s claim to find depths of emotion, new insights into Reality. Or it is possible to argue that Picasso already realized in the 1920s what became evident in America after Abstract Expressionism had run its course in the 1960s—that once you have reached the point of Synthetic Cubism, and your own world has been created, there is no place left to go; only a series of fads and whims can follow. In retrospect, those who simply admire Picasso's wit, who hold that Picasso in those years was simply having great fun spoofing the nonsense which at bottom he always believed this tangible visible world to be, have an easier time proving their case. But today, the

* *Hansard,* November 12, 1936.

42C. *Raoul Dufy:* The Race Track at Deauville. *Cambridge, The Fogg Art Museum, Harvard University, Maurice Wertheim Collection. 1929.*

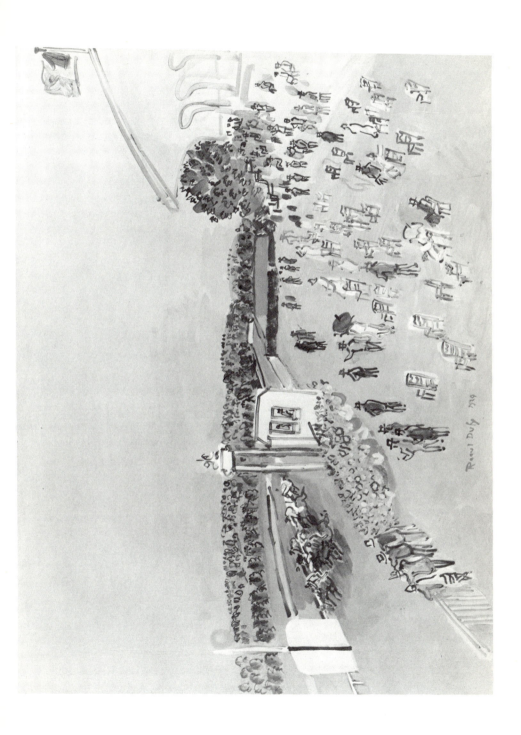

humor is somehow lost, if we look across the Rhine during these same years of Irresponsibility in Paris, and see what was going on in Germany.

NOTES

On Maurice de Vlaminck (1876–1958), see M. Raynal, *Vlaminck* (Geneva, 1949); on Maurice Utrillo (1883–1955), A. Werner, *Maurice Utrillo* (1952); on Fernand Léger (1881–1955), Katharine Kuh, *Léger* (Urbana, Ill., 1953); on Raoul Dufy (1877–1953), the monographs by Sam Hunter (1954), J. Lassaigne (Geneva, 1954), and Marcel Brion (1958); on Amedeo Modigliani (1884–1920), the monographs by J. T. Soby (1951), J. Lipschitz (1952), Claude Roy (1958), and F. Russoli (1959).

"SOCIAL PROTEST" IN GERMAN PAINTING, 1919–1933

Except for inferences in the Dada movement, you would never know from advance-guard French painting of the 1920s that the greatest war in history had just been fought, leaving France decimated, impoverished, and ruined; the subject hardly ever comes up. By contrast, in German painting of the 1920s there is hardly any other. It was in the very air of postwar Germany. As Winston Churchill summarized the situation, "The territorial provisions of the Treaty of Versailles left Germany practically intact . . . , the largest homogeneous racial block in Europe . . . tired and war-scarred, but locally overwhelming.* Though a democratic government had been installed at Weimar, it was staffed with nonentities and resented as an imposition of the conquering Allies, and "beneath this flimsy fabric raged the passions of the mighty, defeated, but substantially uninjured German nation." † The passions rage with equal fury through German painting of the 1920s. Just as we

* *The Gathering Storm* (New York, 1948), p. 10.
† *Ibid.*

42D. *Maurice Utrillo:* Sacre-Coeur de Montmartre et rue St.-Rustique. *Gouache on paper. Indianapolis, Herron Museum of Art. 1934.*

can characterize the common denominator of the School of Paris as elegant futility, so we find the common denominator of painting in Germany during the 1920s in "social protest." Even in those elements in German art most sympathetic to abstract experiment, like the Bauhaus, we find the same preoccupation with positive goals of social analysis and reform—moral, economic, aesthetic.

In aims and outlook, Communist sympathizer Käthe Kollwitz would seem to have had little in common with ex-Dadaist George Grosz, or Expressionist Max Beckmann, or nationalist Otto Dix, or the makers of movies like *The Cabinet of Dr. Caligari* or *The Blue Angel.* But like the political leaders of postwar Germany they too, by however different methods and in whatever different styles, in the end were proved to have been marching down the same road to the same unforeseen goal. For what, ultimately, were they all doing? In sum, their accomplishments amounted to this:

(1) They helped undermine confidence in the new democratic Germany. To be sure, it was not ostensibly the Weimar regime that they attacked; many considered themselves liberals and even radicals, dedicated to destroying "reactionary" and "autocratic" survivals from the social and political institutions of the Kaiser's Empire. Such, for example, was the target of George Grosz's print series *The Face of the Ruling Class,* perhaps the earliest important social protest to appear

43A. *George Grosz:* The Voice of the People Is the Voice of God, *from* The Face of the Ruling Class, *Berlin, 1921.* See also 43B, Dix; 43C, still from 1919 film.

In contrast to the decade of irresponsibility in French painting of the 1920s, a whole school of "social protest" painters arose in Germany. Their means varied, but all were dedicated to the same broad goal of exposing the corrupt Reality of the social structure of Germany, the abuses of science, the sufferings of the German masses, and how the times were out of joint generally. And all found that in the end, by destroying confidence in rational or patient solutions to difficulties, they served not the interests of some higher idealistic Reality, but the primitive, blood-and-soil Realities of National Socialism.

after the war. With a spidery technique derived from Cubist, Dadaist, and Futurist elements, Grosz mercilessly exposed the exploitation of veterans and working classes by the unregenerate militarists and capitalists who still clung to positions of power in the new Germany. Superficially his work seemed a mighty blow on behalf of democracy and equality. But since the Kaiser's Germany was officially dead, since the military caste's power was exercised through underground channels, the net effect of Grosz's protest was to cast discredit on the present and overtly ruling class—on the leaders of the democratic Republic. Unwittingly it served the same end as the harangues of extreme nationalists like Adolf Hitler's nascent party about the "traitors of 1919," an end further served by Grosz's anti-Semitism, evidenced in details like the rich Jew leaning superciliously out the window above the crippled and blinded veteran who is being told that *The Thanks of the Fatherland is enough for you.*

Käthe Kollwitz provides another example. Certainly it was humanitarian impulse that led her to depict Germany as a land of starving wide-eyed children and peasants hitched to plows and mothers clutching aching heads in huge horny hands; her goal was a fairer social order. But she made no attempt to counteract her audience's natural misconception that such things were normal conditions of life under the Weimar Republic, rather than images drawn from the early stages of 19th-century German industrialization and of the Thirty Years War, three centuries before. The net effect of this ambiguity was, then, not only to weaken her own art—for when every line you draw is dedicated to propaganda, artistic integrity is impossible—but also to weaken precisely those democratic and egalitarian forces which she was ostensibly working to encourage.

(2) They undermined confidence in the basic props of civilized society as it had developed in Germany—respect for the law, for morality, for learning, for literature. In this aspect, their works often paralleled line for line the professed views of Adolf Hitler. Intellectuals, Hitler declared, are characteristically confused and weak, so lost in abstractions of thought as to have no power of acting; they "run this way

43B. *Otto Dix:* Portrait of Dr. Mayer-Hermann. *Collection, The Museum of Modern Art, New York, Gift of Philip C. Johnson. 1926.*

344

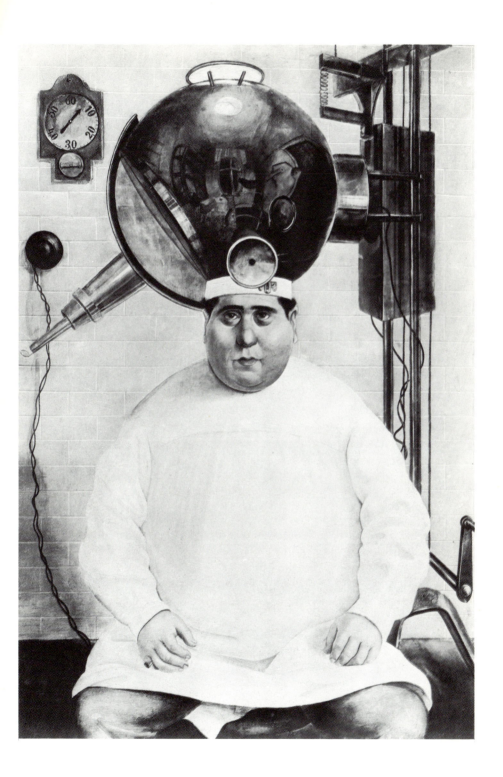

and that, like hens in a poultry yard. With them it is impossible to make history." Just so, the social protesters depicted them: dotards sunk in indolent speculation. The scientist, according to Hitler, was a tool, a machine whose function is to forge powers for the State to use, not to question the State's use of those powers. Just so, he appears in Otto Dix's *Portrait of Dr. Mayer-Hermann* (page 345), a grotesque figure whose equipment seems to grow directly out of his skull, an expressionless hybrid, half man, half machine, that can talk, eat, walk, but never think. Democratic politicians, in Hitler's view, were "little worms," and their so-called parliamentary procedures mere licensed babel; and that is just how the social protesters all exhibited them. In this light, a film like *The Blue Angel* takes on significance far beyond entertainment. See the stern professor, symbol and embodiment of traditional German learning and morality, setting out to find some students whose bragging about their conquests in the Blue Angel nightclub he has been gullible and innocent enough of the world to believe. See how easily, as a whimsical lark, the tart of a dancing girl seduces him in her dressing room; see how the pompous fool returns next day to ask her hand formally in marriage; see how pathetically he trails after her from one town to another—and then ask how the values of people so ignorant of life, so lost in abstraction, can possibly be worth upholding!

(3) In sum, social protest art spread a conviction that life under the Weimar Republic was a hopeless morass of misery and confusion. Frequently the case was so overstated as to become ludicrous to later generations. Max Beckmann's *My Family* of 1920, for instance, irresistibly recalls the old parody to the tune of *Deutschland über Alles:*

> All this world is sad and gloomy
> All is dismal as the tomb
> Father has a stomach ulcer
> Mother has a fallen womb
> Sister Susie in the corner
> Never laughs and never smiles
> What a dreary occupation
> Cracking ice for Brother's piles. . .

43C. *Still from* The Cabinet of Dr. Caligari. *The Museum of Modern Art Film Library, New York. 1919.*

And after spending an afternoon looking at one after another of Käthe Kollwitz's works of supererogation in the social sphere, one emerges less apt to embrace the cause of the working class than to clutch one's own aching head with one's own huge horny hands. But at the time such things were taken very seriously, and contributed to a widespread feeling among all classes of Germans that German society could never rest on democratic institutions, that some other basis must be found.

But what? On this point social protest art had little to say. Its exponents flailed about attacking injustice and misery in general, without ever getting down to particulars. They would not sully themselves by descending to the popular level of, say, newspaper cartoons; they insisted on remaining "fine" artists. Consequently their protests convinced only their own kind of people, whose conversion was superfluous. Like the French painters who made formal disquisitions about picture-making, the German social protest painters were in essence talking to themselves. Though they had many little jokes intelligible to their own in-group, to society at large they appeared entirely humorless, especially as regards themselves; and this quality, combined with their self-consciously Expressionist and quasi-Dada techniques, cut them off from all contact with the masses. What few positive ideas they had were often deleterious. In paintings like Otto Dix's *My Parents,* for instance, a certain mystic faith in The Race is implied—somehow, salvation lies in the sturdy, stolid *deutsche Volk,* whose industry and obedience has always been the real backbone of German society, whose instinctive likings and dislikes have always been the backbone of German art. But since such people are by definition dumb, in every sense of the word, some sort of authoritarian order must be imposed on Germany to utilize their strengths. Käthe Kollwitz looked to the Communist Party to provide that order. But most social protest invoked something more native. It is in this light that the extraordinary popularity of the 1919 shoestring movie, *The Cabinet of Dr. Caligari* (page 347) takes on such significance (in contrast to its apathetic reception in calmer countries). For here, at the very threshold of the supposedly new age for Germany, is a premonition of old things to return. Here is a chaotic world of cardboard stage sets painted like *Die Brücke* woodcuts and intersecting ramps and walls in the manner of Schwitters' *Merzhaus* in Hannover, whose central figure is a corpse in a box, symbol (in retrospect) of the crushed power of martial Germany. And who revives this corpse, and makes it an instrument of fear and conquest once again?

Not sweet reason nor liberal protest, but a magician who weaves spells and dreams visions of world power. . . . All of which in the end could profit only one man, one vision, one party. And so it did.

How much the social protest painters of Germany witlessly helped Hitler's rise to power is not measurable; but certainly they never hindered this maniac, whose appeal rested on belief that Germany's troubles were so hopeless that only a mystic genius could rescue her. The essential point is the contrast between this boiling energy revealed in German social protest painting and the frivolous lethargy of painting in France. When this energy is harnessed and focused, the result of any contest between the two societies they embody must be a foregone conclusion. The events of 1940 are plain to read in the contrasting reactions of French and German painting to the postwar situation.

NOTES

The various streams of social protest in German painting stemming from Expressionism, Dada, and other sources first came together in a 1925 exhibition at Mannheim, where the movement was christened *Die Neue Sachlichkeit* ("New Objectivity"). In this exhibition George Grosz (1893–1959), Max Beckmann (1884–1950), and Otto Dix (1891–) were represented, along with half-a-dozen others. On Grosz, see the biography by H. Bittner (ed.), 1960; and the autobiography, *A Little Yes and a Big No* (1946). On Beckmann, catalogue of the retrospective at the Saint Louis City Art Museum, 1948, by Perry T. Rathbone. On Kollwitz, the biographical introduction by Carl Zigrosser to *Kaethe Kollwitz* (1946), and H. Bittner, *Käthe Kollwitz Drawings* (1959). On the evolution of the German film, Siegfried Kracauer, *From Caligari to Hitler* (Princeton, N. J., 1947).

2

Towards a New Order:
Visionaries, Saviors, and Brave New Worlds

However it may have begun, there could be no doubt about the high moral plane on which the Great War ended, at least officially. To induce submission to regimentation at home and systematic extermination under the name of attrition in the trenches, exhortations about national security or trade protection were not enough. Higher and higher ideals were proclaimed, all the more loudly as the slaughter bungled on. Chief among them were pronouncements that this was a "war to end war," a war to "make the world safe for democracy" once and for all. It was claimed that this war was very different from others, it was a kind of crusade, a painful travail preceding the birth of a brave, new, and different sort of world. Once it was over, people everywhere clamored to make the claims good.

It soon appeared, however, that there were two very different conceptions as to precisely what form this new world should take, and on what foundations it should be built. On one side the liberal idealists, symbolized and in effect led by Woodrow Wilson, argued that in order to realize the new era, one had only to work from the premise that mankind was naturally good. They believed that the war had come about, not through any evil inherent in individuals or nations, but through bad institutions. Man's natural goodness had been frustrated and perverted by the existence of armies, of secret treaties encouraging war, by governments tyrannizing over "minorities." Change these conditions, create a new kind of national order through a League of Nations, and a new atmosphere through disarmament, and peace would spontaneously result. But on the other side there were those who refused to believe that trench warfare had purged the world of Original Sin. Chief among them in the early postwar days seemed to be Georges Clemenceau, the old Tiger of France, who, as the idealist John Maynard Keynes lamented in *The Economic Consequences of the Peace,* maintained that "there is nothing very new to learn about this war," "that essentially the old order does not change, being based on human nature which is always the same." He

350

wanted a peace based not on abstract moral imperatives, but on concrete force—permanent military occupation of the Rhineland, maintenance of strong armies by the Allies for an indefinite period to deter wicked men who might once again rise to threaten the peace of the world by their ambitions.

At Versailles abstract intellectualism won out. Maintenance of the victory bought by four years of horror was staked on the proposition that moral conscience, exercised through the weaponless League of Nations, would be enough; Clemenceau retired in defeat and disgrace. But he was by no means the only believer in building a new world on power and force. The struggle between abstract intellectualism and concrete force went on for nearly two decades, until German tanks and Japanese bombs put a rude end to it. And in painting, if we now turn from considering negative reactions to the War—from Dada and Social Protest—to expressions of creative reconstruction, we find this same issue being fought out.

Painting for Salvation: Abstract Intellectualism, 1920–1940

To Clemenceau's way of thinking, Wilson and his group [at Versailles] . . . were not constructing a better machine for propelling the existing forces; they were constructing a machine for propelling forces better than the existing ones. They were planning improvements not according to eternal human nature, but according to an allegedly changed human nature. The old man knew well that there was no task more thankless than that of confronting enthusiasts with reality . . . Enthusiasts resist reality in a fashion of their own . . .*

In painting of the 1920s it was the same. There, too, all sorts of "enthusiasts" were busy "planning improvements . . . according to an allegedly changed human nature."

Earliest of them was the group making up *De Stijl* movement in Holland, with Theo Van Doesburg as chief spokesman and Piet Mondriaan as the most representative painter. *De Stijl* theory was inspired by Theosophy and particularly by a Neoplatonic philosophical system propounded by one M. H. J. Schoenmaekers called "plastic mathematics" or "positive mysticism"; its forms were derived from Analytical

* Leopold Schwarzschild, *World in Trance* (New York, 1942), pp. 47–48.

351

Cubism and ultimately Cézanne. But its claims went far beyond art. "Neo-plasticism" (as Mondriaan preferred to call his kind of painting) professed to be concerned not merely with ultimate Platonic essences on which the world is built, but with defining ideal relationships among them; furthermore, this "pure plastic art" was one and the same thing as "Universal Truth." Now according to classic Platonic theory, Universal Truth is innate in all men; it follows that the function of *De Stijl* art was not to reveal new Reality but to help us recognize that which we already know by divesting it from obscuring trivia of any and every kind—including alike all specific reference to the objective world and "all . . . temperament, inspiration, sacred fire, and all the attributes of genius that conceal the untidiness of the mind," as Van Doesburg once wrote.

Once the mind learns to recognize the Universal Truth innate there, the art that teaches it will be unnecessary, of course, and Mondriaan happily anticipated such a day. Until that day arrives, however, pure plastic art will perform in its realm of painting much the same function as enthusiasts envisaged for the League of Nations in politics or the dictatorial State which Marxists claimed would fade away once World Revolution was won. Harmonious arrangements of flat primary color areas set in black lines would be an irresistible instrument for assuring world peace. Only let men be surrounded by pure plastic art—not only in the form of easel pictures, but also in house design, in linoleum, in bathroom fixtures, or wherever—and all discordant impulses must die.

44A. *Piet Mondriaan:* Composition in Blue and White. *Hartford, Wadsworth Atheneum. 1935.* See also 44B, Kandinsky.

Painters joined enthusiastically in the general quest for foundations on which to build the new and better world so universally believed in after the War; in their several ways, the Stijl *movement in Holland, the Bauhaus in Germany, Constructivism in Russia were all motivated by an impulse to improve mankind through truer revelations of Reality in painting. Common to all these movements was the conviction that pure painting was a positive force.*

Pure plastic art will bring about an era of perpetual peace and brother-hood with the same effortless inevitability prophesied by advocates of the League of Nations:

> . . . A visual opposition of rectangles of different sizes, an arrange-ment of lines that divides the canvas into parts that are unequal but equivalent . . . gives insight into the unity that would be possible in a cooperative society. Such unity constitutes a vision of reality which serves at once as a model and a spur; men see what they should work for, and thereby renew their strength to accelerate human progress.*

But *De Stijl* was not the only would-be world savior; the postwar years abounded with them. Moscow in the Revolutionary period from 1917 to 1922 was another great center of their activities.

In the prewar decades, easy communications and pastportless frontiers had encouraged all sorts of Russians to live and study in Western Europe. There they had come into contact with advance-guard painting, and the more esoteric and unworldly Reality in painting had become, the more it had appealed to mystic Slavic souls; by 1914 Russians had become prominent everywhere in the modern movement. Establishment of the new Soviet Communist regime in 1917 filled these expatriates with enthusiasm and drew them home, filled with visions of providing their homeland with an artistic counterpart and expression of the New Reality of brotherhood among good-hearted men on which they naively believed the Revolutionary State was being built.

On specific details of this New Reality, the Russian visionaries were far from agreed. The Constructivist brothers Antoine Pevsner and Naum Gabo announced in a 1920 manifesto that "the only way to liberate art from its impasse is to destroy compact mass and look for empty space"; this eventually led them and their associate Vladimir Tatlin in the direction of nonobjective sculpture. Kasimir Malevich, by contrast, already in 1915 had proclaimed a new school, which he called Suprema-tism, dedicated to the proposition that the only elements a painter should

* P. C. Mondriaan, *Plastic Art and Pure Plastic Art* (New York, 1947).

44B. *Wassily Kandinsky:* Blue Circle, No. 242. *New York, The Solo-mon R. Guggenheim Museum Collection. 1922.*

use were rectangles, circles, triangles, and crosses, because

> The representation of an object, in itself . . . is something that has
> nothing to do with art. . . . The object in itself is meaning-
> less . . . and the ideas of the conscious mind are worthless. [Pre-
> sumably excluding the ideas in his own mind, of course!] Feeling is
> the decisive factor . . . and thus art arrives at non-objective repre-
> sentation—at suprematism.

Its supreme accomplishments were a black square on a white ground
(1913) and a white square on a white ground—the famous *White on
White* of 1918. In this work we can certainly recognize a counterpart to
the goals of the Russian Revolutionaries; just as they hoped to freeze the
class struggle at the precise moment when yesterday's middle-class
representatives of the proletariat had become today's upper-class rulers,
so Suprematism proposed to freeze the tides of taste and end art history
at the Russian Revolution. But of such an aim we can only paraphrase,
"C'est magnifique, mais ce n'est pas l'art."

Wassily Kandinsky had yet another approach. His ideal, announced
in the title of a book written while he was working with Der Blaue Reiter
in Munich and published in 1912, was *The Spiritual In Art*.

Like Mondriaan, Kandinsky was a Theosophist, but whereas Mondriaan was a Westerner whose abstractions were still ultimately drawn
from an objective reality (or, in the jargon of the time, proceeded from
"external necessity"), Kandinsky was a Slav, steeped in Byzantine
mysticism, who had no inhibitions about composing pictures nonobjec-
tively, without reference to any reality outside themselves, by "inner
necessity." In his Blaue Reiter period in Munich just before the Great
War, Kandinsky's painting evolved into loose masses of color reminiscent
of the ectoplasmic essences described by his idol and fellow Russian, the
famous spiritualist Madame Helena Petrovna Blavatsky. He developed
an elaborate theory of correspondence between colors and musical
sounds, on grounds that, like music,

> Color is a means of expression that speaks directly to the soul. It is
> not correct drawing that portrays the nature of things, but rather the
> spirited and expressive contour. Things are not things alone if they are
> an expression of the soul.*

The resultant paintings had been well described by his Blaue Reiter
colleague, Franz Marc, as "symbols that belong on the altars of the

* *On the Spiritual in Art* (New York, Solomon R. Guggenheim Foundation,
1946).

coming spiritual religion," and during the intoxicating years of Revolutionary ferment in postwar Moscow it was Kandinsky's dream to establish such a religion in the New Russia as an appropriate (and not entirely illegitimate) successor to the Eastern Orthodox Church of the Old. It seemed logical enough, for both Kandinsky's painting and the theory of the Bolshevik state basically rested on the same premise of the Natural Goodness of Man. If the excesses and terrors of the Revolution could be justified by a necessity to destroy wicked institutions and incorrigibly corrupted classes which stood in the way of "the people" realizing and acting in accordance with their innate goodness, surely its appropriate artistic expression would be a kind of painting which similarly destroyed all reference to corrupt materialistic external reality and, having so cleansed the mind of carnal impurities, served as a medium through which men's natural goodness and spirituality might become dominant.

Unfortunately, the new rulers of Russia proved no more receptive to those who would save the world through art than the old dynasties had been; in fact, they were even less sympathetic than the despised capitalistic *bourgeoisie*. Despite their surface differences, all these advance-guard Russian painters were concerned with a kind of intangible, immeasurable, incommunicable Reality divined by intuition and demanding unconditional and unreasoning acceptance by the masses, which was all too familiar in Russia. How, people asked, do these painters differ from the itinerant holy men who wandered around the country under the old regime, from those starets whose mystic intuitions so often and so curiously seemed to coincide with their personal interests and inclinations? There had been enough Rasputins in Russia. Harassed by the tangible realities of civil war, counterrevolutions, famine, and plague, the Soviet leaders were in no mood to subsidize private little creations of the mind promoted by visionary painters. These people held endless colloquies on the ideal relationship among the various arts, to which the Soviet rulers responded in the disconcertingly bourgeois spirit of Joseph Addison two centuries before:

> I shall add no more to what I have offered than that Music, Architecture, and Painting as well as Poetry and Oratory, are to deduce their Laws and Rules from the general Sense and Taste of Mankind, and not from the Principles of those Arts themselves; or in other words, the Taste is not to conform to the Art, but the Art to the Taste.*

At this particular moment in history the Sense and Taste of Mankind, the Russian rulers in effect declared, demands poetry and painting and music

* *Spectator*, No. 71.

which will rally the people to our cause and explain our goals. What they got were subtle exercises in spatial composition, delicate nonobjective intimations of mystical experience, and endless disquisitions on the fine points of abstract picture-making. By 1922 they had had enough. Denouncing "the infantile disorder of Leftism," Lenin ordered his painters to produce something effectively intelligible to the mass of the people, or take the consequences. The visionaries fled. Back they went to the bourgeois havens whence they had come, where it was still safe to campaign against materialism and science and reason, "making mock of uniforms that guard you while you sleep." It was the first, but not the last time that abstract intellectualism fractured against the solid fact of unregenerate human nature.

Kandinsky was fortunate; almost at once he found a congenial appointment in Germany, at the new Bauhaus school in Weimar, which was perhaps the single most important center of advance-guard art between the wars. Once upon a time it had been a design school patronized by the Grand Duke of Hesse and headed by Art Nouveau champion Henry Van de Velde. But now there were no more Grand Dukes of Hesse and no more Art Nouveau. A new era was in birth, and in 1919 the school was reorganized as Das Staatliche Bauhaus and dedicated to save the new world through art:

> . . . Let us conceive and create the new building of the future [said the first Bauhaus proclamation in 1919] which will embrace architecture *and* painting *and* sculpture in one unity and which will rise one day toward heaven from the hands of a million workers like the crystal symbol of a new faith.

Originally, the Bauhaus concentrated on rethinking basic principles common to all the arts, and in this area lasting contributions and solid accomplishments were made by such serious-minded artists as its director, architect Walter Gropius, furniture designer Marcel Breuer, and painters Johannes Itten and Josef Albers, who applied basic principles drawn from abstract art to practical problems in industrial design. But the appointment of Paul Klee in 1921, Kandinsky in 1922, and Laszlo Moholy-Nagy in 1923 introduced a new element.

At the Bauhaus, Kandinsky changed his style from fuzzy masses of color to bright and brittle geometrical shapes floating in space—circles, attenuated triangles, latticework, and the like. He also began to affect the role of patriarch, lohan, or father-confessor, appropriately enough, since as a man forty-five years of age when Der Blaue Reiter was formed of "young and fermenting elements" in 1911, he had been a painterly equivalent of the world's oldest teen-ager far too long. But his mystic messianic fervor remained unabated. If anything, it increased; for now he had strong allies. Moholy-Nagy was a much more vigorous, inventive, and versatile Constructivist than Pevsner or Gabo or Tatlin. In the words of a 1948–49 prospectus of the Chicago Institute of Design which he later headed, his "new vision" meant specifically, being "able to increase and refine our native ability to react to and to control the physical environment in which we live . . . . , to show the student the power that rests within himself." But perhaps the most striking of all these world saviors—the more significant because consistently misunderstood—was Paul Klee, who in the Bauhaus developed from a minor figure of Der Blaue Reiter into a major force in the New Painting.

In the popular mind, Paul Klee is still too often considered whimsical, a painter of elfin humors; or alternatively, a simple childlike soul. Emphatically, he was neither. Certainly his art exhibits many of the principles of children's and savages' drawing; but there is nothing childlike in its conception. No child would ever do anything like Klee's famous *Man on a Tightrope,* for instance. Children draw what they know is there; Klee's intent, by contrast, was to represent not the outward characteristics of a man on a tightrope, but to express by subtle arrangements of line, pattern, color, and texture what it feels like to walk a tightrope—a vastly different thing. It is the same basic aim as Van Gogh's or Munch's; but Klee carries it much further, and much more systematically. His *Pedagogical Sketchbook* is no child's play. Through systematic experiment, Klee believed that he had discovered the secret of inner power possessed by artists in those ancient primitive ages when painters were considered to be magicians. This secret, he thought, lay in a compulsive power exerted by certain combinations of shapes, lines, and forms on the unconscious mind. In its simplest form this "compulsive symbol" is still familiar to all of us, in such things as the red light at which drivers automatically pull their cars to a halt, or the arrow whose indicated direction we instinctively follow. But once upon a time such compulsive symbols guided and governed whole societies. Egypt, for instance, or Byzantium, where Reality consisted of the symbols made by artists and imposed on the masses through collective solipsism. Klee was

359

a perfect example of the historic frame of mind described by Macaulay, which is

> under a deception similar to that which misleads the travellers in the Arabian desert. Beneath the caravan all is dry and bare; but far in advance, and far in the rear, is the semblance of rushing waters.

His mind was obsessed with the hopeless chaos of life in democratic Germany of the 1920s, and with the beautifully ordered and totally collectivized societies far away in time and space and their re-establishment at some equally far-off time in the future. Somehow, he thought, that order had been, and could be again, achieved through a kind of spiritual power exercised over the masses—something like the extrasensory perception which according to some researchers governs anthills and beehives; and somehow this power was exercised by artists through the compulsive symbols they created. At the moment, this idea had considerable appeal. In it were united many of the most characteristic currents of advance-guard thought: adulation of primitivism, exaltation of intuition at the expense of reason, the ideal of a collectivized society which would rescue men from the agonies of personal responsibility and allow their natural goodness to operate, the dream of artists regaining a useful and powerful place in society through recognition of their command of Reality.

Of all earlier societies, however, the one that most appealed to Klee was the early Byzantine Empire. His visit to Ravenna was one of the

45. *Paul Klee:* Red-Green Steps. *New Haven, Yale University Art Gallery, Collection Société Anonyme. c. 1921.*

Klee shared the obsessive desire of his advance-guard generation for some source of power able to bring order out of postwar German chaos; he found it in the compulsive power of shapes and symbols which enable the mind to impose meaningful patterns on the confusion of sense impressions. He hoped that his "pedagogical pictures," with compulsive arrows, eyes, light movements, and other atavistic symbols ordering multitudes of disparate units, would lead mankind to an understanding of cosmic order which in turn would foster recovery of political and social order.

great experiences of his life. True, Byzantine art had been an inspiration for all participants in Der Blaue Reiter before the War; but Klee put a different interpretation on it. Where Kandinsky was impressed by Byzantine "spiritualism," and Jawlensky by the evocative possibilities of Byzantine (more exactly, Coptic) forms, Klee saw in the mosaics of Ravenna a demonstration of the artist's power to create compulsive images. Even if one knew nothing of the specific history of Emperor Justinian and Empress Theodora, the mosaics commemorating them in San Vitale would remain images of power in themselves, because the form of this art—a few dominant shapes and lines giving order and direction to an otherwise confused and limitless expanse of tiny tesserae —perfectly complements its content, self-evidently manifests how confused masses of insignificant individuals could be given direction and purpose by the compelling will of a great ruler. Here, Klee thought, was a model to follow in creating an art to rejuvenate postwar Europe. Over and over again he worked on the theme—creating pictures composed of masses of intersecting lines, or squares of colors in expanding relationships of intensity, which were given direction by compulsive lines, compelling shapes, commanding colors. Gradually he perfected his expression, producing one intimation after another of chaotic masses of individuals being ordered into purposeful action by compulsive symbols.

Unfortunately, like the Irishman who trained his horse to live on less and less and had just got it to the point of living on nothing at all when it died, Klee had just brought his art to refined perfection when the Nazis seized power and killed it with compulsive symbols of their own. In this there was an ironic twist entirely characteristic of the *World in Trance,* where, as Schwarzschild wrote, ". . . Again and again . . . , ideas of a high-flying idealism had an exact counterpart in the most callous realism." * In the autumn of 1918, Wilson's calculation that a strong German army surviving the Armistice could help force the Allies to accept his idealistic peace terms had corresponded "as the negative of a film to its positive," with Ludendorff's and Hindenburg's calculations that a strong German army surviving the Armistice might yet win the war if a quarrel over those peace terms could be fomented among the Allies. So now Klee's dream of painters using compulsive symbols to bring beneficent order to the chaos of democratic individualism had its exact counterpart in Nazi techniques of mass persuasion. Turn from one of Klee's typical exercises in organizing and unifying myriad elements

* *Op. cit.*

362

through the power of compulsive symbols, to Alan Bullock's description of one of Hitler's big meetings, and you can hardly fail to see the parallel; it is Klee writ large:

> To attend . . . was to go through an emotional experience, not to listen to an argument or a programme. . . . To see the films of the Nuremberg rallies even today is to be recaptured by the hypnotic effect of thousands of men marching in perfect order, the music of the massed bands, the forest of standards and flags, the vast perspectives of the stadium, the smoking torches, the dome of searchlights. The sense of power, of force and unity was irresistible, and all converged with a mounting crescendo of excitement on the supreme moment when the Fuehrer himself made his entry. Paradoxically, the man who was most affected by such spectacles was their originator, Hitler himself, and, as Rosenberg remarks in his memoirs, they played an indispensable part in the process of self-intoxication.*

It is this paradoxical parallel that gives peculiar interest and cultural significance to that otherwise dull, dismal, banal, and sinister creation and phenomenon of the between-Wars years, "totalitarian art."

NOTES

Quotations from L. Schwarzschild, *World in Trance* (1942), pp. 47–48; Alan Bullock, *Adolf Hitler* (1953), Ch. 7; and Frances B. Blanshard, *Retreat from Likeness* (2d ed., 1949). Useful surveys of the personalities and movements in this section are contained in Blanshard's *Retreat;* see also Herbert Read, *A Concise History of Modern Painting* (1959), and Camilla Gray, *The Great Experiment: Russian Art 1863–1922* (1962).

Totalitarian Realism: "Modern Art Inside Out"

It has been customary in the 20th-century West to think of "totalitarian art" as the antithesis of "modern art." Apologists for the advance guard like to think of themselves as champions of free expression in the struggle against reactionary tyranny. For any who persist in thinking that modern art is subversive or "bolshevistic" they have only contempt and supercilious pity, pointing out that in every totalitarian state arising

* *Adolf Hitler* (New York, 1953), Ch. 7, "The Dictator."

during the 1920s and -30s, modern art was early and consistently suppressed in favor of naturalistic pseudoacademic "calendar art," "illustration," or "social realism." All of which is true, certainly. The new totalitarian states did proscribe modern art; and the art they officially encouraged was, by any normal Western standards, stupid, vulgar and pretentious—a bombastic pseudoclassical architecture, and paintings stereotyped in content and style of happy peasants, contented factory workers, bovine nudes, fecund mothers, stern soldiers, and idealized leaders.

But freedom versus tyranny, sensitivity versus banality, is not the whole truth. The bourgeois and the "Philistines" were not entirely wrong when they intimated with alarm that totalitarian and modern art had something in common. In large measure modern artists were persecuted by totalitarians not because they were opponents, like the churches or the free labor unions, but because they were rivals. Germany is the classic example.

Why did Hitler persecute advance-guard painters? Surely not because he was afraid of them; he who contemptuously destroyed the Communist Party, organized labor, even the German General Staff, could hardly have feared the political opposition of a few painters, particularly painters whose work (as he claimed) was unintelligible and uninteresting to the masses. Nor can it be entirely a matter of petty personal revenge, as is often suggested. Alan Bullock describes how when Hitler was in his teens

> vast dreams of his own success as an artist filled his mind. He lived in a world of his own, content to let his mother provide for his needs, scornfully refusing to concern himself with such petty mundane affairs as money or a job. . . .*

how throughout his life he consistently maintained that he was an Artist, keeping pads of paper on his desk for sketching in spare moments, and how time and again he declared that his ultimate ambition in life was to retire from the toils of politics to an artistic career. Since he was at the same time "incapable of any disciplined or systematic work," having "the artist's temperament without either talent, training, or creative energy," so that he was refused admission to the Vienna Academy and received no sort of artistic recognition whatever, it is temptingly obvious to see in his later actions as dictator a delicious revenge for the failure of his early ambition. However, were it that simple, we should have expected him to

* *Op. cit.*

364

attack the kind of painters who had rejected him—the conservatives whom the Vienna Academy represented; instead, his fury fell on modern painters, who, after all, had never done anything to him. It is hard to escape this logic: primarily Hitler attacked modern painters because he saw them as rivals, whose means might differ but whose ends corresponded to his "as the negative of a film to its positive." He and they had ultimately the same ends in view in pursuing their respective arts, politics or painting as the case might be.

For the old-fashioned liberal bourgeois, painters were people who served the simple and specific function of bringing beauties of various kinds into the world. But Hitler agreed with advance-guard painters in claiming for artists the very different role of leaders whose ideas should determine the course of human affairs. Courbet the seer, Picasso the virtuoso, Hitler the "world-historical hero"—all of them claimed superior insights into Reality, on the strength of which they justified extraordinary rights and privileges, including freedom to flout conventions and morality binding on lesser men. However, "Hitler's originality," in Alan Bullock's words, "lay not in his ideas, but in the terrifyingly literal way in which he set to work to translate fantasy into reality, and his unequalled grasp of the means by which to do this." That is, he succeeded in grasping the power of which other artists only dreamed. And once possessing it, he persecuted advance-guard painters not on grounds of aesthetics, but on their own terms, as proponents of a rival religion. Reality, not Beauty, was at issue. He saw them not as infidels whose beliefs were different from his, but as heretics who held the same basic convictions as he, but pursued them by false and feeble means, and so were all the more dangerous. He conceived Nazism, as they conceived modern painting, to be the means towards establishing a New Order—a Church Militant, as it were. To have two rival Churches Militant was intolerable. Hence his intolerance towards modern painting. And hence his establishment of an officially approved Totalitarian Art.

Criticisms of Hitler's totalitarian art—or Lenin's, or Stalin's, or Mussolini's, for they all spring from the same premises—cannot properly be made, then, in terms either of the traditional theory of Beauty or contemporary advance-guard painting. For this art is not concerned either with Beauty or with Reality in the common sense of artists working from personal insights or ideas. Whatever beauties or realities it may involve are not personal at all. In the totalitarian state, personal appreciations of Beauty or personal concepts of Reality are unnecessary and undesirable. State and Party determine what shall be considered Real and what not; and as for interpretations of Beauty, individual interpretations of any kind are potentially subversive, for once allow them in one field and there is no telling when they might spread to politics or economics or anywhere. The totalitarian artist is called on to give tangible form to truths dictated by the State. He is in fact in much the same situation as the artist in Egypt under the Pharaohs. "Pictorial art," says the official catalogue of the *Grosse Deutsche Kunstausstellung 1938 im Haus der deutschen Kunst zu München,*

> must become again something more than an aspect—and if one may believe Hegel, a somewhat antiquated aspect—of human spiritual activity. It must become again the complete expression of the noblest and most heroic aspirations of a whole people.

In other words, it must be a collective expression. In the early years of the 20th century, Picasso and Braque "had been inclined to efface our own personalities in order to find originality" and restore to art the powers it had once had in the collectivized societies of savage peoples and early civilizations; Der Blaue Reiter and Synthetic Cubism had tried to create a Reality independent of the physical world by individual solipsism. Now these same ideals reappeared, but turned inside out, and imposed by collective solipsism.

That vision of a new and vital primitive art which had so long inspired so many advance-guard artists suddenly materialized in a serious, systematic and terrifying form. And just as Hitler's or Stalin's monstrous crimes made Napoleon or the Caesars or the Pharaohs amateurs in tyranny, so beside the fundamental primitivism of totalitarian art, Picasso and Kandinsky and Klee and their followers seemed petty players on a

46. *Elk Eber:* So war S.A. *From the catalogue of the* Great German Art *exhibition, House of German Art, Munich, 1938.*

Official Party dogma given tangible form: Nazi Storm Troops are here made to appear heroic champions of a noble cause. Indeed, in their stiffness of pose and sameness of feature and expression, they have a curious resemblance to those rows of saints in Byzantine church walls so admired by Klee; their swastika imposes order like his compulsive arrows.

hollow stage. So obvious was this fact that by the 1930s even the advance guard, in its remaining bastions in Paris and England, could not help being aware of it. Some reply to the obvious challenge of the weapon totalitarian regimes were forging out of art was clearly in order. It took the form of Surrealism, last of the major movements in the classic period of "modern art."

NOTES

Quotations from Alan Bullock, *Adolf Hitler, passim;* from John A. Wilson, *The Burden of Egypt* (Chicago, 1951), p. 155. Of the comparatively little that has been written on the theory of modern totalitarian art, Hellmut Lehmann-Haupt, *Art Under a Dictatorship* (1954) is noteworthy but, as the author himself notes, only the beginning of an interpretation.

THE VANITY OF HUMAN BRUSHES:
SURREALISM IN THE 1930s

We must not use nationalist weapons, lest we reinforce German unity around Hitler. More than ever, salvation resides in the organization of the peace. Let us not sneer at the value of the world's conscience, whose indignation has already forced Hitler's fascism to retreat.

The date was April 8, 1933; the speaker, French premier Léon Blum, reported in *Le Temps* of Paris. With such statements the leaders of Britain and France served ringing notice that they intended to go on ignoring the unpleasant facts of postwar life as long as possible, even one so obvious and so extraordinarily unpleasant as the rise of a man like Hitler to leadership in Germany; that as far into the 1930s as the totalitarian powers would let them, they would go on relying for security on abstruse schemes of world salvation, from the League of Nations to "pure plastic art."

Yet the harshening political and economic climate could hardly be ignored altogether by the advance guard. Though for them external things were not Real, still some sort of reaction to events seemed called for. In literature it took the form of "social consciousness"—Eliot exchanged for Auden, *Ulysses* for *For Whom The Bell Tolls.* In painting, the chief reaction was Surrealism.

In most people's minds, Surrealism is probably still most closely associated with Salvador Dali. His work exemplified its two most conspicuous characteristics, a quality of extravagant whimsy, and dependence on Freudian psychology. Of course there was nothing new about employing Freudian imagery in painting; the idea of subconscious sexual attitudes influencing certain kinds of behavior and personality had long been explicit in the work of many painters, from Munch's notorious *Madonna* framed by sperms and foetus to Grosz's composite images drawn from spontaneous *graffiti* on lavatory walls. What was new in the Surrealism of the 1930s was a claim that all actions are predetermined by those subconscious drives which are best revealed in dreams; hence that to paint dream images is to deal directly with the "super-Reality" that rules the world. Like all the Surrealists, Dali composed his dream images by illogical juxtaposition of objects; but in contrast to the semi-abstraction of Joan Miro's *Personnage Throwing a Stone at a Bird* or *Dog Barking at the Moon,* or the fantasy of Yves Tanguy's vaguely biomorphic forms, Dali used everyday objects, painted with meticulously literal naturalism. In his work, furthermore, the ponderous and esoteric intellectualism of so much Surrealism in the 1930s was relieved by a humor drawn indirectly from the popular arts; just as the Dadaists of the 1920s had drawn on the whimsical inventiveness of humorists like Edward Lear and Rube Goldberg, so there are evident parallels between Dali's visual puns and animated cartoons like Walt Disney's *Skeleton Dance* of 1929.

For all these reasons, Dali soon became one of the best-known painters of the 1930s; but for the same reasons, most of his advance-guard contemporaries looked on him with disdain. It was not only that they considered his precise and meticulous delineations, by catering to a debased public taste for illustration, vulgarized and demeaned the painter's lofty mission to redeem mankind, or even that he was more interested in publicizing himself than in the cause of art; his great fault in their eyes was making a joke of an intensely serious movement in painting. For them, the true Surrealists were those dedicated to combating totalitarianism generally, and Fascism in particular. Such was Max Beckmann, who worked to transform what had been mere social protest painting in the

369

early 1920s into evocations of primeval passion by the end of the decade, and who in 1932 had begun a famous triptych of *The Departure* (page 373, finished 1935, New York, Museum of Modern Art). According to the authors of *Looking at Modern Painting,* this was meant as an attack on the Nazi regime in Germany and originally entitled *Scenes from Shakespeare's Tempest* "in order to confuse Nazi investigators":

> The painting itself offers no further specific clue to explain the drama or to clarify the relations of the figures. The most that can definitely be said is that the scene on the left of revolting physical torture is a pendant to the maddeningly illogical episode on the right. These contrast strongly with the central event of the departure. But who is travelling, and with whom, and in what direction? These questions are not answered. In spite of these baffling ambiguities, however, we cannot escape the sense of import, of moral judgement. All action seems arrested by the intensity of the artist's feeling. The painting cries out mutely, perhaps offers release, barely suggests the existence of hope.*

Pre-eminent among such artists was Picasso, who in the 1930s maintained his position as leader of the advance guard by becoming the foremost exemplar of a serious Surrealism dedicated to the proposition that, in his own words, "Painting is not meant to decorate houses. It is a weapon of offensive and defensive war against the enemy." Of this

* L. Freedman, ed. (New York, 1957), p. 48.

47A. *Salvador Dali:* Paranoiac-Astral Image. *Hartford, Wadsworth Atheneum. 1934.* See also 47B, Beckmann.

Faced with the tangible Realities of totalitarian police states, the private subjective Realities advance-guard painters had created for themselves in Germany and Russia evaporated. But in democratic countries the trance continued into the 1930s. Characteristic of the decade was Surrealism, and the vogue for "naïve" painting. Superficially, the forms of Surrealism looked in general "more real" than the typical advance-guard painting of the 1920s. And it could be claimed that Surrealistic content, too, was "more real," in that its subjective Reality was now "disciplined" by "scientific" psychology. To that extent Surrealism represented a response to the Reality of totalitarianism.

doctrine the great demonstration was *Guernica* (page 375), painted early in May, 1937.

In many respects *Guernica* was for Picasso what *The Studio* had been for Courbet: "a summation of seven years of my artistic life." Its genesis was in the time-space studies initiated by what for his devoted followers was the astounding new departure of a series of paintings on medieval themes in the early 1930s, most notably a *Crucifixion* in 1930 and the *Girl Before a Mirror* of 1932 (New York, Museum of Modern Art). Here Picasso's concern was neither directly nor indirectly with the specific content of medieval art, of course, but with its time-space conventions used as a vehicle for apocalyptic expression. To the earlier time-space disquisitions of his Cubist days Picasso now added a new dimension: the idea of the cosmic present, which had led medieval artists to discard classical unities of time and place as unreal, and instead depict cause and effect together in one spatial structure, showing past and present and future at once, taking a viewpoint outside of Time. And in this time-space concept, with its plain implications that time as this world knows it is no more than a finite dream, Picasso found a vehicle for expressing in fashionable Surrealist terms his unchanging conviction that the things of this world must pass away; it is no accident that the works of medieval art which most moved him, and which became a major source of *Guernica* imagery, were Spanish illustrated manuscripts of the Apocalypse—the primordial War in Heaven and the Last Days. From 1934 on, Picasso added to these studies yet another theme, the Bull Fight; drawing on his own Spanish background as well as Goya's series on the subject, Picasso found in it subjective symbols of the sublimated love of violence to be found in the heart of every society, and in every man. All these lines of development converged in the *Guernica,* painted in May, 1937.

The overt occasion for the painting was a commission for a great mural in the Spanish Government Building at the Paris World's Fair; its overt subject, newspaper reports of an unprovoked bombing by German and Italian airplanes of the Basque town of Guernica on April 28, 1937. But of course it was understood that the painting would be far more than that. It would be a ringing denunciation of war in general and the

47B. *Max Beckmann:* The Departure. *Collection, The Museum of Modern Art, New York. 1932–33.*

372

Spanish Fascist forces of General Franco in particular; it would be a grand demonstration of that power of painting and painters to change the world in which all the world saviors of the years between the Wars so fervently believed. For had not Picasso himself announced that abstract disquisitions on picture-making were out of date? Here would be proof positive that "Painting is not made to decorate houses. It is a weapon of offensive and defensive war against the enemy." Mere announcement of the project was enough to convince the entire advance-guard world that *Guernica* would be the great monument to the rejuvenation of painting. The future masterpiece was photographed at every stage of its creation— which did not take long, the picture being already outlined in mature form on its twenty-six-foot canvas in only eleven days. Eager apologists could hardly wait for its last stroke to hail *Guernica* as the greatest work of the 20th century and to reiterate, in the spirit of Blum, that before this evidence of opposition by the world's conscience Hitler's Fascism would surely now be forced to retreat.

It should perhaps have been obvious that Picasso's Surrealism would have as little practical influence on the course of human events as Blum's "moral conscience of the world," or Kandinsky's Spiritualism, or Klee's pedagogical sketchbook, or Mondriaan's pure plastic form. Brushes, like pens, may ultimately prove mightier than swords, but the process takes time; and time was lacking. But it may be questioned whether, even with time, Surrealism could ever have functioned as its admirers hoped. The whole concept and ethos of Surrealism in particular, and of

48A. *Pablo Picasso:* Guernica. *Collection, The Museum of Modern Art, New York, on Extended Loan from the Artist. 1937.* See also 48B, Blume.

From c. 1930 on Picasso began to manifest a new "seriousness," applying himself to formal time-space and other problems comparably related to Surrealism. This picture of 1937, interpreting Goya's Disasters of War *in terms of the new psychological Reality, was called by his admirers the greatest painting of the 20th century, if not of all time, and by himself a "mighty weapon" in the "struggle against Fascism." Yet it could convert only those already within the fold; on the unregenerate it had no effect.*

"modern painting" as developed in the 20th century, worked against any such possibility.

The specific basis of Surrealism in subconscious imagery, in ideas and impulses implanted at earlier periods of life, deprived it of immediate impact. Both the two main sources of inspiration for *Guernica,* for example, derived from events much earlier than the situation with which it was supposed to be concerned. One of them, Goya's series on the *Disasters of War,* which provided the monochromatic color scheme and the universal "war is hell" theme, was more than a hundred years old. The other, quite certainly, was World War I; perhaps the closest parallel to the complex of horror images that make up the *Guernica* is to be found in the vivid sequences of memory pictures which make up Remarque's descriptions of combat in *All Quiet on The Western Front,* published in 1929 and stock reading matter for people of any intellectual pretensions in the early 1930s. Effective communication was further stultified by the solipsistic nature of Reality which Surrealism shared with advance-guard painting generally. Juan Larrea meant the highest compliment to *Guernica* as a masterpiece of 20th-century art when he described how

> Everything that has been considered inherent in the art of painting, even by the most advanced schools: light, color precision or plasticity of drawing . . . are here conspicuously lacking. The most that can be said to remain is a clean surface upon which we follow the alternate syncopations of blacks with grays and whites, in a mysterious drama of vital disorder, with a marked tendency towards triangulation. . . . Clearly, then, the reality conveyed by the Guernica is not a physical but a mental reality alike in this to language and writing . . . a dream world, with images flowing together, not related particularly to Guernica, basque country, or anything else . . .*

But such art can hardly be described as a useful ideological weapon, for its symbols can have no fixed meaning. Larrea may well be right when he goes on to claim that "the horse transfixed by a lance or pike . . . stands, in the painter's mind, for nothing more nor less than Nationalist Spain," and thereby "Picasso's brush bursts out, as it were, in a magic imprecation, calling down upon Franco's Fascism a spasm of agony and its final doom"; but he may just as well be wrong, because the painter has done nothing and, by the rules of his own art, can do nothing to prevent our interpreting the picture in an entirely opposite sense. *Guernica* has in fact the same kind of ambiguity as Goya's

* *Guernica* (New York, 1947), pp. 13, 28.

Disasters of War; but whereas in that case the painter had a pragmatic reason to speak obscurely—otherwise he risked his life—Picasso's motivation was the purely doctrinaire advance-guard principle of subjective and solipsistic Reality. "A mysterious drama of vital disorder" may be great art, but is certainly poor propaganda.

The same sort of criticism can be made of Beckmann's *Departure*. It may well be that sensitive intellectuals "in spite of these baffling ambiguities . . . cannot escape the sense of import, of moral judgement," but the general public had no such difficulty. Nor is it at all clear to an ordinary mind how changing titles from *The Departure* to *Scenes from Shakespeare's Tempest* should have helped "to confuse Nazi investigators"; surely, its meaning was already quite obscure enough to make the picture useless as a weapon, however fine it might be as a painting.

In short, concern with Reality alone, however deeply perceived, is not enough to make a painting effective in ideological combat. It can be so only when and if the painter's Reality is of a sort that is communicable, and objectively verifiable. James Gillray's art had that sort of Reality, and in consequence his cartoons were so effective a weapon against Napoleon that the French Emperor personally tried to persuade an English government to jail the obscure nobody who drew them. Daumier's cartoons against the restored Bourbons, Thomas Nast's against Boss Tweed in post-Civil-War New York, David Low's against Hitler, all had this same power. But Picasso's *Guernica* and Beckmann's *Departure,* like Dali's Surrealist paintings on Spanish Civil War themes, did not and could not. For in contrast to the objective, tangible, definable Reality of popular arts, the advance guard's was subjective, intangible, and solipsistic; and long ago Samuel Johnson on the quay at Harwich in 1763 had shown Boswell how to deal with Reality of this kind:

> After we came out of the church, we stood talking for some time together of Bishop Berkeley's ingenious sophistry to prove the non-existence of matter, and that everything in the universe is merely ideal. I observed, that though we are satisfied his doctrine is not true, it is impossible to refute it. I shall never forget the alacrity with which Johnson answered, striking his foot with mighty force against a large stone, till he rebounded from it, "I refute it *thus.*"

Hitler dealt with it in the same brutally effective way.

Not least among the casualties of Hitler's War was the rationale of modern painting as it had evolved over the previous fifty years. When the smoke cleared after 1945, New York had replaced Paris as the world center of painting; "for good or ill [to paraphrase Henry Russell Hitchcock's remark about modern architecture] American painting had come to be synonymous with modern painting"; but it could never be quite the same.

NOTES

Appropriately enough for a movement half literary and half graphic, there have been an extraordinary number of books written about Surrealism. Among those published since World War II are: M. Nadeau, *Histoire du Surréalisme* (2 vols., Paris, 1945), Wallace Fowlie, *Age of Surrealism* (1950), M. Carrouges, *André Breton et les donnés fondamentales du surréalisme* (Paris, 1950), M. Raymond, *From Baudelaire to Surrealism* (1950), F. Alquie, *Philosophie du Surréalisme* (Paris, 1955), A. E. Balakian, *Surrealism, the Road to the Absolute* (1960), Jean Marcel, *A History of Surrealist Painting* (1960), Yves Duplessis, *Surrealism* (1963). Among the many books dealing in whole or part with Picasso's Surrealism are H. F. Mackenzie, *Understanding Picasso* (Chicago, 1940), A. H. Barr, Jr., *Picasso: Fifty Years of His Art*, and *Picasso: 75th Anniversary Exhibition* (New York, Museum of Modern Art, 1946 and 1957); F. Elgar, *Picasso* (1956), R. Arnheim, *Picasso's Guernica* (Berkeley, 1962).

48B. *Peter Blume:* The Eternal City. *Collection, The Museum of Modern Art, New York, Mrs. Simon Guggenheim Fund. 1937.*

Painted in the same year as the Guernica, *in a superficially similar Surrealist vocabulary, and ostensibly with the same didactic and hortative intent, Blume's picture illustrates how fundamental has been the difference between the American and the European advance-guard understanding of the function of painting. The one painting, rooted in a deep tradition of illustration and the empirical Reality of popular arts, is unmistakably about something unmistakable; the other simply is.*

III

The American Experience

1

The "Americanness" of American Art

It has become customary, at least since the 1950s, for studies or surveys of painting to make two assumptions about American art. One is that American and European cultures are fundamentally different, or at best that American culture is no more than a distant colonial reflection of Europe's. The other is that, even granting the possibility of American and European cultures being integral parts of the same whole, America is culturally backward compared to Europe. Though the United States happens temporarily to be of some cultural importance—so this argument runs—through most of its history all of North America has been culturally primitive, its native tradition of folk art only fitfully and sporadically enlivened by visits of European artists on missions of mercy among the savages.

Both views have been and still are widely shared by Americans themselves. For example, as late as 1962 a writer as widely known and respected as John I. H. Baur could propose as a guide for organizing an ideal pavilion of American Art at the New York World's Fair the principle that "from the 17th to the end of the 19th centuries our art was a dialogue between a native folk culture and imported European influences" (*Art in America*, L, 3, 1962, p. 42). Yet neither assumption can stand much close scrutiny.

The fact is that an "International Style" is no sudden invention of the 1920s; historically, styles in European art and architecture have always been international. Since at least the year 1000, Europe has been a close cultural entity; ideas, fashions in dress, forms in art and architecture, technological innovations have always spread rapidly and consistently from wherever they originated all over those territories that comprise what we think of as The West. And from its foundation, America has shared in this dissemination, been part of that entity. Literate Americans in the 17th and 18th centuries read what literate Europeans were reading; American builders used the same forms and composed them on the same principles as their counterparts in Europe. Available resources and materials necessarily varied, and, in the earliest periods of settlement, the cultural lag in transmission of ideas was perhaps longer. But that lag was never as long as popularly imagined, and it rapidly shortened, so that by the 18th century there was no more difference between American colonial architecture and fashionable architecture in London, for example, than between London and provincial building in England. The same is true of painting.

Throughout its history, the tides of taste in American painting have been part of the wider pattern of the history of painting in Europe. And just as there has been "French painting" or "British painting" within the general context of "European painting," so there has been an "American painting" which embodies, reflects, and represents a national variant of European culture as a whole, developed in response to certain distinctive national attitudes produced by the distinctive historical experiences of English-speaking America.

Even when the existence of an American painting in this sense was admitted, however, attempts to define its characteristic qualities in terms other than primitiveness or alienation from Europe have been few and sporadic until quite recent times; historical circumstances dictated that painting never played the same important role in American life as architecture or furniture design, so that the problem never had urgent interest. The second World War radically changed this situation. Quite suddenly, the United States became a world center of painting, and its historical attitude to painting was a matter of important concern for the development and future of painting in general. John McCoubrey's analysis of a formal mode of vision peculiarly characteristic of *American Tradition in Painting* (1963) is one notable essay in this direction. Here I am concerned more with determining the traditional American concept of what painting is fundamentally about, what painters do in and for society. This is not a history of American painting but a *kritik,* an attempt to judge and understand American painting in terms of its own rationale rather than in terms of cultural lag as compared to advance-guard painting in Paris or anywhere else.

Broadly speaking, the advance-guard evolution of painting since 1750 in Europe generally, and particularly in France, has been towards a kind of religious status, a mystically satisfying spiritual experience in itself. That tendency, and its corollary in the concept of painter as godlike creator which we have traced through the 19th century into the 20th, has been patent at least as far back as Manet, who, according to George Bataille, realized that

> . . . in the past, art was the expression of "supreme" forms, divine and royal. . . . the majestic forms of old had drawn their strength from the people's naïveté which was now lost to them. Christianity lived on, but Christian naïveté was no longer a living force. . . . What had to be found, above and beyond conventional majestic forms, was some supreme, unimpeachable reality capable of withstanding the immense pressure of utilitarian tradition. This supreme reality was found in the silence of art. What is supreme and majestic in present-day life is not to be found in present-day forms, which are incapable of giving rise to palaces and temples; it resides in that "secret royalty" which Malraux reads into Cézanne's apples, which made its appearance in *Olympia*, and which is the greatness of *The Execution of Maximilian*. This royalty springs not from any given image, but from the passion of the painter who, within himself, fathoms the depths of supreme silence, in which his painting is transfigured and which becomes the art of wresting objects, and the images of objects, from a world that has surrendered to a bourgeois torpor. André Malraux was the first to state it clearly: the only cathedral raised in our time is the vast collection of modern paintings in our museums.*

But both this European advance-guard concept of the nature of art, and its concept of the nature of religion, have traditionally been uncongenial to the American temperament and fundamentally foreign to the whole American historical experience.

The idea of religion as an end in itself, of religious experience for its own sake, has never flourished in North America. Neither the Puritans who came to New England dedicated to the proposition that social institutions exist in order to further religious experience, nor the Anglicans who tried to establish in Virginia the orthodox doctrine of Richard Hooker that the State depends on and exists to serve the Church, were able to maintain such a position long. Everywhere in the colonies it had become implicitly assumed within a generation or two that religion and

* *Manet* (New York, 1958), pp. 57–58.

religious institutions existed to serve the welfare of society at large, and the State in particular. And when the Republic was founded, that assumption became explicit. The traditional heavenly vision was firmly transferred to earth; the pursuit of happiness had as its goal an ideal social order existing here and now, and the function of formal religious institutions was to assist that pursuit in whatever ways seemed most appropriate—from preaching against drunkenness or adultery to supporting the democratic process by assisting in demonstrations for civil rights. Any number of factors helped shape this characteristic attitude: the frontier experience which necessarily judged activities and institutions primarily in terms of social utility; the historic outlook of the middle-class bourgeois which came to dominate the country within a hundred years of its founding and still does; the Calvinist premium on useful work; the fact that the United States, first of Western nations, decisively rejected the principle of hereditary rule in favor of rule by demonstrable talent and ability; above all, the Protestant insistence on individual responsibility. But whatever its background, historically the fact is that Americans have always taken it for granted that religion is something useful, a means to an end; they put "In God We Trust" on coins and "The Family that Prays Together Stays Together" on billboards. And they have taken precisely the same attitude towards painting.

To most Americans, the Whistler-Pater dogma that "all art constantly aspires to the condition of music" has always seemed nonsense, because the concept of aesthetic experience as an end in itself has never been any more generally acceptable than religious experience in itself. "Art," in short, has always meant something useful in the United States, never a self-justifying or self-sufficient activity. This conviction, rather than any primitiveness or cultural backwardness, explains why, from the beginning, whatever innate sense for Beauty Americans had to express went pre-eminently into the popular and industrial arts; why, from the beginning, their influence on all the "fine arts" in America has been so constant and pervasive that no discussion of American painting can be fully intelligible without taking them into account. In this conviction, then, the "Americanness" of American art is rooted.

2

Industrial Design and Popular Arts
as American Cultural Expression

The definitive book on American industrial design and popular arts as cultural expression, and as significant creations in their own right rather than quaint bits of folksy Americana, has yet to be written. In this context we can do no more than indicate some of the points it might make. It should include the evolution of tool design in response to special American conditions, beginning with the handsome new types of axes developed on the frontier, and making special mention of Eli Whitney's lathes which made mass production possible in the 19th century; it should then go on to discuss the influence of these new tools on product design, from 17th-century furniture to 20th-century automobiles. The several good existing studies of early tombstone carvings should be expanded into the 20th century, and the changes in imagery and sentiment used to illuminate changing currents in American religious life. It should consider why Currier & Ives were so successful, why Lincoln and Longfellow alike admired Rogers groups. A large section should be devoted to the history of political cartooning in America, from broadsheets to tabloids; in it is mirrored and dramatized the creation of that viable political system which has been one of America's greatest historic achievements. Another large section could be devoted to that large body of cartoons, Thomas Nast's and Art Young's pre-eminent among them, which represent the American search for a just social order. The development of advertising arts deserves extended study as a significant expression of the nature and growth of American economic institutions, and in the same way the development of comics can be analyzed in terms of American social values; a book within a book could be written on Popeye's *Thimble Theatre* alone (page 229), for example, as revealing public opinion on major political and social issues of the 1930s. Calendar art and book illustration could be analyzed from the same point of view.

And particular mention needs to be made, of course, of the pervasive influence of all these arts on the character of painting in the United States. In earlier parts of this book we have seen what a large part

384

realism in the popular arts played in affecting the course of evolution of advance-guard painting; in America, where they were so much more pre-eminent, their influence was that much stronger. No matter what it was conventional to proclaim in theory, in practice "art" for most Americans has always meant the kind of values and social function inherent in popular arts and industrial design, and in order to survive and work American painters have had to take account of that fact, by incorporating a high degree of naturalism and popular Realism, and by retaining many traditional functions of communication and entertainment which in Europe were early surrendered to "commercial art."

3

Historic Development
of the American Tradition in Painting

Keeping in mind this constant influence of the popular arts on the historical development of painting in America, we can understand why, whenever it deviates from the broader European tradition of which it is a part, it always deviates in the direction of standards and functions characteristic of the popular arts. This appears very early. Writing in *The Earthly Paradise* of 18th-century painting, for instance, Werner Hofmann declared that

> English historical painting had made its decision, set its face against the glorifying tradition and rejected the rule of the "universal human." West's *Death of General Wolfe* (1771) and Copley's *Boy Attacked by a Shark* are important documents illustrating this trend.*

The fact that these painters were American is not mentioned; yet it is immensely important, as illustrating both the integral relationship of American and European culture, and how early a distinctive American tradition was evident. For what characterize both these pictures, of course, are qualities related to the popular arts—communication, report-age, things as they are rather than as imagined. And the lines of development here apparent continued to govern American painting throughout the 19th century. The painters who failed personally, or who

* (New York, 1961), p. 52.

385

in retrospect were outside the main American tradition (like Vanderlyn at the beginning of the century or Blakelock at its end) were those who tried to idealize, who tried to follow doctrinaire aesthetic systems; the successful painters, those whom we now think of as constituting the core of the American tradition, were men like Charles Willson Peale, with his concern for bringing art to the people; Morse with his interest in photography; the creative illustrators Bingham, Mount, Eakins, and Homer. And at the beginning of the 20th century the situation had not changed.

From the European advance-guard point of view, the "Ash Can School" led by Henri, Sloan, and Luks, which represented advance-guard painting in early 20th-century America, only illustrated how provincial and backward American culture actually was; to Europeans it seemed that the kind of Reality which Americans thought "revolutionary" was no more than what Manet had been proposing in France back in the 1860s —unidealized themes from everyday life, painted as seen. Yet in terms of the historic American tradition, the Ash Can school had a very different significance. Its objective was in fact to rescue American painting from the effete excesses of advance-guard painting in Europe, to break away from Whistler's Aesthetic Impressionism and Sargent's Academic Impressionism as much as from lingering High Victorian Academic painting. Like the "progressive" architects of Chicago and California who wanted to return to basic American traditions and values which had been lost in the current vogue for archaeological Beaux-Arts niceties, so the Ash Can leaders were trying to restore to American painting its traditional values and function, not to introduce any European concepts of Reality. And just as the "progressive" architects found inspiration in ordinary 19th-century American architecture—Wright's "Prairie House" can be traced back through the Shingle Style to High

49. *John Sloan:* McSorley's Bar. *The Detroit Institute of Arts. 1900.*

Social Impressionism, American style. Inviting comparison with Manet's Bar at the Folies-Bergères, *it is in fact fundamentally and typically different, in that the artist's concern is more with content than form, a disquisition on the Reality of American life rather than the Reality of painting.*

Victorian villas and thence to Italianate houses of the 1840s, for instance —so Ash Can painters drew their inspiration, as painters in the historic American tradition always had, from illustration and cartooning; indeed, most of them were cartoonists or illustrators originally. The American experience of 20th-century painting in the European sense did not begin with the Ash Can school, but with the exhibition of modern American and European painting which its leaders organized at the New York Armory in 1913.

4

The American Experience in 20th-Century Painting

To what extent the Armory Show organizers understood the specific character of their own American tradition in painting, as contrasted with what had been developing in advance-guard Paris, is still a question for debate. So is the effect of the Show. Ostensibly, it achieved all that its organizers hoped for. As anticipated, all the new trends in painting were ridiculed, but no more violently than had been feared. In many quarters people were unexpectedly friendly, and there were plenty who found their first exposure to the New Painting inspirational.

In the long run, however, the Show was a disaster for its organizers. The contrast between developments in Europe and those in America was inescapable. European advance-guard painting had by now become a self-sufficient and self-justifying activity; almost all connection with society at large had been abandoned. If this were good painting, if this were the proper condition and function of art, then American painting, with its strong concern for social comment and illustrative qualities rooted in popular realism, must be hopelessly outdated. The chief beneficiary of the Show, financially and in reputation, was the advance-guard school of Paris; for the Ash Can painters, its chief result was the loss of several important patrons to the Europeans without any commensurate gain in public understanding of what they, in distinction to European painters, were doing. The Show thus contributed to the general debacle of the native "progressive" movement in arts and letters that had set in around 1910. By 1920 that movement was so moribund that during the decade of "normalcy" American painters generally were reduced to choosing among the three dismal alternatives of producing pictures on the level of calendar art and magazine illustration, making feeble pastiches of tamely "modernistic" clichés, or becoming expatriates who hung rootlessly on the fringes of the European advance guard; to most people—even the majority of writers and scholars—the very idea of an American tradition seemed contemptible and somehow embarrassing.

The Depression of 1929, and the rise of menacing totalitarian regimes in Europe, combined to change this situation markedly during the 1930s. Two contending parties emerged in American painting, roughly comparable to the two great political parties of the decade. To the one (roughly equivalent to the Republican party) belonged all those who believed in the general principle of returning to past principles and practices as the best solution to present difficulties. It included such painters as Edward Hopper, Peter Hurd, Luigi Lucioni, Aaron Bohrod, and Raphael Soyer, in whose work the inspiration of Eakins and Homer was more or less evident; painters of social protest in the spirit of Thomas Nast and Art Young and the Ash Can school (Sloan himself, Reginald Marsh, William Gropper, and many more). And above all, the "regionalists" led by Thomas Hart Benton, Grant Wood, and John Steuart Curry. Nowadays the regionalists have fallen out of favor, and are often considered little more than illustrators, of (in Curry's case particularly) a not very high or creative order. But in the 1930s they seemed to (and in fact did) represent some measure of return to a tried and true tradition in American painting, comparable to the traditional political principle of noninvolvement in European affairs, and their work appealed to the same isolationalist mood. Until 1941 this conservative kind of painting largely dominated the American scene.

Increasingly, however, its predominance was challenged by a second party in painting—the "moderns," a group as wildly diverse as the Democratic coalition under Roosevelt. Its motivation was the "liberal" view that the old America could never be revived, that change was inevitable and essential, that new experiments ought to be tried, whether or not their nature and implications were fully understood; and in particular, that the old isolation from Europe was impossible, and America must take its full part in Western civilization. Most of the painters in this group had come under strong European influences: John Marin, whose studies in Europe over the years 1905–1911 had resulted in a vaguely Cubist-Expressionist manner of rendering landscapes; Max

389

Weber, born in Russia, come to the United States in 1891, cross product of the studio of Henri Matisse and the Pratt Institute; Morris Graves, Stuart Davis, Peter Blume, Walt Kuhn, Abraham Rattner, and many others. Collectively, they professed to hold the regionalists and American-scene painters generally in contempt.

But in fact the two camps in American painting held a recognizably common core of distinctively American values and outlook, just as the two political parties did, sharing and manifesting a deep concern for objectively real situations which set both camps equally apart from the typical European advance-guard painting of the 1930s with its detached interest in abstract formal picture-making for its own sake. To European advance-guard critics no fact seemed more obvious; in their eyes the differences between "conservative" and "modern" American painters of the 1930s were as miniscule and incomprehensible as the differences between Republicans and Democrats appeared in Europe. It was not only a matter of Americans consistently appropriating and "debasing" the ideas of modern painting for utilitarian and popular uses—Mondriaan appropriated for Kleenex boxes, Klee made into a joke by Steinberg, Picasso parodied by Virgil Partch; even those American painters who considered themselves "modern" seemed unable to "take art seriously." "Though closer to Surrealism than almost any other American painter, he has never belonged to the movement; his whole approach is conscious and rational": what Lloyd Goodrich * perceptively noted about Peter Blume was typical of all the American "moderns" of the 1950s. However many ideas or forms they incorporated from the European advance guard, they would not work on its premises. So "naïve" painting, though originally associated with the advance guard in Europe, in America tended to become a kind of regional expression—compare John Kane with Henri Rousseau, for instance. So did Expressionism, as represented by painters like Morris Graves and even to some extent Stuart Davis. In the hands of painters like Jack Levine or Ben Shahn, by contrast, Expressionism tended to turn into social protest and on occasion even into something perilously close to cartooning. Surrealism also, as Lloyd Goodrich noted, subtly changed its character; comparing what was perhaps its most famous American example in the 1930s, Blume's *Eternal City* of 1936 (page 379), with Picasso's *Guernica,* it is obvious that the American with his pragmatic background and

* *American Art of Our Century,* Part I (New York, Whitney Museum of American Art, 1961).

50. *Grant Wood:* American Gothic. *Chicago, The Art Institute, Friends of American Art Collection. 1935.*

Social protest, American style. Acquainted from studies in Europe with the general development of modern painting in Germany and specifically with the Neue Sachlichkeit *("New Objectivity") school of social protest represented by Dix and Grosz, Wood clearly borrows ideas from Teutonic linear patterns, "magic realism," and compulsive symbols (fork, window, etc.), but makes of them the same kind of portrait that Sinclair Lewis made of* Babbitt—*at once satirical and sympathetic.*

391

tradition oriented towards the popular arts instinctively understood the basic principle involved in using painting "as a weapon"—it must be "about something" and not simply "be."

In the later 1930s the differences between American and European advance-guard painting began to become painfully apparent, as a great wave of refugee painters swept in following the rise of Hitler: Ashile Gorky; Hans Hofmann; Joseph Albers, Lionel Feininger and Laszlo Moholy-Nagy from the Bauhaus; Fritz Glarner of *De Stijl*—to name only a few. At first the American "moderns" thought they were gaining allies; instead, what happened was much more like the ultimate result of the Armory Show. As one art school after another fell into the hands of ex-Bauhausmen, as one 57th-Street gallery after another began featuring fugitives from the School of Paris in preference to American painters, the American "moderns" found themselves in a squeeze. Caught between the regionalists, whom they considered reactionary and provincial, and the European advance guard, whose basic philosophy of self-justifying, nihilistic and abstractly impersonal acts of creation they found abhorrent and pointless, they had nowhere to move, and were crushed where they stood.

Such was the background for American painting after World War II. Once again American painters divided into two broad camps, one conservative and the other liberal; but this time the differences between them seemed much sharper. Composing the conservative party were primarily followers and successors of the regionalists, reinforced and made more sophisticated by elements from the "moderns" of the 1930s. Its most typical and outstanding representative was Andrew Wyeth. His roots in the American tradition were obvious. Whatever depths within depths there may have been in his paintings, they offered some "meaning" for everyone; indeed, for some critics' tastes they were all too close to popular illustration. Others, more severe, declared that Wyeth's work was not painting in the 20th-century sense at all; no one could deny that, however great a perception of Reality his paintings involved, their true concern was with the old goal of Beauty.

By contrast, the advance-guard wing of American painting after 1945 seemed thoroughly Europeanized. Many of those composing it were in fact Europeans from the 1930s who had settled in the United States. But its best-known representatives were Americans, the Abstract Expressionists of New York. Although basically trained in America during the 1930s, most of them by the "moderns," a few even by regionalists

(Jackson Pollock, who had worked with Thomas Hart Benton, is an example), they seemed to many people, including some Europeans, to have thoroughly accepted European advance-guard concepts of the nature of painting, and indeed to be carrying on where the School of Paris left off. So Françoise Choay, for example, wrote in "Modern Art Yesterday and Tomorrow" * that

> Pollock has marked the second stage in the evolution of modern art. The first dates from the first twenty years of this century, and was characterized by Cubism's challenge to the classical "subject" followed by various experiments in non-figuration. Once the intellectual element had been demolished and the claims of the irrational asserted, notably by Surrealism, Pollock's role was to reveal certain regions of being, no longer solely through an unusual use of color, but by means of an entirely new structuration of pictorial space having no connection with classical logic.

But it may be questioned whether Abstract Expressionism was quite as European and remote from the American tradition as it superficially looked. There is considerable reason for doubting that Pollock, in painting something like *Phosphorescence* (page 395), was concerned with pure visual experience to the same extent and degree as Max Ernst when, anticipating Abstract Expressionism,

> on the 10th of August 1925, finding myself one rainy evening in a seaside inn, I was struck by the obsession that showed to my excited gaze the floor-boards upon which a thousand scrubbings had deepened the grooves. I decided then to investigate the symbolism of this obsession, and, in order to aid my meditative and hallucinatory faculties, I made from the boards a series of drawings by placing on them, at random, sheets of paper which I undertook to rub with black lead. In gazing attentively at the drawings thus obtained . . . I was surprised by the sudden identification of my visionary capacities and by the hallucinatory succession of contradictory images superimposed, one upon the other, with the persistence and rapidity characteristic of amorous memories.†

Whether deliberately or not, much Abstract Expressionist painting functioned as a vehicle, not for aesthetic trances or hallucinatory imagery, but for enlarging the capacities of the human mind. Breaking through the

---

* *The Selective Eye* IV (1962).
† Quoted in Marcel Jean, *History of Surrealist Painting* (London, 1959), pp. 126–127.

confines of conventional time and order, these great nonobjective "action" canvases, which themselves were brought into being by acts of spontaneous intuition, could function for spectators like a hypnotist's swinging watch or the rote prayers of a mystic, to lull the conscious, sensuous, rational mind into quiescence so that psychic powers of unsuspected potential might be released from the subconscious. In so functioning, Abstract Expressionist painting contributes to that 20th-century religion which teaches that man is on the point of actually achieving a godlike status; it plays its part in the search for the secrets of life itself, for techniques of transporting matter and energy at will so that time and space fall entirely under man's control and he commands the processes of his own body as well as the stars in their courses. In so functioning, however, Abstract Expressionist painting also changes its character. It becomes a means to an end, rather than an end in itself. Like so many other borrowings from Europe over the three and a half centuries of American history, the New Painting was somehow transformed in its American environment. The implications of all this remain to be seen. But from this ending to two hundred years of evolution in painting, certain conclusions may be hazarded.

It has been apparent for a long time that European advance-guard painting has become an activity of the same order as stamp-collecting, a hobby sustained by, but of no intrinsic value in, an affluent society. Ever since Post-Impressionism the gulf between advance-guard painters and the public at large has been steadily deepening and widening. Attempts at closing it made by Kandinsky with his spiritual art, Klee with his compulsive symbols, Mondriaan with his pure plastic form, or the Surrealists with their weapon against Fascism, all alike proved in the end only that this kind of painting had no practical function in the modern world. Their pictures did retain a certain intrinsic value, however, as

51. *Jackson Pollock:* Phosphorescence. *1950. Andover, Mass., Addison Gallery of American Art.*

"Pollock has marked the second stage in the evolution of modern art" —but perhaps not in quite the way meant by the European critic, Françoise Choay.

pictures. But Abstract Expressionist canvases, by the very token of having a certain demonstrable metaphysical function, lost even that value.

Traditionally art was valued, to use a homely analogy, like a fine whiskey. Just as you take some everyday grain and water, then refine and process and distill them until in the end you get a product far rarer

52. *Fred Shane:* Avant-Garde, 1949. *Kansas City, Mo., Collection of Mr. and Mrs. Bernard Hoffman.*

A characteristic "American Modern," it consummately expresses the traditional American concept of the nature of art—the European advance-guard painter is to be condemned not on aesthetic grounds, but for ignoring both the Beauties which lie crumbling behind him and the Realities before his eyes, to concentrate on creating a useless world of his own making.

and more valuable than the sum of these raw ingredients, so the painter—and this applies to Cézanne and Mondriaan as well as to Raphael or Reynolds—took the raw materials of nature, refined and distilled them, selected and abstracted from them until he had an end product much finer than his original materials; and that is what you paid for. But Abstract Expressionist paintings were not like that. Their primary function was fulfilled in the act that brought them into existence; and even their secondary function of affording spectators a vehicle for psychic release imparted no intrinsic value to them. For just as the hypnotist's swinging watch is of no worth *as a watch,* and the mystic's rote-prayers are of none as communication, so Abstract Expressionist canvases could have no value *as pictures.* They remained at best the shell of an experience. There is something illogical about pricing and exhibiting them in the same way as traditional paintings, and it is possible to see in the sudden appearance and success in the 1960s of "pop" art, of "anti-pictures" ostentatiously composed of trash, a tacit protest against this illogical situation.

It is also possible to recognize in "pop" art implications of significance regarding the future of painting. In part they are ironic: if photographers now perform painting's old function of recording life, if people now turn to advertising or posters when they want life made more beautiful, and go to movies or read comic strips when they want it made more pleasant—if, in short, painting means people talking to themselves and art for all practical intents and purposes means the popular arts, then anyone who still wants to be called an artist might as well recognize that situation by exhibiting stenciled letters and flags and cast bronze beer cans and fragments of comic strips instead of easel paintings in the old sense. But "pop" art has positive implications, too. There is a constructive conclusion to be drawn from the spectacle of popular arts flourishing at the moment when easel painting is moribund as a useful or necessary activity in society, from the fact that industrial designers and photographers and commercial artists and cartoonists live dignified and rewarding lives while advance-guard painters are reduced to quarreling petitioners for government aid. It is simply this: the present dismal state of painting does not mean that art is dead. It means only that the particular line of evolution taken by advance-guard painting over the last hundred years has run into a dead end. When and wherever artists have been content to leave the search for Reality to philosophers or physicists or theologians, and have confined themselves to their traditional function of providing society with Beauty (on whatever level), art is as vital as ever.

What we have here defined as the historic American tradition in painting is still very much alive; many of the leading painters in the United States still work within it. They are flourishing, and unless Western civilization itself is destroyed, they will continue to flourish. For that "American tradition" is of course simply a perpetuation of the traditional Western concept of what painting is and what painters do in society.

NOTES

Milton W. Brown, *The Story of the Armory Show* (1963) presents a vivid picture of the state of American culture and taste in 1913. The Whitney Museum of American Art's *American Art of Our Century* (1961) is perhaps the best general survey of the period (Part I, 1900–1939, by Lloyd Goodrich; Part II, 1940–1960, by John I. H. Baur). Useful studies of Abstract Expressionism are provided by Edward B. Henning, *Paths of Abstract Art* (Cleveland Museum of Art, 1960) and Dore Ashton, *The Unknown Shore* (Boston, 1962).

53. *Robert Indiana:* The Demuth American Dream No. 5. *The Toronto (Ontario) Art Gallery, Gift from the Women's Committee Fund.*

An impressive and typical example of "pop" art, painted in 1963. Characteristic are its great size (five separate panels each four feet square, the whole twelve feet square); its use of the techniques of industrial and commercial art; its parodying of "classic" modern art (with pseudopsychological "slices of life" implications, especially in the autobiographical fragments in the central panel); but above all its only half-deliberate reversion to older ideals of Beauty—the painter selecting and abstracting from the world around him to bring out unsuspected aesthetic satisfactions.

Picture Credits

1. Henry E. Huntington Library and Art Gallery, San Marino, Calif.
2. The Toledo Museum of Art, Toledo, Ohio, Gift of Edward Drummond Libbey.
3. National Gallery of Art, Washington, D.C., Chester Dale Collection.
4. The Metropolitan Museum of Art, Wolfe Fund, 1938.
5. Copyrighted by The Frick Collection, 1936, New York.
6. In The Brooklyn Museum Collection, Gift of Mrs. Horace Havemeyer.
7. Library of Congress, Washington, Lessing J. Rosenwald Collection.
8. Courtesy of the Fogg Art Museum, Harvard University, Bequest of Grenville L. Winthrop.
9. Francisco de Goya, 1746–1828, *The Marquesa de Santa Cruz as a Muse,* 1804. Oil on canvas, 49¾" x 81¾". Collection of the Los Angeles County Museum of Art, Allen C. Balch Endowment Fund.
11. Collection of the City Art Museum, St. Louis.
12. Courtesy, Museum of Fine Arts, Boston.
13A. Courtesy of The Art Institute of Chicago, W. W. Kimball Collection.

16A. By courtesy of the Trustees of the Tate Gallery, London.
  B. Museum of Art, Rhode Island School of Design, Providence, R.I.
  C. The Toledo Museum of Art, Toledo, Ohio, Gift of Sidney Spitzer, 1923.
17A. The Metropolitan Museum of Art, Bequest of Mrs. H. O. Havemeyer, 1929. The H. O. Havemeyer Collection.
  B. Addison Gallery of American Art, Phillips Academy, Andover, Mass.
  C. Fort Worth Art Center, Fort Worth, Tex., Permanent Collection of the Fort Worth Art Association.
  D. The Collection of The Detroit Institute of Arts.
18A. By courtesy of the Trustees of the Tate Gallery, London.
  B. The Wilmington Society of the Fine Arts, Wilmington, Del., Samuel and Mary Bancroft Collection.
  C. City Art Gallery, Manchester, England.
19A. Collection of The Paine Art Center and Arboretum, Oshkosh, Wisconsin.
  B. Courtesy of the Walters Art Gallery, Baltimore.
  C. The Metropolitan Museum of Art, Gift of Cornelius Vanderbilt, 1887.
20. Louvre, Paris.
21A. National Gallery of Art, Washington, D.C., Chester Dale Collection.
  B. National Gallery of Art, Washington, D.C., Chester Dale Collection.
22. The Museum of Fine Arts, Springfield, Mass.

23.   Courtesy of The Art Institute of Chicago, Helen Birch Bartlett Memorial Collection.

24A. The Phillips Collection, Washington.

   B. The Corcoran Gallery of Art, Washington, W. A. Clark Collection.

   C. The Metropolitan Museum of Art, Rogers Fund, 1951.

25.   Worcester Art Museum, Worcester, Mass.

26A. From *Fliegende Blätter*, Munich, published 1865.

   B. From *Collier's Magazine,* published 1901.

   C. King Features Syndicate, New York.

27A. Courtesy of the Gallery of Modern Art including The Huntington Hartford Collection, New York.

   B. Collection, The Museum of Modern Art, New York, Gift of Victor S. Riesenfeld.

28A. Courtesy of the Smithsonian Institution, Freer Gallery of Art, Washington, D.C.

   B. The Baltimore Museum of Art, Cone Collection.

29B. National Gallery of Art, Washington, D.C., Rosenwald Collection.

30A. The Minneapolis Institute of Arts, William Hood Dunwoody Fund, 1949.

   B. Philadelphia Museum of Art, Wilstach Collection.

31A. Municipal Museum, Amsterdam, V. W. Van Gogh Collection.

   B. Courtesy of The Art Institute of Chicago, Helen Birch Bartlett Memorial Collection.

32A. National Gallery of Art, Washington, D.C., Chester Dale Collection.

   B. Courtesy, Museum of Fine Arts, Boston.

33.   Courtesy of the Fogg Art Museum, Harvard University, Collection of Maurice Wertheim.

34.   Collection, The Museum of Modern Art, New York, Lillie P. Bliss Bequest.

35A. Courtesy of The Art Institute of Chicago, Gift of Mrs. Gilbert W. Chapman.

   B. Smith College Museum of Art, Northampton, Mass.

36A. © 1966 by The Barnes Foundation.

   B. Allen Memorial Art Museum, Oberlin College, Oberlin, Ohio, Charles F. Olney Fund.

37.   Museum of Art, Carnegie Institute, Pittsburgh, Pa.

38.   Philadelphia Museum of Art.

39.   Museum of Art, Rhode Island School of Design, Providence, R.I.

40A. Collection, The Museum of Modern Art, New York.

   B. Philadelphia Museum of Art, The Louise and Walter Arensberg Collection.

41A. Collection, The Museum of Modern Art, New York, Gift of Tristan Tzara.

   B. Smith College Museum of Art, Northampton, Mass.

42A. The Solomon R. Guggenheim Museum Collection, New York.

   B. Courtesy Wadsworth Atheneum, Hartford.

   C. Courtesy of the Fogg Art Museum, Harvard University, Collection of Maurice Wertheim.

   D. Herron Museum of Art, Art Association of Indianapolis.

43A. From *The Face of the Ruling Class,* Berlin, Malik Press, 1921; by permission of the Estate of George Grosz, Princeton, N.J.

   B. Collection, The Museum of Modern Art, New York, Gift of Philip C. Johnson.

   C. Courtesy of the Museum of Modern Art Film Library, New York.

44A. Courtesy Wadsworth Atheneum, Hartford.

   B. The Solomon R. Guggenheim Museum Collection, New York.

45. Courtesy Yale University Art Gallery, Collection Société Anonyme.

46. From Grosse Deutsche Kunstaustellung im Haus der deutschen Kunst zu München, 10.juli–16.oktober 1938.

47A. Courtesy Wadsworth Atheneum, Hartford.

   B. Collection, The Museum of Modern Art, New York.

48A. Collection, The Museum of Modern Art, New York, on Extended Loan from the Artist.

   B. Collection, The Museum of Modern Art, New York, Mrs. Simon Guggenheim Fund.

49. The Collection of The Detroit Institute of Arts.

50. Courtesy of The Art Institute of Chicago, Friends of American Art Collection.

51. Addison Gallery of American Art, Phillips Academy, Andover, Mass.

52. Collection of Mr. and Mrs. Bernard Hoffman, Kansas City, Mo.

53. Collection, The Art Gallery of Toronto, Gift from the Women's Committee Fund, 1964.

Index

Note: Titles of pictures discussed in the text proper will be found in this index under the artists' names. The heading "works" under an artist's name indicates where to find such other titles as are listed in the Notes at the end of each chapter. Page numbers in italics indicate illustrations.

Abbreviations:
  bibl: bibliography
  char: character of
  cf.: comparisons with, parallels to
  infc: influence on, from
  qu: quoted